The American Supreme Court

THE CHICAGO HISTORY OF
AMERICAN CIVILIZATION

DANIEL J. BOORSTIN, EDITOR

ROBERT G. MCCLOSKEY

THE
AMERICAN
SUPREME
COURT

FOURTH EDITION

REVISED BY SANFORD LEVINSON

THE UNIVERSITY OF CHICAGO PRESS
Chicago & London

ROBERT G. McCLOSKEY was professor of government at Harvard University. He is the author of *American Conservatism in the Age of Enterprise* and editor of *Essays in Constitutional Law.*

SANFORD LEVINSON is the W. St. John Garwood and W. St. John Garwood Jr. Centennial Chair in Law and professor of government at the University of Texas Law School, the author of *Constitutional Faith,* and the coeditor of *Processes of Constitutional Decisionmaking.*

The University of Chicago Press, Chicago 60637
The University of Chicago Press, Ltd., London
© 1960, 1994, 2000, 2005 by The University of Chicago
All rights reserved. Published 2005
Fourth edition 2005
Printed in the United States of America

14 13 12 11 10 09 08 07 06 05   1 2 3 4 5

ISBN: 0-226-55681-6 (cloth)
ISBN: 0-226-55682-4 (paper)

Library of Congress Cataloging-in-Publication Data

McCloskey, Robert G. (Robert Green)
    The American Supreme Court / Robert G. McCloskey.— 4th ed. / revised by Sanford Levinson.
        p.   cm.—(The Chicago history of American civilization)
    Includes bibliographical references and index.
    ISBN 0-226-55681-6 (cloth : alk. paper)—ISBN 0-226-55682-4 (pbk. : alk. paper)
    1. United States. Supreme Court—History.   2. Courts of last resort—United States—History.   3. Constitutional history—United States.
    I. Levinson, Sanford, 1941–   II. Title.   III. Series.

KF8742.M296 2005
347.73'26—dc22   2004009456

♾ The paper used in this publication meets the minimum requirements of the American National Standard for Information Sciences—Permanence of Paper for Printed Library Materials, ANSI Z39.48-1992.

To My Wife

R. G. McC.

For Rebecca

S. L.

CONTENTS

PREFACE TO THE FOURTH EDITION

I BEGIN THIS PREFACE with the opening words of my preface to the first revised edition in 1994: "This is literally a labor of love," to reflect my deep affection, even thirty-five years after his premature death in 1969, for Robert G. McCloskey. He was my Ph.D. supervisor when I was a graduate student at Harvard and, far more important, was everything a mentor should be. Many, many were the times that we retired, following his lecture in one or another course in which I was a teaching assistant, to a local restaurant to discuss both the subjects raised by the particular lecture and, as Justice Cardozo might put it, "life in all of its fullness."

It is, though, not only my respect for the memory of a wonderful man that has led me to revise his book in the specific manner that I have. *The American Supreme Court* is justifiably regarded as a classic, as signified by the fact that it remained in print, and was assigned in courses, well after most books published in 1960 had been consigned to the remainder heap. It not only presents a remarkably concise descriptive overview of the history of the Supreme Court; it also clearly articulates a particular normative view of the role best played by the Court within the American political system. Though McCloskey may be a voice from the past, he spoke to concerns that certainly remain as we stride further into the twenty-first century.

This accounts, then, for the basic decision to *add to,* rather than genuinely *revise,* his book. The first seven chapters are exactly as he wrote them at the end of the 1950's, save for the silent correction of a very few factual errors and, more important, different titles for chapters 6 and 7. I argue in my own final chapter that the term "welfare state," used in the original title for chapter 6, is better used for the regime that emerged in the United States following Lyndon B. Johnson's "Great Society" and its consolidation by Richard M. Nixon. I thus substitute the term "regulatory state" for "welfare state" in the title of chapter 6. It also seemed obviously desirable to revise the title of chapter 7 insofar as McCloskey's "modern court and modern America" are now more than a generation old.

I certainly do not want to suggest that I would not argue for some changes in McCloskey's own arguments, were this a genuinely coauthored work. Inevitably, both developments in disciplinary scholarship and generational shifts in overarching perspectives would lead to differences in approach. An example of both, probably, is that I would focus much more on slavery as a dominating issue of the Supreme Court's first seventy years, rather than treat it simply as one aspect of the controversies, important as they were, about Federalism. And I have a somewhat different view of John Marshall. McCloskey's romanticized view of this Chief Justice was partly shaped by his being a product, in important senses, of the Great Depression and the New Deal response. (He was born in 1916.) An important part of New Deal judicial theory was the theme that Roosevelt simply wanted to return to Marshall's broad and capacious nationalist vision, almost unaccountably hijacked by Republican conservatives at the turn of the twentieth century. I see far less continuity between Marshall and the New Deal. Were this entirely my own book, moreover, I would spend some pages on the Court's role in the saga of American expansion by which the United States was transformed from a nation of eleven Atlantic coast states at the time of Washington's inauguration in 1789 (North Carolina and Rhode Island had not yet ratified the Constitution) to a country of fifty states—one of them in the mid-Pacific—plus assorted colonies such as Puerto Rico. The Court, as a matter of fact, played no significant role in the most important single event of this transformation, the Louisiana Purchase of 1803, but it played a significantly greater role in legitimizing the new legal order that characterized the relationship with American Indians in the late nineteenth century.

And there are surely other differences as well. One of them involves the role that McCloskey assigns to the Court as the primary agent of American constitutional development. No one can deny that the Court has played a significant role. But it is important for students to be aware of what has come to be called "the Constitution outside the courts." As political scientist–lawyer Mark Graber has argued, Alexis de Tocqueville was wrong insofar as he suggested that Americans tend to turn all issues into judicial ones. He may have been correct that Americans tend to view political issues as legal ones, but the primary venue for much constitutional debate, especially in the nineteenth century, was Congress, not the Supreme Court. Still, even if students should become aware that other institutions besides the American judiciary play a role in constitutional development, it would be foolish to ignore the important role played by the American Supreme Court, and I remain convinced that the book that McCloskey wrote offers a fine introduction to that subject that should remain available for assignment to students.

I view this, therefore, as *McCloskey's* book rather than my own. My task was to try to update it and make it useful even for another third of a century by imagining, as best I can, how he might have responded to the remarkable events of the four decades since he wrote the book. Fortunately, one has some idea what his answer might be for the first of those decades, and I have drawn on some of his articles. For the time since 1969, I can only call on my own imaginative resources.

This being said, I gladly accept full responsibility for the two chapters that I have added. In the new chapter 8, I try primarily to update the story that McCloskey began telling in terms of the Court's role as protector of the civil rights and liberties of vulnerable, often unpopular, minorities. Chapter 9, on the other hand, represents something potentially quite new, for there I argue that this role in significant ways has been supplemented, and, perhaps more accurately, supplanted, by a distinctively new one as "monitor of the welfare state"—a function that I identify with developments occurring in the decade after the initial publication of *The American Supreme Court*. It also appears to be the case that the Court has begun the twenty-first century by attempting to return to a much older role as "umpire" of the federal system and defender of states' rights against an encroaching national government. A number of cases that will be discussed in chapter 9 certainly suggest this. To put it mildly, though, whether the Court will play this role more successfully this time than the last remains to be seen.

After these two new chapters, the reader will find the original epilogue, "The Court of Today and the Lessons of History." In keeping with what I hope is the spirit of this book, I am reprinting it as it was published in 1960, though I have added my own coda that continues a conversation initiated well more than a third of a century ago in Cambridge. Indeed, the theme of intergenerational conversation—so memorably achieved back then as a senior professor took a fledgling graduate student under his wing—ever more resonates in my own consciousness, as I realize that my own students are now the age that I was when I first met Robert McCloskey in 1963. Even if these students (properly) dismiss some of the arguments found in this book as reflecting the particular consciousness-forming experiences first of Robert McCloskey and then of myself, I hope they will nonetheless agree that the conversation about the historical development and normative role of the Supreme Court is one well worth continuing.

Sanford Levinson

ACKNOWLEDGMENTS

A S NOTED IN my preface, my deepest acknowledgment is indeed to Robert McCloskey. It is no coincidence at all that McCloskey is a dedicatee of *Processes of Constitutional Decisionmaking,* a casebook that I coedit with Paul Brest, Jack Balkin, and Akhil Reed Amar, which is organized very much along McCloskean historical lines. Indeed, I suspect that it was my initial training that has made me so unsympathetic to the typical way that constitutional law is taught, which is to engage in clause-by-clause analysis rather than to recognize that *all* doctrines during a particular period are interlaced with the dominant issues of that era.

I am especially grateful to Brest for his inviting me, back in 1979, to collaborate with him on the second edition of his path-breaking casebook. That collaboration has provided me the occasion not only for deepened friendship, but also the opportunity (and necessity) to reflect at length about developments in recent American constitutionalism and how they can best be organized for pedagogical purposes. Chapter 9 of this book would never have taken form in 1994 had I not struggled over several summers to organize a new chapter in the 1992 edition of *Processes* on the Constitution and the modern welfare state. All of my revisions for this new edition of *The American Supreme Court* reflect continuing conversations with our new collaborators (and my close friends) Balkin and Amar.

I have benefited immensely from my two-decade association with the University of Texas Law School and my colleagues there, who have always proved willing to read my drafts and discuss my ideas. I must single out one of them, Scot Powe, for his endless encouragement and help; my own "take" on the Warren Court has certainly been affected by his own magnum opus, *The Warren Court and American Politics*. I am also grateful to many friends and associates, including participants in various internet listserves, for their invaluable help with regard to the bibliography, which I hope will be useful to students (and even professors) who use this book. Mark Graber should be singled out for special thanks in this regard.

Finally, I remain grateful to John Tryneski of the University of Chicago Press, who has been a sympathetic and helpful friend in our joint project of keeping alive Robert McCloskey's marvelous book.

Sanford Levinson

PREFACE TO THE FIRST EDITION

THIS BOOK DEALS with the work of the Supreme Court of the United States as a constitutional tribunal, exercising the power of judicial review. It does not purport to describe the activity of the Court as a whole; much less is it a history of constitutional law in the widest possible sense, treating of constitutional developments that have been brought about by legislative and executive action, or by the more subtle process we call custom. Finally, because it is a brief book, I cannot of course even claim that it covers the story of judicial review comprehensively. The chapters are interpretive essays in the history of judicial review. They deal with aspects of that history that seem to me important and interesting, but they omit material that might legitimately seem equally important or interesting to another.

My aim has been, within this compass, to understand the way the Supreme Court has conducted itself to achieve its results, the role it has played in American life. I have been most concerned, as the text will reveal, to see the Court as an agency in the American governing process, an agency with a mind and a will and an influence of its own. Greatly as we may respect John Marshall, not many sophisticated persons would now take these words of his very seriously: "Judicial power, as contradistinguished from the power of the laws, has no existence. Courts are the mere instruments of the law, and can will nothing."

Yet there has been too little effort, I believe, to project a contrary view back into judicial history in order to see what the Court *was*, if it was not what Marshall asserted. And because this has not been done, as I am at pains to suggest in the epilogue to this volume, we are not prepared as we should be to evaluate the Court of today, either as critics or as defenders.

ONE

THE GENESIS AND NATURE OF
JUDICIAL POWER

O N JUNE 21, 1788, when the convention of New Hampshire
voted 57 to 46 to approve the proposed national constitution,
the requirement of nine ratifying states was fulfilled and the
United States of America sprang into legal being. Opportunity for instant
creation of this magnitude occurs only in fiction and law, and the delegates did not underrate their historic moment. They were careful to specify that it came at one o'clock in the afternoon, for they feared that Virginia might act that very evening and claim a share in the honor. They
need not have worried. The Virginians were in for three more days of
oratory, mostly by Patrick Henry, before their state's proud name could
be added to the list.

Fifteen months later, President Washington accomplished another of
these portentous juridical feats by signing the Judiciary Act of 1789,
which was to be called many years afterward "probably the most important and the most satisfactory Act ever passed by Congress." The latter-
day eulogist was himself a Supreme Court justice, and his good opinion
of a law that made him one of the most august figures in the nation is not
surprising; a long roll of eminent statesmen since 1789 could be called to
testify on the other side. But hardly one of them would dispute his opinion that the Act was extremely important, for it not only established the
far-flung system of federal courts but boldly defined their jurisdiction, and
especially that of the Supreme Court, in such a way that the states, Congress, and the President could be held subject to judicial authority.

Finally, on February 2, 1790, some of the men who had received these
high commissions and whose duty it therefore was to give living force to
these paper enactments, assembled in the Royal Exchange building in
New York and organized as the Supreme Court of the United States. The

I

occasion was solemn, and the newspapers followed it closely, passing on to the people every crumb of detail about this third great department of their young national republic. Yet neither the press nor the people nor the justices themselves could quite know how momentous the day was, and there is good evidence that they did not. Only four of the six men Washington had chosen to adorn the Supreme Court turned up for that first official meeting. Robert H. Harrison declined appointment, apparently because he thought his judicial post as chancellor of Maryland was more important; and John Rutledge, though officially a member of the Court in its first three terms, never attended a session and soon resigned to accept the chief justiceship of South Carolina. Looking back, we can see that the first meeting of the Supreme Court of the United States was one of the mileposts in the history of jurisprudence. We can see that the ratifying of the Constitution and the signing of the Judiciary Act had, when taken together, opened great wells of judicial power, and that the four justices who sat together in the Royal Exchange that winter were inaugurating a governmental enterprise of vast and unprecedented dimensions. But the principals were looking forward, not back, and the future must have seemed cloudy.

In the nature of the case they would not have known much about the prospects of their Court and the Constitution, for the very good reason that so little about either had been firmly decided. The delegates who framed the Constitution have been traditionally and deservedly praised for producing a document that could earn the approval of such diverse states as Massachusetts and Georgia and such diverse men as John Adams and Thomas Jefferson (neither of whom, by the way, attended the Federal Convention). But this congenial result had been achieved not only by compromise but by forbearance. The Constitution clearly established a few principles about which there was no serious colonial disagreement, for example, the representative system for choosing officials and the separation of powers between the departments of the national government. It compromised a few more troublesome issues like the question of equal state representation versus representation based on population, and the question of the slave trade. But still weightier difficulties that might have prevented ratification were either left severely alone by the Founding Fathers or treated in ambiguous clauses that passed the problems on to posterity.

No one quite knew, for example, what was meant when the Constitution endowed Congress with power "to regulate commerce among foreign nations, and among the several states"; or to make all laws "necessary and proper" for carrying out the national government's other powers; or when it was asserted that the Constitution as well as laws and treaties made by the nation were "the supreme law of the land." No one was sure how the "ex post facto" clause or the "contract clause" would restrict state inroads on the rights of property-holders. Some had hopes and others had suspicions about the meaning of these and other enigmatic phrases in the document. But if either the hopes or the suspicions had been fully warranted by clear language in the Constitution itself, it seems most unlikely that ratification would have been possible. The issue underlying these uncertainties was no less than this: whether a nation or a league of sovereign states was created by the Constitution. That was the question still awaiting decision in 1790, and until America began answering it, the full significance of New Hampshire's historic vote was a matter for guess work. If a true nation emerged as the future unfolded, then New Hampshire's action was unforgettable. If not, ratification would be seen as a comparatively minor incident in modern world history.

As for the Supreme Court, its future was even more uncertain. The Constitution has comparatively little to say about the Court or the federal judiciary in general. The "judicial power of the United States," whatever it may be, is vested in the Supreme Court and in such other courts as Congress may establish. But the composition of the Court, including the number of its members, is left for congressional decision; and, while federal judges cannot be removed except by impeachment, there is nothing to prevent Congress from creating additional judgeships whenever it chooses. Furthermore, although the judicial power "extends" to a variety of cases described in Article III, section 2, the second paragraph of that section significantly qualifies what the first seems to have granted, and gives Congress power to control the Supreme Court's jurisdiction over appeals from lower courts. Since the cases that reach the Court directly without first being heard in other courts are comparatively minor in quantity or importance, this legislative authority over appeals (over the "appellate jurisdiction") is a license for Congress to decide whether the Supreme Court will be a significant or a peripheral factor in American government.

Most important of all, the Constitution makes no explicit statement about the nature of the Court's power even when a case admittedly falls within its jurisdiction. Some of the uncertainties outlined above were resolved, temporarily at any rate, by the passage of the Judiciary Act. Its famous Section 25 gave the Supreme Court power to reverse or affirm state court decisions which had denied claims based on the federal Constitution, treaties, or laws. This meant that such cases could be reached by the Supreme Court through its appellate jurisdiction. But suppose a state court had denied such a claim under the federal Constitution and the Supreme Court of the United States reversed on the ground that the state court's interpretation of the Constitution was in error. And suppose further that the state court obstinately continued to insist upon its own interpretation. Was there anything in the Constitution to guarantee that the Supreme Court's opinion would prevail, that the Supreme Court's authority was superior to state courts? Or suppose, to carry the matter a step further, that the state court had held a federal law invalid as conflicting with the *national* Constitution and the Supreme Court *agreed* with this holding, thus asserting its authority to overthrow an act of Congress. Does the Constitution make it *clear* that the Court has this final authority of "judicial review" over national legislative enactments?

The answer to both questions is a fairly solid "no." As for state decisions it has been argued that the "supreme law of the land" clause and the clause extending the judicial power to cases arising under the Constitution do make it clear that the Supreme Court was intended to be preeminent on questions of constitutional interpretation. If the Constitution is supreme and the Supreme Court has jurisdiction over cases involving the Constitution, then it follows that the Court's word on such matters is paramount over all others—so the argument runs. But in the first place this reasoning is not unassailable, for as defenders of states' rights were later passionately to insist, the fact that the Constitution is supreme does not settle the question of who decides what the Constitution means. And in the second place enthusiasts for judicial review have never quite been able to explain why so formidable a power was granted by implication rather than by flat statement. As for judicial review of congressional acts, the support in the language of the Constitution was even more suppositious, and arguments for the authority derived solely from that language seem inevitably to beg the question.

None of this is to say that the framers of the Constitution would have been surprised to see the Supreme Court exercising the power of judicial review in some form, both as against the states and as against Congress. Indeed there is ample evidence that most of them who had thought about it expected that the Court would do so, however distressing it is that they failed to make their expectations explicit. But neither the framers nor the ratifying state conventions (whose views are in some ways more relevant to the issue) had any general understanding about the particular form that the judicial review would take and the role that the Supreme Court would therefore assume.

Some, like Alexander Hamilton, certainly hoped that the justices would act as general monitors, broadly supervising the other branches of government and holding them to the path of constitutional duty, though even he seems to have conceived this exalted notion only after the Convention's adjournment. Others, like Robert Yates, also of New York, feared that the Court would so regard its function. But James Madison, the highest possible authority on the Constitution's intent, though apparently expecting the Supreme Court to disallow laws that *clearly* contravened the Constitution, by no means conceded that the Court could apply its negative judgment to more debatable points or that the judicial pronouncements were intended to be final and binding on the other branches of government. And the evidence of both the Convention and the ratification controversy suggests that other participants were equally doubtful about these questions and that many more had simply not considered the matter at all.

In short, neither the words of the Constitution nor the provable intent of those who framed and ratified it justified in 1790 any certitude about the scope or finality of the Court's power to superintend either the states or Congress. The most that can be said is that language and intent did not *preclude* the Court from becoming the puissant tribunal of later history.

GREAT EXPECTATIONS

Nevertheless those four men in the Royal Exchange, though without any ironclad assurances, might well have had a strong hunch that destiny sat beside them, that the Constitution would be transfigured from a bitterly debated paper enactment into a venerated symbol of Americanism, and that the Court would emerge as the chief expounder of its mysteries and a beneficiary of its prestige. They must have realized that by tradition and temperament the new nation was ripe for such developments.

For the Constitution was potentially the convergence point for all the ideas about fundamental law that had been current in America since the colonization period. Of course the notion of a law-above-government, a "higher" law, was well known throughout the Western world, but the colonists had given it a special domestic cast, infusing it with interpretations drawn from their own unique experience. While most Europeans thought of higher law as exercising a moral restraint on government, they did not argue that this moral limit was legally enforceable, that it was positive law, practically binding the governors. Even before the Revolutionary controversy, Americans had found it easy to assume that it was just that, for their own legislatures had long been literally bound by "higher law" in such forms as the colonial charters and decisions of the British Privy Council. But the struggle with England turned assumption into fiery conviction as the colonists argued that Parliament was forbidden, not only morally but literally, to transgress the rights Americans claimed under their charters and under the British Constitution. And after the break with England this now very American idea of a written, tangible higher law was further embodied in the new state constitutions and in the Articles of Confederation. The document of 1789 then could draw on this enormous fund of prestige that the higher-law idea had assimilated in America.

Such circumstances might help explain, at least initially, why the Constitution won such ready devotion. But the question remains, it might be said, why the Court should be chosen to share in and perpetuate the Constitution's glory. We have seen that the language of the Constitution is inconclusive on this matter and that the intentions of the framers were ambiguous. Jefferson, Madison and many other almost equally illustrious statesmen were later to argue that the Congress, the President, and even the individual states were, no less than the courts, guardians of the Constitution and coequal interpreters of its meaning. What warrant then had our four new judges for hoping that history would reject these rival claimants and confirm the Supreme Court's constitutional prerogative? To put the question somewhat differently, what made it likely, though perhaps not certain, that the Court would play the great part it has played in American life?

THE HIGHER-LAW BACKGROUND AND POPULAR SOVEREIGNTY

With the benefit of hindsight, it is not hard to find a number of answers to these questions. The common law traditions deriving from the great seventeenth-century English jurist, Sir Edward Coke, exalted judges above other folk, and that tradition was cherished by Americans with peculiar tenacity. The Federalists, who enjoyed political ascendancy during the first decade of the Republic's history, tried to use their temporary prestige to implant in the popular mind a respect for judges, so that Federalism might find a haven against the adversity of a Jeffersonian political victory. The very fact that the concept of judicial review was, at the outset, imperfectly understood was a point in its favor, for it enabled judges to build up the Court's power gradually and almost imperceptibly and its opponents thus found themselves in the frustrating position of those who fight shadows. These factors, among others, are surely relevant to the problem. But they are not sufficient to explain the Court's impending future; they seem to rest on a broader, underlying causal condition whose roots drive deeper into the subsoil of American political life.

To understand that condition it is necessary to look again at the climate of political opinion in eighteenth-century America and particularly at the quarter-century that preceded the Constitution. We have seen that the old doctrine of fundamental law was stimulated by the events and idea currents of the Revolutionary era. Now it must be observed that the movement for revolution also supplied a vital impetus for another, and in some ways, contradictory, notion—the theory of popular sovereignty. American pamphleteers had insisted on the principle of home rule; the Declaration of Independence had founded just government on the "consent of the governed"; the next and natural step was to regard the people as not only a consenting but a willing entity and to declare, as Jefferson later said, that "the will of the majority is in all cases to prevail." These reasonable and perhaps inevitable deductions from the Spirit of '76 were widely prevalent in America during the Articles of Confederation period. Many of the solid citizens deplored such "mad democracy" and longed to curb it, but they could not evade the fact that the will-of-the-people concept was now firmly planted in American minds as one of the premises of political thinking.

Yet plainly that concept conflicted with the doctrine of fundamental law which was also, and concurrently, treasured by Americans. Popular sovereignty suggests *will*; fundamental law suggests *limit*. The one idea conjures up the vision of an active, positive state; the other idea emphasizes the negative, restrictive side of the political problem. It may be possible to harmonize these seeming opposites by logical sleight of hand, by arguing that the doctrines of popular sovereignty and fundamental law were fused in the Constitution, which was a popularly willed limitation. But it seems unlikely that Americans in general achieved such a synthesis and far more probable, considering our later political history, that most of them retained the two ideas side by side. This propensity to hold contradictory ideas simultaneously is one of the most significant qualities of the American political mind at all stages of national history, and it helps substantially in explaining the rise to power of the United States Supreme Court.

For with their political hearts thus divided between the will of the people and the rule of law, Americans were naturally receptive to the development of institutions that reflected each of these values separately.

The legislature with its power to initiate programs and policies, to respond to the expressed interest of the public, embodied the doctrine of popular sovereignty. The courts, generally supposed to be without will as Hamilton said, generally revered as impartial and independent, fell heir almost by default to the guardianship of the fundamental law. It did not avail for Jeffersonian enemies of the judicial power to insist that a single department could exercise *both* the willing and the limiting functions. The bifurcation of the two values in the American mind impellingly suggested that the functions should be similarly separated. And the devotion of Americans to both popular sovereignty and fundamental law insured public support for the institution that represented each of them.

CONSEQUENCES FOR AMERICAN CONSTITUTIONALISM

This dualism of the American mind, symbolized on the one hand by "political" institutions like the Congress and the Presidency and on the other hand by the Court and the Constitution, helps account for a good deal that seems baffling in later history. In logical terms it might appear strange that the nation should resoundingly approve the New Deal in 1936 and a few months later stoutly defend against attack the Supreme Court that had cut the heart from the New Deal program. But the paradox is related as branch to root to the historic dualism between popular sovereignty and the doctrine of fundamental law that developed with the birth throes of the American political system. The separation of the two ideas in the American mind had been emphasized by intervening events: strong-minded judges had added new arguments for the Court's constitutional prerogative; congressmen and presidents, busy with more pressing concerns, had been content except for fitful rebellious impulses to let those arguments go unchallenged; and the cake of custom had hardened over the original disjunction. But it was made possible at the outset by our native tendency to harbor conflicting ideas without trying, or caring, to resolve them.

The United States began its history, then, with a Constitution that posed more questions than it answered and with a Supreme Court whose birthright was most uncertain. The temper of the times and the deep-seated inclinations of the American political character favored the future of both these institutions and at the same time prescribed their limits and helped determine their nature. American devotion to the principle of fundamental law gave the Constitution its odor of sanctity, and the American bent for evading contradictions by assigning values to separate compartments allowed the Supreme Court to assume the priestly mantle. But like most successes, in politics and elsewhere, this one had a price. The failure to resolve the conflict between popular sovereignty and fundamental law perhaps saved the latter principle, but by the same token it left the former intact. And this meant that the fundamental law could be enforced only within delicately defined boundaries, that constitutional law though not simply the creature of the popular will nevertheless had always to reckon with it, that the mandates of the Supreme Court must be shaped with an eye not only to legal right and wrong, but with an eye to what popular opinion would tolerate.

We have seen, then, that the Constitution makers postponed some of the most vital questions confronting them, that the Constitution and the Supreme Court inherited the quasi-religious symbolic quality attached to the doctrine of "higher law," but that the dogmas of popular sovereignty also continued to survive and flourish and therefore influence constitutionalism. The consequences of all this were several. For one thing the Constitution itself could not become the certain and immutable code of governmental conduct that some of its latter-day idolators imagined it to be. Conceived in ambiguity as well as liberty, it could never escape that legacy. The framers had said in effect: with respect to certain questions, some of them very momentous, the Constitution means whatever the circumstances of the future will allow it to mean. But since those circumstances were almost sure to vary, the result was that alterability became the law of the Constitution's being: it might mean one thing in 1855, something else in 1905, and something still different in 1955, depending upon what circumstances, including popular expectations, warranted.

To be sure, as the years went on there was a certain accumulation of fairly well-fixed interpretations, and the picture of a constitutional system in eternal flux should not be overdrawn. Some constitutional clauses are explicit enough (and frequently unimportant enough) so that argument about their meaning is improbable. It is unlikely that the states will ever be permitted to grant titles of nobility (Art. I, sec. 10); federal judges, once hired, can feel secure against direct wage cuts (Art. III, sec. 1). Other phrases often rather technical in nature, like the "ex post facto" clause (Art. I, sec. 10), seem to resist the winds of innovation more efficiently than others. Moreover, because the illusion of continuity must be respected, great constitutional changes are likely to come slowly. Nevertheless only a very bold constitutional scholar would declare that he *knows* how the commerce clause or the due process clauses will be understood by the next generation. And when we count up the clauses whose past is variable and whose future is uncertain they far exceed in significance if not in number their more stable fellows.

THE COURT'S CONSTITUTIONAL POWERS AND DUTIES

As for the Supreme Court, its nature has also been heavily and permanently influenced by the factors just described. As might be expected, any description of the judicial function in America is shot through with paradoxes. To begin with, the observer confronts the fact that the Court does inherit a responsibility for helping to guide the nation, especially with respect to those long-term "value questions" that are so vital to the maintenance of a just political order. A good many gallons of ink have been spilled over the issue of whether such a heavy assignment should have devolved on the judiciary. John Marshall, "the great Chief Justice," has been accused of seizing the bitter cup all too gladly and thus setting a pattern of usurpation for future judges to follow. Insofar as this indictment rests on the supposed "intent of the framers," it suffers from the weakness already remarked: that so few of the framers had any clear views one way or another about the subject.

On the other hand, insofar as the charge is that the nation was unwise to delegate this duty to the judges (or allow them to assume it), it may be right, but is also perilously near to irrelevance. For this amounts to saying that America was unwise to be the nation that it was. The American mind conceived a dichotomy between the willed law of legislative enactment and the discovered or pronounced law of the Constitution, and "judicial review" was, as we have seen, one result. The fallacy of making such a distinction may be palpable enough from our modern perspective, but the fact remains that it was not palpable to Marshall's generation, and nothing very helpful is accomplished by arguing that it should have been.

Nor is it much more profitable to urge that the Court should now put off the responsibility it once so eagerly took up, even if it be conceded that the original arrogation was unwise. Historical accident and bad logic may explain the inception of judicial review, but by now the American nation has lived with the consequences for more than 150 years. Our courts and, even more important, our legislatures have been shaped by the understanding that the judiciary will help in charting the path of governmental policy. A rough division of labor has developed from that understanding, for it is assumed that the legislature can focus largely on the task of "interest representation," while passing on to the courts a substantial share of the responsibility for considering the long-term constitutional questions that continually arise. Appearances may be deceptive. Congressmen may self-righteously insist that they serve both the Constitutional Tradition and their Constituents, but the needs of these two masters seem to coincide with remarkable invariability; and it is fair to infer that interests and pressures play the larger part in the legislative process.

Surely this is no indictment of that process, for the American tradition respects, as has been said, the will of today's popular majority, and interests must therefore be paid due heed. But the American tradition also sets great store, as we have also seen, by the set of values associated with the "rule of law," which history has rightly or wrongly consigned in heavy part to the judiciary. In a world of abstractions, one might argue that this historic division, since it defies good sense, ought to be obliterated. But in the world that history has given us, the almost certain result would be that pure calculation of interest-group pressures defined the course of government in the United States. It is too much to ask that a legislative process as interest-dominated as ours abjure its traditions at this late date and take on the functions of a high court as well. Yet until it does, the judiciary must accept its own traditional responsibility, lest the very idea of limited government be lost. Critics may legitimately debate whether the Court should play a greater or lesser part in directing the ship of state. That it must play some part is the penalty of its heritage.

THE CONDITIONS OF JUDICIAL CONTROL

Yet once this is said, it must immediately be added—or reiterated—that the tradition which transmits this power to the Court likewise prescribes the conditions of its exercise. The nation expects the judges to aid in deciding policy questions, but the nation is prone, with sublime inconsistency, to grow fiercely resentful if the aid becomes repression, if the judges bypass certain ill-marked but nevertheless quite real boundaries, two of which merit special consideration.

In the first place, there are the limitations implied by the fact that the Supreme Court is expected to be both a "court" in the orthodox sense of the word and something very much more as well. A full account of the confusions fostered by this seeming contradiction would almost involve a recapitulation of Supreme Court history. Legions of judges and their devotees have believed, or professed to believe, that constitutional law was a technical mystery revealing itself in terms of unmistakable precision to those who had the key, that the Constitution was the record and the judges merely the impartial phonograph that played it, a group of men who somehow managed to stop being men when they put on their robes and would not dream of letting their subjective value judgments affect their understanding of the Constitution. No court was ever like this, no system of law was ever so sure a guide to its interpreters. And the myth of a perfect judiciary perfectly administering a perfect Constitution was therefore deeply impaired in the twentieth century by writers who pointed out what some perceptive observers had always known—that judges are mortal. Like senators and presidents, it was said, judges may have prejudices, and those prejudices may affect their understanding of the Constitution. In fact, the critics went on, the American Supreme Court, so far from merely and imperturbably reflecting eternal constitutional verities, is a willing, policy-making, *political* body.

All this was perfectly true as far as it went, and it provided a useful antidote to previous oversimplifications. But the trouble was that it tended to foster an oversimplification of its own: "legal realists," impressed by the discovery that the Supreme Court was more than a court, were sometimes prone to treat it as if it were not a court at all, as if its "courthood" were a pure façade for political functions indistinguishable from those performed by the legislature. Such a view bypasses everything that is really interesting about the institution and obscures, as much as the discredited old mythology ever did, its true nature.

For the fascinating thing about the Supreme Court has been that it blends orthodox judicial functions with policy-making functions in a complex mixture. And the Court's power is accounted for by the fact that the mixture is maintained in nice balance; but the fact that it *must* be maintained in such a balance accounts for the limitations of that power. The Court's claim on the American mind derives from the myth of an impartial, judicious tribunal whose duty it is to preserve our sense of continuity with the fundamental law. Because that law was initially stated in ambiguous terms, it has been the duty of the Court to make "policy decisions" about it, that is, to decide what it means in the circumstances existing when the question is presented. But though the judges do enter this realm of policy-making, they enter with their robes on, and they can never (or at any rate seldom) take them off; they are both empowered and restricted by their "courtly" attributes.

They cannot, for example, even decide a question unless it is presented in the form of a "case" between two or more interested parties; and the Supreme Court early, and wisely, held that to render "advisory opinions" even to the President would be incongruous with the judicial function. Sometimes the Court is criticized for leaning over backward to find technical and, to a layman, unduly "legalistic" reasons for leaving important constitutional questions unsettled. Often the drag of precedent inhibits the judges from revising constitutional principles as quickly as might be desirable. And finally there are whole large areas of constitutional determination which the Court deliberately and rather consistently leaves alone (for example, the issue of whether a state has "a republican form of government," Art. IV, sec. 4) on the grounds that the questions therein raised are not appropriate for judicial determination.

Any individual decision along any of these lines may well be subject to criticism, for the judges of the Supreme Court, being men, can err. But it is the greatest of nonsense to generalize the criticism into impatience with the Court's "legalistic" demeanor as such, since the logical conclusion of such a criticism is to align the judicial power squarely with the legislative power and to erase the differentiation of function that is the Court's basis for being. And it is also wrong to suppose that the Court's insistence on such attributes of judiciality is a mere pose, designed to hoodwink the public without hampering the judges. In certain spectacular cases in our history the Court has seemed to take leave of courtly procedures in order to remedy an injustice, real or fancied. Such a landmark of judicial temerity was the decision of 1895 which outlawed a national income tax, and no sophisticated student of the Court would deny that it can sometimes forget its "legalistic" trappings and can at other times refashion them to serve the judicial purpose of the moment. But in most cases such technical legal limitations do play a part that is not sham but perfectly real. The judges have usually known what students have sometimes not known—that their tribunal must be a court, as well as seem one, if it is to retain its power. The idea of fundamental law as a force in its own right, distinguishable from today's popular will, can only be maintained by a pattern of Court behavior that emphasizes the separation. If departures from that pattern are too frequent and too extreme, the emphasis will be lost and the idea itself will be imperiled.

One consequence, then, of the Supreme Court's peculiar origins is this necessity that it perform legislative (or quasi-legislative) tasks with judicial tools, which is roughly akin to the assignment of playing baseball with a billiard cue. But its problems do not end there. A second result, as has already been intimated, is the need for the judges to reckon, in making rules and guiding policy, with the imperatives of public opinion no matter how impeccably "judicial" is the method by which the rules are arrived at. This is not to say that the Court should consult the latest bulletins on the popular climate and shape its judgments accordingly. But it is to say that public concurrence sets an outer boundary for judicial policy-making; that judicial ideas of the good society can never be too far removed from the popular ideas. The Republic might have been dedicated at the outset to the principle of pure popular sovereignty, and in that event the Supreme Court would have inherited only the important but secondary responsibility of statutory interpretation. On the other hand, it is imaginatively, though not perhaps practically, conceivable to establish a governmental system in which the fundamental law absolutely controls the public will, and in such a system the Court might enjoy utter independence. But America, as we have seen, chose neither of these worlds, but tried to have the best of them both: the upshot is that the Court, while sometimes checking or at any rate modifying the popular will, is itself in turn checked or modified.

America has thus had two sovereigns, but this somewhat outlandish arrangement has been maintained only because each of the partners has known the meaning of self-restraint. In the critical literature of the past generation or two, one has read much about judicial tyranny, and the vision of a populace bent on social reform but shackled by an unfeeling Court's despotism seems to have beguiled more than one observer. In truth the Supreme Court has seldom, if ever, flatly and for very long resisted a really unmistakable wave of public sentiment. It has worked with the premise that constitutional law, like politics itself, is a science of the possible.

THE CONTOURS OF COURT HISTORY

There is a final point, which is at the same time very much like a summary of the discussion so far. We have seen that both the meaning of the Constitution and the nature of the Supreme Court's authority were left in doubt by the framers, that circumstances nonetheless conspired to favor the early growth of both constitutionalism and judicial power, but that those same circumstances also helped to set the terms within which these institutions would develop. The Constitution became a symbol of American patriotic devotion, but a symbol whose continued force depended on its continued flexibility in the face of shifting national needs. The Supreme Court became a venerated institution, half judicial tribunal and half political preceptor, sensitive but not subservient to popular expectations, obliged by its tradition to share the duties of statesmanship, but equally obliged to be alert that its share did not exceed its capacities.

The history of the Court and its treatment of the Constitution can be broadly understood as an endless search for a position in American government that is appropriate to these conditions imposed by its genesis. The quest is laden with difficulties because the paradoxes of the Court's existence can only be reconciled, even temporarily, by the most delicate balancing of judgments. It is unending because every such tentative reconciliation is sure to be disturbed ultimately by the relentless course of history, and every such major disturbance sends the judges forth on another chapter in their odyssey.

In each chapter certain dominant judicial interests take form, certain dominant values emerge, and the Court can be observed struggling to formulate a judicial role that will reinforce those interests and values within the subtle limits of judicial capability. We need not pause just now over the issue of whether these preoccupations and postures are consciously chosen, nor need we trouble ourselves that individual judges may vary in the degree of their conformity to the pattern, except insofar as this may affect the pattern itself. The refinements of the judicial motivation process are intriguing to be sure, but too much concern with them may cause an observer to miss the broad trends that give meaning to an epoch in constitutional history. Conceding that there are variations within the framework, we can nevertheless identify three great periods in American constitutional development: 1789 to the close of the Civil War; 1865 to the "Court revolution" of 1937; and 1937 to the present. The judicial interests and values that characterize each period are sufficiently articulated to be significant; and the Court's struggle to define its role as great new historical movements alter the backdrop, supplies a further element of dramatic change and uncertainty. If the framers had tried to settle all "constitutional" questions that confronted them; if they had even assumed the more modest task of specifically circumscribing the judicial power; if the doctrine of legislative supremacy had been a little more firmly intrenched in 1789; if judges like Marshall had been a little more inclined toward abnegation and a little less inclined toward politics, the uncertainties would be very different, the tale would be of another order. But then the country it was told about would not be the historical United States.

Two

The Establishment of the
Right to Decide: 1789–1810

A MERICANS HAVE ALWAYS experienced a peculiar difficulty in accommodating themselves to one of the least contestable observations made in the preceding chapter—that the Supreme Court is
a willful, policy-making agency of American government. In the long and
crowded history of antijudicial polemics the most persistent angry charge
has been that the Court, in this situation or that, has been guided by its
prepossessions rather than by the unambiguous mandates of the fundamental law. On the other hand, the defenders of the Court in such debates
(that is, those who approve the policy decisions in question) have ordinarily and with indignation rejected this impeachment, insisting that the
judges were the helpless instruments of constitutional logic. Since the
combatants have a bewildering way of shifting sides from year to year or
at any rate from decade to decade, a watcher of the constitutional skies
might draw a somewhat puzzling conclusion—that for many Americans
the Court is the echo of the Constitution when it agrees with them and
the voice of subjective prejudice when it does not.

The effect of this musical chairs game is unfortunately to obscure any
coherent view of what the Court is really up to at any given time. Those
who like the Court's record in that time are indisposed to admit that it is
up to anything except its mythic business of consulting the oracle; and
those who disapprove its record are too wrathful over the current usurpation to offer reliable judgments.

Nevertheless it is perfectly apparent to the detached observer that the
Court's decisions do tend to fall into patterns that reflect current judicial
views of what ought to be done; and that these views, though heavily
influenced by the nature of the forum that issues them, are nonetheless
policy determinations. The very question of what subjects should claim

judicial attention, involves an avowed or implicit decision about what is most important in the American polity at any given time, for the Court has always enjoyed some leeway in controlling its own jurisdiction (though less in the past than it does now). The Court's "interests" are likely indeed to be affected by the historical context, but historical imperatives can be strengthened or weakened by the Court's eagerness or reluctance to accede to them. And since the constitutional questions that do successfully claim the attention of the Court are often those least answerable by rules of thumb, the predilections, the "values" of the judges, must play a part in supplying answers to them.

From 1789 until the Civil War, the dominant interest of the Supreme Court was in that greatest of all the questions left unsolved by the founders—the nation-state relationship. And the dominant judicial value, underlying the drift of decision in widely different areas, was the value of preserving the American Union. To be sure, the judges of the Supreme Court were not entirely single-minded and so of course other interests, other values, intruded upon the judicial mind and clamored for attention. Marshall and, indeed, the American bench and bar in general, were deeply concerned over the question of property rights, and it is possible to interpret the decisions of the Marshall court in terms that emphasize this preoccupation. Early in Taney's era Jacksonian distrust of finance capitalism found expression in judicial decisions; later the issue of slavery ran its dark course through constitutional law. Such matters as these profoundly engaged the judges' interests, and there is no disposition here to minimize the part they played in shaping legal doctrine or to deny that in isolated cases that part might be the crucial one.

But the question of nation-state relationships was in this era so closely entwined with such issues as property rights and slavery that to touch one was to touch the other, and we can be sure that it was never far from the judges' minds even when they seemed for the moment to be focusing on something else. And the motive of preserving the Union is persistently suggested by decision after decision, the one factor that makes sense out of apparent doctrinal inconsistencies, the often-inarticulate major premise that binds even such disparate spirits as Marshall and Taney together in a common cause.

It is hardly surprising that this should be so considering the drift of American history during the period, the evasiveness of the Constitution on these points, and the extremely tentative nature of the Court's own status. The states' rights and nationalist fetishes were the great herrings across the trail of American politics. Where reason and prudence were arrayed against him, a partisan could always invoke the dogma of states' rights or national sovereignty and feel fairly confident that tempers would rise and good sense depart. The nation lived in a nearly constant alternation of fears that it would cease being a nation altogether or become too much of one. And the Constitution alone could not serve to quiet these misgivings, for, as the warring camps soon discovered, it could be cited on either side, depending on whether a "strict construction" or a "loose construction" were adopted.

These ubiquitous questions thus inhered in almost every constitutional case the Supreme Court faced. At the same time, the Court's very title to decide them depended upon the Union's preservation, and this made it almost sure that the judges would put that value first. Hamilton hoped to strengthen the nation by giving capitalism a stake in its survival. Whatever the failures of that particular program, just such a marriage of interest and principle was accomplished by the establishment of the federal judiciary.

Within this broad category of interests then and with this dominant value of unionism for guidance, the Supreme Court of the pre–Civil War years sought to define its role. The relevant query for the judges—as for a student of the period—was not whether the Union ought to be maintained and made "more perfect"; there was all but unanimous agreement about that. The problem was how the Court could most usefully serve the cause it had espoused, or, to put it in another way, what view of the Constitution was best calculated to preserve the Union—and thereby the Supreme Court.

With the advantage of hindsight we can see that the judges had three major "role problems" before them. In the first place they must establish, not merely in theory but in practice as well, the doctrine of *judicial independence*. It is true that this doctrine was well rooted in colonial tradition and that the framers had tried to implement it by providing life tenure during "good behavior" for federal judges and by prohibiting reduction of their salaries. But it is also true that Congress was given powers, such as impeachment and control of the appellate jurisdiction, which were quite adequate to obliterate judicial independence if Congress were determined to do so.

Second, the Court must gain acceptance for the idea that among the powers thus independently exercised was that of *judicial review*, that is, the power to refuse to enforce an unconstitutional act of either the state or national government. And finally that power itself must be nourished and cultivated so that it will grow into the doctrine of *judicial sovereignty*, or the idea that a law may be held unconstitutional if the Court thinks it is, even though the case is not plain, and that the Court's opinion to this effect is binding on other branches of government. These problems need not be met in just this order; they need not be resolved with absolute finality. But they must be dealt with and partially answered if the Supreme Court is to play a significant part in the long struggle to preserve the Union.

YOUTHFUL UNCERTAINTIES

It is hard for a student of judicial review to avoid feeling that American constitutional history from 1789 to 1801 was marking time. The great shadow of John Marshall, who became Chief Justice in the latter year, falls across our understanding of that first decade; and it has therefore the quality of a play's opening moments with minor characters exchanging trivialities while they and the audience await the appearance of the star.

Such an impression is not altogether unjustified. The Supreme Court was, as we have seen, uncertain of its standing in those early years. When John Jay refused to resume the chief justiceship in 1801, he told President Adams that he had no faith the Court could acquire enough "energy, weight and dignity" to play a salient part in the nation's affairs. Each justice was burdened with the ridiculous chore of riding circuit, turning up twice a year to attend circuit court in each of four or five federal districts, which meant that judicial energies were dissipated in endless travel under the semiprimitive conditions of the day. Several statesmen of distinction like Edmund Pendleton of Virginia and Charles Cotesworth Pinckney of South Carolina refused appointment to the Court, and several more resigned in favor of greener pastures, including two Chief Justices, John Jay and Oliver Ellsworth. Few cases came to the Court compared with the torrents of later years, and even fewer were very important. Not one decision holding a state or federal law unconstitutional was handed down. And in most of the cases that were decided the practice of delivering opinions *seriatim* (a separate opinion by each judge) diffused the impact of the judgments and made it all the less likely that the Court would be regarded as an equal partner in the federal triumvirate.

Of course constitutional questions were arising. It would have been strange if they had not in these years when the Constitution itself was being tried on for size. But for the time being most of them were fought out in the legislative branches, in cabinet meetings, or in the forum of public opinion. The first Congress, acting in accord with the conditions attached to ratification by several of the states, proposed twelve amendments, ten of which were ultimately ratified and became the "Bill of Rights." The bill to incorporate a national bank raised the grave question of whether the national government's authority should be broadly or strictly construed, for no such incorporation power was specifically granted in the Constitution. Madison in Congress and Jefferson in the cabinet sharply opposed the proposal, arguing for strict construction, while Hamilton's astute defense of the broader viewpoint not only won the day but became one of the great state papers of American history. The issue was not to reach the Supreme Court for almost thirty years.

Even when the rod of power was explicitly offered, the judiciary displayed some reluctance about grasping it. Certain ticklish questions of international law were arising in connection with the Neutrality Proclamation of 1793, and, although President Washington wanted the Court's advice in solving them, the Court declined to give him any, arguing that "advisory opinions" were inconsistent with the judicial function. And somewhat earlier, when Congress had tried to invest the judiciary with authority to settle claims of invalid war veterans, two Supreme Court justices sitting on the circuit court joined a district judge in modestly rejecting the assignment. The law, they declared, is unconstitutional, because "the business directed by this act is not of a judicial nature" (first *Hayburn* case). All this suggests a Court bypassed in the major power struggles of the day and by no means eager to have greatness thrust upon it.

But this does not mean that the Court of the 1790's was unmindful of its potential as a factor in American government. In fact, as the *Hayburn* case suggests, the judges were quietly laying the groundwork of power even while power itself was allowed to slip away, were preparing for a time when great matters, such as the issue of the Bank, would come within the judicial purview. The refusal to perform "non-judicial" functions reflected a shrewd insight—that the Court's position would ultimately depend on preserving its difference from the other branches of government. The Congress and the presidency would always have roots in the power structure of American society, while the Court must find its support in the popular belief that the judiciary stands apart and defends the fundamental law. And the decision in *Hayburn*, with all its appearance of self-denial, was bold enough in other respects: it rested on the cardinal premise that the judiciary could disregard a legislative act which it believed was unconstitutional.

That premise, the very essence of the Court's future greatness, was taking vague but perceptible shape throughout these years. Hamilton had supplied an invaluable cue in the *Federalist Papers* by flatly claiming such a power for the judiciary; and those papers were already become a venerated source of constitutional guidance. State court judges were following his lead from time to time, asserting their right to determine the validity of state laws in the light of the state constitutions. The members of the Supreme Court themselves, not only in *Hayburn* but in other cases, were giving voice to the idea of judicial review in ways that allowed them to avoid being called to account for all the idea's implications. Justice Paterson indulged in 1795 in some high-sounding language about the judicial duty to declare unwarranted legislative acts void; but the occasion was a jury charge in the course of circuit court proceedings, and it was not at all clear that the doctrine he enunciated had any practical effect on the outcome of the case. In several other cases, decided by the Supreme Court, the justices quite evidently assumed in their opinions that they *could* set unconstitutional state or federal laws aside, but they elected in these circumstances not to do so. This approach had the double advantage of disarming critics concerned with the outcome of the immediate cause and at the same time adding a brick or two to the edifice of precedent on which the judicial future would depend.

Nor was the Court of this era as neglectful of the nation-state relationship problem as its failure to hold a state act unconstitutional might suggest. In fact, its first real foray into hotly disputed constitutional realms indicated zeal and audacity somewhat in advance of the times. In the course of the ratification controversy, more than one apprehensive Antifederalist had noticed the phrase in Article III which extended the judicial power to controversies "between a State and citizens of another State," and had darkly suspected that it might be invoked to subvert state sovereignty. Did the clause mean that an individual could sue a state in the federal courts? So it might seem from the language alone, but the Constitution's defenders, including Madison, Hamilton, and Marshall, rejected the inference and soothed this fear of its detractors: no state, they said, would be haled into federal courts under the authority of this clause, for the sovereign is not subject to suit. Now however, in 1793, the Supreme Court chose to think otherwise. When two citizens of South Carolina brought an action against Georgia for the recovery of debt and Georgia refused to appear in her own defense, the Court declared that states were suable and rendered judgment for the plaintiff.

The practical consequences of this doctrine were grave enough, for the states had been playing fast and loose in fiscal matters for years; and the doctrine, if enforced, might expose them to harassment by a swarm of creditors. But, even worse, the theoretical premise of the decision was an outright challenge to state sovereignty. The judges had forthrightly recognized that they were being asked to make their first great decision about the nature of the Union and had held, in the words of Justice Wilson, that "*as to the purposes of the Union, therefore, Georgia is not a sovereign state.*" The point seems sensible and indeed almost inevitable if the Union was to have meaning, but 1793 was too soon to state it so baldly. A gale of opposition at once arose from all sides, and a constitutional amendment denying that states were suable in federal courts by citizens of other states, was proposed and later ratified (Amendment XI). The larger question of the nature of the Union was postponed for the more devious talents of Marshall to cope with. The pre-Marshall justices had made two mistakes their great successor usually managed to avoid: in their ardor to establish an ultra-Federalist doctrine they had spoken overplainly; and they had spoken thus in support of a doctrine that immediately imperiled the concrete interests of most of the states. The resulting united protest was too strong for the Court's nascent independence to withstand, and the judges' fingers were badly (though not fatally) singed.

As *Chisholm* v. *Georgia* suggests, then, the pre-Marshall Court was fully conscious that its greatest problem was the nation-state relationship, and it was heavily disposed to create, or to encourage the creation of, a consolidated national union. And as tentative gropings toward a doctrine of judicial review suggest, the Court was also perfectly aware that it could carry out this imposing assignment only if it possessed final authority to decide questions of constitutionality. Why then did it not proceed at once to undermine state sovereignty and to assert the full range of the judicial prerogative? Why, for example, did the Court allow more than a decade to pass without directly invalidating a state law on constitutional grounds? Why are the statements of the doctrine of judicial review artfully concealed in innocuous decisions or pronounced so equivocally as to leave the whole matter in doubt?

In part the answer is that the judges understood, whether consciously or instinctively, their limitations as well as their opportunities. They realized that the Constitution did not explicitly accord them the power they coveted and that public opinion had not yet filled in this gap in the organic law. They realized that the characteristically unqualified logic of Hamilton, however convincing and tempting it might seem, was not quite apt for their purposes. The essayist Hamilton could sweep premises, argument, and conclusions together in a single brave statement at a single moment in time. The constitutional judge—or the would-be constitutional judge—needed time as an ally and could not afford to treat it so cavalierly. The judicial empire, if there was to be one, had to be conquered slowly, piece by piece. An idea could be implied today, obliquely stated tomorrow, and flatly asserted the next day. But months and years had to pass before the judiciary was ready to give that idea fully effective life as a principle of decision. Meanwhile the forthright logic of Hamilton was being transmuted into the less tidy but more potent logic of public consent, as the original idea worked its way into the consciousness of educated Americans. And then, when the moment for real action came, the ground might be ready.

THE MENACE OF JEFFERSON AND THE CAUTION OF MARSHALL

The ground might indeed have been ready in 1800 if the nicely ordered political world of the Federalists' dreams had behaved itself as they thought they had a right to expect. The Court, as we have seen, had laid the basis for judicial review in its pronouncements of the past ten years. The idea was now familiar to most of those who thought about such matters, and there is no reason to believe that many of them staunchly opposed it. Neither, to be sure, is there evidence that they fully understood its implications as a doctrine of judicial *supremacy*, or expected that the Court would use its veto in any but a clear case; but some of those implications could wait a bit longer for the future to unfold them. Judicial nationalism had been set back on its heels by the reaction to the *Chisholm* case, but in 1796 the Court had dealt state sovereignty an almost equally grievous blow when it held that the peace treaty with Great Britain overrode state laws affecting the rights of British creditors, and the reaction had not been disastrous, however ill-tempered. The judiciary's time for greatness might have seemed at hand.

But the world of politics chose this moment to display a mind of its own. The Federalists, in a fine frenzy engendered partly by fear of France and partly by well-founded doubts about their own ability to hold the American electorate's support, had passed the Alien and Sedition Acts in 1798. The judges of the federal bench were almost to a man ardent Federalist partisans, and they had enthusiastically shouldered the task of enforcing the Sedition Act, which was designed, among other things, to visit savage punishment on those who criticized the national administration. Supreme Court justices like Paterson, Iredell, and above all Samuel Chase earned the hatred of Jefferson's fast-growing Republican party, not only by presiding over the convictions of men who had called John Adams names ("hoary headed incendiary") and otherwise maligned Federalism, but by revealing on the bench a vengeful partisanship that rekindled pre-Revolutionary memories of the king's courts. Insult was added to injury when federal judges undertook, even without benefit of a statute, to punish under the English common law those who violated Washington's Neutrality Proclamation or the Treaty of Peace with Great Britain. Justice Chase, not content with giving partisan speeches from the bench, openly and eagerly participated in political campaigns against the monstrous threat of Jeffersonianism.

This would have been a bad sort of game for the judiciary to play under any circumstances, but in light of the political realities of the time it was almost suicidal. The Alien and Sedition Acts called forth the Kentucky and Virginia resolutions which challenged, in language composed by Jefferson and Madison, respectively, the whole doctrine of national supremacy and unity upon which the very existence of the Supreme Court hinged. The party of Jefferson won the election of 1800, and the victors came to office with an understandably bitter distrust of the national judiciary which had so eagerly joined in the persecution of Republicans. The outgoing Federalists did their part to make a bad situation worse by passing the Judiciary Act of 1801, creating a number of new federal judgeships which were hastily filled by Adams, and reducing the number of Supreme Court justices from six to five. This law was not without merits, but those merits were forgotten in the justifiable Republican anger at its obvious partisanship. The Federalists, having lost the other two branches of government, hoped to maintain their control nonetheless by intrenching a pro-Federalist judiciary protected by life tenure.

It is little wonder that the noble rage of Jefferson's party, once focused on the task of winning a national election, was now directed at the federal judiciary and its head and symbol, the Supreme Court. When Adams, as one of the last acts of his administration, appointed the Federalist John Marshall to the Chief Justiceship, the Republicans felt they had endured enough such Parthian salvos and began to map out a counter-campaign of their own. The Judiciary Act of 1801 was repealed only a little more than a year after its passage, notwithstanding Federalist cries that the repealing act was itself unconstitutional. John Adams' "midnight appointments" of new federal judges were thus for the most part wiped away. As for the remaining members of the federal (and Federalist) bench, the awful power of impeachment was to be invoked: the judiciary must bow to the will of the people—which was, of course, in Jeffersonian theory the will of the Republicans—or be turned out. The principle of judicial independence was faced with its first great challenge.

This threat to judicial independence loomed over the Marshall Court during the first few years of his incumbency and inevitably conditioned what might be called the strategy of judicial behavior. Marshall desired, as much as Wilson or Jay had, to establish the power of the judiciary on solid ground and to use the power to defend the cause of national union. Their Court had in its first few years prepared the way for this and was proceeding gradually but surely along the way when the Jeffersonian tempest, generated in part by the judiciary's own folly, burst forth. As a result of it, Marshall's opportunity was perilously difficult for him to grasp, and in fact the great day when the Court would declare a state law unconstitutional was postponed for almost another full decade. Not until then, or nearly then, was it clear that localist sentiment in the American body politic was less robust than he had feared it was. Not until then did he know that judicial prestige was durable enough to warrant some risks, that judicial independence was at least relatively secure. Not until then did the Court begin to be a major factor in American government.

Important as Marshall is in the history of American jurisprudence, it is not his appointment that marks the Court's coming of age, for the Court, like an individual, grew up slowly. Marshall did establish almost at once the custom of letting one justice's opinion, usually his own, stand for the decision of the whole Court, and this custom gave the judicial pronouncements a forceful unity they had formerly lacked. But in spite of this the Court after 1801 was for some time no more formidable than it had been before; judicial independence had not yet been firmly established; the real bite of the doctrine of judicial review had not yet made itself felt; the problem of the Union was still comparatively untouched. Marshall was holding back, awaiting a more propitious future. His preeminence among builders of the American constitutional tradition rests not only on his well-known boldness, his "tiger instinct for the jugular vein" as an enthusiastic metaphorist once called it, but also on his less-noticed sense of self-restraint.

The famous case *Marbury* v. *Madison* in 1803 appears to contradict this proposition but in fact confirms it. The decision is a masterwork of indirection, a brilliant example of Marshall's capacity to sidestep danger while seeming to court it, to advance in one direction while his opponents are looking in another.

In its closing hours the Adams administration had done its competent best, as we have seen, to fill up federal offices with loyal anti-

Jeffersonians. But events were moving rapidly, some details were apt to be neglected, and when Jefferson took over, the commission of one William Marbury to be Justice of the Peace in the District of Columbia had not been delivered to him, though it had been signed and sealed. The new President was indisposed to mend this oversight of his predecessors, so Marbury asked the Supreme Court for a writ which would compel Jefferson's Secretary of State, Madison, to hand over the commission. This created what seemed a painful and unpromising dilemma for Marshall and his Court. If they upheld Marbury and ordered delivery of the commission, the order would surely be ignored by Madison, the Court would be exposed as impotent to enforce its mandates, the shakiness of judicial prestige would be dramatically emphasized. If on the other hand they did not uphold Marbury, they would give aid and comfort to Jefferson and might seem to support his denunciation of the "midnight appointments." The latter course was impossibly distasteful to an ardently Federalist bench; the former was humiliating and might well be risky.

But Marshall was equal to the occasion. Marbury's commission, he said, is being illegally withheld from him by the Jeffersonian administration and a writ can appropriately be directed to a cabinet official when he fails his duty. However, the Supreme Court is not the proper tribunal to supply Marbury with a remedy in this case, for the Court does not possess the power to issue writs in cases of this kind. It is true that Section 13 of the Judiciary Act of 1789 seems to grant the Court such power, but that provision is itself invalid. For the Court's original jurisdiction is defined in the Constitution, and a congressional act like this one, which adds to the original jurisdiction, is therefore unconstitutional. And an unconstitutional law is void and must be so treated by the Supreme Court. Mr. Marbury then must look elsewhere for redress of his just grievance— with the Court's best wishes.

A more adroit series of parries and ripostes would be difficult to imagine. The danger of a head-on clash with the Jeffersonians was averted by the denial of jurisdiction; but, at the same time, the declaration that the commission was illegally withheld scotched any impression that the Court condoned the administration's behavior. These negative maneuvers were artful achievements in their own right. But the touch of genius is evident when Marshall, not content with having rescued a bad situation, seizes the occasion to set forth the doctrine of judicial review. It is easy for us to see in retrospect that the occasion was golden. The attention of the Republicans was focused on the question of Marbury's commission, and they cared very little how the Court went about justifying a hands-off policy so long as that policy was followed. Moreover, the Court was in the delightful position, so common in its history but so confusing to its critics, of rejecting and assuming power in a single breath, for the Congress had tried here to give the judges an authority they could not constitutionally accept and the judges were high-mindedly refusing. The moment for immortal statement was at hand all right, but only a judge of Marshall's discernment could have recognized it.

As for the statement itself, it exemplifies the gift for argumentative effectiveness, the masterful sense of strategy, that is illustrated in Marshall's whole approach to the case and was perhaps his supreme talent. He was able to endow his arguments with the flavor of the irresistible through a combination of lucidity and self-confidence:

> The question of whether an Act repugnant to the Constitution can become the law of the land, is a question deeply interesting to the United States; but, happily, not of an intricacy proportioned to its interest. It seems only necessary to recognize certain principles, supposed to have been long and well-established, to decide it.

Marshall then proceeds to an examination of those principles for the benefit of the few who might not realize how "long and well-established" they were. These hypothetical adversaries are chosen with great care— they are evidently those who would deny the power of judicial review *altogether.* Imagine a law that clearly violates the Constitution, says Marshall, for example, a duty on state exports explicitly violating Article I, section 9. Surely the judges are not bound to enforce such an act, to treat it as valid. Now many, though not all, of Marshall's listeners would probably concede this point as far as it goes; the real questions for them would arise when the statute was not a *clear* violation of the Constitution, or when judges purported to speak on constitutional questions not only for themselves but for the other branches as well, to presume that the judicial finding of invalidity was final. These queries are not met at all in the argument of the *Marbury* case, and by ignoring them Marshall succeeds in beclouding them. Attacks on the discretionary scope and the finality of judicial review are henceforth confused with attacks on the minimal power Marshall here contends for, and the attackers thus find that though they aim for the weakest point in the judicial armor they almost invariably hit the strongest. The *Marbury* argument is justly celebrated, but not the least of its virtues is the fact that it is somewhat beside the point.

The *Marbury* opinion then is far from suggesting that Marshall was rash or even very bold in exercising judicial supervision at this stage of his career as Chief Justice. The decision was criticized for its dictum that the executive *could* be called to account by judicial process, but since the requested writ was in fact denied, no really great heat was generated even on this point. And as for the argument for judicial review, at the time only the Federalists paid much attention to it, and they of course were warmly approving; the Jeffersonians shed few tears over the voiding of a law that had been passed by Federalists in the first place.

The decision does suggest, however, that Marshall, though choosing the path of discretion in the immediate occasion, did not for a moment forget the long-term objectives—enhancement of judicial power in general and diminution of state autonomy in particular. The relevance of the *Marbury* case to the struggle against state autonomy is easy to miss, because the Chief Justice's specific target is a national statute. But the argument for holding an unconstitutional law void is phrased in very broad terms, and it applies equally whether the enacting body is Congress or a state legislature. In fact two of Marshall's three argumentative illustrations of obviously invalid laws would be just as apposite if state, rather than national, power were being called into question. The important point is that the Court may refuse to enforce an unconstitutional law, whatever its source may be. *Marbury* is thus not, as it might appear at first glance, a digression from the long-run struggle against excessive localism; on the contrary, it is a crucial skirmish in that campaign, for when state laws are later judicially challenged, the precedent of *Marbury* stands ready to back up the challenge.

The Ordeal of John Marshall: The Impeachment Threat Subsides

Meanwhile, however, the antijudicial brew of the Republicans was simmering and Marshall was constrained to adhere to the course of measured caution that *Marbury* represents. No one knew better than he that the ambitious assertions of that case would be quite meaningless in the face of concerted political resistance from the other branches, and he had no wish to provoke more united opposition than he already faced. In 1803, the very year of the *Marbury* decision, the Congress proceeded to the impeachment of John Pickering, Judge of the United States Court for the District of New Hampshire. This unfortunate man was hopelessly insane and a drunkard; his behavior on the bench for three years had been picturesquely irrational. There was no doubt that he now lacked the capacity to discharge the duties of office, but the Constitution provides no method for removal except "Impeachment for, and Conviction of, Treason, Bribery, or other high Crimes and Misdemeanors" (Art. II, sec. 4). Could a man who was clearly out of his mind and therefore not responsible be convicted of "high Crimes and Misdemeanors"? If not, could he be impeached?

The answer of the Republicans was to offer a theory of the impeachment power that would transcend such technical limits. As Senator Giles of Virginia was to put it: "Impeachment is nothing more than the enquiry, by the two Houses of Congress, whether the office of any public man might not be better filled by another. . . . A trial and removal of a judge need not imply any criminality or corruption in him." Pickering was convicted of high crimes and misdemeanors in spite of the legal anomaly this involved, the broad theory of the impeachment power being clearly implicit in the finding. But the principal interest of the theory's framers was not of course its first demented victim. Having given the idea a trial run, they now proposed to apply it to Samuel Chase of the Supreme Court, their particular bête noire among Federalist judges, and then to any other judicial menace to Republican aims, including John Marshall.

If the program had succeeded, the doctrine of an independent judiciary would have foundered and the whole future history of the Court might have been profoundly altered. Marshall's alarm can hardly be exaggerated. Apparently despairing of the chances for full independence, he privately suggested that Congress might be given appellate jurisdiction over Supreme Court decisions, as an alternative to impeachment. As a biographer remarks, we could not credit that Marshall ever subscribed to such an extraordinary notion if it had not been set forth in his own hand and the letter preserved. But the suggestion is a measure of his fear for his precious tribunal, of his conviction that a formal surrender of final authority might be the price that had to be paid in order to preserve any authority at all.

But the program did not succeed; it turned out that a lesser price would serve the purpose. The House, under the whip of the malignant John Randolph, duly brought impeachment articles against Chase, charging him with misconduct in the sedition trials of Fries and Callender in 1800, in his treatment of a grand jury at Newcastle in the same year, and in his political harangue of another grand jury in Baltimore in 1803. However, in conducting the impeachment proceedings before the Senate, Randolph and his cohorts seemed unable to decide whether to rest their case on charges of criminality or on the radical Republican theory that Congress could impeach merely for conduct it disapproved. The former charges were hard to prove, especially in the face of the formidable legal counsel that had assembled on Chase's behalf; yet the latter theory might well not receive the support of the necessary two-thirds of the Senate, and the whole cause might thus be lost. Instead of resolving this dilemma, the impeachers mingled criminality and mere objectionable conduct in a hopeless tangle. Those who might have supported one kind of charge were repelled by the other, and the Senate ended by finding Chase not guilty.

Mismanagement by the impeachment leaders undoubtedly contributed to this result. But the essential explanation is that many members of the Senate, including some Republicans, were not yet incensed enough with the judiciary to vote to destroy its independence. And their wrath was moderate or non-existent because the Court under Marshall had really done so little to incite it. The charge that the judiciary was tyrannically imposing a Federalist will on a Republican-minded nation did not square with the immediate facts of judicial behavior, whatever suspicions might be entertained about Marshall's long-term aspirations. And this impression of a non-aggressive bench had been further confirmed when, only a few days after *Marbury*, the Supreme Court sustained the validity of the law repealing the Judiciary Act of 1801. A Court that would pass up an opportunity to strike at this law, which all good Federalists regarded as the acme of Republican wickedness, could hardly be thought of as a despotic monster.

The failure of the Chase impeachment is one of the signal events in the history of the federal judiciary, because it set a precedent against loose construction of the impeachment power and thus supported the doctrine of judicial independence. And the price paid for this benign result was not the great one Marshall had feared—the vesting of an appellate authority in Congress—but simply a measure of present judicial self-restraint. Throughout the nation's future history this lesson can be read again and again: paradoxical though it may seem, the Supreme Court often gains rather than loses power by adopting a policy of forbearance.

THE LION STIRS AT LAST: FLETCHER V. PECK

Marshall at any rate continued to take this lesson to heart for some years after Chase was saved from martyrdom. Of course it was by no means as clear to Marshall and his contemporaries as it is to us that impeachment was no longer an omnipresent danger. After his only real clash with Jefferson's administration, the trial of Aaron Burr for treason in 1807, demands for impeachment were heard once more. In this case Marshall seems to have been provoked by the partisan heat of the moment and by his hatred of Jefferson to depart from the pathway of caution. His interpretation of the treason clause of the Constitution made it quite impossible for Jefferson's administration to convict Burr, and his vulnerability to the consequent Republican attacks might appear all the greater when we reflect that the interpretation was of very doubtful validity.

But this time the antijudicial crusade, though extremely noisy, got nowhere at all. No doubt its progress was to a degree thwarted by the administration's involvement in other concerns, for the War of 1812 was already impending. But surely it can also be inferred that the doctrine of judicial independence had itself become a formidable shield against partisan assaults. The fact that the doctrine was now established and recognized did not mean that the judiciary was henceforth free of any threats from the congressional side. Under sufficient provocation the weapon of impeachment might yet be called into use, and in any event the less drastic but formidable power to restrict appellate jurisdiction was still untried. Henceforward Marshall and his cohorts could feel sure that such antijudicial action would not be undertaken lightly, that the Supreme Court's prestige was a factor to be reckoned with. In those first few stormy years of the Republic's history, the members of Congress and of the executive department had demonstrated over and over that the Constitution was less important to them than were political results. The records of both parties were strewn with evidence of this, but the Federalists' Sedition Act and the Jeffersonians' Louisiana Purchase are enough to illustrate the point. The judiciary had thus been left free to claim the Constitution for its own, to identify its own prestige with the prestige of fundamental law, and Marshall, with his happy combination of audacity and discretion, had made the most of the advantage.

Now at last then, after the reverberations of the Burr incident had subsided, Marshall was ready to follow the course which the judicial maneuvers of the past had made possible. He was ready to declare state law unconstitutional, to show how the judiciary's carefully nurtured power and prestige could be employed to help preserve the Union.

The case, Fletcher v. Peck in 1810, involved the notorious Yazoo land-grant scandal. The details of this outrageous but fascinating affair are too intricate to be traced here; a good, long story must be shortened unmercifully. In 1795, Georgia had sold at a bargain price a huge tract of land comprising most of the modern states of Alabama and Mississippi. It quickly became known that all but one of the members of the legislature who voted for the sale had been bribed to do so, and a newly elected legislature, inflamed with righteous indignation, hastened to rescind the grant. However, before this virtuous step could be taken, the original purchasers had resold millions of acres of the land to supposedly innocent third parties, and the question of their titles' validity now came before the Supreme Court. The argument was that the rescinding act was a violation of the Constitution and that the third-party titles were therefore still sound.

John Marshall and a unanimous Court agreed. The rescinding act was invalid and must be held so by the Supreme Court; this much was clear. But the exact basis for the holding was far from clear, for Marshall seemed reluctant to rest his judgment on one ground alone, probably because of the lingering difficulties each argument separately presented.

At one point he seemed to declare explicitly that the rescinding act impaired the obligation of contracts in violation of Article I, section 10, of the Constitution. But this declaration encountered two serious objections: that the contract clause was probably meant to apply to contracts between private individuals and not between the state and individuals; and that in any event a grant is not a contract carrying an obligation. Marshall met both of these hazards and purported to dispose of them, but we may doubt that he was fully confident he had done so.

At another point he intimated that the Georgia act was a violation of the ex post facto clause, but the trouble here was that the clause had been held applicable only to criminal legislation some twelve years before, and the law now in question of course concerned purely civil matters. At still another point he suggested that the rescinding act might be invalid merely because it offended against "the nature of society and of government," in other words natural law; as Justice Johnson, concurring, put it: "the reason and nature of things: a principle which will impose laws even on the Deity." And in the end Marshall said: "The state of Georgia was restrained, *either* by general principles, which are common to our free institutions, or by the particular provisions of the Constitution of the United States" from passing the rescinding law and applying it to innocent purchasers. (Italics added.) This statement scrambled the various possible arguments in a single indiscriminate mixture.

Yet the importance of the results accomplished by this seemingly turgid rhetoric was considerable. To begin with, it laid the basis for the momentous rule that the state is bound by its own contractual obligations. Marshall may have been toying with the idea of claiming for the Court the power to overthrow laws which violated such agreements on the basis of natural law or "right reason" without reference to any specific constitutional clause. This idea was abroad in the land at the time, and hints of it keep turning up in Supreme Court opinions for many years to come. At first glance it might seem that this carte blanche for judicial governance would be very appealing to Marshall, for it would supply him with a roving commission to invalidate any law he disapproved, subject only to the proviso that the incantations of the natural-law tradition must be recited. But he surely realized that the Court's future lay with the tangible Constitution itself rather than its invisible and most disputable higher-law background, that a Court which claimed the power to go beyond the Constitution would be dispensing with its most valuable support and might end by possessing no power at all. In the long run, therefore, he preferred to moor his arguments in the language of the Constitution. For the moment, however, since the contract clause alone was not yet strong enough to support the great principle that the state must abide by its agreements, he was willing to use the natural law as a supplementary prop. Later, when the contract clause had reached a higher stage of legal maturity, the talk of natural law and right reason was dispensed with and the principle rested squarely and explicitly on the contract clause.

But in the second place and in some ways more important, *Fletcher v. Peck* is the first clear precedent for the general proposition that the Supreme Court is empowered to hold state laws unconstitutional. That this power exists is the unstated premise of the whole decision, unstated because Marshall simply assumed that there was no room for argument on the point. He declared what no one would dispute:

> But Georgia cannot be viewed as a single, unconnected sovereign power, on whose legislature no other restrictions are imposed than may be found in its own constitution. She is a part of a large empire; she is a member of the American Union; and that Union has a constitution the supremacy of which all acknowledge, and which imposes limits to the legislatures of the several states, which none claim a right to pass.

Then he blandly took a long leap from this resounding truism to the holding that the Georgia law was invalid. We have seen with what circumspection the Court had been edging toward this climactic declaration in the preceding two decades; now at length its careful efforts were rewarded. The justification for Marshall's assumption of power is to be found by looking to the past, back to the judicial arguments in such cases as *Hayburn* and *Marbury,* back to the acceptance of jurisdiction in *Chisholm,* back to the whole elaborate process by which Marshall and his predecessors built support for the doctrines of judicial independence and judicial review. The argument need not be stated now because that process has imbedded it in the ideology of the nation.

Fletcher v. *Peck,* then, marks the end of the beginning of the Court's long struggle to find its place in the American governmental system. It is a milestone at which we can pause to assess the accomplishments and lessons of the past, and the problems of the future. Some of the initial uncertainties that confronted the four judges in Philadelphia in 1790 have been at least tentatively resolved. The idea of judicial independence has become an operative doctrine. The power of judicial review over national and state legislation has been not only claimed in theory but applied to concrete cases. The judges have begun to learn the arts of judicial governance: the necessity to avoid, if possible, head-on collisions with the dominant political forces of the moment; the undesirability of claiming too much too soon; the great advantage of taking the long view, especially when others take the short; the usefulness of diverting criticism from weakness to strength; the importance of identifying judicial claims to authority with the claims of the Constitution. These doctrines, these arts, are now available to the judiciary as it turns its attention to the cause of national union, and they are potentially of great service to that cause. But we must not mistake half a loaf for the whole; though the preliminaries are over, much remains undone. Judicial independence is a formidable reality, but it remains to be seen whether it can be sustained in the face of real adversity. Judicial review in Marshall's carefully phrased formulation is fairly well accepted, but judicial sovereignty is not; and until the Court's opinion on constitutionality even in debatable cases is regarded as final, the influence of the judiciary on national affairs can only be peripheral. These remaining problems dominate the agenda of the Court's next twenty-five years; and their resolution depends partly on the roll of the historical dice and partly on the wisdom of the judges in directing the institution that has fallen to their charge.

THREE

THE MARSHALL COURT AND THE SHAPING OF THE NATION: 1810–1835

S
O FAR THE STORY of the Supreme Court has been largely prelude. The judges have been deviled by uncertainties about their own status in the young American polity and about the power and malevolence of the forces that might imperil that status. Since the constitutional agreement of 1789 was inexplicit about the nature and scope of judicial authority, the Court has inherited the responsibility for drawing up its own commission, one line at a time, and the task has been delicate. Only gradually has it become apparent that the Court is being accepted as a symbol of constitutionalism and can therefore count on a solid measure of public support. Only with experience has it become clear to Marshall and his judicial brethren that the Republicans are not after all savage revolutionaries, that their bark is worse than their bite, and that the rule of law can therefore survive even though the Federalist party may not. In such a prelude, amid such uncertainties, the Court has been able to lay the argumentative bases for future accomplishments; it has fashioned some of the tools which may later be used to help govern America. But it has not yet been in a position to exert much real influence on the course of affairs. It has built its own fences with some cunning, but has not so far done much to build the nation.

However, with the War of 1812 and its immediate aftermath a new stage in the Court's history was inaugurated. We have seen that the slow accretion of precedents and confidence culminated in 1810, when the judges at last felt secure enough to hold a state law unconstitutional. Logically, the Court was then ready to begin to make its weight felt in the political order, to defend and foster in a concrete way the principle of national union. Now this logical development was stimulated and strengthened by the war's impact on American attitudes and political alignments.

Many of the old Federalists, especially in New England, had fiercely opposed "Mr. Madison's war," had talked darkly of seceding from the Union, and had espoused a states' rights position strangely reminiscent of the extreme Republicanism of the Virginia and Kentucky resolutions. The politically dominant Republicans, on the other hand, were forced, in defending their war, to embrace the idea of nationalism, and to abjure in part their own localist tradition. Since they were in the ascendancy, this meant that the creed of nationalism enjoyed an unprecedented, if temporary, popularity and—the other side of the coin—that localism was for the moment bereft of really powerful defenders. To be sure localist sentiment soon revived and its exponents were as vocal as ever. But the nationalist spirit, once awakened, could not be dismissed at will. These events had intruded a cross-current in the Republican ideology; leaders like Madison and Monroe though by no means unqualified nationalists were not consistent localists either; the tradition they spoke for was now ambivalent on the great question of the nature of the Union.

This ambivalence persisted for some years and gave John Marshall his opportunity to use the judicial instruments he had been preparing. But his way, though now passable, was still far from easy. The Court after all was in the process of attaining a position more exalted than any attained by a judicial tribunal in modern world history; great tasks were impending. For one thing it was necessary both to confirm and to extend the Court's claim to authority, to transmute "judicial review" into "judicial sovereignty." Granted that it was proper for the Court to adjudge questions of constitutionality, did this imply that the Court's judgment was final? Did it imply that the judges could call the other branches to account even when the question of constitutionality was doubtful? Did it imply that the Court would exercise a general supervision over some governmental affairs that fell outside the traditional judicial orbit?

To Marshall it implied all this, for he was firmly convinced that the more America was guided by judges the happier and more just its system would be. But others, in politics and out, were not ready to bear the Chief Justice's mild yoke, and there was always a threat that overweening judicial power would encounter resistance or counterattack more formidable than its recently established independence could withstand. Though moving onward and upward, then, the Court must still tread carefully.

Secondly and simultaneously, the Court of Marshall's remaining years was engaged in using its still nascent authority to establish the substantive constitutional principles on which the American polity should rest. It was interpreting the document of 1789 so as to provide maximum protection to property rights and maximum support for the idea of nationalism. Usually these two objectives were conjoined, so that a pronationalist constitutional doctrine best served the cause of property rights and vice versa. The national government was not at this time much inclined to interfere in commercial affairs, whereas the states, one or the other, presented a constant threat to the stability of currency, the sanctity of debts, or the freedom of business enterprise. Thus Marshall, happily for his peace of mind, was able to assure himself that he made property rights more secure when he deprived the states of power by enhancing the power of the nation. If these two primary values of his had conflicted, his soul-search would have been agonizing. But they seldom did conflict, and his historic achievements in the cause of union were therefore not clouded by confusion of motives.

He had troubles enough without adding internal uncertainty to them. The antinationalist front of the Republicans (soon to be called Democrats) had indeed been impaired, but specific and bitter centers of opposition still developed when specific provocations aroused them, and almost every major decision was met by a storm of intemperate denunciation from some politically potent quarter. Even worse, as the 1820's neared their end, it became increasingly apparent that the tide of states' rights sentiment was rising if not in volume at any rate in intensity. From time to time he was compellingly reminded of a fact that all Supreme Court justices must learn to live with: that the Court's decrees are backed only by its own prestige and ultimately by the willingness of the President to help enforce them. Over and over he was reminded that Congress could destroy in a day the judicial independence that had been building for decades.

In this context Marshall faced his great task of augmenting the judicial power and shaping the Constitution into a charter for nationalism. These two interwoven themes run through nearly all his decisions; each case raises the question of the Court's authority together with that of nation-state relationship, and the Court must always decide one question in the light of the other, taking care that its nationalist zeal does not compromise its own status or that claims for judicial power are never so extreme as to vitiate the crusade for nationalism. And little by little, in spite of the delicacy of this balancing feat, in spite of the deep antagonism of affected litigants, in spite of the rising wave of states' rights sentiment, the job is done. The Court's empire of decision is extended and stabilized as firmly as it ever can be in a governmental arrangement that rests on inference and acquiescence rather than on final definition. The great operative phrases of the Constitution—the supremacy clause, the contract clause, the necessary and proper clause, the commerce clause—are impregnated with the nationalist meanings so dear to Marshall's heart. And most important of all, these judicially contrived mutations in the character of American constitutionalism are generally accepted by the nation they are designed to guide.

How were these remarkable results achieved? How was the Court able, in the face of these adversities, to have its way? Partly the answer goes back to factors mentioned in previous chapters—the American attachment to the idea of fundamental law and the gradual identification of the Supreme Court with that idea. Partly the answer is to be found in the judges themselves and most of all of course in Marshall—the judicial sense of strategy and timing, the rhetorical virtuosity which should never be undervalued, the capacity to engender respect even among those who disagreed. Partly, as has been said, the difficulties were eased by the temporary ambivalence of Republican opinion on the nature of the Union. But the Court's progress was also aided by a basic disability of the localist movement—its very lack of unity. The states were so individualistic that they defeated themselves, for it was (and is) a peculiarity of the states' rights doctrine that its partisans were devoted to it only when their own oxen were being gored, when nationalism presented a specific threat to a concrete interest. If states' rights could be associated with a common and long-term economic issue like slavery or the tariff, then the affected states would stand long and firm against their mutual adversary. But if Virginia had a problem today that Maryland did not share, Virginia's outraged protest in the name of states' rights would attract little support from Maryland any more than Maryland's similar protest tomorrow would bring Virginia rushing to her standard. Both states were being true to the fractional principle that lay at the heart of the states' rights doctrine. But, because of their adherence to that principle, the Supreme Court, with its eye steadily on a single target, was spared the calamity of confronting a united opposition. The Court left such potentially unifying issues as the tariff and slavery pretty much alone, and it was not even necessary, then, to divide to conquer, for the opposition had thoughtfully divided itself.

THE COURT OVER THE STATES

One of the Court's great problems was presented either by direct or by implied challenge in nearly every significant case of the era: the problem of its right to review decisions of state courts involving the validity of acts undertaken by the state governments. Such a right was granted to the Court under Section 25 of the Judiciary Act of 1789; state court decisions that denied a claim made in the name of the federal Constitution, laws, or treaties could be reviewed by the Supreme Court by a "writ of error." And of course if the state court was thought to have erred, its judgment could be reversed and any state law it rested on invalidated.

That was the Supreme Court's nominal statutory authority, but it was one thing for Congress to pass such an empowering act and another thing to persuade the states to yield to it. From the first, localists had contended that Section 25 involved an unconstitutional encroachment on state sovereignty, and although the Court had several times exercised this supposedly unwarranted power with comparative impunity, the rumbles of protest had never quite been stilled. The case of *Martin v. Hunter's Lessee* in 1816 compelled the Court, which had so far tried to ignore the arguments against Section 25, finally to meet them head on.

The case involved the title to some 300,000 acres of Virginia land which had once belonged to Lord Fairfax but which had been confiscated by the state in Revolutionary times partly on the ground that Fairfax and his heirs were enemy aliens. Virginia had proceeded to grant a section of the land, which it now claimed as its own, to David Hunter, who later sought in the courts of Virginia to eject the Fairfax heirs. But in the meantime of course the Revolution had ended, the Treaty of Peace with Great Britain had been signed, the national Constitution had come into being, and the new national government had been endowed with the power to make treaties. It was argued that both the Treaty of Peace and Jay's Treaty of 1795 confirmed the titles of British subjects to land in America and that the Fairfax title was therefore still valid.

In spite of this, the Virginia Court of Appeals held against the Fairfax heirs, and the Supreme Court of the United States, having granted review of this holding on a writ of error, ordered it reversed. The Virginia court, which was headed by Spencer Roane, an ardent states' righter and bitter foe of Marshall, pondered this order for a while and then decided to ignore it, arguing that Section 25 was itself unconstitutional. The Virginia judges conceded of course that they were bound to observe the federal

Constitution, but they insisted that the meaning of the Constitution was for them to decide and that the Supreme Court had no power to impose its own interpretation upon them. It was this contention, so fatal to the prospects for both judicial supervision and centralism, that faced the Court in *Martin* v. *Hunter's Lessee.* If the Constitution was to mean whatever the various states wanted it to mean, the cause of national union was lost at the outset.

Justice Story spoke for the Court, Marshall having disqualified himself because he had been financially involved with the Fairfax interests. Story had been appointed by Madison in 1811 as a New England Republican, but now, after five years on the Court, he was as nationalistic in his views as Marshall himself. Indeed the supreme bench consisted of two Federalists and five nominal Republicans, and yet Marshall was seldom to have much difficulty enlisting his fellows in the nationalist crusade. His success in doing so has often been attributed to the witchcraft of his strong and charming personality; Jefferson had once predicted that "it will be difficult to find a character with firmness enough to preserve his independence on the same bench with Marshall." There can be no doubt that Marshall was an immensely attractive and convincing colleague, but it seems reasonable to suppose that the judges who came to share his nationalist views were beguiled not only by him but by a growing awareness that the Court's status and their own depended on the strength of the Union. It is hardly surprising that the Supreme Court, an intrinsically national institution, should be drawn to the doctrine of nationalism.

Story's powerful opinion in this case followed a pattern which can be traced through most of the great nationalistic decisions of the era. In the first place, he felt called upon to argue, or rather to assert, that the Constitution was the creation of "the people of the United States" as the Preamble says, and not of the several states. This contention, which may seem merely abstract, was essential to his purpose. Since at least 1776, most Americans had conceded that the people were the ultimate source of sovereignty and that the people could therefore, as Story says, "invest the general government with all powers which they might deem proper and necessary." If the Constitution was the work of the people, the powers it granted the national government *could* be as extensive as sovereignty itself. But if, on the other hand, the states had created the Constitution, it was arguable that the powers of the national government must stop at the point where they encroached on state sovereignty, and this very argument had been insisted upon by the embattled Virginians. The assertion that the Constitution represented the higher sovereignty of the people enabled Story to controvert the argument that state sovereignty is inviolable; if the people, in enacting the Constitution, wanted to modify state sovereignty, they had an incontestable right to do so.

The second great step in the opinion was to contend that the people *did* want to modify state sovereignty and had given evidence of that desire in the language of the Constitution. Article III extends the judicial power to all *cases* arising under the Constitution, laws, or treaties. There is no suggestion that the judicial power must stop short if a case originates in a state court rather than a federal. Since the language is general and is not restricted by the context or by necessary implication, it must be assumed that any case presenting a federal question is within reach of the judicial power, whatever may be the tribunal in which it arises.

This opinion contains, in more or less explicit statement, practically all the major items in the bag of tricks the Marshall Court was to use in future years against the minions of disunion. It invokes the doctrine of popular sovereignty to accomplish traditionally Federalist ends, a gambit that was particularly frustrating to the Court's Republican opponents, who were accustomed to think of themselves as the champions of that doctrine. The doctrine is then used by Story to deprecate the idea that state sovereignty was left intact at the time the Union was formed. Next he sets forth the proposition that national powers should be construed generously, a notion disastrous to states' rights when its implications are developed. From these principles "in respect to which no difference of opinion ought to be indulged," as Story says, he is able to infer a supervisory power for the Supreme Court so broad that it embraces all state tribunals. And finally this panoply of authority is used to defend property rights against spoliation by a capricious public. Each of these themes will be echoed over and over in the decisions of the future; each of them serves a vital purpose in the judges' struggle to make America the nation they believed it ought to be.

The specific problem of the *Martin* case—whether the Court's power under Section 25 could be maintained—was not of course entirely settled by Story's argumentative dexterities. In the years that followed, whenever a state felt aggrieved by a Court decision, the familiar cry against Section 25 was again heard. In 1821, in *Cohens* v. *Virginia,* Marshall not only reiterated Story's basic points but interpreted the Eleventh Amendment, that supposed warranty of states' rights, so as to permit individuals to appeal to the Supreme Court even though a state was the other party in the litigation. The Amendment, said Marshall, prevents individual suits against states only if the action is "commenced" by the individual; if the state has initiated the action (for instance, by arresting a person), the person can still bring the state into the Supreme Court to defend itself against an appeal.

At this point, the Virginian defenders of states' rights felt that judicial sophistry had surpassed itself, since not even a constitutional amendment had arrested its course. They urged that the Court's authority be curbed by statute or by more carefully drawn amendment, and hereafter throughout the 1820's hardly a session of Congress went by without a proposal to modify, in one way or another, the doctrine of judicial control. These threats were serious enough to alarm the Court and its friends, but in truth none of them ever came very close to succeeding. As John Taylor of Caroline complained, the apathy of the "sister states," when one of their number was assailed, for a long time made a united front of states' rights sentiment impossible to assemble. Meanwhile, decision after decision accustomed the nation to accept the Court's view of its own function; each year that passed, each holding that was submitted to, made it a little harder to question that view. When South Carolina radically assailed the whole principle of nationalism in the Nullification Ordinance of 1832, its formidable adversaries included not only Andrew Jackson but a federal judiciary which had become a focus of public respect and a symbol of Union.

THE ENHANCEMENT OF NATIONAL POWER

One handicap of the Supreme Court during these early years and indeed throughout its history was its divorce from the sources of political power. Seven men in Washington, armed with nothing save their robes and their intellects, seem pitiful rivals to state legislatures, congresses, and presidents who command the machinery of government and are backed by the mighty force of the electoral process. But the Court's apparent weakness was also, as we have seen, a kind of opportunity. Because it was an independent, small, cohesive body, it could maintain a long-term view that gave it a decided advantage over opponents divided between a variety of special, temporary concerns and often confused in the basic premises of their opposition.

This advantage is further illustrated by the great Marshallian decisions involving the question of national legislative authority. Story's argument in the *Martin* case that national powers should be liberally construed enabled him to contend that Congress had a right to pass Section 25 and thus to make the Court the dominant tribunal of the nation. But his interest and Marshall's in the doctrine of liberal construction went far beyond its use to bolster judicial status. They wanted to enhance national power in all respects, partly because this would simultaneously restrict the power of the states, but partly too because they anticipated awesome tasks for the nation and wanted to insure that it was constitutionally equipped to deal with them. And the Court's success in accomplishing this aim must be attributed in no small degree to self-contradiction among the forces that opposed it.

McCulloch v. *Maryland* in 1819 is by almost any reckoning the greatest decision John Marshall ever handed down—the one most important to the future of America, most influential in the Court's own doctrinal history, and most revealing of Marshall's unique talent for stately argument. It involved a state tax on note issues of the Bank of the United States, which had been incorporated by act of Congress in 1816. The government argued that such a tax on a federal instrumentality was invalid and need not be paid. The state replied that the incorporation of the Bank exceeded Congress' constitutional powers and that in any event the states could tax as they willed within their own borders. These contentions raised vast and difficult questions both for the present and the future. The Bank was viewed with special loathing by the states' rights advocates; any decision upholding its claim to exist and denying the state's claim to tax could be counted on to infuriate them. And not the least of their heated objections would be the familiar one that the Court had no power in spite of Section 25 to entertain the cause. On the other hand, it was clear to Marshall, as it has been to posterity, that a national government restricted in its powers by Maryland's narrow interpretation would be incapable of the great tasks that might lie before it.

Speaking for a unanimous Court, Marshall therefore upheld the constitutionality of the Bank's incorporation, and in doing so set down the classic statement of the doctrine of national authority. The argument he advanced was not new; its main outlines had been endlessly debated since the first Congress and Hamilton's famous paper urging the Bank's establishment; and much of it had been given judicial expression by Story in 1816. But Marshall deserves the credit for stamping it with the die of his memorable rhetoric and converting it from a political theory into the master doctrine of American constitutional law.

Because the argument is logical it lends itself to summary, falling into three major phases. The first is concerned with the problem of the nature of the Constitution itself. Two crucial premises are laid down: First, the Constitution emanates from the hand of the sovereign people and speaks in broad language so that it can "be adapted to the various crises of human affairs." We must never forget that "it is a *constitution* we are expounding." These premises infuse the second phase, which concerns the nature of the national government the Constitution created. The people made that government supreme over all rivals within the sphere of its powers (Art. VI), and those powers must be construed generously if they are to be sufficient for the "various crises" of the ages to come.

The third phase is simply the application of these weighty principles. The power to incorporate the Bank is upheld under the clause endowing Congress with the power to make all laws "necessary and proper" for carrying into execution the other powers (Art. I, sec. 8); the words "necessary and proper" are interpreted generously, in accord with the principles advanced, to mean "appropriate" and "plainly adapted." The Maryland tax is invalidated, because since "the power to tax involves the power to destroy," to uphold the tax would grant the state the power to defeat the national government's supremacy; an inferior (in these matters) would be empowered to destroy a superior. But no summary can convey the air of high seriousness that pervades the opinion, the magisterial dignity with which it marches to its conclusions, the sense of righteous certitude with which it announces them. It was such qualities as these that made it persuasive to contemporaries and to the generations to come; and to appreciate these qualities the reader must go to the opinion itself.

The reaction was what might have been expected. In the North and the East the decision was praised; in the South and West, where the Bank was especially unpopular, the Court was roundly condemned. But even in Virginia, the fastness of such philosophers of Republicanism as Jefferson, Roane, and Taylor, the assailants curiously compromised their own position by putting the immediate issue of the Bank ahead of the broader issue of principle. Most of them denounced the Court for *not* holding the incorporation statute unconstitutional, thus of course tacitly conceding that the Court had the power to do so. Yet surely if the Court had the exalted power of overthrowing an act of Congress, it was not unreasonable to suppose that it also had the right to disapprove state laws. And if it did have these high prerogatives the Court must have some discretion in exercising them, that is, it could not be condemned merely because Spencer Roane, wielding the same power, would have decided the case differently.

In short most of the critics conceded too much for the good of their own criticisms. Their proper course would have been to deny that the Court had any business judging the validity of either national or state laws. But as usual they were more concerned about the immediate, concrete issue than they were about such a general doctrine as judicial sovereignty or even states' rights; and once again the Court profited from the fact that it alone seemed to understand the value of consistency and generality.

Much the same lesson can be drawn from the "Steamboat Monopoly Case," *Gibbons* v. *Ogden* in 1824, in which the Court was confronted for the first time by the problem of interpreting the commerce clause. A quarter-century before, the New York legislature had granted Robert R. Livingston and Robert Fulton the exclusive right to steamboat navigation in the waters of New York, and in the course of time the monopoly had extracted a similar privilege from Louisiana. The value of this controlling position in the two great port states of the nation was of course enormous, and rival states were deeply resentful of the arrangement. The *Gibbons* case involved an action for encroachment on the monopoly, and the defendant contended that the state had no right to grant it in the first place, because navigation is "commerce among the several states," which is the business of Congress.

This contention raised a series of questions that were destined for long and checkered careers in the development of constitutional law. First, what *is* interstate commerce? Does the term cover only buying and selling, or does it apply to such activities as navigation? Second, once we have determined what interstate commerce is, what is the extent of the power to regulate it? Third, what is the effect on the states of this grant of power to Congress? Must they stay out of the field altogether, or do they have a concurrent right to control it? It is not too much to say that the future of America as a nation depended on the answers that were given to these questions.

And Marshall, with his usual foresight, was well aware that he stood at another major constitutional crossroad. The opinion, like so many of his great ones, is a deft blend of boldness and restraint. In answer to the first two questions, he advanced the kind of broad, nationalistic definitions that the Hamiltonian tradition approved. Commerce, he said, is not merely buying and selling; it includes "every species of commercial intercourse," and this is true whether we are talking of either interstate or foreign commerce. Nor does interstate commerce stop at state boundaries; a journey that begins in Boston and ends in Philadelphia is subject to congressional power from start to finish. Of course, so inclusive a definition amply covers navigation. As for the extent of Congress' power to regulate a subject, once it is found to be in interstate commerce, that power is "complete in itself, may be exercised to its utmost extent, and acknowledges no limitations other than are prescribed in the Constitution." It is no less than the power "to prescribe the rule by which commerce is to be governed."

Perhaps only in the perspective of the future can it be understood how much these words meant; a twentieth-century observer looking back on them is impressed because he knows that the definitions have proved elastic enough to justify all the extensive commercial enterprises in which the national government has since engaged. But to contemporaries the most urgent question was yet to come: are the states precluded from acting in the commercial area thus defined? And at this point Marshall grew curiously evasive. He stated sympathetically the argument that the commerce power is exclusive, remarked that it had "great force" and said: ". . . the court is not satisfied that it has been refuted." He came as close to formally approving the doctrine as he could without quite doing so. But, he went on, it is not now necessary to decide this issue, because the New York monopoly law conflicts with a federal coasting license statute. Whether or not the commerce clause alone would invalidate the state law, surely it must be admitted that the federal coasting license law does, for the Constitution makes congressional enactments "the supreme law of the land." The lucrative but controversial monopoly was thus at last brought to an end.

Once again, as so often in the past, Marshall had managed to achieve imperishable results while sidestepping the area of greatest controversy. In other commerce clause cases he refined the notion of interstate (and foreign) commerce somewhat further by holding that goods were still subject to national control so long as they remained in their original shipping packages (the "original package doctrine"); and confused the question of state regulatory power still more by allowing a state to maintain a dam that blocked a navigable stream. No watchful guardian of states' rights could contend that Marshall had erected constitutional barriers to all state commercial regulation. Surely he had implied that some such regulation might be prohibited by the commerce clause alone, and surely his dicta about the extent of the commerce power had opened up the possibility of prodigious congressional regulation in this field. But it was present actualities, not implications and possibilities, that most concerned his contemporaries, and they found it hard to condemn a judicial stroke that slew the hated monopoly, whatever the flourishes that accompanied it. Jefferson and a few like him were horrified by *Gibbons*, but in general the decision was welcomed; the fact that it did after all overthrow a state law and hammer a few more nails in the coffin of state sovereignty was easy to minimize in the face of its immediately popular conclusion.

JUDICIAL ALLIES AND PRIVATE RIGHTS

One of the Supreme Court's peculiar characteristics is that it attempts to decide questions of policy without the advantage of conventional political resources. The judges have no organized party machine to call on for guidance and encouragement; they are spared both the penalties and the benefits of direct electoral support. But this does not mean of course that the Court has no constituency, if we can use that word in a somewhat looser and more informal sense than is usual. No institution in a democratic society could become and remain potent unless it could count on a solid block of public opinion that would rally to its side in a pinch. And the Supreme Court has historically been blessed with two kinds of supporters—those who venerate it and are prepared to defend it as the symbol of continuity and fairness, who are attached to the idea of the rule of law; and those who happen to be gratified by the course of policy the judges are pursuing at the moment. In practice the latter invariably claim also to be the former, and perhaps the problem of separately identifying the two groups is futile and somewhat academic. It is enough for our purposes to say that the Marshall Court had such a constituency to draw on and that the growth of constitutional doctrine on the subject of private rights is illuminated if we realize that this is so.

An essential element in that constituency, though by no means the whole of it, was the American legal fraternity, or as it has been called in a fine phrase, "the inner republic of bench and bar." In these early days lawyers were already occupying the pivotal position in American political affairs that they have occupied ever since. And they tended to reinforce the Supreme Court, partly no doubt because they represented the affluent "haves" who would profit from the stable, nationalized structure Marshall was building, but partly too because their training had taught them to esteem the rule of law which Marshall and his associates stood for. It was not only that men like William Pinckney and Daniel Webster vindicated Marshallian doctrine with the magic of their oratory in formal argument before the supreme bench; they and their lesser colleagues also helped, in letters, in conversations, in appearances before lower courts, in state legislatures, and in Congress, to generate the atmosphere of consent that made Marshall's achievements possible.

These stout allies played a significant part during Marshall's era in the development and acceptance of doctrines protecting the property owner, most particularly by way of the contract clause of the Constitution. In fact if their activities were not part of the historical record, they would have to be postulated in order to account for a process of legal growth that would otherwise seem autonomous. It will be remembered that Marshall had stepped very tentatively in *Fletcher* v. *Peck,* the first contract clause decision. The principle that the state must abide by its own contractual commitments rested on flimsy historical grounds and presented certain grave logical difficulties; therefore the vague mandates of natural law were invoked to augment the force of the contract clause argument. Two years later, in 1812, he offered an interpretation of *Fletcher* that made it sound less ambiguous than it was: in that case, he said, it was decided "on solemn argument and much deliberation" that the contract clause "extends to contracts to which a State is a party." The statement of the point is clear enough at this stage, but it is after all only a statement; nothing apparent had happened to quiet the misgivings he seemed to have in *Fletcher* about the doctrine's acceptability.

Seven years later the famous case *Dartmouth College* v. *Woodward* came to the Supreme Court. The question was whether the state legislature could validly alter the charter which had been granted to Dartmouth College in 1769 by the British crown. A complex imbroglio of theology and politics had resulted in a law changing the name of the college to Dartmouth University and vesting control over it in trustees and overseers largely appointed by the governor; in effect, Dartmouth was to be converted into a public institution. The old trustees fought back by pointing out that the charter had granted them the sole right to fill vacancies in their number "forever" and contending among other things that the state law violated the federal contract clause. This was a bold assertion and seemingly not a very promising one, since it involved, in addition to the heretofore somewhat doubtful idea that the state is bound by its own contracts, two even more novel propositions: that a charter is such a contract and that it is inviolable even though its holders have no "beneficial interest" at stake.

It might be thought that the burden of all these meanings would be more than the contract clause could bear, especially when we consider that Marshall himself appeared to have so little confidence in it only nine years earlier. But Marshall not only affirmed all three interpretations but did so with an economy of argument unusual for him. On the first he offered no argument at all, simply taking it for granted that the state must stick to its agreements; the trimmings drawn from the natural law tradition were now dispensed with, and the contract clause alone was the basis for decision. The idea that a corporate charter is a contract within the meaning of the clause was also assumed rather than argued. Finally he came to the only point that really troubled him—that the contract clause was primarily designed to protect the private property rights of individuals and that the trustees have no such beneficial interest in Dartmouth College; they would not personally lose anything if the charter were overthrown. But, said Marshall, although the framers of the contract clause may have been chiefly concerned with protecting private property, they did not use language that excludes a charitable institution like Dartmouth, and we must therefore assume it is included. "The case, being within the words of the rule, must be within its operation likewise" unless the result would be "obviously absurd, or mischievous, or repugnant to the general spirit" of the Constitution.

The startling thing about the *Dartmouth College* case is not this last point, which follows reasonably enough if we accept the two that precede it, nor yet those two points themselves; but the fact that they were announced so confidently and seem to have provoked so little dissent. Indeed the Superior Court of New Hampshire, though holding against the trustees, had conceded that the contract clause extended to contracts between states and individuals and had assumed that a charter granting privileges to individuals for their own benefit would be protected by the contract clause. Yet by these concessions the contract clause, once apparently innocuous, became a mighty instrument for the judicial protection of property rights against state abridgment. How did it happen that Marshall could forge such an instrument so off-handedly? How did the tentative suggestion of *Fletcher* in 1810 become the confident assertion of *Dartmouth* in 1819?

The explanation is that the Court's "constituency" had been at work on its behalf in the meantime. The idea that the contract clause might serve to protect private property from the states and the corollary idea that corporate charters could be included in such protection—these embryonic ideas had caught hold in the minds of lawyers and judges, had been fostered and developed by them, and had thereby been raised to the status of mature constitutional doctrines. By 1819, they were so well intrenched that the Supreme Court needed to do little more than stamp them with its formal sanctions. The *Dartmouth* decision is important then, not for its own accomplishments but for its acknowledgment of results already achieved. Businessmen, secure in the possession of inviolable state-granted charters, could thank their stars for "the inner republic of bench and bar" as well as for John Marshall.

Marshall wanted in fact to improve the property holders' lot even further. In the same year he invalidated a New York bankruptcy law on the ground that it infringed the contract clause. The special vice of this law was that it released debtors from obligations contracted before its passage. A creditor might legitimately feel aggrieved if he loaned money under one set of rules and was forced to try to collect it under another. But, it was argued, if the law already exists, the lender knowingly takes the risk that his debtor will be released by bankruptcy and therefore cannot complain of unfairness if it so turns out. However, Marshall, in holding that the Constitution barred retrospective interference with contracts, used language intimating that *prospective* interferences were also prohibited. His ambitious objective was to forbid any state law that impaired contracts in any way, and the acceptance of such a principle would have greatly enhanced the value of the contract clause as an instrument for the protection of private rights. But at this point even his usually acquiescent brethren called a halt, and in 1827 the Court voted, four to three, to uphold a state bankruptcy law as applied to debts contracted after its passage. Marshall dissented, and it is plain that the decision bitterly disappointed him; but he had much reason for self-congratulation all the same. With the help of the contemporary bench and bar, he had transmuted a clause of modest pretensions into a broad inhibition on the commercial laws of the states. He had maneuvered America a few steps closer to his own idea of the good society.

THE ACHIEVEMENT OF JOHN MARSHALL

Few intellectual feats are more difficult than the assessment of history while we are living it, and perhaps the problem is all the greater for those who are themselves playing the leading roles. In his last years, Marshall was beset with misgivings about America's future, full of gloomy convictions that he had failed in his campaign to establish judicial sovereignty and to cement the bonds of national union. The states' rights movement was waxing ever stronger and more vocal under the ministrations of John C. Calhoun; the Court had recently been defied in two spectacular cases by Georgia, and President Jackson's unwillingness to back the judges had underlined the Court's ultimate dependency on external support. The old Federalist dream of rule by "the wise, the rich, and the good" seemed more chimerical than ever, as the spirit of Jacksonian democracy swept the nation.

But, ominous though these developments appeared, Marshall was wrong to think that they spelled the failure of his programs. Not even he, the architect-in-chief, realized how securely the cornerstones of American constitutionalism had been laid. His error probably was that he hoped for absolute certitude in a system that had been dedicated by its framers to the principle of relativism. We cannot say that the doctrine of judicial sovereignty was established beyond the shadow of doubt by *Cohens v. Virginia* in 1821, or that the broad construction of national powers was settled once and for all by *McCulloch v. Maryland* and *Gibbons v. Ogden*, or that the *Dartmouth* case stilled all uncertainties about the contract clause. We cannot say that at one moment the constitutional basis for union was an aspiration and at the next a firm reality, for constitutional history does not move in this way. The vagueness of the Constitution on these issues gave the Court its chance to be creative, but by the same token it was decreed that the creations would never be final and perfect. The Court's title to power, being inferred rather than explicitly stated, must always be somewhat tentative; interpretations of the Constitution, being fashioned by the historical context rather than by the fiat of 1789, must submit to the verdict of later history, as well as the past. With all his subtlety and shrewdness, Marshall's mind was attracted by absolutes, and the contingency of the constitutional universe never ceased to trouble him.

But if we can tolerate, as Marshall could not, a world of half-certainty (and if we enjoy, as he did not, the perspective of the future), we can see that his forebodings were excessive, and his accomplishments greater than he knew. The doctrine of judicial sovereignty was still subject to occasional challenge in moments of stress; men like Jackson and Calhoun were unwilling to admit that the Supreme Court was the *only* authority on the Constitution's meaning. But surely the judicial monopoly, though imperfect, was very impressive. The nation in general thought of the Court as the principal authority and conceded its right to supervise the states in most matters. When the Court impinged on the great primary interests of a state or region, a line might be drawn; but in the considerable distance before that line was reached judicial sovereignty held its sway. The Supreme Court was now far more serene and formidable than the precariously balanced institution Marshall had taken over in 1801. America's devotion to the idea of fundamental law and the Court's ability to capitalize on opponents' errors had made sure of that.

This establishment of judicial hegemony was itself a highly important victory in the struggle to promote the principle of national union, for it meant (with the qualifications already mentioned) that the Constitution spoke with one voice throughout America. But the other substantive principles Marshall had laid down also served that purpose and were also more solidly fixed than Marshall, in his somber old age, imagined. The national-power doctrines of *McCulloch* and *Gibbons* were to have their great day in a more remote future when the national government felt inclined to use the constitutional sinews Marshall's court had provided; until then their significance was more moral than practical. But the corollary doctrine—that the states may not encroach on these federally reserved realms—was well accepted and immediately relevant. These limitations on state power based on the doctrine of national supremacy, plus such specific limitations as those derived from the contract clause, helped open the way to the development of commercial enterprise on a national scale in the next half-century.

Marshall was right in thinking that he had failed to resolve for America the great problem of nation-state relationships. No court could finally settle an issue of such dimensions, an issue that had already brought the nation near the brink of civil war. But he might justifiably have felt that he and his Court had made a priceless contribution to its settlement, had fashioned out of judicial materials an ideology of seasoned strength to which those who cared for the Union could repair, had established a pattern of control that would help to shore up the Union even though nothing but bloodshed could ultimately save it. He could have comforted himself with the thought that no court in world history had ever done so much to affect the destiny of a great nation.

FOUR

THE COURT UNDER TANEY: THE NATURAL HISTORY OF JUDICIAL PRESTIGE

WHEN JOHN MARSHALL DIED in 1835, the anguish of his admirers was compounded partly of grief for a beloved national figure and partly of apprehension that Jackson would appoint Roger B. Taney to succeed him. It is one of the commonplaces of American history that those who have learned to live with the governmental order of their own day nurse an often excessive dread of its passing. They forget how many times their forebodings of the past have turned out to be bugbears; they forget that the bonds of continuity in America are remarkably strong. And so it was in 1835. Taney had been a staunch opponent of the Bank of the United States and had, as Secretary of the Treasury, deprived the Bank of the federal deposits that were its lifeblood. This made him, in the eyes of anti-Jacksonians, a "political hack" and "a supple, cringing tool of power," for the Bank was their darling. The prospect of a Court appointed by Democratic presidents and headed by Taney seemed dark indeed; Marshall's carefully wrought jurisprudence would be demolished and the nation would be exposed to the unchecked ravages of agrarian, states' rights radicalism.

Their depression deepened when the event they had feared actually occurred. Taney was appointed, and confirmed by the Senate after a bitter wrangle in March of 1836; five members of the Court were now Jackson appointees, only Story and Thompson surviving from the Marshallian golden age. Webster, the "godlike Daniel" whose name and heart were so intimately associated with the old Court, wrote: "Judge Story thinks the Supreme Court is *gone,* and I think so too." Then three decisions handed down in Taney's first term seemed to confirm their misgivings. Each of the cases had been heard by Marshall, but decision had been postponed; the holdings of the new Taney Court were in each case at variance with the position Marshall would have taken, according to his close friend Justice Story. The dismay of the Whigs was acute. "Under the progressive genius of the new judicial administration," said one journal, "we can see the whole fair system of the Constitution beginning to dissolve like the baseless fabric of a vision."

For a long time historians accepted these despairing outbursts as if they actually, or at any rate nearly, described the constitutional policies of the Taney Court. The legend of Taney and his brethren as radical democrats, hostile to property rights, nationalism, and Marshall's memory, was stronger than the facts that would have emerged from a reading of the decisions themselves. But as the decisions finally were read and compared with those of Marshall's time, as the whole doctrinal course of the Taney Court was traced, it became apparent that the legend was badly misleading. The old jurisprudence had not been broken down after all, or even very greatly altered: the claims of property were still well protected, the nation was not constitutionally fragmented, judicial power was not surrendered. In fact, the position of the Supreme Court as the final arbiter of constitutional questions had become, within a few years of Taney's accession, more secure than ever before. The concept of judicial sovereignty, which Marshall had nurtured so lovingly and defended against so many challenges, was by 1840 an almost unquestioned premise of American government.

This congenial result, unexpected by the Webster-Story fraternity and long unnoticed by history, was achieved in perfectly unsurprising ways. The living Marshall himself of course deserves much of the credit. Numerous though his enemies were, even they had found it hard to resist being impressed by his dignity, his self-righteousness, and his intellectual power; and his constitutional edifice had been well made.

But the death of the great Chief Justice was almost as decisive as his life in bringing about the triumph of judicial sovereignty. For one thing it made him a saint. Within a surprisingly short time the justices of the Supreme Court, regardless of who appointed them, were paying almost unanimous lip service to his memory; those who had chided him so willingly while he was alive now cited him, like scripture, in their own behalf and flinched at the charge that he would have disagreed with them. For another thing, Marshall's death diverted judicial partisanship, or rather turned it upside down. Though many Americans came to venerate Marshall, many others could never forget that he was a Federalist and a very opinionated one at that, and thus a residue of animosity always handicapped the Marshall Court.

Now the Chief and a majority of his associates were Jackson-approved, and this meant that the anti-judicial tradition of the Democrats lost much of its edge. On the other hand, the Whigs (the successors to the now-dead Federalist party), though they might bemoan the loss of their idol and deplore the advent of Taney, were committed to a projudicial philosophy they could not lightly forswear. Their natural propensity to support the Court could be depended upon to reassert itself when and if they realized that the Taney regime was not likely to attempt a real constitutional revolution. Unless the Court erred on the side of either extreme—unless it enraged the Democrats by an excess of Marshallian nationalism or antagonized the Whigs by an outright reversion to localism—the chances for a kind of judicial "era of good feelings" were very good.

Whether the chance should become a reality depended of course on the wisdom of the judges who confronted this opportunity. The old idea that they seriously undermined Marshall's constitutional structure has already been mentioned; there is very little to it. But in recent years there has been some disposition to reverse the idea, and to treat the Court of the Taney era as if its doctrines were a consistent extension in all important respects of tendencies Marshall set going, as if no concessions at all to shifting political winds had been made.

The trouble is that neither of these comparatively neat analyses will quite square with the untidy, pragmatic welter of doctrines that has actually been bequeathed to us by the Taney Court. It is true that the jurisdiction of the federal courts was in some ways extended beyond the limits Marshall had recognized—in admiralty cases, for example, and in cases involving the right of corporations to bring federal suits. It is true that the basic dogmas of Marshall's contract-clause interpretation were not challenged and that in some cases the Taney Court was as dogmatic about the sanctity of contracts as even Marshall had been. It is true that the national government's supremacy over the states was repeatedly upheld. But it is also true that the Court elsewhere restricted the range of jurisdiction that is asserted or implied in some of Marshall's great opinions, qualified the constitutional privileges enjoyed by corporations, and granted the states a degree of autonomy in commercial matters that Marshall would undoubtedly have denied them.

The fact is that the Court from 1836 until 1857 was pursuing a non-doctrinaire course to which only the loosest kind of descriptive generalizations can apply. The Court was adjusting itself to the contours of a changing America, relaxing the rigidities of Marshallian dogma when that seemed desirable, retaining or strengthening others, and fashioning some new dogmas of its own, producing a constitutional jurisprudence that had been pragmatically fitted to the nation of the day. If we see the process either in terms of pure judicial imperialism or pure judicial abnegation, we are missing the important point—that the Taney Court by giving ground at some salients was able to advance upon others, thus maintaining a quantum of jurisdiction at least equal to that exercised by Marshall but composed of elements somewhat different from those the great Chief Justice himself might have chosen. And we might miss the even more significant point that the result of this adjustment process was to fortify the judicial power by creating an atmosphere of public acceptance more complete than the Court had ever before enjoyed. Marshall's historic task had been to establish the frontiers of judicial supervision; the function of the Court under Taney was to consolidate the most essential of these gains by a deft combination of tenacity and flexibility. The function was so well performed that not even the monumental indiscretion of the *Dred Scott* decision could quite destroy the judicial imperium.

THE NATION-STATE PROBLEM AND
THE COURT'S POLICY OF MODERATION

The theme of the adjustment process by which this result was achieved was compromise. To be sure, this theme was far from new in the Court's history; even Marshall had been well aware that half a loaf is sometimes better than none, and no wise Court has ever forgotten this platitude. But the need to compromise is a matter of degree depending in part on the historic context. Marshall in the most creative period of his tenure faced a situation that permitted the Court to pursue a comparatively bold and unambiguous policy with impunity. In the years from 1836 to 1857, the American political world was torn by conflicts so bitter that a frankly doctrinaire Court would have wounded both itself and the cause of union. As always, the Court was dedicated to keeping the Union secure, if only because its own existence depended on that security. But there is a season for everything, and in the climate of the Taney era the Court could best sustain the Union by preserving its own status as a national tribunal. And that meant that constitutional doctrines must be framed in a spirit of moderation.

One of the 1837 decisions that so alarmed the Whigs was *Mayor of New York* v. *Miln,* in which the Court had upheld a state regulation applying to ships entering the port of New York. The law impinged on foreign commerce, and Marshall's disciple Story argued that it should be overturned under the doctrine, which he derived from the Steamboat Monopoly Case, that Congress' power over foreign and interstate commerce is exclusive. This was of course the extreme nationalist position applied with a rigor that Marshall himself had not insisted upon. The other extreme was Justice Thompson's view that the states could regulate interstate and foreign commerce as much as they chose unless the state law conflicted with an actual federal statute.

But the Court majority steered between, sustaining the law on the ground that the state had merely been exercising its "police power" for the welfare of its citizens, not regulating commerce; thus the question of whether the national commerce power was exclusive did not arise. A flat answer to that question, either yes or no, would have infuriated an important segment of American opinion. The Court's resort to what has been called the "convenient apologetics" of the police power enabled it to avoid both the frying pan and the fire; and the additional advantage was that the doctrine was arguably rooted in one of Marshall's own decisions which had permitted a state, on similar grounds, to block a navigable stream. Even the Whigs, if they had really thought the matter over, could not reasonably contend that a prolocalist revolution had taken place.

Although the police-power doctrine was therefore in some ways very convenient, the distinction it made was always slippery, for it depended, as Taney was to say, on the idea that a state regulation which affected commerce had been passed with the motive of protecting health and welfare, rather than regulating commercial affairs. Motive is always an elusive entity. Moreover, since Revolutionary times, the states had woven a complex network of regulations which were frankly commercial and which often touched foreign and interstate transactions: here the police-power "apologetics" were not even relevant. So the Court found it increasingly difficult to evade the direct question of whether the states could regulate commerce as such. In 1851, they resolved the question, again by compromise. The states, said the Court, are precluded from regulating commerce as such when the particular subjects regulated are "in their nature national, or admit only of one uniform system . . . of regulation." On the other hand, if the subject is one that is local in character, appropriate for diverse plans of regulation, depending on local peculiarities, the states may regulate that commerce until Congress itself chooses to take over the subject (*Cooley* v. *Board of Wardens*).

This ingenious disengagement from the horns of the dilemma was not entirely satisfying to those, like Taney himself, who had argued for full concurrent state power in the commercial field; nor to those all-out nationalists, like Justice McLean, who had insisted that the states must leave commerce strictly alone. But neither localist nor nationalist could claim that the Court had wholly yielded to the other; each could justifiably feel that the announced doctrine in some part embodied his views.

In other fields a comparably moderate realignment of doctrine can be traced. The other two 1837 decisions that had alarmed the disciples of Marshall like a fire bell in the night were *Charles River Bridge* v. *Warren Bridge Co.* and *Briscoe* v. *Bank of Kentucky.* The first involved an application of the contract clause, that sacred cow of Marshall's jurisprudence, and because the Court refused to find in the clause new restrictions on state power, the cry of heresy was raised.

The proprietors of a toll bridge in Massachusetts argued that their state-granted charter implied a promise that the legislature would not authorize a competing bridge; in short that, without explicitly saying so, the state had endowed them with a constitutionally guaranteed monopoly. The Court simply held that no such inferences would be drawn; public grants should be strictly construed. There is no challenge to the basic principles of Marshall's contract-clause doctrine—that a charter is a contract that binds the states—nor is there evidence in later contract-clause cases that the Taney Court was reckless of property rights, as the Whigs had feared. The states were held to the letter of the doctrines Marshall had enunciated, and the most that can be said is that the new Court usually declined to expand those doctrines so as further to inhibit state powers. By thus conceding the states some leeway in commercial affairs and at the same time insisting that they abide by the promises they had actually made, the Court had once more found a middle—and generally popular—ground.

As for the *Briscoe* case, it undoubtedly represents a concession to localism. One of the evils that had most perturbed men of substance during the Articles of Confederation period was state issuance of currency, and the Founding Fathers had hoped to debar a return to that sorry state of affairs by providing, in Article I, section 10, that no states might "emit bills of credit." Marshall had enforced the clause rigorously when Missouri issued interest-bearing certificates receivable for debts due the state. Since they circulated as money, they were bills of credit. But now Justice McLean, in a Court opinion that is a triumph of incoherency, approved the issuance of currency by a bank owned and controlled by Kentucky. An uninitiated observer might protest that such a bank was the equivalent of the state itself and equally bound by the constitutional prohibition. Justice Story, who dissented, had no doubts about it. But the new Court thought otherwise, and state autonomy in money matters was given increased vitality.

But against the centrifugal thrust of such a decision and a few others of a similar tenor, we can balance a series of judgments which reasserted the principle of national supremacy: for example, a ruling that the incomes of federal employees are exempt from state taxation under the doctrine of *McCulloch* v. *Maryland;* a second that the extradition of fugitives from justice to foreign countries is an exclusive prerogative of the national government; and a third permitting a corporation chartered in one state to do business in another unless specifically barred by the second state's laws. In this last case partisans had argued on the one side that Alabama *could* not, under the "privileges and immunities" clause (Art. IV, sec. 2), exclude a Georgia-chartered corporation, and on the other side that the corporation was *automatically* excluded, without a specific Alabama law, because the Georgia charter was useless anywhere else. Characteristically the Taney Court faced by these extreme contentions chose to compromise.

And compromise was appropriate to the Court's historic circumstances in a double sense. After the burst of creative enterprise under Marshall, the judiciary had need to slow the pace of its constitution-making process so that America could grow used to the house John Marshall had built, so that the doctrines could be adjusted a little to fit the facts of the changing economic order, so that the judicial power could be consolidated. Great advances in history, if they endure, are often followed by such a period of retardation and adaptation. But beyond this, a propitiating temper was called for by the conditions of the day, especially when the great question of nation-state relationships was even indirectly raised. For America was moving toward Armageddon with frightening inexorability, and passions were stirring as never before. If the task of the Marshall Court had been to champion nationalism against the states' rights movement, the task of the Court in Taney's era was to champion temperance and reason against the extremism that threatened to dissever the Republic. For a long time it performed that task remarkably well.

THE PRIDE OF POWER AND THE SLAVERY QUESTION

But throughout these years, as the judges charted point by point their path of moderation, a specter stood near their elbows, and as time passed this presence became harder and harder to ignore. Its name, of course, was slavery. In an attempt to exorcise it, the Court mortally endangered the judicial temple which they and their predecessors had so painfully erected. For a time it seemed that the labor of nearly seventy years would be blown away by the holocaust following one dramatic lapse from judicial self-restraint.

It is easy for a modern observer to see, looking back, that the slavery question was too big and too explosive to be decided by a court. We know, whatever mythologists may say, that there are practical as well as technical limits on the Court's jurisdiction. The great fundamental decisions that determine the course of society must ultimately be made by society itself. If they are also, as they are apt to be, decisions that profoundly engage the emotions of the whole people, this is all the more reason for the judiciary to leave them alone; the Court's place is not on the battlefield or in the center of the political arena. And we know that, as it turned out, only bloodshed could settle the slavery issue.

The judges of the 1850's knew some of these things but unfortunately not all, and others were perhaps too easily forgotten in the heat of the moment. They should have realized that their power was built on a lively sense of its own limitations; this was the lesson of the Court's past successes—and failures. They should have known that slavery was a judicial untouchable, for it had already, in 1850, brought the nation to the brink of civil war. But they were children of their time as well as judges. By the 1850's the slavery issue was clouding the gaze of seemingly wise men all over America; it is perhaps too much to expect that the vision of the Supreme Court would remain unimpaired.

For a while the Court majority resisted the temptation to plunge into the flames. To be sure, as early as 1842 Justice Story had struck backhandedly at slavery when, speaking for the Court, he overturned a Pennsylvania law. It conflicted, he said, with the federal Fugitive Slave Law, and he went on gratuitously to hold that *any* state legislation touching fugitive slaves was invalid because the national power over that subject was exclusive. Since the national law was almost unworkable without state co-operation, the effect of this decision was to hamper the apprehension of fugitive slaves under the guise of defending the power to apprehend them. The decision was angrily criticized. But the tumult such as it was soon died down, and the Court thereafter left the slavery question pretty much to the mercies of the political branches of government.

In 1851, it was confronted with the contention that slaves had become free when they entered free states or territories. Behind this argument lurked the perilous question of whether Congress could prohibit slavery in the territories of the United States, as it had done in the Missouri Compromise. With nice discretion, the judges skirted the volcano's edge, holding in *Strader* v. *Graham* that the status of the Negroes in question depended on the laws of the state where they now lived—Kentucky. Since Kentucky regarded them as slaves, the Supreme Court was bound by that fact; and the question of their status during former sojourns in free areas did not arise.

By this kind of circumspection the carefully nurtured judicial prestige was temporarily kept intact in these hazardous hours. But the Court's high repute was in some ways its danger. The political order was abundantly demonstrating its inability to cope with the slavery issue without dissevering the nation. The line defining the practical boundaries of the Court's power, though implicitly recognized in decisions of the past, had seldom been acknowledged, and prevailing mythology tended to obscure its existence. Perhaps, then, this highly esteemed group of nine men could succeed where the political parties were so grievously failing. Perhaps a pronouncement from them would settle the questions evoking the slavery controversy, or at any rate help in settling the thorniest of them all—the question of slavery in the territories. The nation was in deadly jeopardy. It would be tragic for the Court to withhold its hand, if that hand might save the Union.

Such exalted ideas of the Court's power were advanced repeatedly during these years by supposedly responsible statesmen and publicists. The judges were sure to listen, and they were tempted to heed. Perhaps, however, they had also been impressed by the ominous words of Northerners like Seward and Chase, who had accused the Court of partiality to slavery and denied that the country need accept a proslavey decision. The old familiar challenge to judicial sovereignty had not been heard much lately, and its reappearance now may have given the judges pause. At all events a majority of them were still apparently unconvinced that they could bell the cat when *Dred Scott* v. *Sandford* came before them in 1856. Scott had been taken as a slave into Illinois and into the northern part of the Louisiana Purchase. Illinois law forbade slavery, and the Louisiana Purchase territory north of the southern boundary of Missouri had been declared free by the Missouri Compromise in 1820–21. Scott, now in Missouri, sued his present owner in federal court, arguing that these journeys to free areas had made him a free man. This raised the fiery question of whether Congress could bar slavery from the territories, but did not require the Court to answer the question. The judges might have replied, under the analogy of the *Strader* case, that they were bound by Missouri law, regardless of Scott's status when he had lived elsewhere. Since Missouri regarded him as a slave that would settle the matter, and the problem of Congress' power need not be answered, pro or con. A majority of the Supreme Court agreed to take this course; an opinion was actually written by Justice Nelson.

But at least one judge, McLean, was dissatisfied with this prudent arrangement. It became known that he, an ambitious politician and a firm abolitionist, intended to dissent, arguing that Scott became free when he entered the free territory of the Louisiana Purchase. This necessarily involved the contention that Congress had the power to enact the Missouri Compromise which had made that area free. A majority of his fellow judges believed in fact that the Compromise was invalid, and they were unwilling to let McLean go unanswered, if the question was to be posed at all. Besides there was always the beguiling idea that a forthright statement from the Court might settle the whole, terrible issue and retrieve simultaneously the cause of both the Union and the South. Cheered on by his fellows and by the newly elected President James Buchanan, Taney therefore produced the most disastrous opinion the Supreme Court has ever issued. Dred Scott, he said, cannot bring suit in federal courts, first, because Negroes are not and cannot be citizens in the meaning of the federal Constitution; second, because, since the Missouri Compromise exceeded Congress' powers and is unconstitutional, he is still a slave in spite of his sojourn in free territory; and, third, because Missouri law regards him as a slave and the Supreme Court is here bound by Missouri's determination.

Eight separate opinions, including the Chief's, were filed by the judges in this case, and the task of unraveling them is more formidable than it is rewarding. What mattered to the nation was that a six-judge majority had denied the right of Negroes to be citizens and the right of Congress to control slavery in the territories.

The tempest of malediction that burst over the judges seems to have stunned them; far from extinguishing the slavery controversy, they had fanned its flames and had, moreover, deeply endangered the security of the judicial arm of government. No such vilification as this had been heard even in the wrathful days following the Alien and Sedition Acts. Taney's opinion was assailed by the Northern press as a wicked "stump speech" and was shamefully misquoted and distorted. "If the people obey this decision," said one newspaper, "they disobey God." Senator Seward fostered a dramatic but improbable story that Buchanan and Taney had villainously plotted this stroke on behalf of the slavery interests in a whispered tête-à-tête during the President's inauguration ceremonies, and the idea of a corrupt bargain between President, Congress, and Court became a theme of party politics in the next few years.

Of course no such explicit conspiracy existed. But Taney had connived in an exchange of information between Justices Catron and Grier and the incoming President, apparently out of sincere conviction that the leader of the nation in such parlous times should be informed about so grave an issue. It was not the least of his mistakes. The first and greatest had been to imagine that a flaming political issue could be quenched by calling it a "legal" issue and deciding it judicially.

But the notion that the Court could legitimately co-operate with the "political" branches in dealing with such an issue was almost equally self-destructive, for the Court's claim to public regard rested heavily on the belief that its work was distinguishable from "politics." In 1850 the Court enjoyed popular support as nearly unanimous as can ever be expected in a diverse democratic society. It was playing a modest but significant part in the affairs of the nation. Eight years later, it had forfeited that position, and its role in the American polity was nearly negligible. Taney and his fellows had been almost irresistibly provoked to do what they did in the *Dred Scott* case; the Chief's errors were well intended and understandable; he does not deserve the infamy that was so long associated with his name, for he was during most of his tenure a wise and good leader of the Court. But the fact that he had these virtues does not make his errors in this case any the less woeful; the fact that the Court under him had reached the pinnacle of its historic prestige merely heightens the tragedy of its decline.

The extent of that tragedy is revealed by the peculiar transvaluation of values that took place in connection with the case of *Ableman* v. *Booth* in 1859. Ableman, a Milwaukee editor, had assisted a fugitive slave to escape from federal custody, and was therefore arrested for violation of the national Fugitive Slave Law. The Wisconsin Supreme Court ordered him released on a writ of habeas corpus, and the order was obeyed. However, the national government then appealed to the Supreme Court of the United States, which held that the state courts had no business to interfere with the conduct of federal law and that the Fugitive Slave Law was constitutional.

Now the first point was of course the very keystone of the Supreme Court's jurisdictional arch; this was the principle for which Marshall had fought so shrewdly and effectively. If the national government and its judicial arm can operate only by the leave of the several states, the nation is not a nation and the Supreme Court is not a supreme court. Yet the decision was violently attacked, the state was urged to resist, the cry that the Court had no power thus to overrule a state was heard, not only in Wisconsin, but throughout the North.

This was the doctrine of nullification, familiar since the Virginia and Kentucky resolutions of 1798–99, re-energized by the mordant genius of Calhoun in 1832, and now becoming an article of faith below the Mason-Dixon line. That it should be invoked by a northern state as a challenge to the Court is a measure of the witless inconsistency of some Northern opinion but is also a measure of judicial bankruptcy. The Court's effective existence depended on acceptance of the principle of national authority, and there was no hope that this principle would be entertained in the South one minute after an anti-slavery opinion was rendered. The judicial constituency had always been drawn from those who had a stake in nationalism, and in 1859 that meant the North. But the monumental indiscretion of *Dred Scott* had forfeited Northern allegiance. For the first time in its history, the Court seemed almost friendless (for the fair-weather friendship of the South provided very cold comfort).

DECLINE WITHOUT FALL

The gloomy view of the judiciary's estate that is suggested by these events seems confirmed when we glance briefly at the Court's vicissitudes during the war years that followed. War is never a favorable environment for judicial power. It is characterized by emotion and quick, drastic action; and courts are not well equipped to cope with either. But natural handicaps are not enough to account for the impotency of the Supreme Court during the Civil War. It was of course, necessarily, the court of the Union, for the Confederacy was going its own way. But a substantial proportion of Union opinion associated the Court with the Confederate cause, unfairly but nonetheless stubbornly. It was hardly to be expected that its mandates would be eagerly sought or greatly heeded.

Taney, the luckless scapegoat of this judicial ice age, added another item to the Unionist score against him when less than three months after Lincoln's inauguration, he challenged the President's power to suspend the writ of habeas corpus for wartime purposes. He ordered that John Merryman, a Maryland secessionist being held in military prison, be brought before him on the writ, and when the commanding general refused to comply, Taney ordered that the general himself be haled into court in order to be fined and imprisoned for his disobedience. The marshal seeking to carry out this assignment was denied admission to the fort by the general, and Taney addressed himself to the President, calling on Lincoln to "perform his constitutional duty." The President did not reply. The only immediate reward for Taney's zeal was another shower of venom from the Northern press against this "hoary apologist for treason."

The Chief's point was in fact pretty well taken. Lincoln had wielded executive power somewhat recklessly during those early months of hostilities. It is at least doubtful that the President alone had the power to suspend the writ of habeas corpus, and it was not unreasonable to ask that he get congressional approval before he did so. But any chance that the Court might play the role of a moderating force, holding the government within sensible boundaries as it waged the bloody war, had been squandered in 1857.

And the Court majority knew it. Taney's willingness in the *Merryman* case to add to the judicial sea of troubles was not characteristic of the Court as a whole while the shooting continued. The judges found reason to refuse jurisdiction on cases involving such ticklish questions as the trial of civilians by military commission and the Legal Tender Acts. A decision adverse to the Union government in either might well have brought the temple crashing about their ears. The Court also upheld the power of the President to make war in the legal sense without waiting for a congressional declaration. Surely, it might be said, the day of the Supreme Court as a powerful factor in America was done. The Civil War was not only testing whether the nation could long endure; it was also demonstrating that the experiment of an independent and influential national judiciary had failed. The aged Chief Justice was not alone in believing that the Court would never "be restored to the authority and rank which the Constitution intended to confer on it," that is, the status it had attained under Marshall and himself.

But like Marshall, who died with similar forebodings weighing on his spirit, Taney and his colleagues had built better than he knew. On the foundation Marshall had bequeathed, the Taney Court had fashioned a system of jurisprudence and a judicial image; and the nation had learned to accept one and to admire the other. The judges had maintained a clear line of connection between Marshall's doctrines and their own. This was wise because it preserved the essential idea of the fundamental law as a steady river of continuity in otherwise capricious political seas. They had used the judicial veto, and this was important because it not only kept the notion of constitutional limit alive but reminded those who might forget that judicial sovereignty had not atrophied. But their discipleship to Marshall was discriminating; the veto had been handled discreetly; the Taney judges were aware that both the economic and the political world had changed since Marshall's time. They had managed to strike a middle ground that reconciled the American will for change with the desire for order and stability, the American's wish to have his way with his respect for the rule of law. Their reward had been the homage of the nation.

This achievement had been endangered by the audacious assumption in *Dred Scott* that the judiciary could solve the major problem facing America. But the public habit of reverence was strongly ingrained by those years of painstaking cultivation, and not even this calamity could stamp it out altogether. How many such adversities the judiciary could sustain is another question. The fact is that this wound, though grievous, was not fatal. The qualities of the American mind that had made the Court of the past possible had not disappeared. Americans, so to speak, had needed the Supreme Court to help express their own peculiar medley of governmental aspirations. When the war was over that need would reawaken.

FIVE

CONSTITUTIONAL EVOLUTION IN THE GILDED AGE: 1865–1900

IN THE OPENING CHAPTERS of this volume it was suggested that the Civil War marks the close of one great epoch in the history of judicial review, and the beginning of another. For the Court, as for many individuals, the war wrought profound changes both internal and external, changes so basic that it might well take decades to realize their dimensions. No person or institution or nation that had endured that experience could ever be the same as before; men like Henry Adams, who had lived abroad during the conflagration, were astonished—and somewhat appalled—when they returned to see the altered America that had emerged from the flames. And the judges of the Supreme Court, though lacking, perhaps, Adams' peculiar gifts of detachment and insight, had equal reason to rub their eyes. Their constitutional universe had been similarly transfigured.

For one thing, the nation-state problem had changed its nature dramatically. The Marshall and Taney Courts had been perennially haunted by the danger that centrifugal forces would tear the nation apart, and their jurisprudence had been shaped with that terrible threat always in mind. The Northern victory scotched this bugbear; when Chief Justice Chase declared in 1869 that ours was "an indestructible Union, composed of indestructible States," he spoke with a just confidence unknown to his predecessors.

The second great difference between the old constitutional environment and the new was slower to reveal itself fully but in the long run even more important to the future of judicial review. It was, of course, that capitalism, developing at a rapid but relatively moderate tempo in prewar years, had been given an enormous accelerating thrust by the war and was now proceeding at a pace of headlong expansion that was unexampled in the nation's history. The agrarian nation Jefferson and Marshall had known was now the industrial-mercantile nation that Hamilton had envisioned. The change had not really occurred overnight; in the 1850's this metamorphosis had been clearly enough foreshadowed. But in the 1850's the problems of slavery and the Union had claimed a very heavy share of attention from those who had thought about constitutional questions, and the constitutional implications of the rise of capitalism were correspondingly obscured. Now those implications were evident and were soon to be unavoidable. In 1866 the judges faced what was in effect a new judicial environment; and it was getting newer all the time.

For as capitalism expanded, it impinged on the lives of individuals as never before; as it became the most important fact in American life, it became the most troublesome fact as well. Men began to say, first from scattered quarters, then in a steadily augmenting chorus, that the power of government should be used to control this giant, to mitigate the harm to individual and collective welfare that it might do if left unchecked. And, conversely, others began to say, with a vehemence and volume far greater than in the past, that the giant would serve the community best if it were allowed to go its own way, that governmental tinkering with the economy was both futile and mischievous, that laissez faire should be the watchword of the day. The question of whether government should control capitalism, and how much it should control it, moved to the center of the American political arena and was never very far from that center for the next seventy years.

The results of all this for judicial review in the postwar era were several, but the most significant was that the Court's focus of interest was radically modified. The dominant interest of the Court in the past had been the nation-state relationship, and the dominant judicial value, as I have said earlier, was the preservation of the Union. The war did not of course obliterate the nation-state issue, for that issue is interminable in a federal republic. But its importance in the judicial order of things became much less, both absolutely because the very existence of the Union no longer hung in the balance and relatively because the greater issue of economic control had arisen to dominate the political scene. The postwar Court was no more disposed to leave the question of economic control alone than Marshall was disposed to leave the question of federalism alone. He had taught his successors to view themselves as vital factors in the governmental process, he had tried within the limits of judicial capacity to guide and coerce America along paths of his choosing. Whether or not he had succeeded in all his aims, he had at any rate succeeded in planting a judicial tradition of mentorship. The judges who now began coming to the Court—men like Chase and Bradley and Field—felt authorized to help America decide what kind of nation it should be. And since the gravest problem facing America was government regulation of business, that problem gradually became the major interest of America's constitutional court.

But if the Court's tradition helps explain why it was likely to focus now on the economic control issue, the tradition is also useful in predicting where the judges' preferences would lie in the evolving conflict between the proponents of control and of laissez faire. Marshall's darlings had been the nation and the property-owner, and most Supreme Court judges between 1789 and 1860 had shared these twin affections to a greater or lesser degree. Now that the national government had vindicated its existence in trial by battle, its health seemed reasonably assured, and it no longer required the solicitous protection of the Court. But the property-owner (that is, the businessman) began in the 1870's to be harried by government; "legislation by clamor," in William Graham Sumner's phrase, threatened to penalize him and hamper his freedom of action— to prevent him, as his admirers saw it, from helping the community by helping himself. A Court committed by its tradition to the cause of property rights, composed of judges who were inevitably drawn largely from the ranks of the "haves" and who were of course by definition lawyers and thus imbued with the conservative bias that has always characterized the American legal fraternity—such a Court was almost certain to throw its weight against the regulatory movement and on the side of the business community.

In this second great period of constitutional history, then, running roughly from the end of the Civil War to 1937, the major interest of the Supreme Court as a molder of governmental policy became the relationship between government and business; and the major value of the Court (to carry on the terminology used in earlier chapters) was the protection of the business community against government. The nation-state relationship, once salient, was now subordinate; the fear that the states would wound or destroy the nation was replaced by the fear that government, state or national, would unduly hinder business in its mission to make America wealthy and wise.

But to say this is the beginning of analysis, not the end. Historians like Charles Beard and J. Allen Smith and Brooks Adams were telling us, as early as the first decade of the twentieth century, that the Supreme Court was remarkably friendly to the pleas of "vested wealth." Those who at first recoiled in horror from such a suggestion have now generally subsided, and the fact has been incorporated among the standard assumptions of students of the era. The challenging question is not whether the Court of 1865–1937 favored the business community but what was the nature and degree of that favoritism, how was it implemented, to what extent was it qualified and self-restrained? In short, what role did the Court work out for itself in the light of its new interests and values? As suggested earlier in this volume, the Court's whole history can be viewed as a constant, or at least repeated, readjustment of role to suit the circumstances of each succeeding judicial era. What were the readjustment problems faced by the Court in this new age of burgeoning capitalism and regulatory government? How did the Court meet them?

The historical record that supplies the answers to these questions can be divided into two subperiods, the first extending roughly from the Civil War to 1900, the second ending with a bang and a good many whimpers in the fateful spring of 1937. And it is of course the first of these subperiods that concerns us for the remainder of this chapter.

VALOR AND DISCRETION: THE PROBLEM OF MILITARY TRIALS

An unwary reader, examining the behavior of the Court in the early postwar years, might easily get the impression that the foregoing paragraphs exaggerate the predominance of the government-business relationship in this judicial era. For some time after the shooting ended, the Court was heavily concerned with after-echoes of the war and with the knotty problem of Reconstruction for the conquered South. These issues were imposing enough in their own right to preoccupy the minds of the judges, and it would not be surprising if the Court had concentrated on them exclusively. But the significant fact is that even in the thick of these postwar difficulties the problem of economic control persists in peeping through; even while the guns are still reverberating or the "bloody shirt of the Rebellion" being most violently waved, the judicial opinions hint strongly of a quite different world which the judges themselves are perhaps as yet only dimly aware of.

True, there are few such hints in the decisions involving the war-endangered problem of military trials. In 1862, President Lincoln had authorized military commanders to seize and try by military tribunal civilians who engaged in "disloyal practices," even in areas remote from the actual conflict where the civil courts were duly functioning. Although in fact this authority was used quite sparingly, in principle it represented a startling transgression on individual rights, and the executive order was bitterly criticized in some quarters.

However, in 1863 it was applied in Ohio by General Burnside to the notorious "Copperhead" Clement L. Vallandigham who had, in a public meeting, denounced the "wicked, cruel, and unnecessary" war and had urged resistance to such extraordinary powers as those granted by the presidential order. Burnside promptly arrested him, presumably under that very order, and a military commission, finding him guilty of aiding and comforting the enemy, sentenced him to detention for the balance of the war.

Then Lincoln, apparently somewhat embarrassed by Burnside's zeal and always alert to the opportunity for a jest, commuted the sentence and ordered Vallandigham sent into Southern territory, where he could be free to comfort rebels to his heart's content. Meanwhile the prisoner had applied for a writ of habeas corpus to the United States circuit court in Cincinnati, and the writ had been denied. He and his supporters wished of course to pursue the issue to the Supreme Court in the hope that the Lincoln administration might be declared to have acted illegally. But the approach they chose, seemingly on the assumption that it was the only way now available, was to petition that the Supreme Court call up the record of the military commission for review by a writ of certiorari. This writ was, and is, a standard form by which the Court exercises control over inferior tribunals, but the use of the writ is confined by law to certain types of cases. The Court held, quite rightly, that its powers of review consisted only of those granted by the Constitution and Congress, and that it had not been authorized by either of those agents to call up the proceedings of a military commission in this way. Vallandigham was left to seek his satisfaction elsewhere, and he did, running for governor of Ohio in 1864 and polling nearly 40 per cent of the total vote.

The members of the Court may well have thanked providence for the jurisdictional technicalities that removed Vallandigham's cause from their ken, for the scars of the *Dred Scott* decision were as yet by no means healed, and a "pro-Copperhead" decision would not have been received kindly by Unionist opinion. However, in 1866, when *Ex Parte Milligan* came before them, the fighting was over, and the judges felt that a backward slap at the wartime military trials was now in order. In 1864, Lambdin P. Milligan, a citizen of Indiana, had played a leading part in a plot by the Order of the Sons of Liberty to set free prisoners of war and take over by armed force the state governments in Indiana, Ohio, and Illinois. He had been tried by a military tribunal and sentenced to hang. Milligan, like Vallandigham, then asked the circuit court in Indianapolis for a writ of habeas corpus.

So far the cases of Vallandigham and Milligan would appear to be kindred in all important respects. But from the viewpoint of the Supreme Court when it received Milligan's appeal, there were two significant differences. For one thing, a law of March 3, 1863, though suspending the privilege of the writ of habeas corpus, had provided that if a grand jury had met after a man was taken into custody and had failed to indict him, the prisoner could require the court concerned to order his release. This seemed to give the circuit court undoubted authority to hear Milligan's case, and moreover it strongly suggested that Congress had tacitly forbidden military trial if the civil courts were open and grand juries were duly being assembled. The circuit court to which Milligan applied professed doubts on these and other points and passed the issues up to the Supreme Court by the process known as "certification." This mode of appellate jurisdiction is provided in the Judiciary Act, and thus the jurisdictional difficulties that barred the way in the case of Vallandigham did not arise. The question of the validity of the military trials was clearly and regularly before the Court.

The second difference between the two cases was of course that the war had ended by the time Milligan's case reached the Supreme Court. Some commentators have made more of this point than is warranted, suggesting that the Court gratuitously seized upon a technicality to escape jurisdiction in the first case because the atmosphere was supercharged with danger for a Court that presumed to interfere with the conduct of the war. As we have seen, there was nothing gratuitous about it; in order to reach Vallandigham's case, the judges would have had to invent jurisdiction that was not provided by law. But this is not to say that they were unaware of the difference between the military trial question in 1863 and in 1866. Their awareness shows in a contrast of the spirits of the two decisions, the cautious opinion of Justice Wayne in the first case, restricting himself to the jurisdictional issue, eschewing any implications about the propriety of such trials, and the boldly venturesome majority opinion in *Milligan*, suggesting with oratorical flourishes that the Court was now ready to resume its place as a leading participant in the councils of the nation.

A majority of five now felt prepared to say that no one, not even Congress, could authorize military trial of civilians when the civil courts were still open. The remaining four judges were not willing to go so far, but they concurred that Congress though possessing the power to authorize military trials in war, had not exerted it here, and that Milligan must go free. Justice Davis' majority opinion is the more remarkable in that he not only deals with an issue unnecessary to the decision (for he agrees that Congress had not authorized the trial, and the question of whether it could have done so is thus hypothetical) but intrepidly asserts, in effect, that the Supreme Court is the final judge of what constitutes military necessity.

This is not the Court of the wartime years, smarting under the lash of criticism that had immediately followed *Dred Scott,* modestly forbearing from interference in the great affairs of state. It has shown itself willing to wait until the national temperature has dropped somewhat below the boiling point, but there is no mistaking the intimation, made as soon as that stage of excessive peril is past, that the Court is moving back to its accustomed seat of power as fast as circumstances will allow. There is no danger that America will be deprived of judicial guidance in coping with the problems that the postwar era has in store.

Unfortunately one of those problems, though temporary, was calculated to generate almost as much heat as the war itself. This was the problem of Reconstruction in the South, for the Republican party, now riding high, was determined upon a policy of revenge and self-perpetuation. To those ends Congress had divided the South into military districts under military commanders and had provided for military trials in the areas at the commanders' discretion. Under the rule of the *Milligan* case such trials were plainly invalid, but in that case the Court had been looking back at a situation in the past, and now it was looking squarely at a present danger.

The enemies of Reconstruction hastened to bring up a case that would force the Court to stand on the *Milligan* logic and declare the Reconstruction Acts unconstitutional, but they encountered a series of jurisdictional checks. A request for an injunction to prevent Johnson from enforcing the laws was turned down on the ground that an injunction could not lie against the President. Similar suits against the Secretary of War and military officials encountered from the Court the declaration that they presented "political questions" (that is, abstract questions of sovereignty rather than the immediate question of whether John Doe was being deprived of particular rights) and were not justiciable. The would-be litigants seemed on the point of success in *Ex Parte McCardle,* involving a Mississippi editor arrested by a military commander, for his right to appeal in a habeas corpus proceeding seemed clearly guaranteed by federal law. But the Court delayed action until Congress itself provided a checkmate by passing a bill that deprived the Court of the jurisdiction under which McCardle's cause had been brought. The Court unanimously—and, we may guess, thankfully—held that this act was valid, that Congress' power over appellate jurisdiction was plenary. And the upshot was that the Reconstruction Acts, though palpably unconstitutional under the *Milligan* doctrine, were never tested in the Supreme Court.

THE COURT'S NEW SPIRIT AND THE LEGAL TENDER ISSUE

The generalizations that can be drawn from the military trial cases are two. The first is that the postwar Court is wary of involving itself in issues so emotionally charged that a decision might precipitate ruthless counterattack from the dominant political forces of the nation. But the second is that, with this caveat duly in mind, the judges still feel it their right and duty to help America decide the fundamental issues that confront it. An understanding of the delicate distinction that is here implied is crucial to an understanding of the Court's historic place in American life. The Court tacitly acknowledges an informal but very real limit on its jurisdiction: the most explosive issues are "non-justiciable." Sometimes (as in war) the most explosive issues will also be the most "important," and then the Court is likely to play a rather modest role in national affairs. But this modesty is brought on by knowledge of the explosiveness of the question rather than by awe at its importance. Neither Marshall nor his predecessors nor his successors have, until lately at any rate, displayed much diffidence about substituting their judgment for that of others when the moment for doing so seemed auspicious. But they have displayed a fairly consistent awareness that for everything on earth there is a season.

The willingness of the postwar Court to remount the heights of power, foreshadowed in the *Milligan* case, is further illustrated in a series of other cases involving problems of war and Reconstruction. And now the King Charles's head of economic control does begin to break through the more immediate judicial preoccupations.

Perhaps the most ambitious, though abortive, of these early postwar ventures into judicial supervision was the attempt to adjudicate the weighty issue of legal tender. During the war the Union government, being in some fiscal difficulties, had issued $450,000,000 in "greenbacks" (that is, paper money which was not redeemable in coin and thus owed its value, if any, to the government's declaration that it was legal tender for "payment of all debts, public and private"). The question of whether Congress had power to issue such fiat money and compel creditors to accept it was an old one, and a case (*Roosevelt* v. *Meyer*) challenging the law's validity reached the Supreme Court in 1863. But the Court escaped jurisdiction by the simple, if inexcusable expedient of misreading the Judiciary Act in such a way as to prohibit a Supreme Court hearing. We must assume either that the judges were unfamiliar with the law that furnishes their very basis for being, or that they deliberately chose a Pickwickian interpretation in order to avoid deciding, in wartime, a question so central to the conduct of the war. It is hard to think of a third reasonable explanation.

At any rate this decision postponed the constitutional issue of legal tender, as *Vallandigham* had postponed the war trials issue, until the war was over. Even then the Court approached the matter cautiously, avoiding constitutional problems by strict construction of the statutes, agreeing that Congress had power to issue greenbacks, but not grappling with the ultimate question, which was whether creditors must accept them. However, in 1869 this question was squarely presented by a creditor who refused to take payment in paper for a debt contracted in 1860, before the passage of the Legal Tender Acts. And in 1870 a Court majority held in *Hepburn* v. *Griswold* that the refusal was justified because the law, at least as applied to debts contracted before its passage, was unconstitutional.

Chief Justice Chase's opinion for the majority has been roundly criticized by generations of observers, not only on the ground that it undertook to argue and decide a question inappropriate for judicial treatment, but also on the ground that the Chief Justice failed to make a good case for the point of view he did adopt. His argument was that the legal tender requirement was not a "necessary and proper" means of carrying out the war powers, and this involved him in an essentially economic treatise on the evils of soft money, hardly a matter that falls within the range of judicial expertness. He further sought to prop up this slender reed of logic by contending that the law violated the "spirit" of the Constitution because it was unjust; and the letter as well because, by decreasing the value of the creditor's accounts receivable, it took money without "due process of law."

The noteworthy things about the decision from the viewpoint of this chapter are that it illustrates, as *Milligan* did, the postwar Court's eagerness to impose its wisdom on the government in connection with momentous issues, and more particularly a growing compulsion to defend property rights against all who might assail them. The question at stake was the power of the national government to control its own currency, a power which, as Justice Bradley was to say, may be "absolutely essential to independent national existence." The audacity of the Court's decision to restrict this authority by its own fiat is breathtaking when we consider that the *Dred Scott* case lay only thirteen years in the past. And the invocation of the due process clause, though it seems a kind of afterthought here, is prophetic. For it was by way of this clause that the Court was ultimately to claim the overloadship of economic policy that is asserted so daringly, though lamely, in the *Hepburn* case.

But the *Hepburn* doctrine itself, including its novel gloss of due process, enjoyed the shortest life of any important doctrine ever promulgated by the Court. Justice Grier, who helped to make up the five-man majority, had retired before the decision was announced, and on the very day of announcement President Grant nominated two new justices, Strong and Bradley, to bring the Court to its full complement of nine. The *Hepburn* vote had been on strict party lines—five Democrats against the law (counting Chase who was busily becoming a Democrat at this time) and three Republicans for. The two new appointees were of course Republicans and could presumably be counted on to uphold the Legal Tender Acts, if they got a chance to do so. They helped to provide that chance by voting to accept jurisdiction in two cases which raised an issue similar to *Hepburn* and agreeing to reconsider the constitutional issue. And in 1871, only fifteen months after *Hepburn*, a new majority held that the Acts were constitutional in all respects (the *Legal Tender Cases*). Thus Chief Justice Chase's tortured logic and his doubtful interpretations of constitutional doctrine died in infancy. But the spirit of his opinion—the implied superiority of judicial wisdom, the insistence that no issue is too big or too intricate for judicial governance, the solicitude for the aggrieved possessing class—these lived on in decisions of the future, as we shall see.

The Fourteenth Amendment and the Slaughter-House Cases

The *Legal Tender Cases* then blended the motifs of war and Reconstruction with the more purely economic themes that were to dominate the Court's value system in the near future. Somewhat the same qualities were apparent in the *Slaughter-House Cases* of 1873, one of the great landmarks in American constitutional history. But here the harmonies were even more complicated, for the eternal issue of federalism could also be detected, running through the opinions and influencing their result.

The cases involved the Fourteenth Amendment, the second and, as it turned out, most pregnant of the three major constitutional changes that had been imposed by the triumphant Republicans on the nation in general and the defeated South in particular. In its first section the Amendment declared that:

> No State shall make or enforce any law which shall abridge the privileges or immunities of citizens of the United States; nor shall any State deprive any person of life, liberty, or property, without due process of law; nor deny to any person within its jurisdiction the equal protection of the laws.

This sentence, especially in its last two clauses, was to become perhaps the most adjudicated and discussed sentence in the federal Constitution, but in 1873 its meaning was uncertain and its significance highly conjectural. In order to understand both its future importance and its contemporary ambiguity, we must glance backward again at pre–Civil War constitutional history.

For one thing it must be realized that the Bill of Rights (Amendments I–VIII) had been held to limit the federal government alone, not the states. This was Marshall's doctrine in *Barron* v. *Baltimore* (1833); it had never been seriously controverted; the states could therefore infringe on individual liberties as they willed, except for relatively mild restrictions like the contract clause or the ex post facto clause. The second point worth special note is that the due process clause, which appears in both the Fifth Amendment as a limit on the nation and in the Fourteenth as a limit on the states, had usually been interpreted as having only a procedural meaning. That is, it did not prevent government from depriving a person of life, liberty, or property, but simply guaranteed that certain standard procedures would be observed before a person was so deprived. In this sense the concept of due process did not import a very strict curb on government power, for it meant that only the *manner,* not the *object,* of legislation was subject to judicial scrutiny. And yet having said this, we must also admit that the difference between manner and object, between procedure and substance, is not always so clear-cut in practice as it may appear in conception, and that there had existed for some time an undercurrent of feeling that the due process requirement could be, and perhaps should be, enlarged into a general prohibition against "unjust" or "arbitrary" legislation. Such a prohibition, if recognized, could now apply to both the national government and the states through the Fifth and Fourteenth Amendments, respectively.

These two points lead to a question or rather a series of them: what was the quoted sentence of the Fourteenth Amendment designed to accomplish? Was it intended to reverse *Barron* v. *Baltimore* and make the Bill of Rights applicable to the states, that is, were the "privileges or immunities" it speaks of those that have heretofore been protected against national action alone by the Bill of Rights (free speech, jury trial, etc.)? Was the due process clause merely meant to outlaw unfair legal procedures in the states or to forbid all governmental action infringing on property which a court might regard as unjust? Was the "equal protection" clause to be taken literally? Did it mean that the states' laws could enforce no discriminations at all between persons? If the sentence meant all of these things, or even a substantial part of them, then the federal system had been drastically revised, for the whole domain of civil rights now fell under the protection of the national judiciary.

Unfortunately these questions are easier to state than to answer. The best evidence is that the Congress that passed, and the state legislators who ratified, the Amendment had extremely mixed or extremely vague ideas about the meaning of these terms. Only the query about due process can be answered with anything resembling confidence; it is most unlikely that those who participated in establishing the Amendment expected it to protect property in a broad way from all forms of state-imposed injustice, for the phrase had usually been construed much more narrowly. Yet even here there is a modicum of doubt, and with respect to the other clauses the doubt becomes full-fledged confusion.

However, as has been remarked earlier in this volume, ambiguity of constitutional language and uncertainty about constitution-makers' intent is the very *sine qua non* of judicial review as it has operated in the United States. The Court itself could not have been the institution it was if the framers in 1789 had spoken more plainly about the judicial power. Great clauses like the commerce clause and the contract clause could not have been shaped to the judicial purpose if they had been drawn more precisely. It is arguable that the Fourteenth Amendment was a kind of license for the Court to proceed at will within broad limits, to make of these phrases what it felt was right and feasible. That is, after all, what the Court had done with other imprecise mandates. If the framers of the Fourteenth wanted their brainchild to be treated otherwise, nothing would have been easier than for them to say so. They did not, and their failure to clarify their intentions provided the Court with a golden opportunity to inaugurate a new era in the history of judicial review.

Now to return to the *Slaughter-House Cases*. In 1869, a "carpetbag" legislature in Louisiana had passed a law granting a monopoly in the slaughtering of livestock to a single New Orleans corporation. Other

New Orleans butchers were understandably outraged by this invasion of their occupational freedom, but under traditional interpretations of the Constitution it seemed that they would be forced to grin and bear it unless the legislature could be persuaded to change its mind. The pre-war Constitution would have offered the Supreme Court no way to redress their grievance, even if it had the will to do so, for the states' control of such economic matters had been recognized as plenary so long as the contract clause was not violated.

But now the butchers had two new cards to play. The first was the Fourteenth Amendment ratified in 1868 and hence applicable to the legislation. And the second was the Honorable John A. Campbell, one-time Supreme Court justice and now one of the greatly successful lawyers of the day. There was a saying, "Leave it to God and Mr. Campbell," and the butchers gladly put their case in the hands of those high authorities. Mr. Campbell rose to the occasion with a lengthy, scholarly, and powerful argument that the Fourteenth Amendment had revolutionized the American system by bringing the rights of man, including of course the right to occupational freedom, under national judicial protection. Already, in 1873, he was showing the Court the way to provide business with relief from governmental meddling: the Fourteenth Amendment had enacted the principle of laissez faire into the American Constitution.

The Court was visibly shaken by this brilliant improvisation, but a majority was not quite convinced. Five to four, through Justice Miller, it rejected the butchers' claims. The "privileges or immunities" clause, said Miller, does not secure against state action the great basic rights that are protected against national action by the Bill of Rights. It refers only to certain special rights of national citizenship, such as the right to travel freely about the country, the "right to use the navigable waters of the United States," etc. The freedoms guaranteed against national action by the Bill of Rights are at the mercy of the states, just as they have been since Barron v. Baltimore. As for the argument that the due process clause accomplished Mr. Campbell's aims, it is not sustained by any "construction of that phrase that we have ever seen, or any that we deem admissible." And as for the equal protection clause, it is clearly a provision to protect the Negroes in their newly won freedom and has no applications to the case in hand.

One interesting thing about this decision is the contrast between what it seemed to do and what it actually did. It seemed to slam the door on the question of whether the Amendment had radically altered the federal relationship, and on the subquestion of whether property rights were to be granted broad national protection. The answers, one might think, were both emphatically "no." But, in the event, the decision turned out to mean only that these two great developments were postponed until the magical process of "judicial inclusion and exclusion" could bring them about more subtly and gradually. Outright acceptance of Campbell's argument would have imposed upon the Court the vast and perhaps unmanageable problem of protecting all civil rights against state abridgment; moreover, it would have left the Court small room to maneuver, to feel its way toward self-chosen goals within the limits of the politically possible. While seeming to dash all hopes for a constitutional check of this sort, Miller had actually made it possible for the American constitutional system to evolve, as it always has, by slow "Burkean" accretions rather than by a single great mutation; and he had left the Court free to define, as it had in the past, its own role in the national polity.

Moreover, this process of closing the door but leaving it unbolted served another purpose, probably unsuspected by Justice Miller, but nonetheless important in the Court's dawning future. It helped to consign the redoubtable problem of Negro rights to a rather trivial place in the judicial agenda and thus removed an incumbrance that might have been most troublesome. With nicely mingled idealism and opportunism, the victorious Republicans had forced through not only the "War Amendments" (XIII, XIV, XV) but a series of "civil rights acts" designed to secure the Negroes in their newly won privileges of citizenship. Miller's narrow definition of "privileges or immunities" disposed of any likelihood that that constitutional clause would help the freedmen. And a few years later the national civil rights acts were emasculated by the holding that the "enforcement clause" of the Fourteenth Amendment did not authorize Congress to legislate against transgression by private persons on the rights of individuals, Negro or white. This left only the due process and equal protection clauses which Miller had brushed aside so disrespectfully and which for a good many years were to play little part in insuring such meager privileges as the Negro enjoyed. Outright and flagrant state discriminations based on race might be struck down by the judicial arm, but indirect and informal distinctions were tolerated, and legally enforced segregation of races were permitted so long as the facilities provided were "substantially equal" (the adverb was generously construed). And of course, except in very special circumstances, the discriminatory behavior of private persons was beyond the reach of the courts and Congress alike. The judges thus avoided the distractions and the diffusion of energy that might have hampered them, if they had chosen to defend both the businessman and the Negro at the same time.

THE DRIFT TOWARD CONSTITUTIONAL LAISSEZ FAIRE

Now, and to an increasing degree as war and Reconstruction recede into the past, the Court's history becomes a history of response to the advance of what was later to be called "the general-welfare state." The development of this preoccupation is foreshadowed, as I have suggested, in such immediately post-war decisions as *Hepburn* and in the opinions of *Slaughter-House* dissenters like Field and Bradley. Whether they were more prescient than their majority associates or simply more passionately devoted to the defense of property, the fact is that these judges were ready in 1873 to interpret the Fourteenth Amendment as a general restriction on economic legislation.

But the Court majority was more hesitant, and for good reasons. For one thing, some, like Justice Miller, were undoubtedly disturbed by the enormity of the assignment Mr. Campbell had urged upon them. Miller may have been, as his biographer says, more "reconciled to the exercise of power by the political branches of government" than most of his colleagues, but others probably shared some of his misgivings and had to be won over gradually to the radical construction espoused by Bradley and Field. For another thing, it is probably true that the judges in 1873 had not yet become fully alert to the nature and extent of the welfare state "menace." The Granger Movement, an attack on corporate autonomy and especially the railroads, was already under way in the Midwest; but it was still possible in 1873 to view such developments as atypical, temporary, and therefore only mildly alarming. The specter of full-fledged paternal government, of state socialism, had already begun to haunt the dreams of Field, but others still slept fairly soundly.

And finally, as I have intimated, traditional legal doctrine hindered the program of judicial empire-building that Mr. Campbell proposed. The states had always been allowed a pretty free hand to regulate economic affairs under their reserved "police power." The Marshall-Taney view of national power under the "necessary and proper" clause had been uniformly permissive. The term "privileges and immunities" had reposed innocuously in Article IV of the Constitution since 1789, and no court had forced it to bear the weight of implications that Campbell now suggested. Due process had been regarded chiefly as a procedural guarantee.

In these early postwar years, then, and partly for these reasons, the majority seemed willing, if not entirely content, to leave economic affairs to the "political branches of government." The self-denial of the majority in *Slaughter-House* was matched in 1869 by *Paul* v. *Virginia,* sustaining state regulation of the insurance business and as late as 1879 by *Stone* v. *Mississippi,* which held that the state could prohibit lotteries, even when conducted by a corporation that had formerly enjoyed a state-chartered right to do so. Corporate charters are protected by the contract clause but, said the Court, this protection is subject to the implied qualification that "the public health or public morals" cannot be bargained away; that is, in these fields the state can change its mind and retract privileges it has previously granted.

These decisions, and others that might be cited, do suggest a judicial temper that was temporarily tolerant toward some forms of state interference with property rights. But as the years passed this indulgent mood became harder and harder for the Court to sustain and the threat of economic control became more real and more perturbing. Little by little the urge to intrude in economic affairs waxed stronger and stronger, the desire of Field and Bradley, expressed in *Slaughter-House,* was converted into the desire of the Court as a whole. By 1880 the majority was coming fully alive to the danger of economic control and to the need for some judicial action that would check it.

However, at this point, as I have suggested, the Court was handicapped in assuming this weighty but attractive assignment by its own inherited legal traditions. The judges had the will but not the way to protect business against what Joseph Choate was to call, in 1895, the "onward march of communism." What they needed was the due process clause in its 1900 form; what they had was the vague and relatively feeble clause of the Anglo-American legal tradition.

Their willingness to take to the ramparts on behalf of laissez faire is made clear enough in the decisions involving the commerce clause. When the weapons were at hand the judges were ready to use them. In this field, it will be remembered, the Court had available the doctrine of federal preemption (see pp. 56–57), drawn from such old decisions as *Gibbons* v. *Ogden* and *Cooley* v. *Board of Wardens;* and it was relatively easy to find state economic regulations invalid because they encroached on interstate commerce. The Court proceeded to do so in a series of decisions running in a seldom broken line from the year of Chief Justice Waite's appointment (1874) to the turn of the century. The states' power to tax interstate business activity was seriously impaired in such decisions as the *Philadel-*

phia and Reading Rail Road case in 1873, which outlawed freight tonnage taxes on interstate shipments; and other state attempts to control business within their borders fell under a similar ban in the 1870's. Perhaps the most important of these early decisions was the *Pensacola Telegraph* case in 1877, which precluded the states from granting telegraph monopolies, but it is only one of several. The rise of the regulatory movement was bringing commerce cases to the Court in growing numbers, and the judges were giving notice that state laws in this field would be scrutinized with a sharp eye.

This promise was honored with increasing consistency as time went on. There were some fourteen cases between 1877 and 1886 in which state regulations of commerce were held invalid, most of them on the ground that the subject in question was national in character and required a uniform rule which only Congress could provide. Nor does this include the most far-reaching of all, the *Wabash* case in 1886 which effectively forbade the states to regulate interstate railroad rates. And after this date, the tempo of such decisions increased still further; the states' power to tax and regulate business was more and more constrained by the doctrine that national commerce must be nationally controlled, if it is to be controlled at all.

Charles Warren, in his admirable history of the Supreme Court, describes Waite's tenure (1874–88) in terms of the ebb and flow of "nationalism." The non-nationalist period runs through 1880; thereafter nationalist tendencies begin to display themselves. The fact that the pre-1880 Court struck down a healthy number of state laws under the *Cooley* rule is apparently viewed as an enigmatic exception to its general attitude of tolerance toward state regulations, and that tolerance is otherwise evidenced by the judiciary's willingness to leave to the states the problem of Negro rights and by its failure in these years to use the Fourteenth Amendment to invalidate state business regulations.

This analysis mistakes the secondary for the primary. Of course the judges had opinions on the subject of nationalism, and they were growing increasingly aware during this period that business was becoming national in character. Truly intrastate commercial activity was far less common than it had been; more and more businesses had ramifications beyond the borders of a single state and were thus inappropriate for local regulation. The judges knew this and it was reflected, among other things, in their opinions.

But along with this knowledge there developed a complementary and to some extent transcendent feeling that government regulation in general was dangerously increasing and that the judiciary had a holy obligation to help avert the peril if it could. In the early stage the feeling could not be implemented via the Fourteenth Amendment, because judicial conscience did not permit an interpretation of the Amendment that was unwarranted by precedent. But in the commerce field, as we have noted, the precedent did exist, and the Court was inclined from the first to use the *Cooley* rule and related ideas against the regulatory threat. The fact that the decisions invoked the new realities of commercial nationalism was important; these realities added a significant weight to the balance, supplying a powerful argument and sometimes no doubt helping to change a judge's mind. But to suggest that considerations of nationalism were predominant is to confuse the postwar Court with its predecessors, to forget that the old issue of federalism was now becoming subordinate to the "higher" issue of economic control.

That subordination was made abundantly clear in the 1890's, when the Court was finally confronted with national regulatory statutes of major dimensions. Two cases in point are enough to illuminate the matter. After the *Wabash* decision, Congress finally bestirred itself to pass the act which established the Interstate Commerce Commission for regulating the railroads. The Commission's efforts were impeded from the onset by corporate opposition and court-contrived incumbrances. But the great blow fell in 1896 when the Supreme Court announced that the act did not endow the Commission with the power to fix railroad rates (*Cincinnati, New Orleans, and Texas Pacific Railway Co. v. I.C.C.*). As Justice Harlan remarked a year later, the Commission was now left with power "to make reports, and to issue protests. But it has been shorn, by judicial interpretation, of authority to do anything of an effective character."

The second illustrative case is equally edifying. It involved the Sherman Act, which had been passed by Congress in 1890 to "protect trade and commerce against unlawful restraints and monopolies." In 1895, the Court held that the law did not, and indeed could not, forbid monopolies in manufacturing, because manufacturing is not a part of interstate commerce and affects interstate commerce only "indirectly." To allow the national government to regulate this subject would be to permit encroachment on the reserved powers of the states (*United States v. E. C. Knight Co.*).

In the face of these decisions handcuffing national authority and in the face of the line of decisions already discussed which correspondingly restricted state control of commerce, it is a little hard to think of "nationalist" or "localist" considerations as dominant in the Court's value scale.

The inescapable implication is, on the contrary, that the Court's chief concern was to defend the principle of laissez faire and that both nationalist and localist doctrine were being pressed to subserve that end. The minions of the "onward march of communism" would find no comfort in the commerce clause, if the Supreme Court could prevent it. And to an impressive degree the Court could.

THE NEW FOURTEENTH AMENDMENT:
THE TRIUMPH OF JUDICIAL CONSTITUTION-MAKING

However, if the battle of laissez faire was to be waged with effectiveness, some more potent weapon than the commerce clause was needed, for, versatile though that instrument was, it was not a universal answer to the individualist's prayers. Suppose a business falls clearly within the range of interstate or intrastate commerce; what is to save it then? Not the distinctions just discussed; they have been eliminated by definition. Yet unless some alternate doctrine can be discovered, the state and national governments will be left free to impose the most arbitrary restraints on business, and laissez faire will be, as far as constitutional limitations are concerned, a lost cause.

Precisely this point was made by counsel in *Munn* v. *Illinois,* the "Granger case" decided in 1877. Illinois and other western states had recently witnessed popular uprisings against the rate-fixing practices of the railroads and associated enterprises; the state law in question here set limits on the charges for grain storage in the Chicago area, but Illinois and her neighbors had also passed measures fixing maximum railroad rates, and conservative opinion had been deeply agitated by these assaults on free enterprise. Yet the lawyers who spoke for that element—specifically in this case for the grain elevators—were in rather the position of Mr. Campbell in *Slaughter-House:* their passionate conviction that the Constitution ought to prohibit these outrages was more impressive than their legal arguments that the Fourteenth Amendment had been designed to provide such a prohibition. Consequently, their arguments were heavily tinged with the idea that the Court had a moral duty to remake the Amendment into a bastion "behind which private rights and private property may shelter themselves and be safe" from "the will of the majority."

And this plea was meanwhile being echoed in the argument of other Granger cases before the Court, in speeches and legal periodicals, indeed almost everywhere the judges might turn, except of course in the "radical" press. The judiciary (and in fact America as a whole) were being deluged by a potpourri composed of Social Darwinist philosophy about the survival of the fittest and the virtues of economic freedom; scholarly appearing but largely irrelevant citations from the Anglo-American legal past; and admonitions that the judicial power alone had the means at its disposal to save the nation from suicide-by-regulation.

In the face of all this, it speaks well for the self-restraint of the Court that it rejected the immediate call to duty and upheld the Granger acts, including the grain elevator statute. Businesses like the present one, said Chief Justice Waite in the *Munn* case, are "affected with a public interest," because their owners have chosen to use their property "in a manner to make it of public consequence, and affect the community at large." When property is so used, its possessor must submit to public control, including rate regulation.

But the consternation of the proponents of laissez faire at this outcome demonstrates that they had not read the opinion carefully, or perhaps that, like so many critics of the Court in American history, they were more interested in an immediately favorable decision than in the long-term principle they had so fervently espoused. Had they read more attentively and thought more farsightedly, they must have seen that the majority's sales resistance was really weaker than a superficial reading might reveal, that their arguments had, after all, struck home. For Waite was careful to say that "under some circumstances" a regulatory statute might be so arbitrary as to be unconstitutional, and these mild words implied for the business community a concession whose value was beyond emeralds and rubies. It meant that the Court recognized, back-handedly to be sure but without question, that the due process clause of the Fourteenth Amendment imposed a substantive limit on economic legislation. Such an interpretation was too novel in 1877 to support an outright holding of unconstitutionality, but Waite had given the supplicants notice that their prayers were not unheeded, and also a kind of promissory note, redeemable when precedents had ripened a bit further and judicial backs had been stiffened a bit more.

The history of the Fourteenth Amendment for the remainder of the nineteenth century is one of gradual redemption of that promise made in 1877. But for some years the approach to the question was oblique, and the cumulative tendency of the decisions must have seemed equivocal to contemporaries. Instead of forthrightly invalidating a statute by applying a substantive view of due process, the judges chose to uphold the challenged laws, and concurrently to issue more or less explicit warnings that other laws in other circumstances might not be treated so tenderly. In 1886, for example, Waite allowed a Mississippi statute endowing a railroad commission with the power to fix rates, but he seized the occasion to remark that the Commission must beware of fixing charges so low that it might amount "to a taking of private property for public use without just compensation or without due process of law." If "due process" simply meant "due procedure," its historic connotation, the actual amount of the rates established was beyond judicial cognizance so long as the Commission observed procedural amenities like notice and hearing. Quite evidently Waite was assuming, though not for the moment employing, judicial power to restrain "injustice" if it should occur.

This assumption was a product, no doubt, of many converging factors: the multiplication of "welfare state" threats, the Macedonian cries of the business community and its legal and academic defenders, a growing awareness that an interpretation of due process which seemed impossibly novel and probably unnecessary a decade before could be made acceptable by slow accretion and might prove very useful in the cause of righteousness. As Waite wrote, the voices of two great contemporaries, Thomas M. Cooley and Stephen J. Field, must have been echoing in his mind. Cooley's classic treatise on *Constitutional Limitations,* first published in 1868, had become a canonical text for jurists, and his support of due process in its emerging form gave the stamp of scholarly approval to an interpretation that seemed ethically more and more imperative. Field had been from the start eager to embrace an interpretation that would protect freedom of contract; his dissents had been resounding in the supreme courtroom for years, and each term these organ tones must have seemed a little more compelling. Justice Harlan, perhaps the strongest-minded on the bench at the time except Field, was patently moved by the impact of all these gathering forces. In 1887, though upholding a Kansas prohibition law against due process attack, he remarked that the Court in evaluating such legislation is not bound by "mere forms," and continued:

> If, therefore, a statute purporting to have been enacted to protect the public health, the public morals, or the public safety, has no real or substantial relation to those objects . . . it is the duty of the courts so to adjudge and thereby give effect to the Constitution.

By the 1890's the development signalized by such pronouncements had run its course, and the concept of due process as a judicially enforced bar to arbitrary economic legislation was ready for action. Judicial minds had been gradually accommodated to an idea that had long since found its place in their hearts; dicta such as those just cited had accumulated in sufficient numbers so that "precedents" for the new doctrine could be readily invoked to satisfy a lawyer-like conscience. In 1890, the Court overturned a Minnesota railroad commission law on the ground that it "deprived the company of its right to a judicial investigation, by due process of law" of the reasonableness of rates. This seemed to mean that rates fixed by law or by commissions acting under law were subject to approval of courts, and ultimately the Supreme Court. There yet remained a margin of vagueness at this point, though the judges were obviously edging closer to their historic goal. But at all events doubts were swept away five years later in *Smyth* v. *Ames,* which flatly held that the judiciary has the last word on the reasonableness of rates, and even went on to propound what a later jurist called a "mischievous formula" for determining them. In 1897 the concept of "liberty of contract," so dear to Herbert Spencer and other defenders of laissez faire, was used as the basis for invalidating a state law; the Court as B. F. Wright says, "simply wrote the dissenting opinions of Justices Swayne and Bradley in the *Slaughter-House Cases* into the Fourteenth Amendment."

This holding completed the process of constitution-making that had begun with the dissents in that case. Ten years before, the Court had conceded, rather offhandedly, that corporations were "persons" within the meaning of the Amendment, and that concession was now seen to be of epic importance and of incalculable value to the business community. Combined with the now accepted idea of due process as a substantive limit on "arbitrary" laws, it meant that business, whether incorporated or not, was no longer wholly at the mercy of the popular will.

The development just chronicled is beyond much question the classic example of "government by judiciary" in the United States, and it is worthwhile to pause for a moment to underline some of its features. In the first place, it is noteworthy that the Court did not proceed by a single bound to this new doctrine and the new role that it made possible. This was the course urged by Field and other cheerleaders, but the majority preferred to grope more deliberately through the tangled thicket of modern government, to plant the judicial feet more warily. Strong men like Field, with a tinge of dogmatism, play an important part in American constitutional history, but less positive types like Waite are often more interesting because the problem of evaluating them is more subtle, and they tend to exemplify more faithfully the actual nature of American constitutional history.

For Field the problem was fairly simple: here is the businessman whom any just-minded judge should be honored to defend; and here is the due process clause; why not use it for that benign purpose? But the majority of his colleagues saw cross-threads in the tapestry: the proposed doctrine was strange and ill supported by precedent or public acceptance; impetuous and untimely decisions to assume the task of supervision might trap the judiciary in an impossible role of its own contriving. They held back, and this reluctance to make radical departures, to generalize adventurously, is characteristic of the historical Court. But it is also characteristic that their negative opinions provided an escape, that their "no" was qualified by a "perhaps."

That "perhaps" could swell to a certainty in the fullness of time by a process so subtle and complex that not even the craftsmen themselves would be fully aware of what was happening, and in the end both they and their observers could feel that the doctrine they applied was a familiar, indeed an immemorial, rule of law. Justice could be served, but the illusion of a changeless constitution need not be abandoned. And all this was achieved because the Court realized, whether instinctively or analytically does not matter, that the ambiguity of its mandate is both its limitation and its opportunity.

If due process had emerged as a dogmatic "rule" in 1873, it might have saved some corporate profits for a while, but the pressures of the welfare state would have forced the Court to scuttle it before long. The mature doctrine that became explicit in the 1890's was a far more effective tool of judicial governance, not only because it was now more securely backed by use and wont, but because it was flexible enough to mean anything the judiciary wanted it to mean. The Court could now help shape social policy toward capitalism, yet respect the boundaries imposed by economic necessity and political possibility.

The Tools of Judicial Supervision

With the maturation of substantive due process in the closing years of the nineteenth century, the Supreme Court was at length adequately equipped to play a part in resolving the major issue of the era—that of business-government relationships. The new Fourteenth Amendment and the commerce clause doctrines earlier described made almost every governmental intervention in economic affairs the business of the judiciary, to approve or disapprove, as discretion might dictate. The Court had finally adjusted itself and the Constitution to the altered conditions of the postwar order.

Old problems like slavery had been forgotten. The question of Negro rights, and with it the question of civil rights in general, had been relegated to a minor and almost negligible place among the Court's concerns. The once preponderant issue of federalism was now subordinated to the government-business preoccupation: the formerly ruling value of nationalism was replaced by a judicial ideal called economic freedom. The process of redefining the Court's role, a process impelled by the transfiguration of the nation itself, was not complete to be sure. But the enabling conditions had been met; the judges had surmounted traditional interpretations which would have left them impotent to play any significant role at all. They now had the tools, so to speak, to do the job to which they felt they were summoned by their legacy and their consciences. How they would use those tools, what role they would actually assume, what result they would work for arbitrating the business-government relationship—are questions for the next chapter.

Six

The Judiciary and the
Regulatory State: 1900–1937

I<small>N 1900 THE SUPREME COURT'S POSITION</small> is somewhat that of a
medieval knight-bachelor on the morning after his accolade. The long
novitiate as a squire has been served, the vigil has been kept, the rituals have been performed. The gilded spurs and the sword are ready, and
the world is waiting. Will the chevalier at once launch an intrepid campaign to slay all the dragons of "socialism" and rescue all the maidens of
"free enterprise"? Or will he exercise his hard-won rights and powers
moderately, bearing in mind that there are differences in vulnerability
even among dragons and that some maidens may be more virtuous than
others and more worthy of chivalry's attentions?

These were the two clear-cut alternatives open to the Court, and for
clarity's sake it would be gratifying to record that the judges elected one
or the other. But the fact of the matter is a little more intricate. Instead
of adopting either of these courses of action wholeheartedly, the Court
established a kind of dialectic involving both of them and managed to live
in this apparently uneasy state for the next thirty-odd years. Sometimes
the judges talked in this period as if they were determined to halt the
regulatory movement in its tracks and as if they had the will and power
to veto any political impulse they disapproved. Yet at other times, and
often even concurrently, they ratified many inroads on the free enterprise
ideal and sought only to moderate, not to stop, the growth of government intervention.

Such judicial dualism is easy enough to understand. The first notion—that the Court could and should use its new armaments to arrest
the drift toward regulation—had its origin partly in the deep sense of
horror that words like "socialism" generated in judicial breasts, and
partly in the rhetoric of judicial supremacy that had been accumulating

for over a century. Marshall's assertion in *Marbury* that "there is no middle ground" between the idea of judicial control and the idea of unlimited government; the statement of Davis in *Milligan* that the Constitution "covers with the shield of its protection all classes of men, at all times, and under all circumstances"; Field's repeated contentions that the Court had the authority and duty to defend "inalienable rights, rights which are the gift of the Creator" against all comers—such words had a certain impact on the minds of the judges themselves as well as of their auditors. The priesthood more than half believed the mythology it had helped to create; and the impulse to monarchize and kill with looks was therefore very strong.

But the same judges were at the same time more or less dimly aware of certain other factors and shared certain other attributes. Most of them had played some part in practical affairs, and their hostility to regulation in general was tempered by the realization that particular circumstances cannot always be governed by dogmatism. Moreover, the record of judicial history on which they drew was replete not only with mythic incantations like those of Marshall, Davis, and Field, but also with concrete examples of judicial forbearance. In a word, the Court of the past had often talked in absolutist terms, but had usually acted discreetly and flexibly. And the judges of the twentieth century were thus torn between the rhetorical and the historic forms of the judicial image. In general they used the veto power inherent in such doctrines as commerce and due process far more selectively and judiciously than the fierce champions of laissez faire would have preferred. The vision of judicial tyranny that emerges from some of the critical literature of the 1920's and 1930's, the picture of a great nation shackled helplessly by judge-made law, is pretty remote from the fact. Even in the heyday of judicial negativism, the affirmative note was also frequently sounding; many of the most notable negative decisions turned out upon close examination to be less absolutist than they at first appeared.

Yet neither can it be denied that the judges seemed recurrently tempted during these years to have done with temporizing, to attack with their bright new weapons, to rule by flat decree. This impulse emerged most often in dissenting opinions where language was least likely to be qualified by considerations of responsibility; it showed itself in an occasional majority decision during the first three decades, in cases which peculiarly outraged judicial sensibilities. Evidently there was a certain tension between the desire to influence and the desire to rule. In general, the chevalier conducted himself with reasonable modesty and decorum. But always in the background was the fond idea that a really intrepid assault might dispose of the dragons and that a world without them would be a pleasant place. Throughout the period there was a constant undercurrent of threat that the rhetorical could become the actual, if the provocation were great enough.

THE POWER TO TAX AND JUDICIAL SUBJECTIVISM

As the judges of the Supreme Court looked about them in the closing years of the nineteenth century and the early years of the twentieth, they could see threats to free enterprise rearing up on every side in numbers that seemed to increase year by year. They had rejected, as we have seen, the politically impossible plea of Mr. Campbell in the *Slaughter-House Cases* to establish a wall against all such invasions; and they were now faced with the nice task of distinguishing between interlopers that were tolerable and others that were not. Their moral instincts might be thought a sufficient guide by some, but what was needed was a legal rule, and it is hard to translate a moral instinct into a legal rule without losing something in the translation. The judges yearned for a formula, or set of them, which would objectively discriminate between permissible and impermissible economic statutes. If they acted merely in terms of a subjective ethic, they exposed themselves to the suggestion that perhaps the next man's ethic was as good as their own.

The power of taxation illustrates these problems with special force, for the power can be used, unless somehow checked, to accomplish prodigies of public control; yet it is peculiarly hard to formulate a rule that will limit it reasonably. And the Constitution provides little help; the clauses relating to taxation are few and hardly self-explanatory. It is not surprising, as the clamor for social justice grew, that the tax power was called upon to right wrongs, as well as to fill the public treasury.

From the point of view of the businessman, the most horrendous of these forays against capital was the federal income tax law, passed in 1894, which exempted incomes up to $4,000 and imposed a levy of 2 per cent above that amount. The law had been squeezed through Congress only after years of agitation; it was frankly an attempt to tax the well-to-do; and it seemed to many as it did to Justice Field "but the beginning" of "a war of poor against the rich" which would threaten the foundations of the Republic. Certainly it would at any rate deplete the pocketbooks of a good many solid citizens, and a constitutional challenge was rushed to the courts. It was argued among other things that the tax was invalid as applied to the income from real estate (that is, rents) and from personal property, because these were "direct taxes" and must be apportioned among the states in accordance with their population (Art. I, sec. 2). Apportionment by population would of course kill the principle of apportionment on the basis of ability to pay, which was the major concern of those who passed the law.

But the challengers faced the apparently grave difficulty that the Court had, in 1881, unanimously upheld the income tax that had been levied during the immediately after the Civil War; and their case was further undermined in advance by the ancient *Hylton* decision of 1796, in which it had been intimated that only "head taxes" and real estate taxes were "direct" within the meaning of the Constitution and thus subject to the apportionment requirement. Their glittering array of high-priced counsel, including such ornaments of the contemporary bar as George F. Edmunds and Joseph Choate, was therefore forced to argue that the Court should reverse "a century of error" in order to stop the "communistic march." Five members of the Court were ultimately persuaded, after elaborate argument and reargument, that this was indeed their duty, and the income tax law was scuttled by judicial fiat. The direct tax clause, so long neglected as a constitutional restraint, provided the judges with an objective formulation of their prejudice in favor of wealth. It is a kind of anticlimax that the enactment of the Sixteenth Amendment in 1913 deprived them of this self-created mooring post. It declared that Congress could, without apportionment, tax incomes "from whatever source derived" and most of the nice distinctions of the Income Tax decision came tumbling down; capital was again exposed to the communistic threat from which Choate and the Court had temporarily rescued it.

One of those distinctions, however, had long antedated 1895 and was destined to survive for many years thereafter. Among the vices of the income tax had been the fact that it applied to income from municipal bonds. It was thus, the Court had said, a tax upon the powers and instrumentalities of the state, and such intergovernmental taxation is forbidden by the principles of the federal system. This doctrine derived originally from Marshall's pronouncement in *McCulloch* v. *Maryland* (1819) that "the power to tax involves the power to destroy." It followed, thought Marshall's successors, that neither the state nor the national government could tax the other's instrumentalities, for the Constitution supposes the independent existence of both governments, and to allow such taxes would be to allow the taxing government to destroy the taxed government.

With the aid of such reasoning the Court had woven a complex web of reciprocal tax immunities, and it would be more wearisome than profitable to explore them in detail. It might be thought that the Sixteenth Amendment, empowering the federal government to tax incomes without apportionment "from whatever source derived," had relieved Congress of worries about taxing the income of state employees (whose offices had been held many years before to be state instrumentalities and thus exempt from federal taxation). But the Supreme Court ruled otherwise. From the point of view of this volume perhaps the chief significance of this whole doctrine is the light it sheds on the Court's prevailing habit of mind—the idea that government cannot be left judicially unsupervised in possession of a power that *might* be abused. It was suggested from time to time that it would be soon enough to worry when one government actually did seek to destroy or burden another by taxing its instrumentalities unreasonably, and that meanwhile the judiciary should leave the tax policy alone. But the Court of the twentieth century was not disposed to lift its hand from the reins even so conditionally.

Still another problem raised by taxation was presented when the taxing power was used to accomplish regulatory purposes. Such laws of course might endanger the sacrosanct principle of laissez faire, and some restraint on them was, therefore, evidently desirable, but how to frame such a restraint without frankly admitting that the Court was simply second-guessing the legislature on a question of social policy?

The difficulty is illustrated when we compare *McCray v. United States* in 1904, with the Child Labor Tax Case in 1922. In the former, the Court upheld a federal law imposing a heavy tax on oleomargarine colored to resemble butter, the obvious effect and purpose of the tax being to discourage manufacture of the product. The Court, said Justice White, cannot condemn an otherwise valid tax because it objects to the motives that prompted the law's passage, for those motives are not within the scope of proper judicial inquiry. This seemed to mean that regulatory results could be achieved by taxation without fear of court interference, a doctrine that would create vast opportunities for control. However, in later cases the Court began to hint that regulatory taxes might be subject to scrutiny if the provisions for collecting them were not clearly related to the gathering of revenue, and in the Child Labor Tax Case these hints were confirmed. Congress had laid a tax of 10 per cent on the profits of production industries that employed children, obviously banking on the assumption that the regulatory purpose of the tax would be beyond judicial cognizance. But, said the Court, "there comes a time in the extension of the penalizing features of the so-called tax when it loses it character as such and becomes a mere penalty with the characteristics of regulation and punishment. Such is the case in the law before us." The difference between this law and the law in the *McCray* case is that the purpose to control child labor is evident *on the law's face;* the purpose to inhibit manufacture and sale of colored margarine was not similarly evident.

But the trouble is that it *was*. Plainly the Court's ruling in the later case was prompted by the feeling that control over child labor was not and should not be vested in the national government, just as its ruling in *McCray* was explained by the feeling among the judiciary that it did no great harm to restrict the production of colored margarine. As judgments of social policy either of these pronouncements might be open to argument, but at least the argument would be relevant. The Court's difficulty was that it must try to cloak the social judgments in the form of constitutional rules, and the attempt was ultimately unavailing. A flat rule that the motivations of a tax could not be scrutinized would clarify the constitutional process, but it would allow governmental interference in fields which the judges thought best left free from interference. The alternative was the doctrine that the tax would be disallowed if its regulatory purpose was evident "on its face," and this reintroduced the subjective factor in judicial decision-making. For whether the judge finds an intent to penalize on the face of the law is likely to depend on whether he smiles or frowns on the purpose of the penalty. As so often in the cases of this era, the Court had been unable to develop an objective formula that would distinguish between acceptable and unacceptable departures from the free enterprise ideal. By their ultimate resort to subjectivism, the judges kept their hands on the reins and retained their freedom of discretion. But they made it harder to convince observers that judicial review was more than another step in the legislative process.

NEW CHECKREINS ON THE COMMERCE POWER

This subjectivism of judicial control, evident enough in the tax field, becomes even plainer when we examine the Court's decisions involving interstate commerce. The judicial problem here was especially difficult to cope with though it is comparatively easy to state. The commerce clause is a grant of power to the national government, and the pre–Civil War courts had uniformly interpreted that power broadly. Unless such affirmative interpretations are qualified, they make it possible for national statutes to regulate the national economy unmercifully, and the battle for constitutional laissez faire is lost in advance. Negative formulas must, therefore, be devised, and in the *E. C. Knight* case of 1895, as we have seen, the Court answered this challenge by forbidding federal control of manufacturing on the ground that Congress may regulate only interstate commerce itself and that which affects interstate commerce "directly."

Another potent array of negativisms was assembled in *Hammer v. Dagenhart* in 1918. Spurred by the same reformers who were later to bring about the passage of the Child Labor Tax discussed in the preceding section, Congress had forbidden the passage through interstate commerce of products manufactured by firms that employed children. Under the *Knight* doctrines Congress could not directly forbid child labor, for the control of production was vested exclusively in the states; but the legislators evidently assumed that they could strike at the product of such labor *after* it entered interstate commerce, for they had often been told that Congress' power over that commerce was plenary. In fact the Supreme Court had previously upheld national laws that seemed clearly analogous, such as the Mann Act, which barred prostitutes from interstate commerce, and the Pure Food and Drug Act, which barred adulterated food.

The hearts of the judges were troubled, however. If the Congress could exclude from interstate commerce any article it chose to exclude, then it could in effect control production, for most firms were dependent upon interstate commerce for their market. Therefore, the Court in a triumphantly negative mood announced that the power to prohibit goods from moving through interstate commerce was subject to limitations previously unknown. Congress could bar such goods if their transportation was followed by "harmful results" (for example, immorality in the case of prostitutes, ptomaine poisoning in the case of adulterated foods). But since the evil aimed at here, child labor, occurs *before* interstate commerce begins, and since the product transported (for example, a can of shrimp) is in itself harmless, the law must fall. The act is repugnant to the Constitution "in a twofold sense."

> It not only transcends the authority delegated to Congress over commerce but also exerts a power as to a purely local matter to which the federal authority cannot extend. . . . if Congress can thus regulate matters entrusted to local authority . . . the power of the States over local matters may be eliminated, and thus our system of government be practically destroyed.

Here then, it might be thought, was a whole set of criteria, of legal rules, that could be used by the Court to mitigate the headlong advance toward public control of the nation's economy. But there was a fly or two in the ointment. For one thing, it was becoming increasingly apparent to those of even modest political sensitivity that the public demand for some form of economic regulation was rising and could not be altogether gainsaid. The first decade of the twentieth century had witnessed after all "the progressive era"; the revelations of the muckrakers had stirred the popular consciousness; one president had publicly chided "the malefactors of great wealth" and another had spoken eloquently about "the new freedom." For another thing, as has been suggested earlier, the members of the Court were not simple obstructionists. Most of them were flexible enough to realize that Herbert Spencer's ideal order was not literally attainable, that in some circumstances government interference with economic activity could serve a useful end. And the case for such interference was likely to seem especially strong when the challenged statute was designed to protect and promote commerce rather than to shackle it, or was designed to stamp out evils that the judges themselves regarded as objectionable, morally or otherwise.

As a consequence of such considerations, the Court proceeded to qualify and attenuate the negative doctrines of the *Knight* and *Dagenhart* cases in a long series of decisions that exude a quite different spirit. But it is both characteristic and significant that these affirmative doctrines were created, not to replace the negativisms just described, but to exist side by side with them as alternative formulations.

This process is illustrated in two fields involving two of the most awesome problems of modern American industrial society—the trusts and the railroads. It will be remembered that the *Knight* decision had gravely crippled the Sherman Antitrust Act, since it amounted to a judicial veto of the program to control the trusts. Within a very few years, however, the judges began to have second thoughts, and they upheld antitrust proceedings in a number of decisions that seemed to reflect a mood of tolerance toward the necessities of government control. The sharp distinction of the *Knight* case between local and national affairs had indeed the merit of clarity, but it had the defect of impracticality. It made no sense to insist that an activity was "local" in character when its effects were unquestionably national; a tidal wave may originate in mid-ocean yet flood the shores of New York.

These realities were trenchantly acknowledged by Justice Holmes in 1905 in a case involving prosecution of the "beef trust." The packers had conspired to control the sale of meat in Chicago, which was of course the "hog butcher of the world." These sales agreements were evidently as local as the manufacturing agreements of the *Knight* case, but the Court's approach to them was very different:

> Commerce among the States is not a technical legal conception, but a practical one, drawn from the course of business. When cattle are sent for sale from a place in one state, with the expectation that they will end their transit, after purchase, in another, and when in effect they do so, with only the interruption necessary to find a purchaser at the stock yards, and when this is a typical, constant recurring course, the current thus existing is a current of commerce among the states, and that purchase of the cattle is a part and incident of such commerce.

In short, the whole "stream of commerce" including sales is subject to federal control; the Court, as Chief Justice Taft was to remark in a later case, would not frustrate antitrust policy by indulging in a "nice and technical inquiry" to distinguish between the local and the national. Indeed it was precisely such a "nice and technical" excursion which the Court had allowed itself in the *Knight* case, but a petty consistency, as Emerson said, is the hobgoblin of little minds.

As for federal railroad regulation, the Court here displayed an acquiescent temper that was often shocking to the proponents of laissez faire and is most difficult to reconcile with the dogmatisms of the *Knight* and *Dagenhart* decisions. The statutory interpretations of the 1890's had shorn the Interstate Commerce Commission of effective power, but Congress duly repaired the damage, endowing the Commission with ample authority, including control over rates. It might be expected that the Court would greet these developments coldly and would assail them with all the resources of the constitutional armory. But in fact the judges cheerfully upheld the laws and approved Commission orders that deeply impaired the supposedly sacred reserved powers of the states.

Perhaps the high point of such judicial toleration was reached in the *Dayton-Goose Creek Railway* case of 1924, which upheld the Transportation Act of 1920. This law required railroads which earned more than a certain fixed "fair return" to turn over one-half of the excess to the Commission and to hold the rest in a reserve fund to be used as the Commission directed. Even worse, the requirement applied to income earned on wholly intrastate business. But the provisions gave the Court no constitutional qualms. The power to regulate commerce, said Chief Justice Taft for a unanimous Court, is a power "to foster, protect and control the commerce with appropriate regard to the welfare of those who are immediately concerned, as well as the public at large, and to promote its growth and insure its safety." In exercising this wide authority over interstate affairs, Congress may also control intrastate commerce, if state and interstate operations are "inextricably commingled." In short, the whole national railway system is subject to federal control, and the "nice and technical" distinctions based on the Tenth Amendment have little or no bearing in this field.

The contrast between the *Knight* and *Dagenhart* doctrines on the one hand and these antitrust and railway doctrines on the other would be bewildering if it were not for the hint the Chief Justice drops in the words just quoted. Congress, he tells us, may "foster, protect and control" commerce to its heart's content; that is, it may do things that are "good" for commerce, but not (so the implication runs) things that are "bad" for it. This point is comparable to the one made in the *Dagenhart* case: that the law can bar "bad" things from interstate commerce, but not "good" things. The translation of both dicta is this: that the Constitution forbids those departures from laissez faire that the Court disapproves, and permits those departures that the Court thinks reasonable and proper. And obviously this is not a legal "rule" in any understandable sense of the word, but a statement of social policy, or rather an assertion of the power to determine it. Under these loose standards the Court can either uphold or overthrow almost any commercial regulation it encounters, depending on whether the judges approve or disapprove the economic policy the law represents. The advantages of this arrangement is that it enables the Court to choose discreetly the dragons it will fight and the maidens it will rescue. But the disadvantage, as in the tax cases, is that it becomes harder and harder to sustain the illusion that the judicial yes or no is based on inexorable constitutional commands, and it becomes easier and easier for observers to see that judicial review is operating as a subjective and quasilegislative process.

DUE PROCESS AND THE COURT'S REARGUARD ACTION

In the tax cases and in the commerce cases, as we have seen, the Supreme Court had conducted only occasional and rather limited forays against the welfare state. America had been notified that there were limits on these two great powers, and this in itself was important, for it preserved the idea of judicial sovereignty, and the knowledge that the Court was keeping an eye on things might discourage some socialistic ventures before their start. But the actual negative decisions of importance were few, and the march toward regulation had been at most deflected slightly and, here and there, somewhat delayed. However, the sharpest weapon in the judicial panoply, as the last chapter suggested, was the due process clause. That clause was available as a limit on both federal and state government. In its modern form it allowed the Court to reach not only procedural but also substantive questions. If the Court was to control American economic policy in any significant way, due process was obviously its major resource.

The feats that were accomplished with this clause in the 1900–1937 period are by no means unimpressive. B. F. Wright has counted some 184 decisions between 1899 and 1937 which invalidated state laws on the basis of either the due process or equal protection clause (the two were frequently used by the judiciary in tandem; it is often, though not invariably, true that a denial of equal protection is also regarded as a denial of due process). Those involving federal laws were far fewer. But according to accepted doctrine, the term "due process" has the same meaning in both the Fifth and Fourteenth Amendments, and it follows that the prohibitions announced against state action were usually presumptively applicable to national laws as well, if Congress might venture to enact them. There is no way of estimating reliably the restraining effect of this cloud of negativisms on state legislators and congressmen who might otherwise have made haste more speedily along the road to the welfare state. No doubt the pace of social change was moderated; a respectable number of "excesses" were prevented; a respectable amount of money was saved for the businessman; a good many laborers were left a little hungrier than they might have been if the Court had not been there to defend economic liberty.

Yet it is highly questionable that the due process clause was a major factor in determining the drift of American economic policy during this period. Most of the important legislative measures that were really demanded by public opinion did pass and did manage to survive the gauntlet of judicial review. In some conspicuous areas, like maximum hours legislation, the Court found a delaying action for a few years and then, when the trend of public demand became unmistakable, gave in. In only a few instances was its position really adamant, and even here the restraining effect of judicial pronouncements is conjectural. Laws are not automatically invalidated because they happen to conflict logically with the doctrine of a previous Supreme Court decision; a case must be brought against each one, and that case must often be carried through extensive labyrinths of the judicial system for years before the law can be pronounced technically dead. Because of such circumstances a great mass of regulatory legislation survived untouched even in these halcyon days of due process. The fact that there was not more such legislation, the fact that Americans during the 1920's tolerated so great a measure of social injustice—this is to be attributed to public apathy amounting to callousness, not to the Supreme Court. To be sure, the Court did its bit to generate and encourage that public mood. But this is very different from saying that the Court rather than the nation was primarily responsible for the failures of public policy.

The virtue of the modern concept of due process was its remarkable flexibility. It allowed the Court to invalidate any law that struck a majority of the members as "arbitrary" or "capricious." These wonderfully ambiguous definitions brought practically the whole world of regulatory legislation within the potential reach of a judicial veto. But, even better, their ambiguity permitted the judiciary to exercise or withhold that veto in any given case, subject to no guiding principles except the judges' own sense of discretion.

The network of "ayes" and "nays" that they fashioned with the help of this carte blanche is too complex for brief summary. A great variety of regulatory measures were scrutinized. Tax laws were queried and sometimes overthrown on the ground that the state had no "jurisdiction to tax" the source in question, or simply on the ground that the tax was arbitrarily administered. State legislation regulating the weight of loaves of bread, prohibiting the use of "shoddy" in quilts, requiring a railroad to construct an underpass for a farmer's personal convenience, were held to deny due process or equal protection of the laws.

But perhaps the most important and instructive pattern of judicial intervention was developed in connection with the problem of rates—prices and wages. And there is a special significance in this field from the judicial point of view, because rates for goods sold or services performed are the very keystone of the free enterprise system. Any state interference with them impinges vitally on freedom of contract, which is the holy of holies for the knights-errant of laissez faire. It might well be expected that the Court would look hard at legislative innovation in this field.

In *Lochner* v. *New York* (1905) this expectation was amply fulfilled. The case concerned working hours rather than wages, but as Chief Justice Taft was later to say, the one is the multiplier and the other the multiplicand, and the operative point for the Court was that the state was seeking to control the heart of the working contract. The law restricted the hours of bakers in New York to ten per day or sixty per week. To Justice Peckham and the majority, this presented a grave challenge to the principle of contractual freedom, for if bakers' hours could be regulated, then so, presumably, could the hours of all other workers. The Court was prepared to concede that working hours in particularly dangerous conditions could be controlled in order to protect the workers' health. Or it would allow hours regulation if it could be shown that long hours might adversely affect the health of the public at large (for example, by leading to the production of unhealthful bread). But neither of these statements can be made about the baking trade, which is not perhaps "absolutely and perfectly healthy" but is "vastly more healthy than [certain] others." To permit its regulation then would expose all or most occupations to hours regulation, would subject the working contract to "the mercy of legislative majorities." The police power cannot be allowed to reach so far; the law is an example of "meddlesome interferences with the rights of the individual," and it violates due process.

The *Lochner* decision represents one of those moments in the Court's twentieth-century history when the judges temporarily embraced the illusion that the regulatory movement could be halted, rather than merely delayed, by judicial pronouncement. The exceptions they allow to the rule against hours laws—the particularly unhealthy occupation principle—should not obscure the fact that a hard line has been drawn. Hereafter, if constitutional limits are as immutable as the mythology attests, American workmen shall be generally free from restraints on their right to work a twelve-hour day. Departures from the model of Herbert Spencer's *Social Statics* will be permitted up to a point, but at that point they must stop.

But in the actual event the process of judicial governance did not work that way. It seldom has. Justice Holmes, filing one of his earliest and most powerful dissents in this case, said:

> I think that the word liberty in the Fourteenth Amendment is perverted when it is held to prevent the natural outcome of a dominant opinion unless it can be said that a rational and fair man necessarily would admit that the statute proposed would infringe fundamental principles as they have been understood by the traditions of our people and our law. It does not need research to show that no such sweeping condemnation can be passed upon the statute before us.

The majority opinion had stated, or implied, that "dominant opinion" does not matter, that the criterion of constitutionality is not traditional fundamental principles, but the individual conscience of the judge, and

that a flat rule against general hours regulation was now laid down. However, when we follow the course of doctrine through the next twenty
years, we find that it often runs closer to Holmes' standards than the
judges themselves may have realized. Or perhaps it would be more accurate to say that it alternates between Peckham's uncompromising defense
of free enterprise and Holmes' extreme permissiveness, with the balance
of decisions on the latter side.

Three years after *Lochner* the Court found an exception to the flat
rule of that case when faced by a statute regulating the hours of females.
The social and physical characteristics of women, said the Court, put
them at a special disadvantage in the struggle for subsistence, and it is
therefore reasonable for the state to limit the hours they can be worked.
And in 1917, a new majority took leave of the *Lochner* doctrine altogether, upholding an hours law for manufacturing establishments as a
health measure (*Bunting* v. *Oregon*). The startling thing about this opinion by Justice McKenna was that it seemed to assume the validity of hours
regulation and focused most of the argument on an answer to the charge
that the law sought to regulate *wages* indirectly. *Lochner* was not even
mentioned, though counsel had invoked it repeatedly in the briefs. Plainly
the Court was showing itself more sensitive to "dominant opinions" than
the pristine view of judicial sovereignty would allow. Yet it should not be
thought that the Court was giving up contractual freedom entirely to "the
mercy of legislative majorities." Only two years before, the judges had
affirmed that the state could not, in order to equalize the parties engaged
in collective bargaining, outlaw "yellow dog" contracts (agreements, as a
condition of employment, that an employee will not join a labor union).
Even in *Bunting* there was a hint that the wage contract was still sacrosanct, though hours regulations were not. The Court had taken advantage
of the flexibility of due process to yield an outpost or two; for the moment
the counsel of modesty and discretion had prevailed. But the *Lochner*
spirit of hostility to social change, the *Lochner* illusion of judicial om-
nipotence, were not dead; they only slept. And a new majority, confronted
by new threats to the wage-price nexus, might at any time call them to
action again.

A rather similar pattern of judicial outlook and behavior can be
traced in the cases involving the doctrine of "business affected with a
public interest." This doctrine, it will be remembered, enjoyed its modern
rebirth in *Munn* v. *Illinois*, in which Waite had used it to distinguish between rate regulations that would violate due process and those that

would not. A business affected with a public interest or "devoted to a public use" was subject to rate regulation. This emphatically did not mean that the state could impose such rates as whimsy dictated; and after 1895 the Court records are dotted with decisions holding that the rates prescribed for a railroad or other public utility were unreasonably low. But if a business could be judicially classified as falling within the rubric of "public interest," its rates could be subjected to some measure of government control.

The problem, of course, was what criteria to use in making such a classification. One possibility would be to adopt the commonsense idea that any business important to the public was "affected with a public interest." But this would legitimize rate regulation on a vast scale, and rates were so crucial to the capitalist system as the judges understood it that they could not in conscience make so unqualified a concession. (Compare their reluctance in *Lochner* to accede to a similarly general ratification of hours regulation.) Yet as the complexities of commercial life multiplied in the twentieth century, it became evident even to conservative judges that there were many businesses whose prices could not be allowed to run wild.

The judicial solution was to allow rate regulation of a variety of businesses under the public interest principle, but to avoid commitment on the question of just what the principle meant, and thus to retain a potential veto. Franchise industries (those enjoying special, government-granted privileges) and public service industries like railroads and electric power companies, clearly fell within the charmed circle. So did certain traditionally regulated occupations like hotel-keeping and taxicab service. Finally, as Chief Justice Taft was to explain, there is another group of industries which have come to be public because "the owner, by devoting his business to the public use, in effect grants the public an interest in that use and subjects himself to public regulation. . . ." The Court so classified, for example, the business of fire insurance and the business of renting real estate in the District of Columbia during the war-engendered emergency. In fact, before 1923, the doctrine of public interest was never used restrictively, to hamper the development of the regulatory movement. But the rhetoric itself implied the possibility of restriction; the Court in making its concessions had been careful not to rule that possibility out. The affirmations of the past in this field were no more binding on the future than the acceptance of hours legislation in *Bunting* was a guaranty against judicial concern for the labor contract.

NORMALCY AND JUDICIAL LAISSEZ FAIRE

With the advent of the 1920's the tone of judicial decisions, especially under the due process clause, was subtly altered. We have seen that the modern Court had developed in this area, as in others, an elaborate set of both negative and affirmative doctrines, thus establishing for the judiciary what Benjamin Cardozo called "the sovereign prerogative of choice." And we have further seen that the Court had so far been disposed to wield that prerogative discreetly, upholding many regulatory and welfare measures and using the veto more as a salutary threat than an instrument of continuous control.

In the 1920–29 period the number of negative decisions under the Fourteenth Amendment was almost double the number in the preceding decade. These figures themselves suggest some change in the constitutional climate, and the suggestion is confirmed by examination of individual decisions. True, a great many economic statutes still survived the judicial ordeal; prudent self-restraint was still an important Court theme. But the temper of the times, signalized by conservative Republican electoral triumphs and by the withering of the progressive spirit in public policy, was infectious. The spread of the infection was made somewhat more likely by the coming of men like Taft, Sutherland, and Butler to the bench, for all of them were deeply convinced foes of the welfare state. Now the judges were more confident that they spoke for the nation when they defended laissez faire. And the tension between modesty and boldness became greater; the illusion that the judiciary could really govern became a little more obtrusive, was reflected a little more often in actual decisions rather than mere rhetoric.

The spirit of the *Lochner* case, with its jealous concern for the sanctity of the labor contract, revived impressively in *Adkins v. Children's Hospital* (1923). Congress had established a board authorized to prescribe minimum wages for women and minors in the District of Columbia. The approval by the Court of hours regulation in *Bunting,* and of the Adamson Act (which controlled both wages and hours in the railroad industry in the war emergency) in a 1916 decision, had nourished reformist hopes that wage control would now be upheld. But the Court had carefully confined itself in those two opinions to the particular situation presented, and the implied reservations were now invoked. Justice Sutherland declared for the majority that the regulatory movement had once again gone too far. His opinion is an extremely able statement of the argument that minimum wage laws are unjust, mainly because they impose on the employer the burden to support partially indigent persons. This burden, he tells us, "if it belongs to anybody, belongs to society as a whole." Furthermore the statute is faulty in that the standard it sets for the board's guidance is impossibly vague. The board is required to set wages that will maintain the woman worker in good health and protect her morals. But no general wage standard can accomplish reliably the first aim for any particular person, because particular circumstances may vary. For example, "to those who practice economy, a given sum will afford comfort, while to those of contrary habit the same sum will be wholly inadequate." As for morals, "it cannot be shown that well paid women safeguard their morals more carefully than those who are poorly paid." Though liberty of contract is not absolute, it is "the general rule and restraint the exception." For the reasons given, the exception embodied in this law overpasses the limits of state power, and it is "the plain duty of the courts in the proper exercise of their authority to so declare."

Here again, then, as in *Lochner*, the Court had chosen a milepost on the road to the welfare state and elected to make a stand; here again was the idea that the judiciary could and should decide by flat decree great issues of economic control. Justice Sutherland's opinion was memorable because it reflected in classic form both the free enterprise position (exemplified in some of the gems just quoted) and the uncompromising conception of judicial authority and duty that never seems quite to die. And as the 1920's proceeded, the reminders that this conception was viable became more frequent.

It is particularly appropriate that that decade saw the negative threats of the public interest doctrine develop into realities. Chief Justice Taft used it in 1923 against a Kansas law that empowered a court of industrial relations to fix wages in the meat-packing industry, among others. Without deciding whether the meat-packing business was affected with a public interest in any sense, the Chief Justice held that it was not so *much* affected as to warrant wage-fixing. At this point the now mature and no longer innocuous doctrine was tendered into the care of Justice Sutherland who produced, in 1927, 1928, and 1932, three Court opinions that developed the negative implications most thoroughly. Theater ticket brokers, employment agencies, and ice companies were all excluded from the magic circle, which meant that their rates could not be publicly controlled and that certain regulations which the Court regarded as excessive were likewise forbidden.

It became plain as the decisions proceeded that their effect was to protect all the "common callings" (the grocer, the dairyman, the butcher) from the peril of public rate control, and this interpretation, if adhered to, would indeed have been a significant restraint on the regulatory movement. But Sutherland's zeal for free enterprise and his absolutist approach to judicial duty were a trifle too extreme for his brethren. These unqualified rulings under the public interest doctrine had the effect of narrowing the range of judicial discretion, and the instinct for a more flexible standard asserted itself at last. In 1934, in *Nebbia* v. *New York,* the Court upheld a state law fixing minimum and maximum prices for milk, and took the occasion to announce that "there is no closed category of businesses affected with a public interest." The cherished idea that "there is something peculiarly sacrosanct" about prices was shattered by this announcement, and the Court's freedom of action in this field was restored. And simultaneously, of course, another obstacle in the path of the regulatory movement was cleared away.

THE JUDICIAL CHALLENGE TO THE NEW DEAL

The Supreme Court now stood, in 1934, at one of the great crossroads of its history. In the latter part of the nineteenth century it had built up, laboriously and piece by piece, a set of doctrines that could be employed for judicial supervision of the business-government relationship. By 1900 or thereabouts the doctrines were ready for service, but their existence did not settle the question of how the Court would employ them. Economic measures were now subject to judicial supervision, but the supervision could be strict and constant or lax and occasional, as the bench preferred. This freedom of choice was inherent in the tax doctrines, in the commerce doctrines, and above all in the due process doctrines that have been described. The Court could use them to govern marginally, to moderate the pace of social reform, to force the nation to take a second look at extreme programs. It could, in short, operate as one influential factor among others in the process of social decision-making. Or it could alternatively seek to decide all the great political-economic questions that faced America, to halt the trend toward government intervention, to use its veto absolutely rather than suspensively.

The majority of the cases of the twentieth century though 1934 seem to reflect, as has been suggested, the former, modest approach. And this approach, for better or for worse, is surely the one most congruous with the Court's past history and most consistent with the conditions and limitations that were imposed on the judicial power by the peculiar circumstances of its origin in the United States. But a modest stance is often hard to maintain, perhaps especially in a democracy, and even more especially when myth and rhetoric encourage illusions of grandeur. So from time to time during these years, we find the other, monarchical vision emerging in a resounding decision, like *Dagenhart* or *Lochner* or *Adkins,* and we can observe this attractive self-imge becoming stronger in the 1920's as forceful personalities like Sutherland speak for it in bold tones. In 1934, the Court seems balanced almost perfectly between these two conceptions of its role. With the elaborately varied precedents at the judges' disposal, they can swing either way. The regulatory trend that began so long ago in post–Civil War years has culminated in the New Deal; the welfare state, which Field and Cooley and Choate dreaded, seems at hand. The judiciary is bound to respond to it somehow, because for seventy years the judges have been sedulously cultivating the idea that the business-government relationship is, in part, at least, a judicial responsibility. The only question is which form the response will take.

For a time the issue hung in doubt, and there was even reason to believe that the Court would call upon its affirmative precedents, uphold national and state New Dealish innovations, and thus maintain a position on the margin of the political arena. After all, America was now beset by the gravest economic depression in her history, an emergency, as Justice Brandeis had remarked, "more serious than war." The decisions of the past three decades which had presumed to thwart economic legislation had been subjected to trenchant scholarly criticism, and the critics, such as Frankfurter, Corwin, and Powell, had been at pains to dispel the myth that the judges were mere agents of the Constitution, bound by its inexorable commands. Indeed the judges themselves had done their part to discredit that myth by insisting upon doctrinal flexibility in all the major areas of judicial control, by eschewing the objective rule. Most important of all perhaps, the New Deal was at this time enjoying a kind of honeymoon. The swift, decisive actions taken by Congress in the early days of Franklin Roosevelt's leadership were startling, but they seemed, to many at least, an improvement on the policy of stark inaction that had preceded them, and it was some time before doubts, even among the business community, were hardened into staunch opposition. The Supreme Court, despite protestations to the contrary, has seldom been insensitive to such considerations.

The *Nebbia* decision of 1934 had strongly suggested an acquiescent judicial temper. In the same year, the Court sustained a Minnesota law allowing courts to postpone mortgage foreclosures during the economic emergency. The law seemed to impair the obligation of contract, but Chief

Justice Hughes held for a five-man majority that, in view of the emergency, some restraint on the enforcement of contractual rights was reasonable. The idea appeared to be that the states could now violate the contract clause so long as they were "reasonable" about it, and the existence of an emergency would be recognized as reflecting on the judgment of reasonableness. It is not surprising that the exponents of economic reform legislation began to hope for judicial approval of their programs. If the Court was willing to ratify departures in a field like the contract clause, where orthodoxy was fairly well defined, then the commerce clause, the tax power, and due process fields, where the precedents themselves pointed both ways, should create little trouble.

But the balance in favor of the laws in such cases as these was precarious. The affirmative judgments were made possible in both decisions by a bare majority of five including the Chief Justice and a new appointee, Owen Roberts. The four other judges had joined in bitter dissents, rejecting the idea that emergency can affect constitutional results (the Court must not "yield to the voice of an impatient majority when stirred by distressful exigency") and warning of "the far more serious and dangerous inroads upon the limitations of the Constitution which are almost certain to ensue as a consequence naturally following any step beyond the boundaries fixed by that instrument." Such a call to arms was not likely to have much effect on Stone, Brandeis, and Cardozo, the three firm "liberals," for they had no great regard for the laissez-faire order they were being solicited to protect and at all events they doubted that the constitutional boundaries had ever been as clearly fixed as the quoted sentence implies. But Roberts was considerably less settled in his views, and as the New Deal was revealed in all its terrifying dimensions to the conservatives of the nation, he became ready for persuasion. As for the Chief Justice, he was neither clearly liberal nor stubbornly conservative, but he seemed to be much concerned for the Court's own dignity and was likely sometimes to swing with a conservative majority to avoid the criticism that might follow a five-to-four decision.

In 1935, therefore, the majority shifted, and for two busy terms the Court waged what is surely the most ambitious dragon-fight in its long and checkered history. The tension between modesty and temerity was temporarily resolved; the autocratic instinct was triumphant. Negative doctrines that had been accumulating for a century were brought to bear on the New Deal program and on kindred heresies; the affirmative doctrines that might have been invoked to produce contrary results were conveniently ignored or distinguished. And throughout the holocaust perorations from the bench and applause from outside the courtroom made it plain that the myths of judicial supremacy had been translated into reality in the minds of the Court majority. The idea of a changeless Constitution, the idea of judicial review as an exact science, the idea that "dominant opinion" is irrelevant, the idea that a nine-man Court can and should save society from itself and the past from the present—these ideas were no longer rhetoric; they had become the wellsprings of action.

With a salvo of decisions during 1935–36, the Court tore great holes in the New Deal program of recovery legislation. The doctrine of "direct-indirect effects" derived from the *Knight* case was used to help dispose of such major laws as the National Industrial Recovery Act and the Bituminous Coal Act. The distinction between production and commerce, stemming from *Knight* and *Dagenhart,* was used against the Agriculture Adjustment Act, which had sought to regulate farm production. The same law ran afoul of the rule of the Child Labor Tax Case that taxes must not operate as penalties to control what is otherwise beyond congressional reach. The due process clause was present in several decisions though sometimes only murkily visible, and the "sovereign prerogative of choice" which the Court had established in interpretation of that clause was of course here seized upon to negate the legislation. The Tenth Amendment, interpreted as a limit on Congress' delegated power rather than as a prohibition against the exercise of powers not delegated, acted as a makeweight wherever it seemed remotely applicable. Even a doctrine which had never been employed negatively before—and has never been since— had its fleeting moments of effectiveness during those years. The NIRA and the Bituminous Coal Act were condemned because, among other things, they had delegated legislative authority to the executive and thus violated the principle of separation of powers.

The final barrage was fired in June of 1936 as the Court reached the close of its two-year joust with the New Deal, and it was directed against a state law. New York had dared to enact a measure providing minimum wages for women. The legislative draftsmen had tried to meet one of the major objections raised by the Court against the law struck down in the *Adkins* case—that the wage-setting board need not consider the value of services rendered. The New York board was authorized to consider this factor, and it was hoped that the law might thus be saved. But the intransigence of the majority seemed to wax rather than wane with the passing months. Justice Butler now announced as a flat rule "that the state is without power by any form of legislation to prohibit, change or nullify contracts between employers and adult women workers as to the amount of wages to be paid." The argument of the Chief Justice, who dissented, that the *Adkins* precedent need not be followed because of "material differences" in the two laws; the argument of Stone, Brandeis, and Cardozo, also dissenting, that precedent since *Adkins* and "what is more important, reason" support state power to control wages, had no weight for five men now thoroughly deluded by the notion that the welfare state could be judicially throttled and the brave old world of their youth restored.

This New York Minimum Wage decision is a fair example of the judicial attitudes that characterized those two years, and it is an example that merits some reflection. By this time—the spring of 1936—the Court's assault on the New Deal had produced a tempest of antijudicial criticism, and as the presidential campaign of that year whetted political feeling, the critics, and of course the defenders as well, became angrier and more extreme (though the President himself said little in the campaign). Much of the criticism simply reflected the bad old American propensity to traduce the law whenever it conflicts with immediate interests, and perhaps the only thing worth saying about this is that, like most deplorable facts, it cannot be safely ignored. Another line of attack, not always distinguishable but with some claim to respectability as a separate point, was to challenge the Court's right and competence to hinder the democratic will, especially in the economic field. However, the Court had made it plain to the nation long ago that it proposed to play some part in defining government-business relationships, and the nation had tacitly acquiesced. It seems a little hard that the judiciary should now be assailed merely for participating in affairs that had been regarded for almost fifty years as judicial business.

But a telling and legitimate criticism of the Court's attitude can nevertheless be made out. The fault was not that the judges meddled in economic affairs at all, but that they meddled with them on a level too high for judicial governance, and imposed constitutional restraints so rigid that no popular government could tolerate them. As Robert Jackson has said, the anti–New Deal decisions had not:

... been confined to the limited issues actually involved in the immediate controversies and the way left clear for the Congress to improve and perfect its remedies. . . . [I]n striking at New Deal laws, the Court allowed its language to run riot. . . . In overthrowing the A.A.A. the Court cast doubt upon all federal aid to agriculture; in laying low the N.R.A., the Court struck at all national effort to maintain fair labor standards; and in outlawing the New York Minimum Wage Law . . . the Court deliberately attempted to outlaw any form of state legislation to protect minimum wage standards. The Court not merely challenged the policies of the New Deal but erected judicial barriers to the reasonable exercise of legislative powers, both state and national, to meet the urgent needs of a twentieth-century community.

The historic Court (as distinguished from the Court of myth and rhetoric) had very seldom behaved this way, and the exceptions in the record seemed hardly calculated to inspire imitation. Even in the modern period the dominant tendency had been to moderate the regulatory movement without attempting to destroy it, to nudge and advise democracy rather than to frustrate it. The majority had for the time being forgotten this, had forgotten that the Constitution's strength was its flexibility and that the Court's own strength rested on a tradition of judicious self-restraint.

The price of forgetfulness threatened to be a high one. Franklin Roosevelt was re-elected in November, 1936, by a stunning majority, and, after the dust of the campaign had settled a little, he turned his attention to the hostile Supreme Court, just as Jefferson had in 1801 trained his sights on Marshall and his Federalist brethren. Roosevelt, with characteristic indirection, presented Congress with a judiciary plan that purported to cope with the supposed problem of overcrowded federal court dockets. It would have enabled him to appoint a new judge to supplement any judge over seventy who failed to retire (retirement could not of course be made compulsory, for the Constitution protects judicial tenure "during good behavior"). The significant fact was that the plan would permit the President to appoint six new Supreme Court justices, and thus to insure approval of the New Deal program. It was, as it was called, a "court-packing plan," and its passage would set a precedent from which the institution of judicial review might never recover. It is not too much to say that the ambiguous and delicately balanced American tradition of limited government was mortally endangered by this bill. And it was offered by a President who had just received an overwhelming popular vote of confidence and who had not yet been denied in Congress any of his important demands. Even the five or six judges who had provoked this threat must have slept rather uneasily for a few months.

ECHOES OF THE FUTURE: THE EMERGING PROBLEM OF CIVIL RIGHTS

Like the scenario writer who leaves the heroine hanging from a cliff while he takes up another thread of the narrative, we must now digress for a time in order to touch on a development contemporary with the events so far described in this chapter. It is a characteristic of history, often noted, that the present bears the seeds of the future; and it is therefore hardly surprising that the Court of this era, even at the height of its concern for economic matters, should have devoted a small but increasing portion of its time to a widely different subject which was destined to loom very large in the judicial world yet to come. The subject was "civil rights," that is, the liberties of man as man and not primarily as an economic animal.

During most of its history, the court had paid comparatively little attention to this problem. The Bill of Rights, it will be remembered, had been held inapplicable to the states in 1833. That meant that free expression (Amendment I) and the personal procedural rights connected with arrest and trial (Amendments IV–VIII) could be abridged by the states without raising a federal constitutional question. The ratification of the Fourteenth Amendment in 1868 had created some doubts on this score, but the *Slaughter-House* decision in 1873 had rejected the contention that the privileges or immunities clause protected such rights.

Ten years later it was held in *Hurtado* v. *California* that the due process clause did not require the states to conform to the Bill of Rights in their criminal procedures, and as late as 1922 the Court denied that the Amendment restricted the states in dealing with freedom of expression. As for the equal protection clause, it had been used a few times to invalidate explicit racial discrimination in state law, but its effectiveness in deterring Jim Crow had been at best marginal. Like the due process clause it had been chiefly important in this era as a shield for business enterprise.

The states, then, were for some time relatively unconfined by constitutional doctrine in the civil rights field. On the other hand the national government had so far had little occasion to encroach on civil rights except in wartime, for police regulation that raised questions of this kind was left almost exclusively to the states. Given these facts, it is easy to see why civil rights cases had been a minor item on the Court's docket.

But now logic was working on behalf of civil rights. And although Justice Holmes was no doubt right when he once remarked that logic is not the "life of the law," still logic must not be thought of as irrelevant to the judicial process. The Court had provided the businessman with a generous measure of protection under the Fourteenth Amendment, and particularly the due process clause. Could it really be successfully contended that the "liberty" mentioned in that clause meant the liberty of economic man, and that only? Was there any rational basis for setting economic freedom so high above such basic rights as the right to a fair trial or liberty of expression? And if not, was it possible to maintain a constitutional discrimination against those rights for very long? In a way the development of the due process clause to protect economic rights made the ultimate protection of other rights logically inescapable.

The force of this logic was strengthened, it should be said, by certain personal factors in the 1920's and 30's, notably the presence on the Court of such brilliant libertarians as Holmes and Brandeis. And the First World War and the Russian Revolution played their part in precipitating the growth of constitutional doctrine, for they led to an assortment of state and federal laws infringing on freedom of expression, and the enforcement of these laws thrust the whole question into the judiciary's hands.

The free speech story properly begins in 1919 when the Court was presented with a constitutional claim brought by a man being punished under the federal Espionage Act of 1917 for mailing antidraft pamphlets to draftees. The defendant argued that his right to distribute such pamphlets was protected against national action by the First Amendment, but Justice Holmes for the Court rejected the claim. This speech is not protected, said Holmes, because it is used in such circumstances and is of such a nature as to create "a clear and present danger" of "substantive evils that Congress has a right to prevent" (that is, obstruction of the draft and mutiny in the armed forces). It followed of course that the Constitution *did* protect speech which did *not* present such a clear and present danger. Thus, although the individual conviction was here upheld, Holmes had scotched an old and persistent idea that the protection of the First Amendment was very narrow, and had committed the Court to an essentially libertarian formula for determining when speech may be abridged (*Schenck* v. *United States*).

The *Schenck* case involved a federal law, and the question of whether the free speech guarantees applied to the states by way of the Fourteenth Amendment was still comparatively untouched. However, the Court in 1925, confronted by a New York law punishing "criminal anarchy," declared "we may and do assume" that freedom of speech and press "are protected by the due process clause of the Fourteenth Amendment from impairment by the States." This was said with an offhandedness reminiscent of the concession in 1886 that corporations are persons in the meaning of the Amendment; and it was to be no less important in the long run. Again, as in *Schenck*, the particular prosecution was upheld, and the majority in fact repudiated the clear and present danger rule, holding that speech could be punished even if the danger of evil results was remote and conjectural. Nonetheless, the principle was now established that state action infringing free expression raised a federal constitutional question, and cases began making their way to the Court in increasing number. In 1931 the Court made its first important ruling against a state law in this field. Evidently a whole new dimension of constitutional jurisprudence had been opened up.

Meanwhile a somewhat similar development had been running its course in connection with the procedural rights of fair trial for accused persons. Although it had been held that the states were not bound by the specific procedural mandates of the Bill of Rights (for instance, they need not provide grand jury indictment as required by Amendment V) the Court had never quite gone so far as to say that the Fourteenth Amendment set no restrictions on state criminal procedures. The formula, stated in 1908, was that a procedural right was protected against state action only if it was "a fundamental principle of liberty and justice which inheres in the very idea of free government." This might seem an empty incantation, particularly since for a long time no decision upholding such a right was handed down. But in the 1920's the Court began to pour some content into it, for much the same reasons that prompted the concomitant drift toward protection of free expression; and in the early 1930's it was clearly held that state denials of the right to counsel and state use of forced confessions had offended this canon of due process. "The rack and the torture chamber," remarked Chief Justice Hughes, "may not be substituted for the witness stand."

As for the problem of racial discrimination in this period, it is hard to find the signs of doctrinal growth that are discernible in the fields of free expression and procedural rights (though it is perhaps worth remarking that the right-to-counsel case and the forced-confession case just mentioned, involved Negroes in the South). The Court had not yet challenged the doctrine that state law could require separation of races in schools, parks, and other facilities, so long as the accommodations provided were substantially equal. Indeed the standard of equality required was still very loose. The states had encountered a judicial setback or two in their attempts to exclude Negroes from the election process and from white residential areas, but by a modest amount of ingenuity they were able to evade these rulings with the acquiescence of the Court. Jim Crow was still constitutional.

But anyone able to think analogically might predict that he would have his judicial troubles before long. The logical process that had helped impel the Court to move from protection of economic liberty to protection of free expression and fair trial was equally relevant to the next step—the judicial defense of the right to racial equality. It would be too much to say that any of these developments became factually inevitable simply because the natural trend of logic supported them. Indeed the constitutional protection provided for these crucial rights was still, in spite of logic, skimpy and occasional. But the path was now open, in case the course of other historical events should provide a stimulus, for the Court to tread it more frequently.

THE CONSTITUTIONAL REVOLUTION OF 1937

In fact the occasion was already in the making, and, as it turned out, the time was nearly ripe. Having constructed with the greatest of pains a doctrinal tradition that allowed judicial intervention in economic affairs, and having administered those doctrines with reasonable discretion for some years, the Court had finally and dangerously overstepped the line that marks the limits of its authority. At a moment when the political pressure for economic legislation was greater than ever before, the Court had chosen to call a halt; at a moment when the Constitution's famous flexibility was most required, the Court had chosen to regard judicial review as the automatic application of static principles. The depression, and the New Deal which was its reflex, were forces too cosmic for those Canutes to withstand. Finally, the waves dislodged even the partial and contingent grip on economic affairs that the judiciary had once enjoyed. If the judges had stood firm in the position they assumed in 1935–36, there seems a good chance they would have been submerged altogether.

But they did not stand firm, or at any rate Justice Roberts did not, and he was the man who most mattered. The Roosevelt electoral victory in the fall of 1936 was impressive enough to convince all but those who would not listen that the American people wanted the New Deal. An outbreak of labor-management disputes, some of them accompanied by violence, had graphically illustrated the grim fact that the national economic dilemma was still very acute. On February 5, 1937, the President's "court-packing plan" had been set before Congress. No one, perhaps not even Justice Roberts, could say which of these circumstances was decisive for him; but it is hard to doubt that they played a part in the new tone of judicial decision that began to be sounded in the early months of that year.

It was first heard on March 29, 1937, less than two months after the Court plan was submitted and while the war of words over it was raging.

The Court was presented with a state minimum wage law applying to women and minors, a law not materially different from the one overturned in the New York Minimum Wage Case only nine months before. But now, by a vote of five to four, the judges upheld the law, rejecting both the *Adkins* precedent of 1923 and the New York decision. Chief Justice Hughes for the majority denied that freedom of contract was especially sanctified in the American system of constitutional restraints, declared that the Court must take judicial notice of the depression prostrating the nation, and found without difficulty that a minimum wage law was reasonably related to the legitimate end of preserving the workers' health. Justice Roberts, who had seen the matter differently nine months earlier, silently concurred.

Observers were still recovering from their surprise two weeks later when the Court astonished them again. This time the law in question was one of those major statutes that Congress had passed to cope with the national economic impasse—the National Labor Relations Act. In four decisions the law was upheld in spite of the fact that it controlled labor relations in production industries and in spite of the reiteration only a year before of the doctrine that production affected commerce "indirectly" and was therefore immune from congressional regulation. The direct-indirect distinction was in effect discarded. Again the vote was five to four; again the switch in the position of Justice Roberts tipped the scales.

Finally, on May 24, the Court backtracked dramatically once more. The Social Security Act of 1935 was for most exponents of laissez faire the very symbol of the paternalist theory of government which the New Deal represented and which they found so odious. Moreover, it offended the old negativisms of constitutional jurisprudence in a multiple sense, for it used the tax power to accomplish social ends and induced the states to participate in the plan and conform to nationally prescribed standards. On the authority of the *Butler* decision of 1936, this apparent encroachment on the states' reserved powers was most dubious, but again the Court upheld the law, again by a vote of five to four. Justice Roberts, the author of the *Butler* decision, had again changed his mind.

Meanwhile the controversy over the court-packing plan had been bitterly fought in the Congress and in the forum of public opinion. But although the drive to enact the President's proposal continued after the decisions just described, it had lost much of its force and more of its point. In the long run it failed, and the failure is a significant testimonial to the prestige that attached to the Court's Constitution in the American mind.

Not all the influence of a master politician in the prime of his popularity was quite enough to carry a program that would impair judicial review. Yet the Court's defenders were hardly entitled to be complacent. The Court's recantation had helped save the day; certain fortuitous circumstances relating to legislative strategy had made a difference, too. The danger had been great. Even a close call can teach a lesson.

Constitutional doctrine emerged from those months of crisis profoundly altered. The Court's relationship to the American polity had undergone a fundamental change. Quite probably the judges themselves did not understand how great a withdrawal was portended by their about-face in 1937. But within a few years it would be plain to all that another constitutional era had ended and a new one had begun. As the Civil War had settled the basic question underlying the nation-state conflict, so the Depression and the New Deal had resolved the basic question of economic control. Significant economic issues remained to be decided, of course, even after the nation had made the basic decision against laissez faire, but the Court by its own intransigence had disqualified itself to assist in the process by which those decisions were reached. When the extreme negativist position of 1935–36 was forsaken, as it had to be, the Court could find no stopping place short of abdication.

One aspect of the 1937 judicial revolution then was full-scale rejection of the idea that economic legislation was open to constitutional challenge on the basis of its "unreasonableness." The businessman, so long the Court's darling, was shorn of his constitutional fleece and now faced popular sovereignty protected by nothing save his own ample private resources. The second aspect was judicial acceptance of the idea, almost always implicit in the Court's actual past behavior, that constitutional rules must be flexible within broad limits and that as Justice Stone had put it, "the only check upon our own exercise of power is our own sense of self-restraint." The judicial sovereignty of rhetoric and myth, inexorably holding an irresponsible nation to an objectively ascertainable path of constitutional duty, had died the death with *Lochner, Adkins,* and *United States* v. *Butler.*

The Court therefore faced a future in which its interests of seventy years past were no longer relevant and in which myths of even longer standing would be deeply impaired. But recent experience, with all its hazards, had not stifled the remarkable institutional vitality that had sustained the Court throughout its stormy history. The old interests and values were gone, but a new set would arise to replace them. It is significant and far from a coincidence that 1937, the year of the great recantation, was also the year in which the Court revived, by implication at least, the clear and present danger test as a standard for judgment questions of free speech (*Herndon* v. *Lowry*). The same year saw the doctrine of judicial control over state criminal procedures stated more explicitly than ever before (*Palko* v. *Connecticut*). One year later the Court for the first time enforced the equal protection clause on behalf of Negro rights in the field of education (*Missouri* v. *Canada*). With or without myths, the future was on its way.

SEVEN

THE MODERN COURT AND
POSTWAR AMERICA: 1937–1959

THE SITUATION OF THE SUPREME COURT immediately after the constitutional revolution of 1937 was in many ways analogous to its situation at the close of the Civil War. Then as now prodigious national events had conspired to decide the question which had heretofore been the main focus of the Court's interest; then as now the nation's decision had left the judges in the status of men who are threatened by technological unemployment. In 1866 as in 1938 the Court was still smarting from wounds incurred by its own rashness. An observer viewing the Court at either of these hours in its history might have felt warranted to predict that judicial review had reached its twilight period, that the Court's career as an important factor in the American political process was drawing to a close.

But such an observer making such a judgment would be reckoning without the durability and elasticity of the institution Marshall and Taney and Field and Holmes had nurtured. He would be leaving out of account the qualities of the American political character that had led to the development of judicial review in the first place and had sustained and encouraged its continuance for so many years. In 1937 the people had again given testimony to the existence of that quality by refusing to abet an assault on the Court even though it was carried on in their name to chastise the Court for thwarting their will. With such a fund of support to draw on and with their august tradition to inspirit them, the judges were not apt to recede into humble obscurity unless they had no other choice.

If they were to play a real part, however, in the modern affairs of the Republic, they needed to evolve a new sphere of interests and a new set of values to guide them within that sphere. The problems of their past—the nation-state problem, the business-government problem—had successively been snatched from their grasp by history. It was necessary once more to reorient the Court's interests, to formulate another system of judicial values, and to develop a role for the Court in these new terms.

The interest that was to dominate this third great era of judicial history was, as has been intimated in the preceding chapter, civil rights. The Court which had once been primarily occupied with the nation-state relationship and, some time later, with the business-government relationship now became more and more concerned with the relationship between the individual and government. And the values that it now chose to cherish and defend were those embraced by Justice Frankfurter's phrase: "the free play of the human spirit."

History, which had displaced the Court's old ideal of free enterprise, was quick to provide material to fill the gap. The rise of totalitarianism created new problems for America and cast a different light on problems that were old. The nation faced mortal threats of a degree it had not known since the Civil War and of a kind that it had never known before. The freedom of political dissent had formerly been preserved without much difficulty simply because there had been little occasion for government to challenge it; but now fear generated repressive political impulses.

Yet at the same time the spectacle of the police state in Germany and Russia and elsewhere caused many Americans to revere freedom of expression more consciously than they had in the past and to resist attempts to inhibit it. The racist doctrines of Adolf Hitler and the frightful implementation of those doctrines in Nazi policy helped provoke a feeling of dissatisfaction and guilt over America's own patterns of race discrimination. The right of fair trial, once taken for granted, assumed new layers of significance in the minds of men repelled by the totalitarian image. For some, the concern for the civil rights issue was enhanced by awareness that America had become willy-nilly the leader of the free world and must set a responsible leader's example. And because these three categories of rights were logically hard to separate, alertness to one tended to stimulate alertness to all, so that they mutually animated one another. This is how self-consciousness about the civil rights problem was heightened in the 1930's and 40's and how the Supreme Court was impelled to focus on that problem. For, as history has repeatedly attested, the members of the Supreme Court are children of their times, and a chronicle of Court doctrine tends to be, in a general way, an intellectual history of America.

However, in the post-1937 period as in earlier periods, the Court's adoption of a new congeries of interests and values created the problem of working out a judicial role that would best serve these new purposes. The doctrines of the past, forged to serve past aims, had to be reconstructed, as the due process clause for example was altered in the 1880's and 90's to suit the circumstances of that era. The judges had to rethink the question of the Court's place in the American polity, to feel their way to a *modus operandi* that would enable the Court to defend its new values with reasonable effectiveness but would simultaneously take due account of the limits of judicial control.

And the problem of role definition was all the more acute, as was suggested at the close of the last chapter, because the Court's own behavior and a generation of criticism by "judicial realists" had undermined the myths of judicial supremacy and objectivity. The Court of the early twentieth century had flagrantly confirmed the thesis of this school of critics by refusing to bind itself to objective standards in any of the great areas of judicial supervision. The judges who came to the supreme bench after the constitutional revolution (Justice Van Devanter was the first of the old guard to resign, to be succeeded by Justice Black) were men who had been reared in that school, and they joined Justice Stone, one of its leading spokesmen. They had reason to be more explicitly aware than perhaps any Court of the past had been that theirs was "not the only agency of government that must be assumed to have capacity to govern" and that "the criterion of constitutionality is not whether [judges] believe the law to be for the public good." Their task of finding a place for themselves in the new order was made more difficult, though perhaps clearer, by this fact that self-deception was no longer so reliable an ally.

THE END OF ECONOMIC SUPERVISION

The first order of business was to convince the informed public, including an almost incorrigibly hopeful legal fraternity, that the Court really meant what it implied in 1937: that economic issues were no longer of much constitutional relevance. Businessmen were so accustomed to the Court's favors that they found it hard to adjust to the new dispensation. Yet the judicial drift quickly became unmistakable, as the old negative doctrines were discarded or refined to the point of disappearance. The restrictive interpretations of the tax power, which had served so well in the Child Labor Tax Case and the AAA case, had been pretty well scuttled in the spring of 1937 by the Social Security Act decisions. Congress could tax and spend for the "general welfare" (Art. I, sec. 8 [1]) and the fact that a tax controlled local affairs would make no constitutional difference so long as the general welfare, as Congress saw it, would be served. Even the ancient ban on "intergovernmental taxation" was drastically moderated in 1939. The Court formally repudiated Marshall's aphorism that "the power to tax involves the power to destroy," and thus wiped out more than a century's accumulation of intricate doctrine. State and nation could now tax each other's instrumentalities so long as the tax was neither discriminatory nor "unduly" burdensome.

In the commerce clause field, too, the hardy old negativisms were mowed down with rude abandon. The second Agricultural Adjustment Act of 1938 was upheld despite the fact that it excluded "harmless" commodities from interstate commerce by establishing quotas on the amount that could be sold, and indirectly regulated production. In 1942 the Court sustained an even more venturesome amendment which imposed limits on wheat grown for on-the-farm uses even though no part of it was sold in interstate trade. A year before it had upheld the Fair Labor Standards Act which prescribed wages and hours for firms engaged in or producing goods for interstate commerce. The idea that production was beyond congressional reach, the distinction between direct and indirect effects were all given the quietus. As Justice Jackson remarked for a unanimous bench in the wheat quotas case: "The Court's recognition of the relevance of the economic effects in the application of the Commerce Clause . . . has made the mechanical application of legal formulas no longer feasible" (*Wickard* v. *Filburn*).

It was now evident that Congress could reach just about any commercial subject it might want to reach and could do to that subject just about anything it was likely to want to do, whether for economic, humanitarian, or other purposes. The decisions, it is true, offer a hint that some regulations might go too far, that some local activities might be exempt from federal control because their effect on interstate commerce was not substantial. But these hints were small comfort to businessmen appealing for present relief; and business was thoroughly warranted in inferring that the constitutional distinction between intrastate and interstate commerce was no longer a practical limit on federal power.

This was a bitter pill to swallow for those who had benefited from the Old Court's solicitous jurisprudence, but the enfeeblement of the due process clause as a substantive limit on economic legislation was even more dismaying. The post-1937 Court in effect adopted the criterion urged by Justice Holmes in his classic series of dissents during the first three decades of the century. It was authoritatively expressed in 1938 by Justice Stone in *United States* v. *Carolene Products:*

> . . . regulatory legislation affecting ordinary commercial transactions is not to be pronounced unconstitutional unless in the light of the facts made known or generally assumed it is of such a character as to preclude the assumption that it rests upon some rational basis within the knowledge and experience of the legislators.

It is hard to conceive a law so patently unreasonable that it would fail under this test, and it is therefore not surprising that the Court since 1937 has never encountered one. And the Court showed itself ready to make a loose standard even looser by stretching its imagination to the limits to find *some* sensible reason for the law and impute that motive to the legislative authors. Not even the most optimistic litigant could persuade himself for very long after 1938 than an economic statute would be held unreasonable on substantive grounds.

Of course the Court had always paid lip service to the principle that a law should be presumed valid "until its violation of the Constitution is proved beyond reasonable doubt" (*Ogden* v. *Saunders*, 1827). But/ the judges had breached this precept in such decisions as *Lochner, Adkins,* and the anti–New Deal cases, for the very good reason that compliance with it would have forced them to uphold the questioned laws. Now this "presumption of constitutionality" was reinstated with a vengeance, and the extreme form it took is a measure of the Court's determination to have done with economic affairs in the due process area. A state law forbidding women to work as barmaids; another forcing employers to pay employees for hours not worked on election day; still another in effect restricting the river-boat pilot profession to relatives and friends of present pilots—all these were upheld against due process and equal protection attack. The ghosts of Field and Peckham and Sutherland must have stirred restlessly to see freedom of contract so hardly used. But it was not their shades, but those of Holmes and Brandeis that now dominated the course of decision. Constitutional laissez faire was as dead as mutton.

This is not to say that the post-1937 Court was able to ignore the economic world altogether. Though substantive due process in this area was virtually abandoned, the older and historically more legitimate concept of procedural due process survived, and a businessman could still hope for constitutional recourse if, for example, a law took his property without notice or fair hearing. And although the commerce power of

Congress was no longer subject to serious constitutional question, the problem of whether state action impinged on interstate commerce (the old problem of the *Cooley* case) still absorbed a respectable share of the Court's attention. The principle seemed to be that such a state law was acceptable if it did not discriminate against interstate commerce (that is, if it treated the state's own commerce and that of the nation equally) and if the Court felt that the state interest served by the law outweighed "whatever national interest there might be in the prevention of state restrictions." But this form of supervision over economic matters, though not insignificant, is a far cry from the sovereignty once claimed over the whole business-government relationship. And the crucial point is that the Court's doctrines were no longer set up as a barrier against regulations as such. The question of whether America should become a welfare state was now referred strictly to the political branches of government.

HUMILITY VERSUS PRIDE:
INTERNATIONAL AGREEMENTS AND EXECUTIVE POWER

All this suggests a judiciary overwhelmed by considerations of modesty and resolved to interfere as little as possible in the conduct of government, particularly when national power is involved. And the impression seems confirmed by certain other doctrinal tendencies of the era. The rule against undue delegation of legislative power, invoked by the Old Court to help extinguish the New Deal, was now so attenuated that it took on the quality of a moral admonition rather than a legal limitation. In a case involving the validity of federal price control legislation, for example, the Court upheld the law even though it empowered the administrator to issue price regulations subject only to the requirement that they tend to effectuate the very broad purposes of the Act (essentially to prevent inflation), that they be "fair and equitable" (whatever that may mean), and that the administrator "so far as practicable" give "due consideration" to the prices prevailing in October, 1941. The arguments of the judges in the NRA case almost ten years before, that executive discretion under the recovery act was "virtually unfettered" and not "canalized within banks that keep it from overflowing," seem equally apposite here. But now only Justice Roberts dissented from the holding that the standards provided for the administrator's guidance were constitutionally adequate. Even before the 1937 revolution the Court had approved the delegation of very broad discretion to the President in the field of foreign affairs (*United*

States v. *Curtiss-Wright,* 1936). Now it appeared that the rule was similarly permissive when applied to domestic administration.

Nor was the conduct of foreign policy hampered by other sorts of judicially contrived restraints. As long ago as 1920, Justice Holmes, speaking for the Court, had declared that a treaty might accomplish results that a mere act of Congress could not, that the limits of the Constitution applied "in a different way" when the treaty-making power was called into question (Art. II, sec. 2 [2]). In view of this decision and in view of the fact that no treaty had ever been held to exceed constitutional bounds, some alarmed observers have suspected that no such bounds exist as far as the judiciary is concerned. And their apprehension about the danger of arbitrary government in the foreign affairs area was hardly quelled by a 1942 decision holding that an "executive agreement" made by the President with a foreign government (without the concurrence of the Senate, which is required for a treaty) was paramount to state laws.

It is a pretty safe bet that the Court would invalidate a treaty or executive agreement that bartered away all or part of the Bill of Rights; the power to make such international compacts could not avail to deprive Americans of free speech or fair trial. But aside from such an unlikely eventuality, it must be conceded that the chances of judicial interference with this authority are very remote. In connection with the power over foreign affairs, as in connection with national power over economic affairs, the modern Court has for practical purposes abandoned the concept of judicial control and has thrust the responsibility for worrying about constitutional limits on the shoulders of the President and Congress. The argument for this policy of abnegation is that government must have great leeway to act effectively in these two intricate and technical fields, and that judicial review is too restricted in its sources of information and too cumbersome in its procedures to supervise such action adequately. The danger is of course that the other branches of government will fail to assume the constitutional responsibility which the Court has tendered to them, and will interpret the assignment as a license to act arbitrarily. But for better or for worse the fact remains that these two great and increasingly important areas of public affairs are now subject to constitutional limits only in the sense that the British Parliament is constitutionally limited, that is, by legislative and executive self-restraint and by the force of public opinion.

Yet in spite of all these evidences of judicial humility in these areas, it would be an error to assume that the judiciary had lost self-confidence altogether as a result of its chastening experience in the 1930's. One of the best single illustrations of the fact that it had not is to be found in the Steel Seizure decision of 1952. In order to avert a nationwide steel strike which he thought would imperil America's defense, President Truman had seized the steel mills on behalf of the United States government by executive order. Mr. Truman's authority to take such action was not specifically granted by statute, and his right, if any, to seize the mills, therefore, had to rest on the old idea that the President possesses certain "inherent powers" to act for the national welfare even without specific statutory authorization. The Court had tacitly recognized some such prerogative in a few opinions during its history, but in general the concept of inherent power had developed extra-judicially as a result of presidential practice and congressional acquiescence. The Court of the past had seemed to feel about this question the way the modern Court felt about the commerce power and the treaty power—that it was best left to the political branches of government.

But now the Court of 1952, otherwise so skittish about intruding in economic affairs, undertook to mediate this hot dispute between the President and one of the great economic forces of the nation. The "opinion of the Court" by Justice Black boldly held that the President had no authority to act as he did because the subject was within the sphere of Congress' authority; when the President entered that sphere without congressional permission, he violated the principle of separation of powers. Some of the other majority judges did not concur in this definition of executive power that would confine it to matters outside Congress' range (what those matters might be would be hard to say considering the modern scope of legislative power). But they did argue that the President had erred in this instance because, said they, certain federal statutes forbid Mr. Truman to do what he did, and surely inherent executive power, even if there is such a thing, does not license the President to violate statutes.

To that proposition all the judges agreed, and so would most observers, including President Truman (who contended that the supposedly prohibitory statutes were being wrongly interpreted). But such a consensus should not obscure the very real question of whether the Supreme Court should have tried to resolve a controversy so heatedly fought at the bar of public opinion, so loaded with immediate and grave national consequences. At all events the decision reminds us that judicial self-restraint is not the only theme of the modern era. The modern judges have been torn, as were their predecessors of the early twentieth century, between the impulse to wield the scepter and the impulse to remain "lions under the throne." A similar tension has been set up; similar lines of division have been drawn. And the Steel Seizure case represents, as *Adkins* did, a breaking-out and temporary assertion of the old urge to monarchize.

THE COURT SEEKS A ROLE:
THE PROBLEM OF FREEDOM OF EXPRESSION

The tension between the instinct to dominate and the instinct to forbear has been most clearly evident in connection with the subject the modern Court seems to care most about—civil rights. And the competing considerations that have helped to generate the tensions here have been by no means easy to resolve. On the one hand, there has been the feeling, more or less deeply shared by all the modern judges, that "those liberties of the individual which history has attested as the indispensable conditions of an open as against a closed society come to the Court with a momentum for respect lacking when appeal is made to liberties which derive merely from shifting economic arrangements." The words are those of Justice Frankfurter and some of the reasons for the rise of the sentiment have already been discussed. It can be judicially implemented, as Justice Stone once intimated, by subjecting to "more exacting judicial scrutiny" legislation "which restricts the political processes which can ordinarily be expected to bring about repeal of undesirable legislation" and which reflect "prejudices against discrete and insular minorities" (*United States v. Carolene Products Co.*, 1938). Coupled with and supporting this modern concern for civil rights as a value, has been the tradition, running back to Marshall and beyond, that the Court has the power and duty to right wrongs, to translate its moral convictions into constitutional limitations.

On the other hand, of course, there were ranged all the notions about judicial humility that had been generated by the iconoclastic movement of the preceding decades, and an awareness—on the part of at least some of the judges—that the historic Court had usually accomplished more by moderation than by arrogance. These notions, well-grounded enough in any event, could be reinforced in the post-1937 era by a special circumstance of the times: the fact that *crisis* seemed to have become a chronic condition. The concept of constitutional limitation had never functioned very well in emergencies. In moments of great peril, when the temper of the populace was likely to be superheated, the judicial tendency had been to withdraw and wait for more auspicious, normal times. This had been Marshall's policy in the dangerous years after the Jeffersonian revolution, and it had been adopted by the Court with varying degrees of frankness in critical periods that followed. The exceptions have not made very pleasant readings for the Court's friends. Judicial attempts to control policy in such times have seldom been ultimately very successful. In the years after 1937, as wars hot and cold posed awesome problems and frayed public nerves, the case for judicial modesty was not easy to refute. But neither was it easy to dismiss the argument that civil rights are the essence of democratic government and that the Court must do its best to preserve them. The difficulty was to decide what its best was.

The Court's erratic pattern of response to the issue of free expression illustrates these judicial perplexities with special force. In the first few years after 1937, the judges seemed inclined to stand the old constitutional order on its head, and to assert a power of review over free speech statutes that was unmodified by considerations of judicial self-restraint. Holmes's clear and present danger principle, ignored by the majority since 1919, was now revitalized and put forward as a talismanic standard to be applied to all categories of free speech problems. Moreover the Holmesian rubric was strengthened in its negative implications by an amendment that had been proposed by Justice Brandeis in a 1927 concurring opinion. In order to sustain a statute inhibiting freedom of speech, he had suggested, the Court must find a clear and present danger of a *serious* evil; "prohibition of free speech and assembly is a measure so stringent that it would not be appropriate as the means for averting a relatively trivial harm to society" (*Whitney* v. *California*).

Now the rhetoric of clear and present danger in this form expresses well enough some of the factors that might guide the citizen or his legislative representative in deciding whether free expression should be restrained; and it is no doubt advisable that the judicial process take account of these factors, too. But in some of the early decisions of this era the Court gave the impression that its opinion about clear and present danger was the only one that counted and that the "presumption of constitutionality," once denied in *Lochner* and *Adkins* to statutes touching freedom of contract, was now denied to those infringing freedom of speech. The doctrine seemed to be, pressing Justice Stone's *Carolene Products* logic hard, that free expression (including of course religious expression) occupied a "preferred position" in America's constellation of constitutional rights, and that government action impinging on it was presumptively invalid. Armed with these concepts and attitudes, the Court disapproved a considerable number of state actions, including a law forbidding peaceful picketing, another requiring union organizers to register, state court contempt holdings against those who were accused of using the press to influence judicial proceedings, and a state law requiring school children to salute the flag in spite of their contrary religious convictions.

Most of the state measures invalidated in this period were foolish or pernicious, and some of them might well have been overthrown even by a judiciary fully alive to the virtue of modesty. But the decisions nevertheless were vulnerable to criticism on at least two grounds. In the first place the opinions that accompanied them were barren of evidence that the Court was taking adequate account of the legislature's claim to share in "the power to govern." It is one thing to decide that a state action exceeds the bounds of reason and quite another, as Sir Frederick Pollock once said, to treat the legislature "like an inferior court which had to give proof of its competence." The judges had long ago been powerfully admonished by Justice Holmes: "It must be remembered that legislators are the ultimate guardians of the liberties and welfare of the people in quite as great a degree as the courts." Now, with respect to free speech statutes, that reminder seemed to be forgotten.

But second, and in practical terms even more important, the opinions assumed a role for the Court and a rigidity of constitutional limits that could not be sustained in the face of real adversity. The idea seemed to be that the Court would hold government action aimed at free speech to the same kind of strict substantive limits that had been applied, in *Adkins* and similar cases, to inhibitions on freedom of contract. This failed to reckon with the possibility of extreme public need or (what is pretty much the same thing as far as the Court is concerned) extreme public demand for repressive legislation. The doctrines and assumptions of these cases proved no more tenable as the totalitarian threat became acute than the similar doctrines and assumptions of *Adkins* had been tenable in the Great Depression.

What was especially unfortunate about all this is that it left the Court unprepared to cope with adversity when it did come. Instead of working out a viable judicial attitude toward infringements on free speech, the Court had enunciated a policy of flat negation; and when that policy had to be abandoned, there was nothing to take its place except uncritical acquiescence to the legislative will. Growing national awareness of the totalitarian threat in the years after 1945 generated a national mood toward "subversion" that sometimes approached hysteria. Government action in response to that mood was often savagely hostile to freedom of expression. If the judges had been thinking their problem through in the years just preceding, they might have been ready with an approach that could have moderated the tempest and contributed usefully to the resolution of a grave national quandary. But since most of them had been orating rather than thinking, and since the uncompromising policy set forth in the oratory had become impossible, the only alternative seemed to be judicial collapse. At no time in its history had the Court been able to maintain a position squarely opposed to a strong popular majority. There was no reason to expect that it could do so now. In contrast to the negativism of the first few post-1937 years, the Court now became so tolerant of governmental restriction on freedom of expression as to suggest that it was abdicating the field.

The two decisions that exemplified this phase of modern judicial history were *American Communication Ass'n* v. *Douds* (1950) and *Dennis* v. *United States* (1951). Both involved national statutes visiting penalties on Communists, and in both the Court upheld the government actions, painfully swallowing its brave libertarian protestations of a few years before. However the most troubling thing about the decisions was not so much that they sustained the government, but that they came close to abandoning altogether the concept of judicial limitation. The *Douds* opinion by Chief Justice Vinson suggested, about as strongly as words might, that Congress could use the commerce power to interfere with free speech and association without fear of *any* constitutional hindrance. In *Dennis* the language was somewhat more guarded, but the result was not very different. The clear and present danger doctrine, put forward in recent opinions as a kind of universal rule, was now redefined in such a way as to make it meaningless and, for practical purposes, useless. The Court's role as the uncompromising defender of liberty against all comers, also so recently asserted and reasserted, was likewise abandoned. The implication was that judicial review could contribute nothing to the solution of America's "subversion problem" and that the Court's only course was to stand aside while the winds howled on Capitol Hill and elsewhere.

However, it turned out that another phase in this history of judicial responses was already taking shape at the very time that these spectacularly acquiescent decisions were handed down. For one thing, though shying off from the issue of subversion, the Court had continued to widen the area of freedom in cases involving what might be called "nonseditious free speech." For the first time in history, for example, the Court had overturned state laws censoring magazines and motion pictures. These decisions were couched in careful language; they did not condemn all censorship per se. But they made it clear that censorship does raise a constitutional question and thereby opened up a whole new area of judicial supervision. A comparable development was meanwhile taking place in cases involving both the "free exercise of religion" and the "no establishment" clauses of the First Amendment. The substance of those clauses had been held to be binding on the states by way of the Fourteenth Amendment. Now the Court struck down state aid to religion on the ground that it breached the "wall of separation" between church and state and on the ground that it infringed religious liberty. Again the decisions were so framed as to leave some leeway for state policy; but again it had been made plain that a subject highly relevant to free expression was subject to constitutional control.

In the second place, as public enthusiasm for domestic red-hunting subsided somewhat, and as the Court had a chance to take new bearings, the outlines of a mature policy in the subversive field began to emerge. In the stormy times of the *Douds* and *Dennis* cases, the judges seemed to have forgotten that there is more than one way to skin a cat. Awed by the dimensions of the subversion problem and loath to challenge the substantive power of Congress on an issue related to national defense, they had chosen to do nothing. As their history should have informed them, however, there is a middle way between over-assertiveness and abdication even when congressional statutes are concerned. National laws must be *interpreted* by the federal courts, and judicial misgivings about the wisdom or necessity of such laws can be expressed through "the alchemy of construction." In short, the Supreme Court can often so interpret a law invading free speech as to moderate its virulence. This serves to remind Congress and country that a zone of doubt has been entered and encourages them to take a second look at their problem. Yet it leaves Congress free to correct the judicial gloss if convinced, after reflection, that a harsher interpretation should prevail. A further advantage from the viewpoint of democratic values is that the approach focuses responsibility by requiring Congress to speak unmistakably when it wishes to impinge on freedom of expression.

In the 1950's the Supreme Court rediscovered this item in its bag of tricks and began to use it to exert a significant influence on national policy relating to subversion and allied phenomena. Perhaps the most far-reaching case in point was *Pennsylvania* v. *Nelson* which involved the jailing of a Communist party member under a state sedition law. By this time (1956) the national government had added three major peace-time sedition statutes to its books, and most of the states had been stirred by the postwar excitement over such matters to elaborate and intensify their own antisubversive programs. This added up to a bewildering number and variety of governmental restrictions on freedom of expression, and in the *Nelson* case the Court simplified the situation by wiping the state laws, temporarily at least, off the slate. The Court argued that Congress, in passing the national sedition laws, had superseded the state laws by implication. Since the problem dealt with by the laws—national defense—is obviously national in character, there could be no doubt that Congress *could* override state laws if it chose to do so. By holding that the Congress *had* so chosen, the Court threw its weight on the side of rationality and liberty, yet avoided the heavy responsibility of an irrevocable constitutional pronouncement against such state activity.

With respect to free expression, then, the modern Court seems to have established, temporarily at least, a balance between the extremes of judicial supremacy and judicial abdication. Doctrines have been reshaped and jurisdiction widened so as to bring a new range of subjects under potential constitutional control. This development of a jurisprudence of free expression has been in many ways comparable to the development of a jurisprudence of laissez faire in the closing decades of the nineteenth century. And now, as then, the Court, having evolved the tools of judicial supervision, has been faced by the problem of how to use them. The current answer seems to be twofold: government is held to a fairly strict but not inflexible standard in fields unrelated to subversion; in fields that do involve the subversion issue, Congress is left free within wide limits, and the Court employs the device of statutory interpretations to mitigate the asperities of repressive laws and insure that the legislative will is clearly expressed. This adds up to a comparatively modest version of the doctrine of judicial supremacy. It constitutes the judiciary as a significant but not dominant partner in the American governmental enterprise. Throughout the modern period there have been members of the bench who chafed under the limitations of this role and yearned to play a greater part in shaping the decisions of the nation. It remains to be seen whether they will ultimately succeed in launching the Court on one of those campaigns of derring-do that have from time to time marked its history.

JUDICIAL SUCCESSES AND FAILURES: THE PROBLEM OF PROCEDURAL RIGHTS

The modern drive to harry subversives by inhibiting their freedom of expression has also been hampered to some extent by the Supreme Court's insistence that the procedural guarantees of the Constitution must be observed. Like the approach to statutory interpretation just described, this procedural fastidiousness represents a nice compromise between too much judicial review and too little. When Congress is told that it must respect the procedural rights of persons even though they are suspected of subversion, this preserves the substantive power of Congress to accomplish its basic objects and at the same time acts as a reminder that the idea of constitutional limit still lives.

The Court's zeal in enforcing procedural standards has been tempered by an awareness that government needs elbow room to operate effectively, and it is arguable that this spirit of judicial tolerance has sometimes been overdone. During the Second World War, for example, the military authorities (backed, it should be said, by the President and Congress) decided that some 112,000 Japanese-Americans must be moved out of the West Coast military area as a security measure. The decision was carried out in spite of the fact that about 70,000 of the victims were United States citizens and that no crime could be charged, much less proved, against them. The Supreme Court upheld this wholesale invasion of procedural rights, arguing that it could not second-guess the military on a question relating to national defense and calling for swift action. The case provides another illustration—if one is needed—of the proposition that judicial review is likely to be weakest during grave national emergencies. It also illustrates the curious tendency to polarized thinking that occasionally besets the American judiciary. The idea that the Court must either uphold a governmental policy in all respects or disapprove it altogether was controlling in the *Milligan* case in 1866 and in this case almost a century later. Yet the Court's whole history is a refutation of that black-and-white idea.

Procedural rules were sometimes interpreted rather generously in other areas as well. The right against "unreasonable searches and seizures" (Amendment IV) did not avail, for example, to prevent federal officers from searching the premises of an arrested person even though they bore no warrant to conduct the search and there had been ample time to get one before making the arrest. Evidence obtained by wiretapping was not admissible in federal tribunals because wiretapping was forbidden by federal statute, but the Court steadily refused to hold that wiretapping violated the Fourth Amendment, and it allowed the admission of evidence obtained by various hidden listening devices like radio transmitters.

The procedural protection of those threatened by such grave penalties as deportation was not all that it might be. The Court permitted the government to hold a man in prison without bail while deportation proceedings were pending, even though no deportable offense had yet been proved against him and the proceedings might well drag on for years. A federal law of 1954 required witnesses to answer questions that might ordinarily incriminate them and granted them immunity from prosecution on the matters disclosed. The Court upheld the law against the argument that it impaired the privilege against self-incrimination guaranteed by the Fifth Amendment. The statutory immunity from criminal prosecution could not of course protect a man from the other penalties of his testimony, such as loss of employment and "infamy" but the Court declined to extend the right so as to cover such hazards.

Yet the procedural rights that the Court did secure or enlarge during the modern period were by no means insignificant, particularly in their bearing on freedom of expression. In spite of the Immunity Act decision and others which construed the Fifth Amendment narrowly, the Court approached the right against self-incrimination, as Justice Frankfurter said "in a spirit of strict, not lax, observance of the constitutional protection of the individual." The Court made it clear for example in 1950 that the right was available to those who were asked about Communist activities by courts, congressional committees, or any other federal agency. The refusal to enlarge the privilege into a general right of silence or to extend it otherwise by interpretation reflects unwillingness to go forward, not a disposition to go back. And in the field of deportation and denaturalization, although the Court did sometimes uphold rather arbitrary government behavior, it also established in the modern period the important principle that a man threatened by deportation or denaturalization was entitled to *some* procedural rights under the due process clause. The old doctrine, arguably supported by some court decisions, had been that constitutional limits did not apply at all in these areas of governmental power.

Furthermore due process in the procedural sense was increasingly held to be relevant to statutes directly inhibiting freedom of expression. The vice of "vagueness" in a legal prohibition can always be challenged on due process grounds, for a man cannot be fairly punished unless he has a reasonable basis for knowing that his act was forbidden. But vagueness was regarded as particularly objectionable in free speech statutes, and this judicial stand helped to overthrow or discourage the kind of shotgun enactments that legislators sometimes pass, because it takes time and knowledge to draw a statute carefully.

In a similar vein, a "loyalty oath" requirement applied to public college teachers was held invalid on the essentially procedural ground that it penalized innocent as well as knowing membership in "subversive organization" and thus violated due process. The opinions emphasized that such thoughtlessly broad statutes affected not only the immediate litigants but the atmosphere of freedom generally, because they may "chill that free play of the spirit which all teachers ought especially to cultivate and practice." This decision (*Wiemann* v. *Updegraff*, 1952) was important, too, because it flatly rejected the old, bad idea that "there is no constitutionally protected right to public employment." The government may not exclude a public servant from employment on arbitrary or discriminatory grounds.

This attitude toward procedures, combined with the policy of interpreting free speech laws strictly, enabled the modern Court to reconcile its feelings of modesty with its modern solicitude for individual rights, and to contribute to the solution of the subversion problem. The realm of procedure is after all the judge's special domain; the construction of statutes is a peculiarly judicial art; and the Court's ipse dixit seems more authoritative in these areas than it might if substantive issues of policy were being decided.

Like considerations might seem to have a bearing on another great question in the modern jurisprudence of civil rights—the extent to which the *states* are bound by a federal constitutional standard in their general criminal procedures. But here the problem has been complicated by the Court's respect for a value that ranks very high in the lexicon of some of the judges—the value of federalism. Justice Holmes once said (though not, as it happens, in reference to a procedural issue) that he deprecated the use of the Fourteenth Amendment to prevent experiments "in the insulated chambers afforded by the several States." The modern Court has been troubled by the fear that overly strict constitutional supervision of state law enforcement would impede the evolution of new and more effective methods and would dampen the state's sense of responsibility for policing its own standard.

These misgivings help account for the fact that the Court has advanced more slowly in this field than some libertarians might wish. It will be remembered that by the 1930's the Court had clearly accepted the idea that some procedural rights protected against national action by Amendments IV–VIII, were also protected against state action by the Fourteenth Amendment. The problem then was to determine what those rights were and how they should be applied to limit the states. In 1937 in the *Palko* case Justice Cardozo laid it down that the rights protected were those principles of justice "so rooted in the traditions and conscience of our people as to be ranked as fundamental." Unhappily however this principle, like others that have been encountered in this chronicle, was not quite self-explanatory. Suppose it is decided that the right to counsel is fundamental in the sense intended by the *Palko* doctrine. Does that mean that the right must be granted in every kind of proceeding even down to traffic court cases? Does it mean that the state is obliged to provide counsel for the indigent even in those cases? Or is it necessary, once a right has been identified as worthy of protection, to discriminate between denials of it that are offensive and those that are not?

The modern Court met these difficulties, or attempted to meet them, by developing the "fair trial rule." The right to counsel, for example, *had* been recognized to be protected by the Amendment as long ago as 1932. But, said the Court ten years later, in determining whether a *given* denial of counsel is a denial of due process, we will ask whether "the totality of facts" in the case "constitute a denial of fundamental fairness." Thus an indigent farm laborer was not deprived of due process when the state refused his request to supply counsel in a trial for robbery, because the Supreme Court reading the printed record felt that the trial had been fair.

One trouble with this rule, apart from its possible harshness to the defendant, was its extreme uncertainty. If the totality of facts in a given case was the only basis for determining fairness, it seemed impossible to predict whether a conviction would be upheld unless the predicter could anticipate the thought processes of five members of the Supreme Court. This objection, together with a strong disposition to favor the individual in cases of doubt, led to a series of powerful minority dissents in cases following 1942, and finally in *Adamson* v. *California* (1947) the judges engaged in a full-dress verbal conflict. Justice Black argued eloquently and at length that the Court should take leave of the *Palko* doctrine and its subsidiary, the fair trial rule. Both the intent of the Fourteenth Amendment's framers and considerations of sound judicial policy suggest, he said, that Amendments IV–VIII should be incorporated *in toto* in the Fourteenth. Thus the Court would be deprived of the "boundless power" to expand or contract procedural guarantees; the course of the law would be more certain; and the Court would "extend to all the people of the nation the complete protection of the Bill of Rights."

But Justice Black's assault failed to carry the Court majority. Five members joined in reaffirming the established rules. Justice Frankfurter sharply queried the Black interpretation of the framers' intent, denounced the "incorporation" proposal on the ground that it would imprison the states in eighteenth-century legal concepts, and denied that the *Palko* standard was unduly subjective. On the historical point Frankfurter later received valuable extra-judicial support from Professor Charles Fairman, whose researches into contemporary documents raised serious doubts that the framers had a clear-cut intention to embody the Bill of Rights in the Amendment. The suggestion that the states should be allowed leeway to experiment with reforms has obvious force, but one's ultimate assessment of it will depend on a judgment of whether the leeway is likely to be used for good or ill. And that judgment in turn is related to the weight that is assigned federalism as a value: does state autonomy work against individual liberty or tend to promote it?

As for the charge of subjectivity, perhaps the best answer is what lawyers call a plea in confession and avoidance. The question of subjectivity versus objectivity is as old as the Supreme Court (in fact, of course, a great deal older). Critics have perennially urged the Court to abolish uncertainties by pronouncing a sweeping rule, but historical experience suggests that such advice is dubious, however well intended. The broadly generalized dogmatism has usually created more mischief than it has cured, both from the Court's own viewpoint and from the viewpoint of public policy. It is reasonable therefore to expect that the rules will emerge gradually as inferences from a multitude of decisions, and to hope that they will be well adapted to reality by the nature of their evolution.

But on the other hand the fair trial rule with its emphasis on the "totality of facts" in each discrete situation seems a barrier to the development of any rule at all, and the Court does have an obligation to make the law as understandable as reality permits. The all-out incorporation principle espoused by Black seems to have provoked a similarly extreme contradictory doctrine. It is not the first time in this history that we have seen wisdom fall between two opposite poles. The list of decisions since 1937 in which procedural rights have been defended against state action is a long one. Here as elsewhere during the modern era the Court has been more vigilant to protect the individual than it was in the past. But it has failed to develop in this field a criterion of decision that seems intellectually defensible or practically tenable.

RACIAL DISCRIMINATION AND THE BOUNDARIES OF JUDICIAL POWER

In connection with free speech and procedural rights, as we have seen, the modern Court has pursued a somewhat irregular course, alternating between modesty and self-assertion, retreating and advancing by turns. But the third great civil rights problem—racial discrimination—has been handled quite differently. Here the Court has been more venturesome, more confident in announcing its proscriptions. Moreover the doctrinal direction has been consistently (though not unhesitatingly) forward toward a more generous view of the rights of racial minorities and a more daring assessment of the Court's capacity to protect them. And the radical conflicts of opinion among the judges themselves, so frequent in the other cases discussed, have in this field been far less common.

The explanation for this contrast is not hard to guess. With one or two possible exceptions all of the judges appointed to the bench since 1937 shared a general civil rights ethos. Their commitments to it might vary in degree, and the judges might differ in their ideas for implementing it, but they shared it nonetheless. And in that mutual value system the goal of racial equality assumed a special place for several reasons. Partly, no doubt, it was because persecution on the basis of race seemed the most gratuitously evil of totalitarian malignancies. Partly it was because America's primary racial minority, the Negroes, lagged so patently and woefully behind the rest of the nation in their privileges: this problem seemed the greatest because it involved the most glaring injustice. There is usually an arguable justification for restrictions on speech or denial of procedural rights—the state must be defended, the "war against crime" must not be hindered unduly. For racial discrimination there is no such generally commended rationale, but only prejudice. Add to these considerations the fact that Amendments XIV and XV were passed originally to secure Negro rights, though the former amendment had been diverted to other uses. And further add, as has been suggested earlier, that the modern judges were pervasively conscious of America's position as a symbol of the free world and of the new importance of the "non-White" nations in the world arena. The judicial impulse to act forthrightly in this field is easy to understand.

But, however grievous the wrongs and however strong the will to right them, the problems of judicial governance remain problems still. The Court was spared in this field the old self-questioning about whether the challenged state policy was actually justifiable—were the rights of employers to untrammeled economic freedom really superior to the rights of scrubwomen to a living wage? No such baffling calculus need be conducted here, for the side of justice seemed to the Court unarguably manifest. But another question, the sheer issue of judicial power, was not to be similarly bypassed. The authority of the Court is supported (in theory at least) by the force of the national government, and especially the President. But if such support is not accorded, the judiciary's only remaining mainstay is its own prestige. The nation's respect for the judiciary has been great enough, as we have seen, so that the Court can affect policy in marginal ways. It has not usually been so great that the Court can bank on it against a clear-cut and deeply felt political impulse of the majority of the people. In assailing the problem of Negro rights, the Court challenged a significant segment, not a majority, of the nation. But the strain on judicial capacities was not, as it turned out, to be taken lightly.

The modern chapter of the narrative begins in 1938 with *Missouri v. Canada.* It will be remembered that the nineteenth-century Court had diminished the possible effect of the Fourteenth Amendment by denying that Congress could reach private persons under the enforcement clause, and by upholding state-required segregation of races (*Civil Rights Cases,* 1883, and *Plessy v. Ferguson,* 1896). The first of these doctrines was fairly well supported by the language of the Amendment: "no *State . . .* shall deny to any person . . . the equal protection of the laws." This means, or has meant to the Court, that the Amendment has no bearing on private discriminatory behavior and that Congress' "power to enforce . . . the provisions of this article" extends only to states and to state officials acting under state law. This confining interpretation is not entirely inevitable; Justice Harlan suggested a plausible contrary gloss in his *Civil Rights Cases* dissent. But the Court has never been disposed to follow these suggestions, perhaps feeling that the majority doctrine, whether right or wrong to begin with, was now unshakably established in the constitutional tradition. There seemed then little room for maneuver on this point; private persons could discriminate at will if their own states would tolerate it.

Moreover, as has been remarked earlier, even the states themselves were not seriously embarrassed by the Amendment for some time after *Plessy*'s announcement of the doctrine that the races could be legally separated so long as facilities were equal. The facilities did not have to be *very* equal to pass the Court's mild inspection. However, the "separate but equal" doctrine, even with its dubious acceptance of segregation as a principle, did contain a restrictive potential, in case a libertarian-minded Court should be inclined to turn it into a reality by insisting on true equality.

In the *Missouri* case that note was finally sounded loud and clear. In accordance with the casual standards acceptable in the past, Missouri had never bothered to establish a Negro law school, although it did maintain one limited to whites. Now a Negro student, duly qualified except for his color, sought entrance to this University of Missouri law school and was of course denied. The state argued that there were too few Negro applicants to warrant the setting-up of a special school; and that, pending the day when the number of such applicants would be substantial, Missouri had done its constitutional duty by offering to pay this Negro's tuition at a university in another state. But these evasions, though once serviceable enough, did not impress a Court now coming alive to the problem of civil rights on many fronts. It was held that the right to equality does not "depend upon the number of persons who may be discriminated against," that the discrimination was not excused by its supposititiously "temporary character," and that Missouri could not pass on to some other state its own obligation to provide equality. In short, equal means equal.

The *Missouri* decision signalized a new judicial mood toward Negro rights. It was followed in the next twenty years by the development of an elaborate jurisprudence of equality extending into a large variety of fields. For example, the Court applied the hoary *Cooley* rule to forbid segregation on interstate transportation, this being a subject that required a uniform national rule; and the Interstate Commerce Act was also construed to outlaw segregation. Attempts to discriminate on racial grounds in the real estate field were seriously undermined by the judicial decision that "restrictive covenants" (agreements that a buyer will not resell to Negroes, Jews, etc.) cannot be enforced in state courts, since such enforcement would be "state action" forbidden by the Fourteenth Amendment. Even the enforcement clause of that Amendment was to some extent revitalized by a holding that a state officer who used the power of his office to encroach on an individual's constitutional rights could be punished by federal law (*Screws* v. *United States,* 1945). The Court still adhered to the "state action" limit on the Amendment's range, but it was evidently prepared to interpret that interpretation as generously as reason would allow.

These were important developments; and there were others. But there were two kinds of race discrimination that mattered more than any of the rest: denial of the voting right and denial of adequate education. Inequality in these fields not only deprived the Negro of his present rights, but impaired his chance to improve his lot in the future. And therefore the Court moved in these fields with special determination.

The constitutional problem of voting rights was complicated. The Fifteenth Amendment forbids the states to abridge the right to vote on account of race or color. A state law directly denying Negroes the right would be overthrown as a matter of course, and in 1915 the Court had invalidated a so-called "grandfather clause" which required literacy tests of those who were *not* descendants of those who could vote in 1867. But two difficulties arose. For one thing, the primary was of course the only election that mattered in the one-party South, yet primaries had not been known by the Constitution's framers, and in 1920 the Court had seemed to say that they were, therefore, not elections in the meaning of the Constitution. For another thing, although the state was prohibited by the equal protection clause of the Fourteenth Amendment from excluding Negroes from primaries by law, the Democratic party (a "private" group and therefore untouched by the Amendment) could accomplish the same result by denying them party membership. This indirect abridgment of the voting right was allowed by the Court in a 1935 decision, and the White Primary seemed securely entrenched against Court interference (*Grovey* v. *Townsend*).

But the tide of civil rights sentiment in the country and on the bench could not be checked long by such sophistries. A constitution, intended as Story said to endure for ages, cannot be confined by static definitions that ignore changing realities. In 1941, the Court recognized this, upholding Congress' right to prevent fraud in a primary election for congressional representatives, and conceding that primaries are elections in the constitutional sense. Then in 1944 the White Primary question once more reached the Court (*Smith* v. *Allwright*). Texas had barred Negroes from participation in the Democratic primary by the simple expedient of denying them party membership. Indeed the membership resolution here drawn in question was the same one upheld in 1935. Now, however, the Court was in a different mood, and the recognition that primaries were elections had made the *Grovey* doctrine seem all the more anomalous. The judges therefore held that the action of the party was constitutionally forbidden, because the association between state and party stamped the party's doings as state action:

> If the state requires a certain election procedure, prescribes a general election ballot made up of party nominees so chosen and limits the choice of the electorate in general elections for state offices, practically speaking, to those whose names appear on such a ballot, it endorses, adopts and enforces the discrimination against Negroes, practiced by a party entrusted by Texas law with the determination of the qualifications of participants in the primary. This is state action within the meaning of the Fifteenth Amendment.

In other words, the mere fact that the state makes use of the primary results brings the primary procedures within the scope of the Constitution. In the face of this reasoning it became impossible to devise a White Primary arrangement that would not be technically unconstitutional, and the Court made it clear in subsequent decisions that the Fifteenth Amendment "nullifies sophisticated as well as simple-minded modes of discrimination." To be sure, the Court alone could not insure Negroes access to the ballot box; discriminatory administrative practices and the tactics of terror are not always within judicial reach. But the Court had done its part to preserve the idea that the United States is a constitutional democracy.

While these decisions in themselves did not solve the problem of racial disfranchisement, they helped stimulate a movement in that direction, and Negro voting substantially increased in southern states after *Smith* v. *Allwright*. The white Southern reaction was far from joyful of course, but neither was it in general militantly antagonistic to the Court. The truth is that the new doctrine was hard to criticize without challenging the Constitution itself, and the habit of venerating that document was strong. The Constitution does after all enjoin equality in the election process; and no person could rationally deny that the White Primary abridged voting equality. The Constitution and reason were on the judges' side, and these were potent allies.

A similar point can be made concerning *Missouri* v. *Canada* and the question of educational segregation. Not even Justice McReynolds, who dissented in the *Missouri* case, could contend that the state was granting the colored applicant equality of treatment. The best he could offer was his argument that the state had made a "fair effort" to do so. The majority could serenely answer that the Constitution required not efforts but results.

This continued for some time to be the Court's answer. The equality requirement was progressively tightened notch after notch, though segregation itself was not yet queried. In 1950, it was held that Texas had violated the equal protection clause when it denied a Negro entrance to the University of Texas, even though a separate law school for Negroes had been established. The separate school, said the Court unanimously, was not equal to the University of Texas "in those qualities which are incapable of objective measurement but which make for greatness in a law school." By logical extension this opinion certainly condemned all segregation in public professional schools and probably colleges as well. Indeed it can be argued that public school segregation of any kind was inferentially outlawed by the decision. But the Court itself did not draw the inference; it merely decided the instant case. And again, as in the White Primary Case, its position was rationally powerful. For equality *is* constitutionally commanded, and no fair observer could believe that the special Negro school matched the University of Texas.

However, the judges were continually being pressed, by liberal commentators, by counsel, and no doubt by their own consciences, to take the further step of declaring explicitly that segregation per se violated the equal protection clause. And in 1954, they did so, again speaking unanimously. The opinion of Chief Justice Warren was to be, as all members of the Court surely knew, a state paper of enormous importance; inevitably it would be exposed to the most searching criticism. Yet it does not seem in perspective to have been very well thought out. The Chief Justice was forced to admit that the historical intent of the Amendment's framers was inconclusive on the specific question of segregation. He was compelled to reject the contention that the *Plessy* doctrine was currently binding. But he might have made out a strong argument that the framers intended to create an elastic general standard, which could alter and grow with the times; and this argument would help to justify a Court interpretation based on conditions in 1954 rather than 1868. Further, the opinion might have claimed powerful support in precedent both before and after *Plessy*, and thereby undermined in advance the criticism that the decision "was sheer judicial legislation."

Instead the Chief Justice chose to go, almost without preliminary, to the question of whether segregation necessarily involved inequality in contemporary America and to rest his affirmative answer heavily on psychological and sociological literature. If one of the aims of a judicial opinion is to persuade the persuadable, this selection of citations was, to say the least, uninspired. The decision called for the argumentative talents of Marshall and Story rolled into one, and that ideal is rather a lot to hope for. But it is not unfair to wish that the opinion had come a little closer to it.

However, the impact of the opinion, whatever its deficiencies, was not to be mistaken. "Separate facilities are inherently unequal." For the time being the judges postponed any judgment about how the decision should be implemented, but a year later the lower federal courts were ordered to fashion their desegregation decrees in the light of the principles that guide the law of equity (that is, flexibility in the shaping of remedies and due consideration for the problem of adjusting public and private needs). Although this order was obviously designed to permit the states some leeway, the Court was undeviating in its insistence that the states concerned must make "a prompt and reasonable start" toward desegregation and that "the vitality of these constitutional principles cannot be allowed to yield simply because of disagreement with them."

The reaction of the white South to this judicial onslaught on its institutions was noisy and stubborn. Certain "border states," which had formerly maintained segregated school systems, did integrate, and others permitted the token admission of a few Negro students to schools that had once been racially unmixed. However, the Deep South made no moves to obey the judicial command, and in some districts there can be no doubt that the Desegregation decision hardened resistance to integration proposals. The moral support of the President, which might have helped to muster obedience, was accorded too grudgingly and tardily to do much good. The situation settled down into a quasi-stalemate in which the Court steadily reiterated its doctrine as specific cases arose, and the South passionately vowed that it would never yield. The decision had done much good and no doubt some harm. Whether it would ultimately achieve the moral end it contemplated was a question locked, in Justice Story's words, "in the inscrutable purposes of Providence."

The final effect on the judiciary of the decision's backlash is also a matter for conjecture. For the southern foes of the Desegregation doctrine were not content with passive resistance; they mounted a counterattack against the Court. At first the attack was largely rhetorical: the Calhounian slogan of "interposition" was heard in the land once more, with states earnestly proclaiming their sovereignty and impeaching the nation's, as if *Cohens* v. *Virginia* had never been decided and the Civil War never fought. This kind of thing was no cause for perturbation except among those who were already perturbed.

But then, ironically, the Court itself provided an element that made the situation more serious. In 1956 and 1957 it handed down a group of decisions hopefully calculated to moderate the venom of certain "antisubversive" measures. These judicial pronouncements have been touched on earlier in this chapter and their general drift described. They manifestly were not direct challenges of government's power to deal with subversion. The emphasis was on statutory interpretation and procedural caveats throughout. But they furnished the necessary ingredient for an alliance between Southern segregationists and Northerners fearful of domestic subversion and made it possible to shift the attack on the Court from the realm of mere polemics to the much more dangerous arena of Congress. The judgments in the subversive field were catechized as denying the nation the right of self-preservation and Congress the right to function as a co-ordinate branch of government; and the fact that these charges were wildly incongruous with the actual decisions was conveniently ignored. Southerners who frankly favored segregation and Northerners who welcomed a pretext to join them, eagerly supported proposals to "curb" the Court by modifying its appellate jurisdiction.

If the Courts of John Marshall and Morrison R. Waite could have been on hand to observe this development and the twenty-odd years of constitutional history that preceded it, they might well have experienced the shock of recognition. They, too, had been faced by the problem of enforcing a value system that was still a subject of popular controversy. Like the judges of the modern era, they had taken up constitutional clauses of vague and seemingly limited content and had shaped them into the tools of a new jurisprudence. They, too, had struggled to evolve a role for the Court that was adequate to the tasks it faced, yet not beyond its capacities. They, too, had seen the Court assailed and defended for its acts and its failures to act. They, too, were often reminded, as the modern Court has been, that the Constitution's meaning is never quite settled, that the judicial tasks can never be quite done, that the ordeal of self-appraisal is never quite over, and that the challenges to the Court's authority can never quite be stilled. These are the prices that they paid—and the modern judges pay—for maintaining a tribunal that is a vital factor in the American political system.

EIGHT

CIVIL LIBERTIES, CIVIL RIGHTS, AND THE SUPREME COURT

s ROBERT McCLOSKEY finished his book in 1958, he could reasonably believe that the Court—with some dramatic exceptions
such as the Steel Seizure and School Segregation Cases—had indeed learned the lesson he believed taught by history: The Court max-
imized its impact on the actualities of American life by limiting itself to
relatively modest efforts of refining (according to the Court's scheme of
values) the course that history was taking. Should, however, the Court
instead engage in sweeping programmatic pronouncements designed to
fend off powerful political currents, thereby keeping them tightly chan-
neled within the Court's conception of a proper course, it would only
make trouble for itself—especially if the judicially constructed levees
were breached by a floodtide of popular discontent over the Court's
clumsy attempts to thwart popular will. Such opposition, even if generated by dismay over one particular case, could ultimately lead to more
general attacks on the Court's role as the instantiation of constitutionalism and on the rule of law itself. And McCloskey, for all of his criticism
of the Court's past performance, undeniably viewed the Court as a vital
actor in the epic of constitutionalism.

The two cases mentioned, however dramatic, could even, with some
effort, be shoehorned to fit his thesis: The Steel Seizure Case was in many
ways a "one-time-only" decision; it struck down the action of a notably
unpopular President, who would most certainly not defy the Court, and
it required no reshaping of American political institutions or even significant modification of received doctrine. Moreover, even with regard to
civil rights, it is important to recognize that the Court was building on developments already occurring within American society. President Harry

Truman had, after all, displayed great courage in ordering, against the opposition of many military leaders, the desegregation of the armed forces in 1948; he gained his memorable re-election that year in part by running on a civil rights platform strong enough to compel then-Democratic Governor Strom Thurmond of South Carolina to bolt the party and run an independent campaign for the Presidency as a Dixiecrat. Nor should one underestimate the importance of Jackie Robinson's (and others') integration of America's "national pastime," baseball, in the late 1940's and early 1950's. Finally, one should note that Southern segregation was an international embarrassment in the cold war being entered into with the Soviet Union and its allies, who pointed up the unjust treatment of African-Americans whenever Western anticommunists criticized what was happening in Eastern Europe. In its brief to the Court in *Brown*, the United States explicitly brought up "the problem of racial discrimination . . . in the context of the present world struggle between freedom and tyranny" and noted segregation's "adverse effect" on America's winning that struggle. And the Court was surely aware that both the Truman and Eisenhower administrations supported the claims of the plaintiffs in *Brown*. (The latter support reflected more the strong commitments of Eisenhower's Attorney General, Herbert Brownell of New York, than of Ike himself, who had private doubts about desegregation, though this was not publicly known at the time.)

As for *Brown* itself, the Court in 1954 deferred any decision as to remedy and declared in 1955 that "all deliberate speed" would be its operative decision rule. Moreover, it placed implementation of this rule in the hands of federal district judges, who, after all, owed their appointments to close association with the senators from their home states—and were thus unlikely to be far in advance of the dominant political culture. In announcing that the traditional mores of the South would have to change, albeit with less than lightning speed, the Court could easily imagine itself as applying increasingly accepted national norms to what could be dismissed as a "deviant" part of the country. When all is said and done, though, the Court can be seen as having accepted a rather modest conception of its own role in bringing about the necessary changes; as shall be seen in the next chapter, astonishingly little change of behavior took place in the states of the old Confederacy between 1954 and 1960, and the Court gave little sign of genuinely trying to transform this situation.

By 1965, however, McCloskey would write that "the Court of the past dozen years has developed judicial activism to a degree that at least matches the record of the Old Court of the 1920's and 1930's and that certainly exceeds the record of any other Court in our constitutional history." More particularly, he described the four-year period between 1961 and 1965 "as one of the most creative and daring periods in constitutional history," during which "the remarkable extent of the Warren Court's will to govern bec[ame] fully manifest." Whatever lessons of history it was purporting to follow were surely different from those elaborated in the earlier part of this book, and McCloskey concluded his 1965 article by wondering if the American people genuinely had "a so-far unsatiated appetite for government by judiciary." It is not so much that the Supreme Court had taken on a dramatically new role—its primary concern at this period continued to be civil liberties and civil rights—as that it displayed a willingness to confront a host of important issues head-on and become, in important ways, a significant agenda setter for domestic policy.

It is crucial to note that McCloskey dated the rise of "Warren Court" activism at 1961, though Earl Warren, of course, had come to the Court in 1954. Warren's replacement of Fred Vinson clearly made *some* difference to the Court prior to 1961, but it would not be an easy matter to specify it. Some believe that Warren's personal skills helped to account for the crucial achievement of unanimity in *Brown;* others point to his providing the fifth vote in some liberal civil liberties decisions in the mid-1950's. But, as McCloskey pointed out, the Court had scarcely struck out in systematically bold new courses by the end of the 1950's, and it quickly seemed to retreat from its foray into protecting the civil liberties of Communists. Although it would have been a mistake to view the Court circa 1960 as a mere tabby cat, it would have been a far greater error to have confused it with a tiger.

What happened to change the perception? One might point to changes of membership: By 1962 Byron White and Arthur Goldberg had been appointed by President John F. Kennedy to replace Charles Whittaker, a conservative nonentity, and Felix Frankfurter, the titan of judicial restraint. Both White and Goldberg (who had been active for many years as a lawyer for organized labor) were considerably more liberal than their predecessors. But, it should be said, Dwight Eisenhower's appointees, save for Whittaker, had not been particularly conservative. Potter Stewart and John Marshall Harlan (grandson of the author of the immortal dissents in the *Civil Rights Cases* and *Plessy* v. *Ferguson*) were both relatively moderate—indeed, from the perspective of the post-Reagan Republican Party, extremely liberal—Republicans. And one of Ike's picks, William J. Brennan, was a New Jersey Democrat appointed late in the 1956 election campaign in an effort to appeal to Northeastern Catholics; he proved to be the anchor for the next thirty years of the liberal coalition within the Court. (It would not be much of an exaggeration to label the Court between 1958 and, say, 1983 "the Brennan Court" in recognition of his import, which was far greater, practically speaking, than that of either of the two Chief Justices, Earl Warren and Warren Burger, who served during that period.)

But the Court, of course, is embedded within a wider political context. In addition to the examples offered above of significant postwar developments, one can scarcely ignore the fact of Kennedy's election itself. To the astonishment of many, the American electorate had been willing to vote for a forty-two-year-old Roman Catholic from Massachusetts who had run on the theme that the United States must be ready to "move" toward bold new courses. Not the least important moment of the campaign—some commentators at the time ascribed his extraordinarily narrow victory to it—was a telephone call to the family of Martin Luther King, Jr., the leader of the Southern civil rights movement, expressing Kennedy's concern over King's having been arrested and jailed by Georgia authorities for participating in a civil rights demonstration. The country, however tenuously, seemed to endorse a liberal resurgence after the perceived quiescence of the 1950's, and the Supreme Court seemingly enlisted to do its part.

THE CIVIL RIGHTS MOVEMENT AND THE CONSTITUTION

The civil rights movement furnished many occasions for the Court to decide what role it wished to play in the struggle for racial justice. One form the movement took, for example, was "sitting in" at restaurants that refused to serve African-Americans. This action inevitably led to the arrest (and convictions in state courts) of both African-Americans and their white allies for violating the property rights of the affected restaurant owners. Would the Court uphold these convictions against constitutional challenge? Or would it interpret the Fourteenth Amendment as barring them because the property owners were so clearly trying to use the state to reinforce their own racially discriminatory policies? (By this point, it was clearly unconstitutional for states to *require* segregated service; the question was whether states could enforce the ostensibly private wishes of restaurant operators to exclude racially "inappropriate" parties from their property.) In a series of decisions from 1961 to 1964, the Court re-

versed all such convictions on a variety of increasingly strained technicalities, even as it resolutely avoided coming to any clear decision on the basic underlying issue.

Congress, by breaking a months-long Southern filibuster and passing
the Civil Rights Act of 1964, which outlawed racial discrimination in
restaurants and other public accommodations, relieved the Court of having to decide this most delicate issue of constitutional law—and to run
the political risk of yet another spate of headlines throughout the South
about overruling an eighty-year-old precedent like the *Civil Rights Cases,*
which had seemingly placed beyond federal power such "private" decisions as those of the restaurant owners. Indeed, many Southerners, led by
Senator Sam Ervin of North Carolina, argued that Congress lacked the
power to pass the Civil Rights Act because it was not the genuine "regulation of commerce" that its supporters described it as being. When, however, the Act came before the Court within months after its passage, in
Katzenbach v. *McClung,* it was unanimously upheld as well within the
post-1937 understanding of Congress' wide expanse of power under the
commerce clause. The *Civil Rights Cases,* though neither mentioned nor
overruled, were treated as a dead letter for all practical purposes, though
some liberal commentators continued to criticize both Congress and the
Court for treating the fight against racial discrimination as an issue of
"commerce" rather than as a long-overdue effort by Congress to assure
the full measure of "equal protection" (and equal citizenship) promised
by the Fourteenth Amendment.

Indeed, given the general thrust in this and the next chapter on the
"activist" role of the Warren Court, it is worth emphasizing that in some
important respects, it should also be understood as almost "hyperdefer-
ential" with regard to congressional legislation. This is clearly manifested
in its decisions upholding the Civil Rights Act. Most legal observers drew
from those cases (which rested, of course, on the post-1937 repudiation
of the earlier, more constrained, reading of the Commerce Clause) the lesson that, in effect, Congress could do whatever it wished so long as there
was the slightest connection with interstate commerce *and* the legislation
in question did not limit rights protected against governmental interference. Even more dramatic, in this context, was another case involving
Nicholas Katzenbach in his role as Attorney General. In *Katzenbach* v.
Morgan (1966), the Court upheld Congress's power to outlaw English-
language literacy tests as a precondition for voting (at least for Spanish
speakers who had been educated in Puerto Rico) even though there is
no reason to believe that the Court itself would have struck down New

York's law had it been challenged in a standard-form Equal Protection Case. Both of the *Katzenbach* cases were distinguished by the Court's citation of Marshall's opinion in *McCulloch* v. *Maryland* and its capacious reading of congressional power under the "necessary and proper" clause. (Within five years, the Court allowed Congress to ban *any* literacy tests as a prerequisite for the vote, even though the Court in 1957 had unanimously upheld the constitutionality of such tests.) Such legislation represented—as is true, of course, of the Civil Rights Act itself—the triumphant moment of the civil rights movement, a triumph reflected in the actions of all branches of the national government.

Exemplary of the Court's willingness to forge new doctrines as affirmative response to the civil rights movement of the 1960's was *New York Times* v. *Sullivan* (1964), in which the Court had to consider the constitutionality of a $500,000 damage award to the supervisor of the Montgomery, Alabama, police. The damages were assessed by an all-white state-court jury against the *New York Times* for its having published an advertisement that had concededly contained some errors about the commissioner's efforts to stymie the local civil rights movement. Sullivan claimed that relatively minor errors in the advertisement's narrative harmed his reputation (a wildly implausible notion, unless one assumes that Montgomery's white denizens were in fact supportive of the civil rights movement); Alabama, like many states, allowed juries to find newspapers liable for damages on proof of error alone. Not even "negligence" needed to be demonstrated. That truth was always a winning defense was irrelevant, for the problem was that errors had in fact been published.

The Court unanimously reversed the Alabama jury. Justice Brennan wrote an opinion for the majority that envisioned the First Amendment as providing breathing space for "uninhibited, robust, and wide open" public debate, thereby requiring the legal protection even of erroneous statements—especially those regarding "public officials." Indeed, Brennan analogized the situation to old attempts to punish sedition—criticism of governmental officials—and he declared that the First Amendment simply prohibited any punishment for seditious speech. Thus, according to the majority, a newspaper could be liable for misstatements involving public officials only if they were published "knowingly" or in "reckless disregard" of the possibility of their being false. Otherwise, the newspaper would be free from liability. Justices Hugo Black and William O. Douglas would have gone further and freed media from liability under any and all conditions, including the knowing publication of harmful lies. Subsequently, in the context of an Associated Press report on the riot over

James Meredith's admission to the University of Mississippi (in which two people died and federal troops were called out), the Court extended the "*New York Times* rule" to "public figures"—government officials or otherwise.

It is, of course, possible that the Court would have gone down this path had the *Times* been found liable by a New York jury after mistakenly reporting that the local parking commissioner had engaged in financial misdealing. But it seems impossible to understand *Sullivan* without acknowledging its origin within the context of the civil rights movement, surely the most important (and inspiring) domestic social struggle since at least the great union organizing drives of the 1930's. Moreover, the particular case considered in *Sullivan* was simply the tip of an iceberg. At the time the Supreme Court heard it, libel claims totaling more than $300 million (the equivalent of at least $1 billion today) had been brought by white Southerners against various, almost always Northern, media. Local juries, invariably all white, seemed more than happy to send a message to the interloping media that they entered the Southern states at their peril, with bankruptcy a possible result of any misstep, however innocent.

Clearly, the media needed protection, and the Court provided it, to the great applause of liberals in general and newspapers in particular. In later decades, newspapers would complain that the *New York Times* test still allowed too much extremely expensive litigation in contrast to the more "absolutist" approach of Justices Black and Douglas, which would have eliminated the libel action entirely. Victims of media misrepresentation, on the other hand, claimed that the Court had in effect licensed the news media to be careless in checking facts, with the price of such carelessness being paid by those falsely portrayed. Both sides are correct.

THE SUPREME COURT AND FREEDOM OF SPEECH

New York Times was only one among many cases of the 1960's that tested the resolve of the Court to protect unpopular dissenters from conventional norms. As the typical defendant shifted from being a member of the Communist Party—the norm during the late 1940's and the 1950's—to a civil rights activist, whether African-American or white, the Court was far more willing to protect what local authorities deemed "subversive" speech. Indeed, by 1969, in *Brandenburg* v. *Ohio,* a case involving, ironically enough, a member of the Ku Klux Klan, the Court delivered the most speech-protective opinion in American history. It held that a speaker could be punished only if (a) he was inciting an audience to commit an unlawful act *and* (b) there was in fact an "imminent likelihood" that the act would be committed by the affected audience. This test has survived the significant changes of membership throughout the intervening decades, and in the quarter century since *Brandenburg* there were no prosecutions similar in character to the *Debs* and *Dennis* cases that blighted earlier periods of American history.

The Court was also willing, by and large, to turn "freedom of speech" into a more general "freedom of expression." For example, it protected the wearing of a black armband by a high-school student in protest of the Vietnam War. Even more dramatic, perhaps, was its 1971 decision, *Cohen v. California,* which upheld Paul Cohen's right to wear in a courthouse a jacket with "Fuck the Draft" on its back. Ironically enough, Justice Black dissented in both cases, claiming that neither genuinely involved "speech." The Court did not, however, extend its protection to David O'Brien's burning his draft card in protest of the Vietnam War; it upheld a conviction under a statute rushed through an angry Congress that wished to suppress draft-card burning as a form of dissent.

Later Courts, even when dominated by political conservatives, would continue to be relatively protective of unpopular "expression" in general. Thus the Court in 1989 and 1990 struck down Texas and federal laws, respectively, that in effect barred the burning of an American flag as a form of protest. Although the liberal Justice Brennan wrote the decisions in both cases, he was joined by the arch-conservative Justice Antonin Scalia, who adopted Justice Black's view that the First Amendment really did mean, with almost no exceptions, that "no law" could legitimately criminalize speech. Scalia, unlike Black, was quite willing to agree that "speech" included a great deal of "expression" of ideas. He thus wrote a majority opinion in a 1992 case, *R.A.V. v. St. Paul,* that involved the punishment, under an "offensive conduct" ordinance, of someone who burned a cross across the street from the home of an African-American in St. Paul, Minnesota. Reversing the conviction, Scalia held that St. Paul simply had no power to decide which forms of expression were offensive to the population.

The Court also proved far more willing to protect a variety of "nonpolitical" speech that had traditionally been given far less protection than "political speech" directed at public issues. For example, although the Court had in 1957 held that "obscene" speech was totally unprotected by the First Amendment, it also stated that sex was not synonymous with obscenity, thus undermining the basis of existing obscenity law. A number of decisions in the 1960's offered protection to literature and movies, deemed pornographic by authorities, if the material in question—however sexually explicit—had at least some "redeeming social value." Later decisions in the 1970's would offer communities somewhat more leeway in regulating pornography. Relative to the legal standards prior to the Warren-Brennan years, however, communities remained vastly more constrained than before in regulating sexually explicit material. For better or worse, such material would become far more easily available than it had been in earlier years. One should be wary, though, of giving too much credit (or blame) to the Court: The United States as a whole was undergoing what many described as a "sexual revolution," and the Court could scarcely have stopped it even if it wanted to. Nonetheless, at key moments of the "revolution" during the 1960's, the Court appeared to ally itself with the partisans of new sexual freedom against the denizens of more traditionally repressive culture. (It is worth noting, though, that Chief Justice Warren, the father of five daughters, was notably less eager to offer legal protection to sexually explicit materials, so it may be especially unfair to identify such protection with the "Warren Court.")

Similar latitude was revealed by the Court with regard to advertising, another area of traditionally regulated speech. In 1942, the Court almost casually dismissed the claim that "commercial speech" was protected by the First Amendment. By 1976, however, it would find such speech protected, even if somewhat less so than core "political speech." That is, whereas both the *Brandenburg* and *New York Times* tests allowed regulating political speech only in extreme circumstances, the state could prohibit false advertising entirely and could subject even accurate advertisements to significant constraints. But "unreasonable" regulations were now regularly struck down by the Court. As a consequence, for the first time in American history major businesses became warm partisans of the First Amendment. This was no small development inasmuch as many of the decisions of the post-1937 Court in general, and the Warren-Brennan Court in particular, had cost it the support of its traditional allies within the economic elite.

By the 1970's the major focus of "free speech" litigation had shifted away from the unpopular dissenters who had been the subjects of classic earlier cases. Three issues now predominated: the financing of political campaigns; the regulation of nonprint media; and access to public property to convey one's views.

In the aftermath of the Watergate scandal, triggered by abuses in the re-election campaign of Richard Nixon in 1972, Congress amended existing campaign finance laws to limit the amounts that could be contributed to, or spent by, political campaigns. In addition, presidential campaigns would, for the first time in American history, be eligible for public funds. The Court considered these new regulations in *Buckley* v. *Valeo* (1976) and made absolute hash of the legislation. A majority of justices held first that spending money on speech is the constitutional equivalent of speech itself and therefore protected by the First Amendment. Shifting majorities of justices, who could not agree on a single majority opinion, treated other aspects of the 1974 legislation quite differently. Thus the contribution limits were upheld, though the spending limits were struck down. Finally, it upheld a public-financing scheme for presidential elections that patently discriminated in favor of the established Democratic and Republican parties (by paying them in advance of the elections) and against third parties (who had to gain at least 5 percent of the national vote before being compensated for any of their expenditures in the course of the campaign). One consequence of the Court's decision was that millionaires, constitutionally protected in unlimited spending on their own campaigns, were given significant advantages over less wealthy opponents. And, of course, the existing two parties were given a major hedge against possible third-party competition—unless the third party was headed by someone like the Texas billionaire Ross Perot who had no need to garner contributions in order to run for office.

One should be wary of overestimating the influence of any given Supreme Court decision, including *Buckley*. It is hard, nonetheless, to avoid blaming this decision—which in effect established a system of electoral finance law that never received the formal support of even a single legislator—for the increasing prominence of many unusually wealthy candidates who swamped less affluent opponents, not to mention the disgust expressed by nonwealthy candidates over the increasing amount of time they had to spend raising money in self-defense. The role of money in politics is a basic issue of democratic politics. It is impossible to view the Court as having contributed to any kind of cogent resolution of the problem in *Buckley* or a variety of subsequent decisions—sometimes upholding regulations, sometimes striking them down—that constitute our contemporary crazy quilt of election regulation. One might be especially dubious of the Court's particular competence to speak cogently to the issue inasmuch as none of the justices on the Court in 1976—and only one appointed since then, Sandra Day O'Connor—had any kind of experience themselves as candidates running for elective office before appointment (and O'Connor's was limited to being elected to the Arizona state legislature).

A new day is definitely dawning at the Court, though only by one vote. Many observers were surprised by *Nixon* v. *Shrink Missouri Government PAC* (2000), in which six justices upheld state legislation that significantly limited the contributions one could make to a political campaign. Justice Souter's opinion almost seemed to invite further litigation devoted to reopening the entire *Buckley* framework in the direction of allowing further regulation. Justice Kennedy, in dissent, seemed no happier with *Buckley*, writing that "*Buckley* has not worked" and that it has "created a misshapen system." The three dissenters all called for the overruling of *Buckley*.

The Court's current stance with regard to campaign finance was fully tested by Congress's passage in 2002 of the so-called McCain-Feingold bill (tellingly titled the "Bipartisan Campaign Reform Act") that puts significant new limits on the financing of elections. The Court recognized the practical importance of the issues raised by holding an extremely rare special term in September 2003—the Court usually begins its yearly term on the first Monday in October—in order to allow copious argument regarding an elephantine 1800-page decision from the court below that had upheld and struck down various parts of the legislation. In December 2003, the Court delivered its own almost 300-page opinion in *McConnell* v. *Federal Election Commission*. Or, more accurately, several opinions, dealing with different parts of the statute, were issued. Most important was the upholding, by a five-to-four vote, of rigorous prohibitions on "soft money" given to national, state, and local political parties that would (or at least might likely) be used to supplement "hard-money" contributions to political candidates themselves. Thus, for example, the Act prohibits state parties from using soft money to fund "get-out-the-vote" campaigns because that would redound to the benefit of the parties' national candidates; a similar analysis allowed the prohibition of soft-money-funded advertisements in behalf of the party's candidates for national office, even if they lack such "magic words" as "vote for" or "vote against" respective candidates. Equally significant (and, from the view of traditional civil libertarians, an even greater incursion on free speech) was the Court's upholding bans within thirty days of primaries and sixty days of the general election of certain kinds of televised "electioneering communications"; these bans extended to such incorporated interest groups as the National Rifle Association and the American Civil Liberties Union (which joined, along with many other similar groups, in challenging the law).

It is not clear, as a practical matter, how important *McConnell* will turn out to be. Early predictions are that it will further weaken the institutional role of political parties and, because of the limitations on incorporated groups, increase the importance of newspapers and other media, as well as of wealthy individuals like the billionaire George Soros, who has pledged to spend many millions of his own dollars to try to defeat George Bush in the 2004 election. One might also predict that groups like the NRA or the Sierra Club will increasingly claim that their "newsletters" are in fact "newspapers" entitled to the same freedoms to take positions on political candidates right before election day that are possessed by, say, the *New York Times* or *Wall Street Journal*. Finally, one can anticipate that celebrities will become ever more important as potential candidates inasmuch as the very definition of "celebrity" is the enjoyment of wide name recognition that can serve to "swamp" unknown candidates who would have to engage in expensive advertising in order to make themselves known to the public.

What is clear is that the Court remains sharply divided on the major issues; the dissenters in *McConnell* described the majority opinions as constituting a full-scale assault on traditional notions of the First Amendment. Just as importantly, money is very likely to continue to structure the actualities of American politics. George W. Bush had by the end of 2003 amassed over $110 million of hard-money funds for his reelection drive, and both Howard Dean, the Democratic front-runner at the time and Senator John Kerry, the subsequent front-runner, had announced that they would, like Bush in both 2000 and 2004, renounce federally provided campaign funds that would have required them to accept spending limits for their campaigns. *McConnell,* though extremely long, will not be the last word in a debate that goes to the very heart of what it means to call the United States a functioning democracy. (See also the discussion later in this chapter about the implications of politically partisan gerrymandering of legislative districts, the key topic of a case that was decided in 2004.) The majority opinions are replete with language referring to the reasonableness of Congress's believing that soft-money contributions "give rise to corruption and the appearance of corruption." The majority opinions also state that the Court should substantially defer to the judgment of Congress as to what is necessary to forestall such realities (and appearances), though some might regard it as naïve to believe that Congress and the President, the beneficiaries of the present system, are likely to pass effective legislation that will genuinely stop this "corruption." What is even more certain is that the Court itself can do very little to help, at least with regard to campaign financing. (Gerrymandering might be another matter.) Its role in this area is almost completely *reactive* to proposals made by other branches of government rather than *proactive* in initiating change on its own.

As *New York Times* v. *Sullivan* itself revealed, the print media were a special object of solicitude of the Court. But what about the increasingly important nonprint media, including radio and television? The Federal Communications Act of 1934, one of the basic New Deal regulatory measures, authorized the Federal Communications Commission to regulate the electronic media—which at that time, of course, consisted only of radio—in the "public interest." This led fairly rapidly to FCC requirements of "fairness" in programming, including a "right to reply" by persons who had been criticized in a program. Moreover, stations were required to provide "equal time" to all other candidates for a political office if they gave any time (excluding news coverage) to one of the candidates.

The first major test of such requirements took place only in 1969. *Red Lion Broadcasting Co.* v. *FCC* challenged the order by the federal agency that a religiously conservative radio station offer a "right to reply" to a secular liberal who had been accused of "communist affiliations." A unanimous Court (though the libertarian Justice Douglas did not participate in the decision), which implicitly recognized the illegitimacy of any such regulation if applied to newspapers, nevertheless upheld the FCC. (Indeed, in the 1974 *Tornillo* case, the Court unanimously struck down a Florida "right-to-reply" law that applied to newspapers.) The Court focused on the alleged "scarcity" of places on the electromagnetic spectrum used by radio and television stations. Although it has been justifiably subjected to withering criticism—most cities have far more radio and television outlets than newspapers—it has never repudiated *Red Lion*.

During the Reagan-Bush era, the FCC itself rejected *Red Lion*'s view of its own powers and declared that "fairness" and "right-to-reply" rules violated the First Amendment. Even though the Clinton Administration indicated its desire to reinstate some of these regulations, it never actually did so; consequently, the Court has not had the opportunity to revisit the issue. What this demonstrates, among other things, is that other branches of government sometimes feel free to come to their own conclusions as to what the Constitution requires. If they believe that the Constitution permits more regulation than the Court has allowed, judicial tests will inevitably (and quickly) follow. When, however, as here, the determination is that the Constitution allows *less* regulation, then it may be considerably more difficult to generate litigation.

Moreover, the "cable revolution" and, more recently, the remarkable development of the Internet, with its "information highway," have exploded completely any neat distinctions between "print" and "nonprint" media, as more and more newspapers and magazines make their stories freely available over the Net. Can the *New York Times* really receive greater protection for its hard-copy version than for the one distributed over the Internet? As for cable television, the principal controversy has involved "must carry" rules, in which Congress has required cable companies to provide channels to carry all locally originated television signals within their community. (Newspapers could presumably not be required to carry columnists that their editors and owners deemed unworthy of presentation.) In cases involving the Turner Broadcasting Company, a highly fragmented Supreme Court upheld such rules. Justice Souter, in particular, wrote a concurring opinion cautioning his colleagues against moving too quickly to decide issues involving such a rapidly developing area as the electronic media.

The principal Internet decision so far is *ACLU* v. *Reno* (1997): The Court, by a five-to-four vote, struck down a federal law that attempted to limit the availability of sexually explicit (but not legally pornographic) material on the Net. Because the law was couched as a means of protecting children against easy access to objectionable material—and because in fact it *is* probably far easier for a computer-literate child to find such sites than to find comparable material at newsstands or libraries—the issue remains very much on the political agenda, and the Court will have additional opportunities to consider the question as Congress passes new legislation attempting to regulate the Internet. Indeed, a 2002 decision allowed Congress to condition federal aid on libraries installing certain filters on their computers that endeavor to prevent children from logging on to sexually explicit sites.

The Court this past century has tended to be far more protective of "old" media than new (which helps to explain the print media–electronic media distinction), even as members of upcoming generations find the alleged distinctions between "old" and "new" media to be unpersuasive. It is therefore premature to place substantial bets on what the Court will be saying even ten years from now, when Presidents will almost undoubtedly have the opportunity to make several new appointments to replace septuagenarian justices who came to adulthood before anyone envisioned the personal computer, let alone the Internet.

The final issue on the contemporary free-speech docket of the Court involves the state's power "indirectly" to regulate speech through exertion of its power as a property owner. Several cases in the 1960's, during the heyday of the civil rights movement, had protected civil rights demonstrations occurring even in such venues as public libraries (it was a *very* quiet demonstration!). Building on decisions going back to 1939, the Court seemed to be on the verge of placing a significant burden of proof on the state to justify prohibitory regulation of speech on public property. In the absence of such justification, some justices suggested, citizens were entitled access to the property in question. Indeed, in the 1968 *Logan Valley* case involving the prosecution for trespass of union leafleteers within a privately owned shopping mall, the Court described the malls as performing basically "public" functions and thus controlled by the First Amendment, which in turn protected the leafleteers against prosecution. (Justice Black wrote the dissent, describing the decision as an assault on the rights of private property.)

Once again, however, the Court backtracked. It increasingly accepted governmental arguments that "public" ownership of property did not amount to a right of members of the public to use it as a "public forum" for unregulated speech. The Court distinguished between "traditional" public forums, such as public parks and streets, and others such as post offices, airline terminals, military bases, and the like. The state was given far more latitude regarding the latter than the former. Similarly, the Court by 1972 limited and in 1976 flatly overruled *Logan Valley*, and it has subsequently offered no succor to anyone seeking access to private property. (It did, however, uphold a California state supreme court decision that granted such access under the *state* constitution against the claim of a shopping mall owner that it violated his constitutionally protected property right to exclude anyone whose major purpose in being at the shopping center was something other than shopping.) Some critics charged that the Court's decisions after 1970 signified that it was willing to protect more and more speech in fewer and fewer places.

THE COURT CONFRONTS THE CRIMINAL JUSTICE SYSTEM

Many of these preceding cases illustrate, among other things, the extent to which the Warren-Brennan Court was a *nationalist* body, exhibiting relatively little respect for states' decisions on conducting their affairs. As noted earlier, this did not differentiate the Court significantly from the Democratic Congresses that reflected the new moods revealed in the 1960 election of Kennedy and, even more so, Lyndon Johnson's landslide triumph in 1964. Almost all of the "activist" decisions of the Court involved the invalidation of *state* legislation and the attempt to create (or impose) more monolithic values and procedures upon what were often perceived as "backward" states.

To be sure, much of this disdain for "states'-rights" arguments was triggered by the traditional use of such arguments to justify racial oppression or the harassment of those with unpopular political or cultural views. But Felix Frankfurter, among others, had insisted, even as he endorsed the constitutional power of Congress to pass sweeping legislation deemed necessary in the national interest, that the Court respect the values of localism and diversity that Federalism at its best could be said to protect. The Court would, during the 1960's, exhibit little respect for such points of view. Indeed, the Warren-Brennan Court was probably the most truly nationalist Court in American history—save, perhaps, for the Marshall Court in its first two decades, and there the nationalism often took the form of expansive rhetoric in cases dealing with what were rather modest exertions of national power. (*Gibbons* v. *Ogden,* for example, contains paragraphs that would be eagerly seized upon 110 years later by lawyers eager to justify the New Deal, but the actual federal legislation at issue in the case was the rather trivial licensing of vessels travelling along navigable rivers.) And, of course, Marshall himself, in *Barron* v. *Baltimore* (1833), had refused to read the Bill of Rights as applying to the states; only the national government, he held, was obligated to respect the rights found there.

As seen earlier, especially with reference to the First Amendment, this limitation was under attack, as provisions of the Bill of Rights were "incorporated" as part of the Fourteenth Amendment limitation on state autonomy. By and large, however, states remained free to run their criminal justice systems as they saw fit. Such state autonomy was not destined to last, and dramatic illustrations of the actively nationalist Court are provided by its decisions involving the procedures used by states in enforcing their criminal law. States were, as never before, subject to scrutiny regarding their practices of apprehending and convicting alleged criminals.

Between 1953 and 1960, the "Warren Court" had decided fifty-five cases testing these practices. It had upheld the states twenty times and ruled against them thirty-five times, indicating that even then, to paraphrase Bob Dylan, "the times, they were a'changin'." After all, in the five years before Earl Warren's arrival, the Court had decided only twelve of thirty-three claims against the state. But in the five years following 1960, the states would be successful only about 15 percent of the time: eleven times out of seventy-five cases. And far more important than the sheer numbers was the Court's abandonment of its practice of fact-bound, case-by-case scrutiny in favor of the enunciation of sharply defined rules designed to transform the practices of police departments and courts nationwide.

The principal vehicle of change was the "selective incorporation" of most of the criminal-procedure provisions of the Bill of Rights into the Fourteenth Amendment as a limit on the states. Hugo Black had lost the great battle of 1947 in the *Adamson* case, where he made the case for "full incorporation," but he won the more general war. In the spring of 1961, for example, came *Mapp* v. *Ohio,* in which the majority held that states that had seized evidence in violation of the Fourth Amendment would no longer be allowed to offer that evidence in trials, as allowed by a 1949 decision that "incorporated" the Amendment against the states, but, in effect, left it up to the state courts to determine the remedy for violation of the Amendment. Now, instead, state courts would have to follow the "exclusionary rule," which had operated against the federal government since 1914; this dramatically changed the formal rules of the criminal-law game in most of the states (though empirically oriented analysts questioned the actual extent to which the decision changed police practices). Two years later, in *Gideon* v. *Wainwright* (discussed at greater length in the next chapter), the Court ruled unanimously that due process required that indigent criminal defendants be supplied counsel by the state. No conviction resulting in a jail sentence could stand if the indigent was not represented by counsel. Similarly, the Fifth Amendment's protection against compulsory self-incrimination was applied to the states in *Malloy* v. *Hogan,* and prosecutors were later disallowed from even commenting to the jury about defendants' having not testified in their own defense.

Undoubtedly the most controversial decision was *Miranda* v. *Arizona* (1966), in which Chief Justice Warren, for a five-justice majority, held that anyone arrested had the right to be told that he was legally entitled to counsel and to remain silent and, therefore, had the right as well to refuse to answer any questions asked him by the police. A distinctive feature of *Miranda* was the Court's legislaturelike enunciation of a specific set of "*Miranda* warnings" that the police could literally copy on a card and read off to suspects. (Later research demonstrated that an astonishing number of Americans knew about *Miranda* from watching television police dramas.) The case served as a rallying point for conservatives who argued both that the Court was ignoring the legitimate needs of the police and that it had forgotten the difference between itself and a legislature. Indeed, Congress in 1968 passed legislation ostensibly modifying the

Miranda doctrine, but no Justice Department, whether Democrat or Republican, liberal or conservative, allowed United States Attorneys to invoke the legislation.

Then, in an exceedingly odd 1999 decision, the Fourth Circuit Court of Appeals on its own berated the federal prosecutor for ignoring the law and upheld its efficacy as a modification of *Miranda*. The Supreme Court could scarcely ignore the decision, and it indeed reviewed the Fourth Circuit decision. To the surprise of many observers, it reversed the Fourth Circuit in *Dickerson* v. *United States* (2000), in an opinion written by Chief Justice Rehnquist himself; for the first time, the *Miranda* rules were declared to be solidly based on constitutional requirements. It is worth noting that this review of an archetypal Warren Court decision was provoked by a very activist, very conservative federal appeals court, encouraged by the intervention of a conservative "public interest" legal organization, rather than by any public demand. As a matter of fact, most police departments have long since learned to live with *Miranda,* and few analysts believe that it makes a significant difference in the ability to ferret out crime (unlike, possibly, restrictions on police ability to "search and seize" evidence of crime, where, as then-Judge Benjamin Cardozo put it so memorably, an undoubtedly guilty "criminal goes free because the constable blundered"). The willingness of Rehnquist in effect to endorse *Miranda* may as much speak to its basic irrelevance as offer evidence of the Supreme Court's deep commitment to protecting the rights of criminal defendants.

The Warren Court undoubtedly read the Constitution more generously than did prior Courts in terms of the formal legal rights offered criminal defendants. In other ways, though, the Warren Court was scarcely generous to defendants. It refused, for example, to examine the extent to which continued reliance on monetary bail systems meant that those having insufficient economic resources would be kept in jail while wealthier defendants could purchase their freedom at least before trial and conviction. And several decisions in 1970 upheld the practice of "plea bargaining," which in effect allows the state to encourage (its detractors would say "force") criminal defendants to waive many of their constitutional rights in return for a lesser sentence than might be received after full trial and enjoyment of one's formal rights. The United States is unique among nations in its reliance on plea bargaining to dispose of criminal cases; more than 90 percent of all cases are settled in this manner. Not surprisingly, it is those who are most vulnerable to pressure who must in fact accept the state's offers.

Still, the perception of the Warren Court was that it was unduly solicitous to the rights of criminal defendants, and the specific beneficiaries of such decisions—the actual defendants whose convictions were reversed—scarcely had significant political clout that the Court could use in defending itself against its detractors. Indeed, many future presidential campaigns would be run against this aspect of the Warren Court legacy; although conservative Republicans were most eager to attack the Court, liberal Democrats were certainly not eager to offer public defenses of its criminal-justice legacy. It can occasion little surprise, then, that later Courts backtracked on legal rights accorded criminal defendants.

None of the decisions mentioned above was flatly overruled, however, with *Dickerson* being the most dramatic example of the formal continuity of Warren- and Rehnquist-Court doctrine. Instead, later Courts "distinguished" the facts of newer cases or, for example, allowed warrantless searches ordinarily disallowed by the exclusionary rule if the police in "good faith" believed that they were legal. The Reagan-Bush Supreme Court of the 1980's, led by Chief Justice William Rehnquist, also exhibited sometimes extraordinary activism in cutting down the practical ability of those convicted of criminal offenses to complain before federal courts that they had been deprived of their federal constitutional rights in trials that occurred in state courts. Rehnquist could counter, however, that the earlier Court had itself exhibited equal activism in welcoming defendants to federal courts.

But even the far more conservative Court of the 1980's was willing, on occasion, to forge relatively new paths. Thus it held, in *Batson* v. *Kentucky* (1986), that the ages-old practice of "peremptory challenges," by which prosecutors were allowed to keep a selected number of persons from jury impanelment without giving any reason at all, was subject to challenge at least where prosecutors used this power to get rid of all potential minority-group jurors in trials involving defendants of the given group. Within five years, the principle would be extended to defense attorneys as well as prosecutors (and, indeed, to civil as well as criminal trials), and it was no longer necessary that the jurors struck be the same race as the defendant. In 1994 the Court applied the same principle to gender, and it will undoubtedly have to address in the future whether lawyers will be allowed to eliminate potential jurors because of their religious affiliation, national origin, and other attributes that lawyers commonly use in selecting juries. As is so often the case, though, there were significant gaps between the vision of criminal justice articulated by the Court and the actualities found below. Thus all that *Batson* required was that prosecutors, in some circumstances, present "race-neutral" defenses for striking given persons from the jury. As a matter of fact, many courts were remarkably generous in regard to deeming explanations to have passed the *Batson* test, and the Supreme Court did almost nothing to rein in such generosity. It will take much more empirical study to determine whether *Batson* was anything more than an "expressive" decision by which the Court articulates the ideals of American constitutionalism without, however, being willing to devote genuine resources to the intense monitoring of other decision-making bodies actually charged with realizing (or hindering) the Court's vision.

During the 1960's, the Court also began to scrutinize the imposition of the death penalty; by 1972, five justices were willing, in *Furman* v. *Georgia,* to declare the procedures by which it was imposed unconstitutional (and Justices Brennan and Thurgood Marshall, in particular, denied that *any* procedure could legitimize the penalty). Many pronounced the death penalty in America to be at an end, thanks to the leadership of the Court. If, however, the Court believed that it was accurately reading the pulse of the public—as Justice Marshall claimed to be doing when he argued that capital punishment violated the norms of contemporary American culture—it was disastrously wrong. Many states passed new death penalty laws, and by 1976 the Court, almost as if consciously adopting a McCloskean approach, began to pull back significantly from its abolitionist posture and to get more in step with what was arguably the will of the energized political majority. Still, a majority in *Coker* v. *Georgia* (1977), by invalidating a death sentence imposed for rape, seemed to suggest that the death penalty was unconstitutional for any crime short of murder—though their emphasis in *Coker* that the victim was an "adult" left open the question whether death could be a constitutionally appropriate punishment for the rape of a juvenile. Although several states have in fact passed statutes imposing the death penalty for crimes other than murder—Louisiana, for example, would allow it for the rape of a child— the Court has not been presented with an actual case testing the current meaning of *Coker*. In this respect, at least, liberal abolitionists may have won a significant victory, even as they were otherwise routed.

With subsequent changes of membership, by the mid-1980's a firm majority of justices supported the constitutionality of the death penalty; indeed, they seemed positively disdainful of those who continued to register constitutional opposition to its infliction. The Court upheld its imposition on minors and the mentally retarded. And it found irrelevant, in *McCleskey* v. *Kemp* (1987), the fact that Georgia juries were far more likely to impose capital punishment on black murderers of whites than on white murderers in general or black murderers of blacks. Congress—supported by President Bill Clinton, whose campaign for the Presidency had in part been based on his being a "new-style Democrat" who enthusiastically supported the death penalty—engaged in its own efforts to cut back substantially on the access of state criminal defendants to hearings in federal courts via petitions for writs of habeas corpus. Several circuit courts, especially those having jurisdiction over the Southern states that account for the overwhelming majority of actual executions, have seemed more than willing to enforce this legislation with vigor.

The Court, however, has refused to read certain congressional statutes to deprive prisoners of *any* significant review by federal courts of the constitutional adequacy of the procedures by which they were convicted (and sentenced to death). Moreover, in *Atkins* v. *Virginia* (2000), the Court, over the acid dissent of Justice Scalia, read the Constitution as prohibiting the execution of the mentally retarded.

The most important criminal-law cases in the next decade are likely to involve the ability of the Executive Branch to incarcerate suspected terrorists or "illegal combatants," including United States citizens, for an unlimited time without giving them any chance to defend themselves (or, indeed, even to consult with an attorney). This could be discussed as a "criminal-justice" issue; it can also, of course, be viewed as a "war powers" issue, a topic that will be discussed further at the end of this chapter.

EQUAL PROTECTION COMES INTO ITS OWN

Justice Oliver Wendell Holmes in 1927, with characteristic acerbity, described arguments based on the equal protection clause of the Fourteenth Amendment as "the usual last resort of constitutional arguments," offered only (and almost invariably unsuccessfully) when nothing better was available. If equality means that like cases should be treated alike, then it seems logically entailed that unlike cases can legitimately be treated differently. Thus Holmes cautioned against being seduced by arguments that "introduc[e] a factitious equality without regard to practical differences that are best met by corresponding differences of treatment." Given that one of the central meanings of 1937 was the adoption of a Holmesian stance of judicial deference toward legislative decision-making, it is surely no surprise that his disdain for the equal protection clause was reflected in the Court's jurisprudence, at least where the treatment of racial minorities was not at issue. State legislatures were basically given carte blanche to classify as they wished.

Whether because of the pressure of the race-relations cases, including *Brown* v. *Board of Education,* or because of a more general cultural interest in egalitarianism, the Court in the 1960's would engage in the most systematic exploration of the meaning of equality in American history. It would move well beyond the racial dimension, which had, after all, been a steady part of the Court's docket ever since the addition of the Fourteenth Amendment, and confront issues that had not theretofore been accepted by the justices as fit for judicial resolution.

Perhaps the most dramatic symbol of the Court's newfound willingness to confront—and try to resolve from Washington—basic issues of American political life was its 1962 decision in *Baker* v. *Carr.* There a sharply split Court, in an opinion written by Justice Brennan, overruled several prior decisions, including one as recent as 1946, and declared that the issue of legislative districting was "justiciable." This meant that the Court would now assess the fairness of the electorate's representation in state legislatures by reference to the equal protection clause of the Fourteenth Amendment. In the particular case, Tennessee had not redrawn political boundary lines for its state legislature since 1901; as a consequence, the urbanites in Memphis and Nashville received far fewer representatives than an equal number of farmers in thinly populated districts. Had earlier decisions been followed, the suit would simply have been dismissed as raising a "political question" inappropriate for judicial resolution. Now, instead, the Court ordered the Tennessee federal court in which suit had originally been filed to consider the merits of the claim.

Justice Frankfurter, in his last great opinion before a stroke forced him to leave the Court, denounced the majority not only for deviating from precedent but also for taking the Court into a "political thicket" that could easily ensnarl it in partisan political conflicts and rob it of the legitimacy derived from public perception of a body above such conflicts. Frankfurter summarized the thought of a lifetime in declaring that "[i]n a democratic society like ours, relief must come through an aroused popular conscience that sears the conscience of the people's representatives" rather than through judicial mandate. How an "aroused" public was supposed to be effective in the absence of voting power commensurate with their numbers was left undiscussed.

No one could doubt that *Baker* represented a bold departure for the Court. One should note, though, that this change was warmly supported by the new administration of John F. Kennedy and his Solicitor General, Harvard law professor Archibald Cox. Almost by definition, one was unlikely to find enthusiastic majority support for the status quo, a system of representation that entrenched minority rule. By no means, therefore, could the Court be accused of gratuitously seizing new power or standing steadfast against the wishes of newly empowered majorities, as had presumably been the case during the *Lochner* era or, most dramatically, during its efforts in the 1930's to stave off the New Deal. Instead, it basically represented what were widely perceived as majoritarian (and "enlightened") urban interests fighting against parochial farmers for their "fair share" of seats in legislative bodies.

Robert McCloskey, in a 1962 article in the *Harvard Law Review* on *Baker,* noted that it had received wide-scale applause from the public, but he cautioned the Court against moving too boldly in implementing its decision, which, after all, said only that the Court would address, rather than dismiss, issues raised by political districting. In particular, he expressed great fears that the Court's prestige would be significantly diminished as angry politicians and voters who opposed judicially mandated reapportionment would go on the attack. As political scientist John Roche put it, "Power corrupts, and the prospect of losing power corrupts absolutely." The struggle over legislative districting was precisely about the ability of established political elites to maintain power, and there was no reason to believe that they would relinquish it and go gently into the political night. Many other writers, however, saw Frankfurter's appeal to politicians' consciences or McCloskey's prudential concerns over the consequences of judicial assertion as representing an almost willful blindness to the political pathology mocking the majoritarian underpinnings of the American political system.

McCloskey hoped that the Court would confine its intervention into legislative districting to a relatively few, particularly egregious, incidents; any such hopes (or, from the perspective of others, fears) were dashed in *Reynolds* v. *Sims* (1964). The Court, this time through Chief Justice Warren, almost blithely struck down the state legislative systems in most of the states insofar as they had adopted some form of "little Federalism" that, as in the United States Senate, apportioned representatives by political subdivisions (usually counties) rather than by population. "Legislators represent people," wrote Warren, "not trees or acres. Legislators are elected by voters, not farms or cities or economic interests." The mandate, then, was for "one person, one vote," and the Court later extended this principle to almost all popularly elected, multimember decision-making bodies within states. And an earlier decision that same year had required strict equality of population in regard to congressional districts. (It is obvious that the United States Senate does not conform to the Court's new notion of equality; what justifies it, presumably, is a combination of historical inertia and whatever lingering commitment there is to a sufficient notion of "state sovereignty" that will justify Vermont's having the same power in the Senate as does California.)

To a remarkable extent, however, little of the strong counterattack feared by McCloskey took place. To be sure, the House of Representatives, whose current members stood to face future political instability because of the necessity to redraw electoral districts, passed a bill that would have withdrawn jurisdiction over legislative apportionment from the judiciary. And some members of Congress promoted a constitutional amendment that would have had the same consequences. Liberals were, however, able to stave off such attacks on the Court, and "one person, one vote" quickly became accepted by the public as the new status quo.

One result of these decisions is that legislative districting has now become a permanent part of the Court's docket, particularly during the years immediately following the constitutionally required decennial census that reveals which states (and which regions within the states) gained or lost population. Although the Court has remained almost rigidly devoted to a strict equi-population standard in congressional districting, it has adopted a somewhat more relaxed attitude about districting in regard to state institutions. Never in the forty years since *Reynolds* has it precisely explained why populations must be equal given the obvious fact equi-population districts may well not be equal in the number of voters. Consider districts with a high concentration of youngsters—for example, "bedroom suburbs"—against districts that consist of an unusually high percentage of retired adults. Or, perhaps even more important, voting-ineligible noncitizens or felons are counted toward the representation "denominator." Districts high in noncitizens or felons will inevitably have fewer voters than districts without such persons; moreover, it is difficult to believe that voter-oriented representatives will be particularly sensitive to the interests of these nonvoters. "One person, one vote" has turned out to be more of an unanalyzed mantra than a genuinely cogent approach to understanding the Constitution's role in structuring the American electoral process, though it has undoubtedly become a "settled" part of the American constitutional fabric.

Increasingly important on the Court's docket are cases involving gerrymandering, the drawing of electoral districts so that they promote

desirable political outcomes, whether defined as the victory of a given political party or, quite commonly, the protection of incumbent politicians.
(Given Roche's dictum, one could readily, and accurately, predict that
much energy is put into protecting those with power against the possibility of effective challenge, even accepting the new rule of equal-population
districts.) Not until 1986 did the Court formally hold that gerrymandering was subject to review, though, as a practical matter, it indicated that it
would almost never override gerrymanders. The Court in 2004 rejected a
challenge to a highly partisan Pennsylvania gerrymander. Four justices
would have dismissed the case as "nonjusticiable," thus rejecting any judicial role in assessing non-racial gerrymanders. Four justices believed
that gerrymanders are justiciable and that the Pennsylvania legislators
had indeed gone too far. Justice Kennedy was the "swing Justice." He
agreed that gerrymandering was justiciable, but he also wrote that no
one had yet presented an appropriate standard for judicial enforcement.
So the Pennsylvania gerrymander stood. Partisan gerrymandering aims
both to create basically "one-party" districts (and thus effectively to eliminate competitive general elections) and to minimize the number of districts
that the minority party predictably might win. Many observers increasingly see this as light-years from the "republican form of government"
guaranteed to the states (and their citizens) by Article IV of the Constitution. Politicians basically pick their voters, rather than the other way
around. There is no reason to believe that politicians who benefit from the
current process will be eager to reform it, though it obviously remains to
be seen if the Court will ever take the plunge into trying to do something
about it.

Gerrymandering usually evokes oddly shaped single-member districts,
but it can also include the adoption of "multimember" districts offering
the majority of the district the opportunity to elect all of the district's representatives—and, concomitantly, the opportunity to deprive the minority of the ability to elect any representatives sympathetic to their own
views. The Court held in the 1970's that nothing in the Constitution forbids such multimember districts, even if breaking down the district into
single-member entities would allow the minority to prevail in at least one
of the new districts.

The Court has, however, invalidated multimember districting moti-
vated by the desire to limit the practical ability of a racial minority to elect
a representative. That is, a Democratic or Republican legislature could do
almost everything it could to reduce the likely electoral success of their

partisan opponents, but it could not act to reduce the prospects of racial minorities. Indeed, under the Voting Rights Act of 1965 and subsequent amendments passed by Congress, state legislatures appeared to be obligated to *enhance* the prospects of African-Americans and other victims of racial discrimination.

In *Shaw* v. *Reno* (1993), however, the Court called into question (but did not declare unconstitutional) the ability of states to consider race when drawing electoral districts, even if the motivation was to assure the election of minority representatives. Not surprisingly, *Shaw* occasioned heated dissent from four of the justices, who found it almost perverse to hold that states might be barred from taking measures designed to increase the presence of minorities in legislatures or Congress. The 1993 decision was only the first of four that the Court would decide during the next decade regarding the North Carolina redistricting alone, and few lawyers in this new millennium possess a clear understanding of the current Supreme Court doctrine, given a series of sharply split, five-to-four decisions in cases arising out of North Carolina, Georgia, and Texas. For example, the Georgia case, *Miller* v. *Johnson* (1995), held that race could not be the "predominant" factor in drawing legislative lines, but this decision presumably leaves open the ability of race to serve as one factor among many.

Here, as with many other issues discussed in these latter chapters of the book, one must always remember that one of the Court's most important roles is statutory interpretation. Thus, for example, a five-justice majority in *Reno* v. *Bossier Parish* [Louisiana] *School Board* (2000) refused to accept the interpretation by the United States Justice Department of the Voting Rights Act of 1965 as entitling it to refuse to "preclear" changes in districting that, as in the given instance, effectively work to maintain the advantages of white voters in the electoral process. According to the majority, only "retrogression," by which blacks are made worse off than before, justifies rejection by the Justice Department, whereas maintaining a disadvantageous status quo must be tolerated. Justice Souter, in dissent, said that the department would now be forced to approve "unconstitutional voting schemes patently intended to perpetuate discrimination." (As he suggests, it is not that the new districting will be immune to legal challenge, but, rather, that the challenge will, as a practical matter, be far more expensive and time-consuming than is a process in which the Justice Department can simply refuse to approve the new scheme.)

A SPECIAL NOTE ON *BUSH* v. *GORE*

No discussion of the role of the United States Supreme Court in the electoral process could possibly ignore its intervention in the 2000 presidential election. To the surprise of most analysts, the Court first took the case challenging the fairness of the vote-counting procedures in the remarkably close Florida election and then, in a five-to-four decision that provoked extraordinarily hostile dissents, effectively shut down the Florida process, thereby assuring the election of George W. Bush.

My task here is to try to determine what Robert McCloskey might have said about the decision in *Bush* v. *Gore*. I am quite confident that he would have been stunned almost to disbelief by the Court's willingness in effect to name the next President (who would, of course, be able to nominate new members of the Court itself, not to mention the appellate and district courts that, as a practical matter, may be even more important than the Supreme Court). But further reflection led me to conclude that I cannot use McCloskey's book (and presumptive voice) to issue a denunciation of the decision that simply reflects my own distaste for it.

Discussion of the point may help the reader to understand some of the tensions within McCloskey's own approach to the Court. In a marvelously supple 1964 essay, he suggested that "our evaluation of a Supreme Court decision . . . ordinarily depends on one or more of three different judgment components." The first of these components is what we might refer to as traditional "legalism," that is, the "fit" between the decision in question and our ordinary notions of interpretive propriety. In addition, McCloskey offered two other components, the first involving "the question of power," the second, "the question of value." In summary, he wrote, "[I]n criticizing a judicial action we say that the Court has misread the Constitution, or that it has overtaxed its power capabilities, or that it has chosen the wrong ethical solution." Quite obviously, if it has done all three, there is no difficulty at all in criticizing—indeed, castigating—the decision in question. Difficulties emerge, of course, if the components seem to point in different directions.

It is at this point that the task of figuring out what McCloskey might have said about *Bush* v. *Gore* becomes especially challenging. Consider, for example, his analysis of *Marbury* v. *Madison* earlier in this book. That account represents an early version of what political scientists know as "rational choice" theorizing about the behavior of politicians and their institutions. Rational choice theory includes some version of the following propositions:

a) All political actors have agendas of their own, ranging from crass desire for reelection to attaining majestic visions of what constitutes a truly admirable polity, and they respond with alacrity to various incentives (or disincentives) with regard to achieving their goals.

b) Politicians do not operate atomistically but instead must work in and through institutions.

c) The ambitions of any given politician, as James Madison suggested long ago in *Federalist* 51, tend to become attached to the interests of the particular institution within which he or she is serving, especially if one envisions oneself as spending a significant amount of time—perhaps even the remainder of one's active life—within the institution.

d) Institutions must always be analyzed structurally, which is to say that any given institution—the presidency, an administrative agency, a branch of Congress, or the United States Supreme Court—is involved in a complex matrix that consists of a variety of competing institutions (and of political actors occupying those institutions). This means, among other things, that the "interests" of a particular institution may counsel, at any given time, either coalition with or opposition to other institutions (and their leaders), with the institutions in question offering a variety of incentives to cooperate, or at least disincentives against opposition.

Consider *Marbury* in the context of these assumptions. McCloskey was certainly no great admirer of what might be termed the purely "legal" aspects of the opinion. Instead, he praised Marshall's cleverness in manipulating the legal materials in order to achieve his own ends, which included strengthening the power of the Court by illustrating its power of judicial review (by invalidating a federal law), even as Marshall very cleverly avoided the direct challenge to Thomas Jefferson (and James Madison) that would have accompanied an order that they in fact give Marbury the commission to which Marshall thought he was entitled. McCloskey presents Marshall and the institution he loved as the overall winners in the great political shoot-out that was *Marbury*. Given McCloskey's own view that judicial review, on balance, was a good thing, Marshall's strategic cleverness was a cause for celebration rather than critique.

So is it possible that *Bush* v. *Gore* would (or should) also have elicited McCloskey's admiration rather than denunciation? Most of the critics of *Bush* v. *Gore* have emphasized the party identity of the Justices in the majority and have inferred that these justices warmly approved of George W. Bush's becoming President and were therefore inclined to interpret the "great generalities" of the Constitution—and the "greatest generality" is surely the Equal Protection Clause—in a way that would bring about this happy ending. This does not require any conscious dissimulation on the part of the affected Justices. All it requires is a view of human psychology by which intellectual tensions will be resolved in a way that brings about the happiest of endings, in this case the movement of George W. Bush from the governor's mansion in Austin to the White House in Washington, D.C.

Beyond speculations about judicial psychology is an awareness of the institutional context of the decision. One must realize exactly how far removed from any "veil of ignorance" the Court was in December 2000. They not only knew the identity of the specific presidential candidate who would benefit from their decisions, they also knew the outcome of the elections with regard to the House of Representatives and the Senate of the United States. The first, of course, remained Republican. The Senate was a bit more complex, given the uncertainty about who would represent the State of Washington in the Senate. It was clear, though, that the Democrats would have no more than fifty seats (as turned out to be the case until Vermont Senator James Jeffords's entirely unexpected decision in 2001 to leave the Republican Party), which meant that a Republican Vice-President could assure the organization of the Senate for the Republicans.

Just as Marshall, according to McCloskey's analysis, had one eye on Jeffersonians in Congress and their capacity for exercising retribution against a decision they found unacceptable, one might suggest that the majority might have realized that a pro-Bush decision would guarantee it multiple friends. The most obvious would be George W. Bush, who, as President, would manifest his friendship by nominating to the federal judiciary (including, in due time, the Supreme Court itself) persons committed to the ideological agenda set forth by its conservative Republican majority over the past decade. And one ought not underestimate the importance of the House and the Senate as potential friends. An anti-Bush decision would obviously not have pleased congressional Republicans. To be sure, House and Senate Republicans might well have engineered the election of George W. Bush, given the declared willingness of the Florida legislature to ignore the results of the recount if it came up with the wrong outcome (that is, a Gore victory) and instead to name a slate of electors committed to Governor Bush, as arguably allowed by Article II of the Constitution. But the Court's decision took them off the hook. One can easily imagine that they were exceedingly grateful to the Court for getting them off the hook, unlike a decision that would have either (a) risked the possibility that Al Gore would become President after all or (b) forced the congressional Republicans to take the political hit for defying the choice of a majority of American voters, who rejected George W. Bush (and, possibly, of a majority of Florida voters as demonstrated in a recount whose results would be contemptuously cast aside by a partisan Florida State Legislature).

What about public opinion, insofar as one aspect of McCloskey's analysis involved the Court's interest in maintaining its stature in the minds of the general public? The importance of public opinion, for McCloskey, was demonstrated with special vividness in the rejection by the public of Franklin Delano Roosevelt's altogether understandable desire to pack the Supreme Court with justices more favorable to the political views that had just been overwhelmingly endorsed by the public. So what might a "rational" justice, in December 2000, believe about public opinion?

The American public was obviously split roughly down the middle as to the comparative merits of George Bush and Al Gore as a potential president. If Democrats would likely be antagonistic, even furious, at a decision favoring Bush, one might expect joyful approval from grateful Republicans, leaving the Court's general approval relatively unchanged. The majority might have expected a lambasting from legal academics, most of whom are Democrats, but it could have discounted the importance of any such opposition; few people outside the academy are even remotely interested in the views of law professors.

Research conducted prior to the presidential election and then after *Bush* v. *Gore* is extremely suggestive. Gallup Poll numbers show that around Labor Day of 2000, 62 percent of the public approved of the "way the Supreme Court is handling its job" and only 25 percent disapproved. At that time Democrats were more inclined to approve (70 percent) than were Republicans (60 percent), which lends credence to the argument of some political conservatives that the Court remains considerably more liberal than is suggested by some liberal opponents of the current Court. Pre-election, independent voters were least enthusiastic about the way the Supreme Court was handling its job, with 57 percent approval.

The Supreme Court's approval ratings dropped only three percentage points (to 59 percent) after its decision in *Bush* v. *Gore,* though disapproval ratings jumped from 25 percent to 34 percent. Not surprisingly, Republican approval had jumped by a full one-third, from 60 percent to 80 percent. Democratic support had plunged by a similar rate; now only 42 percent of Democrats approved of the Court, and 50 percent disapproved. Independents basically remained stable, going down from 57 percent approval in September to 54 percent in January.

A June 2001 poll revealed that the overall approval-disapproval figures were identical to what they had been the year before, 62 percent to 25 percent. Democrats had clearly learned to live with, if not to love, the

Court: as 54 percent approved, the 50 percent who had registered disapproval in January were reduced to a mere 32 percent. Republican enthusiasm diminished a bit, though it remained at a robust 74 percent. Independents' regard for the Court was at a peak of 59 percent approval.

Similarly, the public's "confidence" in the Court actually seemed to increase from 2000 to 2001: Whereas only 47 percent of the public indicated in June 2000 that they had a "great deal" or "quite a lot" of confidence in the Court (as against 49 percent who had only "some" or "very little"), 50 percent of the sample polled indicated such levels of confidence in June 2001. (Indeed, even in mid-December of 2000, 49 percent manifested the highest levels of confidence.) Not surprisingly, Democrats and Republicans responded differently to the Court's decision in *Bush* v. *Gore.* If, however, the Court was gambling that it could maintain broad public support even while throwing the election to George W. Bush and establishing ever better relations with the congressional Republicans, it was a winning decision.

To summarize, then, with regard to McCloskey's possible response to *Bush* v. *Gore:* If one adopts even a moderately rational choice institutionalist approach to understanding the role (and behavior) of the Supreme Court, the decision in *Bush* v. *Gore* appears almost inevitable. Even if one agrees that the legal arguments are less than impeccable, considerations of judicial power strongly counseled doing exactly what the Court did. A contrary decision would have required almost monumental restraint on the part of the Court's Republican majority, given the overall institutional context in December 2000. Moreover, if one shares Judge Richard Posner's dire warnings about the consequences of further uncertainty as to the identity of our new President, then the decision easily passes the "value" test. According to Posner, the Court saved the country from potential instability that it could ill afford. As it happens, I disagree with him, but one can hardly dismiss Posner's arguments. It is, therefore, more difficult than I would have hoped to figure out exactly how McCloskey the detached political scientist would have responded to the decision, even as I am relatively confident than his more "personal" response would have been as negative as my own.

GENDER AND EQUAL PROTECTION

In 1948 the Court almost casually upheld a Michigan law prohibiting women other than bar owners' wives from tending bar. It clearly had no interest in seriously examining the legitimacy of gender classifications.

States could, practically speaking, do as they wished. And the Warren Court in 1960 sustained a Florida law that operated to make it relatively unlikely that women would in fact serve on juries (even as it would have instantly struck such a law applying to blacks).

Interestingly enough, it was Earl Warren's successor, the considerably more conservative Warren Burger, who wrote a 1971 opinion in *Reed* v. *Reed* that ushered in the age of scrutinizing legislation that classified on the basis of sex. (That opinion struck down as "irrational" a preference by Idaho for male over female administrators of estates because, according to the state, men would be more likely to have had relevant business experience. As many observers noted at the time, this assumption was scarcely crazy and would easily pass the "minimum rationality test" that the Court used to assess routine socioeconomic regulation after 1937.) Justice Brennan was able in 1973 to gain three other justices to subscribe to the proposition that gender classifications should receive the "strict scrutiny" given racial classifications, but he could not get the key fifth vote. Finally, in *Craig* v. *Boren* (1976) the Court coalesced around an "intermediate" test, in which the state would have to show a "substantial" interest to justify gender classifications.

Not surprisingly, this ostensible test would prove quite fluid in its actual application. Over the next twenty years the Court would sometimes uphold gender classifications—Congress was allowed to require only men to register for the draft—and would sometimes strike them down—Mississippi was disallowed from prohibiting men from taking nursing classes at the Mississippi University for Women. (One might note that the plaintiffs in the named cases, as was true in *Craig* v. *Boren,* were men complaining about the ostensibly favorable treatment that women received.) And in 1996 the Court, over the heated dissent of Justice Scalia, invalidated the male-only status of the Virginia Military Institute. Writing for the Court, Justice Ruth Bader Ginsburg, who litigated many important women's-rights cases during the 1970's before being appointed to the Court of Appeals for the District of Columbia by President Jimmy Carter, held that Virginia had not presented the requisite "exceedingly persuasive justification" for such segregation. (Even most lawyers could not discern the distinction between a "compelling interest" and an "exceedingly persuasive justification.")

Far more important in fact than anything the Court said were rapid changes in the surrounding American culture, ranging from the "sexual revolution" to the increasing number of women entering the job market. And far more significant legally was antidiscrimination legislation passed by many state legislatures and Congress. The Civil Rights Act of 1964, for example, had included, almost inadvertently, a prohibition against sex discrimination, and the Court was reasonably vigorous in enforcing the statute. The contemporary law of "sexual harassment," for example, has been largely generated by arguably generous judicial interpretation of congressional statutes, backed in turn by public support most obviously from politically active women.

One of the major controversies of the 1970's concerned the Equal Rights Amendment (ERA), which had been proposed in 1972 by Congress and provided that "Equality of rights under the law shall not be denied or abridged by the United States or by any State on account of sex." Although it was quickly ratified by thirty of the thirty-eight needed states, it thereafter was successfully blocked by vigorous opponents. Although some of them could easily be described as being against gender equality, at least some of them based their opposition on a mixture of plausible doubt about the meaning of the language and, more to the point, an unwillingness to trust the Supreme Court to give acceptable specific meanings to the Amendment. As a matter of fact, few supporters of the Amendment believed that the Supreme Court was barred from reading the Fourteenth Amendment to offer whatever protection would be given women by the ERA. To this day, it remains unclear whether the battle over the ERA was merely symbolic of wider cultural struggles within American society or whether it would have, if adopted, required genuinely transformative legal decisions, going beyond current law, with regard to women's rights.

Enter Privacy: A Second Era of "Substantive Due Process"?

What Justice Stewart termed an "uncommonly silly law" triggered perhaps the most controversial set of "individual-rights" decisions of the Court during the last third of the twentieth century. Connecticut made it criminal to sell, use, or counsel the use of contraceptives for the purpose of birth control. (One could sell and use contraceptives for disease prevention.) Participants in a Planned Parenthood organization working out of New Haven, Connecticut, were charged with violating this law. The majority of the Court struck down the conviction in *Griswold* v. *Connecticut* (1965). Justice Douglas wrote for the majority that the written text of the Bill of Rights contained "penumbras and emanations" that protected marital privacy against the invasion represented by Connecticut's law. Justices Harlan and Goldberg, in separate concurrences, more unabashedly endorsed the Court's ability to identify "unenumerated rights" as part of the Constitution.

Stewart made his comment about Connecticut's law in a dissent, arguing that the meaning of the post-1937, post-*Lochner* Court was that it would forego attempting to identify "unenumerated rights" in the Constitution, of which, he said, "privacy" most certainly was one. Hugo Black, the great textual absolutist of the mid-twentieth century, agreed. Though he described the Connecticut law as "offensive," he went on to argue that the Constitution simply did not include the requisite language limiting a state's right to regulate contraception however it wished. He, too, accused the majority of returning to the discredited era of *Lochner.*

Had the issue been confined to the "silly" and "offensive" Connecticut law, it is hard to believe that anyone besides law professors would really have cared. *Griswold* was widely popular, as demonstrated vividly some twenty-two years later when the appointment of Robert Bork, Ronald Reagan's conservative nominee for a seat on the Supreme Court, was derailed in part because of his derision of the case. What made the situation entirely different was the Court's willingness to extend the protection of "privacy" announced in that decision first to the distribution of contraceptives to unmarried adults and even minors and, most fatefully, to the issue of abortion.

There can be almost no doubt that *Roe* v. *Wade* (1973) is the most important Court decision at least since *Brown,* especially if measured by the consequences for the American polity. (The only other serious candidates would be *Buckley* v. *Valeo,* which saddled the country with its present dysfunctional system of election finance; and the Apportionment Cases, which ended the rural domination of legislative institutions and led not to the urban domination that had been predicted—and, by many, desired—but to dominance of suburban interests in state and national legislatures.) In *Roe,* the Court, in an opinion written by Justice Blackmun, joined by two of the three other Nixon appointees as well as "holdover" justices Brennan, Marshall, Stewart, and Douglas, struck down the antiabortion laws of forty-six states. The Court held that protected "privacy" included the basic right of a woman to procure an abortion from a doctor in the first trimester of pregnancy. States were allowed to exercise some measure of regulation in the second trimester and to prohibit abortion entirely in the third. "Privacy" had replaced "freedom of contract," and there could be little doubt that the Court was stunningly willing to read the Constitution as containing rights not obvious from reading the text. Justices White and Rehnquist heatedly dissented. Stewart, interestingly enough, concurred, saying that the Court had clearly decided to return to the substantive due-process business and that he agreed that abortion should be protected.

Justice Blackmun mentioned in his *Roe* opinion that many states were in fact liberalizing their abortion laws, so it is possible that neither he nor his colleagues in the majority had any inkling of the firestorm they were about to ignite. One message of the 1960's, after all, had been what McCloskey had called the remarkable willingness of the public to accept government by judiciary. To be sure, criticisms had been voiced, and Blackmun owed his own place on the Court to the election of a Republican President who had in many ways run against the Court. (And Blackmun actually was, at least early in his judicial career, quite conservative regarding the criminal-justice issues that were the focus of Nixon's concern.) But, taken as a whole, the level of resistance to the Court could be dismissed as relatively minimal, especially given the scope of the changes promoted by the Court during the 1960's. Fulminating members of Congress could not gain the support necessary to mount a genuine assault on the Court's citadel.

Abortion rights could well be seen as widely supported by the national political and cultural elites (usually secular) to whom the Court justices were likely to be most attentive. Blackmun himself had served as counsel to the Mayo Clinic, the world-famous medical facility in his home state of Minnesota, and he clearly shared its sympathy for the plight of women who wished to terminate unwanted—and possibly dangerous—pregnancies. Indeed, whatever the cogency of "privacy" as a legal rationale, the *Roe* decision quickly became part of the debate about the role of women and, concomitantly, the role of the state in enabling or impeding them from foregoing "traditional" burdens of childbearing and instead entering the workforce or, at the least, from timing their pregnancies congruently with general life plans.

Whatever the perceptions of the Court about its ability to control public response, opponents of the decision, many of whom saw it basically as offering constitutional protection to the mass murder of innocent fetuses, mobilized against it. Although it is not self-evident that one's views on abortion would necessarily correlate with more typical measures of "liberalism" or "conservatism," the antiabortion movement quickly allied itself with the Republican Party, especially the wing sharply critical of the permissive cultural trends of the 1960's. By 1978 several Democratic supporters of abortion rights lost their seats in the United States

Senate, and there can be little doubt that the rise to power of Ronald Reagan and the Republican capture of the Senate in 1980 were considerably helped along by the energies of the "right-to-life" movement. The Republican Party platform by 1980 included specific opposition to *Roe* and the promise that justices would be appointed who would overrule it.

In fact, that never occurred, even though by 1991 a majority of the Court had been appointed by Presidents Reagan and George H. W. Bush (and the original dissenters, White and Rehnquist, remained, with the latter as Chief Justice). Although the Court throughout the 1980's allowed much more state regulation than would have been upheld by Justice Blackmun and other partisans of *Roe* (who dissented from several of these rulings), it always "distinguished," rather than overruled, *Roe*. Finally, in the *Casey* case of 1992, the most direct test of the vitality of *Roe*, a five-justice majority that included Justices O'Connor, Kennedy, and Souter—all Reagan-Bush appointees—announced their refusal to overrule the decision insofar as it offered basic support for a woman's right to choose abortion and a concomitant protection against the state's placing "undue burdens" on the exercise of this right. The three justices named above issued a remarkable opinion that, without ever suggesting that *Roe* had been rightly decided, said that the Court would suffer institutionally if it overruled the case in effect because of changing membership. Precedent had its claims, the three emphasized. Justice Scalia wrote a mocking dissent, joined by Chief Justice Rehnquist and Justices White and Clarence Thomas; they would have returned control of reproductive rights to the states. Justices Blackmun and Stevens dissented, from the opposite direction; they would have struck down a number of Pennsylvania's restrictions that were upheld by the majority. With the 1993 retirement of White and his replacement by Ruth Bader Ginsburg, who had argued many of the classic women's-rights cases for the American Civil Liberties Union and who clearly supported the right to choose, it is extremely unlikely that *Roe* (or at least those portions of *Roe* that survived *Casey*) will be overruled.

Further evidence of the current Court's unwillingness to reconsider its basic position was provided by the 2000 decision invalidating a Nebraska law that prohibited late-term, or what proponents of the ban call "partial-birth," abortions. (It should go without saying that the vote was five to four, with Justice O'Connor providing the vital fifth vote to strike down the legislation.) The Court will probably have the opportunity to revisit this specific issue following the signing by George W. Bush of a 2003 state statute passed by Congress that criminalized such abortions. A district court immediately enjoined enforcement of the law on the grounds that, contrary to the claims of its supporters, it did not differ in any significant way from the invalidated Nebraska statute. Even if Justice O'Connor joins her four conservative colleagues in upholding the new statute, that would leave the basic *Roe-Casey* regime unchanged. No fundamental change is likely unless George W. Bush has the opportunity in coming years to replace two "pro-*Roe*" justices with their ideological opponents.

Far more important than intra-Court arguments, including the claims of precedent evoked by O'Connor in *Casey*, is the fact that some version of a woman's right to choose appears to be supported by a fairly wide majority of Americans. The somewhat clumsy compromises—at least from a traditional doctrinal view—made by the Court during this period allow limitations on abortion so long as they are not "undue," and this position might well enjoy the support of that majority. This leads one to wonder whether Reagan and George H. W. Bush, who supported abortion rights earlier in their political careers before aligning themselves with the antiabortion movement in the 1980's, might in fact have had mixed feelings about returning abortion to the full-scale political process. When abortion rights were directly tested in the political marketplace, Democratic supporters, especially if "moderate," tended to prevail over hard-line Republican opponents. There was no reason to believe that the political interests of the Republican Party would have been served by the actual demise of *Roe*, however much they were helped by incessantly denouncing the decision and promising to seek its overruling. There is no evidence that Reagan and Bush put O'Connor, Kennedy, and Souter on the bench in order to preserve abortion rights, but it is certainly possible that these Presidents were less than zealous in applying a "litmus test" of opposition to *Roe* in deciding whom to nominate to the Court; at least in private, they might well be satisfied with the intermediate position between Blackmun and Scalia taken by the Court's majority. This might also explain why Texas Governor George W. Bush did not seem eager during his 2000 campaign for the presidency to pledge that he would appoint justices likely to overrule *Roe*. Only the future will show whether Bush has the opportunity to nominate someone to the Court and, if so, if he chooses to nominate someone who is perceived as a strong opponent of abortion rights.

Another issue generated by *Griswold* and *Roe* was the protection to be accorded unconventional sexual practices. By far the most important was gay and lesbian sexuality, which was criminalized in many states under the rubric of antisodomy laws. (Some states prohibited sodomy only by homosexuals or bisexuals, while allowing it between married couples or even unmarried heterosexuals.) In *Bowers* v. *Hardwick,* a bitterly split five-to-four Court rejected the argument that the Constitution protected what Justice White for the majority insisted on calling "homosexual sodomy" and what Justice Blackmun in dissent labeled rights of personal sexual intimacy. The crucial fifth vote was provided by Lewis Powell, who remarked shortly after his retirement that he wished he had voted with the dissenters and thus helped to compose a new majority. At the time of the decision, Powell apparently claimed that he did not personally know any homosexuals; in fact, one of his clerks at the time was gay, although he did not reveal it to the justice. One may take this as evidence either of the extent that gays and lesbians remained closeted or of the remarkable isolation of many Supreme Court justices from ordinary American life.

Bowers was, in its way, almost as offensive as *Dred Scott,* with its notorious emphasis that blacks simply were not part of the American political community and, indeed, were "so far inferior, that they had no rights which the white man was bound to respect." If one takes seriously a constitutional vision that offers "equal concern and respect" to the members of the American polity, then *Bowers* betrays it. It must be noted, though, that anyone adopting the general approach articulated by Robert Mc-Closkey might well stress the imprudence of the Court's taking the lead in granting full-scale legal rights to a minority that was, at the time, highly unpopular among much of the public. Indeed, the storm of controversy in 1993 that defeated President Clinton's attempt to lift the ban on openly homosexual people serving in the armed forces indicated the extent of the public antipathy toward accepting gays and lesbians as full members of the American community. Given the Court's unpopularity with many elements of society; it should always be concerned, according to a McCloskean analysis, with carefully nurturing what capital it retains rather than profligately spending it in a venture that is likely to spark far more opposition than support.

Finally, it must be acknowledged that in many ways the criminalization of sodomy is more a symbolic than a "real" issue. Anyone even minimally familiar with American culture and society in recent decades knows that gays and lesbians are an increasingly visible part of the political community, earnestly solicited by many office seekers and holders as part of their political coalition and increasingly elected or appointed to public office themselves. Least of all, it might be argued, should the Court invest its scarce resources in basically symbolic gestures. Victims of very real homophobia would, of course, dispute that the issue is "merely" symbolic and would emphasize the Court's role—which, whatever the reality, it rhetorically embraced after 1937 and especially after World War II — of protecting vulnerable minorities against majority tyranny.

The Court left many observers confused when, in *Romer* v. *Evans* (1996), it struck down an amendment to the Colorado constitution that prohibited both state and local governments from passing laws or otherwise adopting policies that would protect persons against discrimination on grounds of "homosexual, lesbian or bisexual orientation, conduct, practices or relationships." Writing for the Court, Justice Anthony Kennedy described the amendment as striving "not to further a proper legislative end but to make [homosexuals] unequal to everybody else." Justice Scalia, joined by Chief Justice Rehnquist and Justice Thomas, filed a scathing dissent accusing the Court of doing little more than reflecting the opinion of legal elites with regard to an extraordinarily controversial cultural divide within American society. He also noted that Kennedy's opinion never referred to *Bowers,* therefore leaving almost everyone on both sides of the divide wondering why (or if) it is legitimate to criminalize certain sexual behavior while at the same time it is constitutionally illegitimate to discriminate against persons who are likely to engage in it.

Justice Kennedy in effect corroborated Scalia's critique by writing the majority opinion for the Court in *Lawrence* v. *Texas* (2003), which not only forthrightly invalidated Texas's "anti-sodomy" law, but also overruled *Bowers.* Kennedy described the case as involving "two adults who, with full and mutual consent from each other, engaged in sexual practices common to a homosexual lifestyle. [They] are entitled to respect for their private lives. The State cannot demand their existence or control their destiny by making their private sexual conduct a crime." Justice O'Connor, who had voted with the majority in *Bowers,* agreed that the Texas statute was illegitimate, but she wrote a separate concurring opinion based on the Equal Protection Clause, unlike Kennedy, who relied on the Due Process Clause. Justice Scalia wrote an ever-more-caustic dissent accusing his colleagues of "largely sign[ing] on to the so-called homosexual agenda, by which I mean the agenda promoted by some homosexual activists directed at eliminating the moral opprobrium that has traditionally attached to homosexual conduct."

Hovering over all of the opinions was the issue of gay and lesbian marriage. Both Kennedy and O'Connor seemed to go out of their way to insist that their arguments did not have the consequences that Scalia insisted they did. Interestingly enough, the Massachusetts Supreme Judicial Court in November 2003 cited *Lawrence* in striking down the Massachusetts refusal to allow same-sex marriage. Because the decision was ultimately based on the Massachusetts, and not the United States, constitution, there will be no Supreme Court review of at least that decision, though one can anticipate that, sooner or later, a state or federal court will indeed reach a similar decision based on the Court's interpretation of the Constitution in *Lawrence*.

The controversy over gay and lesbian rights underscores how mistaken it may be to view the Court as truly "leading" popular opinion rather than following it or, at best, nudging it further along in directions it is already going. Given that support for gay and lesbian rights seems to be a function of age—the younger the person polled, the more likely he or she is to disapprove of state regulation of sexuality—as those who are now in their twenties and thirties inevitably take their place in positions of leadership (and on the Court), it is readily predictable that future decisions will in fact build on *Lawrence*.

This point about the Court's rather cautious role is probably underscored by the final issue raised by the Court's post-*Griswold* venture into determining the protections "privacy" affords citizens against state control: the regulation of death and dying. The Court's entry into this field occurred with *Cruzan* v. *Missouri Department of Health* (1990), which involved the rights of Nancy Cruzan's parents to order that her treatment be terminated because her coma, caused by an auto accident, left her in a "permanent vegetative state." Although the majority required that a high burden of proof lay on the parents to demonstrate Nancy's ostensible wishes in the matter (which, in this case, they could not meet), the Court, with only Justice Scalia disagreeing, seemed to agree that the Constitution did indeed give a person some right to control the circumstances of his or her death. The broad issue came up again in *Washington* v. *Glucksberg* (1997), in which terminally ill persons claimed the right to access to drugs that would end their lives. Although the Court refused to overturn a Washington state law forbidding such "assisted suicide," again a majority of the justices seemed to agree that under some circumstances it would indeed be unconstitutional for the state, in effect, to condemn a person to extraordinary suffering in lieu of suicide. One suspects that the Court will find that such circumstances obtain only after society begins to reach some degree of closure as part of its own intense discussion about the public policy of death. One also suspects that McCloskey would heartily agree with University of Chicago law professor Cass Sunstein, a recent defender of what he terms judicial "minimalism," that "it is not the Supreme Court but these arenas—state legislatures, prosecutors' offices, hospitals, and private homes—that should decide whether, when, and how to legitimate a 'right to die'"—even if, on occasion, the cost of this minimalism will be paid by the pain of the terminally ill and their families.

"WHEN A NATION IS AT WAR": THE SUPREME COURT, HOT WAR, AND COLD WAR

No survey of the Court's willingness to protect individual rights can ignore the fact of war (a topic of considerably more importance in 2004 than at the last time this book was revised in 2000). As Justice Holmes wrote in 1919, "When a nation is at war many things that might be said in time of peace are such a hindrance to its effort that their utterance will not be endured so long as men fight." One might well lament Holmes's comment, but his description seems accurate enough as an empirical matter. The previous chapter certainly made clear the willingness of the pre-1960's Court to enlist in the cold war struggle against communism and the Soviet Union by upholding the criminalization of much communist speech and conduct. It is therefore all the more remarkable that the U.S. entry into the distinctly "hot" Vietnam War during the 1960's provoked astonishingly little official suppression of speech as such, and the Court generally protected protesters. Earlier paragraphs mentioned the black armband worn to school by Mary Beth Tinker to protest the war and the vivid jacket worn in court by Paul Cohen to protest the military draft—actions deemed protected by the First Amendment.

Many of the Court's most significant war-related cases involved the administration of the Selective Service System, and it generally cracked down on local draft boards that sped up the induction of war protesters or otherwise seemed to be making its selections on blatantly political grounds. As noted earlier, though, the Court, through Chief Justice Warren, upheld a prohibition against burning one's draft card in 1968.

The Court also had to decide several cases involving the meaning of "religion" in statutes that offered conscientious objector status to those who opposed all war on the basis of their "religious" beliefs. The Court read "religion" extremely expansively to include basically any kind of belief that functioned similarly to ordinary religious belief as the foundation of one's stance toward life. However, the Court refused to grant conscientious objector status to a traditionally religious man who denounced the Vietnam War as immoral under the classical just-war theory, but conceded that he would participate in a "just" war.

Surely the most remarkable protection of speech by the Court during the Vietnam era was in the so-called Pentagon Papers case of 1971. It was triggered by the decision of the *New York Times* and other newspapers to publish secret documents compiled by the United States Defense Department concerning the major escalation of the war by the United States in 1964 and 1965. Although the documents dealt only with the Kennedy and Johnson Administrations, the Nixon Administration, citing the general importance of the Executive Branch's being able to preserve the secrecy of its materials, sought an injunction against further publication of any of the documents. Since 1931, the Court had read the First Amendment as being especially weighted against "prior restraints," which prevented speech, through licensing requirements or otherwise, from being delivered at all. The majority thus refused to issue the injunction and protected initial publication, though several of the justices suggested that the United States could criminally prosecute the newspapers subsequent to publication. (No such prosecutions were filed.) Three justices, including Chief Justice Burger, wrote heated dissents.

The Vietnam War clearly divided American society, especially at the elite level, as no previous foreign war had. Lyndon Johnson, elected in an overwhelming landslide in 1964, withdrew from the 1968 campaign after being challenged in the New Hampshire Primary by antiwar Democratic Senator Eugene McCarthy of Minnesota, and the 1968 Democratic Convention in Chicago was literally the most riotous such gathering in history. The very willingness of America's leading newspapers, such as the *New York Times* and *Washington Post,* to publish the Pentagon Papers illustrated their own disinclination to be cheerleaders for American foreign policy any longer, even in a time of war when many American troops (not to mention Vietnamese) were dying. The Court deserves credit for protecting the newspapers, but it can scarcely be described as climbing far out on a limb to rescue truly unpopular and vulnerable dissenters.

What the Court exhibited no interest at all in doing was accepting any of the challenges to the very legality of the Vietnam War itself. The war was never formally "declared" by Congress. Instead, its legal basis was the so-called Gulf of Tonkin resolution in 1964 that authorized the President to take such measures as he deemed necessary to rebuff purported attacks on American forces then in South Vietnam. The legal argument against the war was scarcely frivolous. Although there were many episodes of military conflict that had not been preceded by any official declarations of war (including the Korean "police action" of 1950–53), the Vietnam War, which left more than 50,000 Americans dead, seemed of significantly greater magnitude. And one of the enduring issues of American constitutionalism, going back to the initial debates about the 1787 Constitution, was the power granted the President regarding the disposition of American armed forces. All of this being said, the Court, over consistent dissents by Justice Douglas, avoided taking any of the cases raising such fundamental issues.

Again, one can have no doubt that McCloskey would have been appalled had the Court done otherwise. Imagine, for example, the Court's issuing an injunction ordering the President or the Secretary of Defense to withdraw American armed forces from Vietnam. That might have worked with Harry Truman and the steel mills, though McCloskey was scarcely an enthusiast even in those circumstances. It is immensely more difficult to contemplate an injunction working when the lives of soldiers are even more directly at stake and, just as important, the society is sharply divided about the underlying merits of the war itself. After all, millions of Americans, led by the President of the United States, defended American participation in what others perceived as a Vietnamese civil war, and the Court could scarcely have expected general public approbation had it chosen to adjudicate the legal merits of the Vietnam War. Although the Court would sometimes set up barriers to the unfettered cold war state—in 1972 a unanimous Court (Justice Rehnquist not participating) rejected the government's claim that it could wiretap individuals without warrants in "national security" cases—it scarcely was eager to address the constitutional problems posed by such a state. It refused, for example, to accept a challenge to the constitutionally dubious practices of Congress regarding the secret funding of intelligence agencies like the CIA, holding that no one had "standing" to invoke the Court's jurisdiction. And a sharply divided Court in 1972 refused to enjoin the army from engaging in the surveillance of lawful civilian political activities. The decision was based on a legal technicality, but most observers inferred that the Court would not stand in the way of the executive's being able to ferret out information about its domestic antagonists.

Even more striking in its way was *Dames & Moore* v. *Reagan,* a 1981 case in which the Court upheld an agreement between President Carter (defended by President Reagan) and the government of Iran, which had been holding more than four hundred Americans hostage in Tehran for well over a year. In return for releasing the hostages, Carter agreed, among other things, to suspend certain legal claims that had been filed in American courts by private businesses against the Iranian government. The Court exhibited no qualms about accepting the President's authority in effect to deprive these businesses of their legal rights. What distinguishes the Iranian and Steel Seizure cases, of course, is not only that the latter involved a politically vulnerable President and the former a brand-new chief executive, but also that a contrary decision in the Iranian case might well have triggered an international crisis.

By the end of the 1980's, and, even more so, after the Persian Gulf War of 1991, it was hard indeed to view the Court as interested in playing any role at all in curbing executive power relative to the basic conduct of American foreign policy and the engagement in foreign hostilities. That, for better or worse, would be left up to Congress, with its own power of the purse and other political resources. Indeed, when President Clinton in 1999 committed the American armed forces to join with NATO in engaging in war against Serbia, relatively few protested that he had no constitutional authority to do so.

All of the propositions suggested above will most certainly be tested as challenges to the Bush Administration's assertions of power with regard to the "War on Terrorism" make their way to the Court. In November 2003, for example, the Court agreed to hear a case testing whether foreign detainees at American facilities in Guantanamo Bay, Cuba, have any constitutional rights at all, including the basic right to make the government present even a bit of evidence that their detention can be justified. The administration denies that the Court has any jurisdiction at all to hear the case, as it reaches back to the 1901 *Insular Cases,* in which the Court stated that the Constitution did not necessarily "follow the flag" as the United States took over Puerto Rico as a result of the Spanish-American war. (Although the United States did not annex Cuba, it procured its control over Guantanamo in the aftermath of that war, a control that obviously survived the coming to power of Fidel Castro in 1960.)

Even if the Court accepts jurisdiction, an entirely separate issue will be whether the Court will require the Executive to present anything more than the most minimal evidence of culpability. The Second Circuit Court of Appeals in November 2003 heard a case involving Jose Padilla, an American citizen who was arrested a O'Hare airport in Chicago in 2002 on suspicion of terrorism and who has been detained since then in a military brig in South Carolina without any access to counsel or actual filing of charges. Not surprisingly, *Korematsu* has returned to the center of attention, as well as a 1942 case that allowed the President basically to order summary punishment of Nazi saboteurs who had landed in the United States in order to commit espionage. Given that the War on Terrorism will undoubtedly last the rest of our lives, the Court's decisions may have more fundamental consequences for American life than even *Korematsu,* which could be viewed as referring to a specific war that in fact was already moving toward its end by 1944, when *Korematsu* was decided. (Although the Reagan Administration in the 1980's supported an "apology" and $20,000/person reparations for the relocations upheld in *Korematsu*, Reagan's Attorney General, Edwin Meese, Jr., emphasized, at a University of Chicago conference in 2001, that he did not view this as a concession that *Korematsu* was in fact wrong as a matter of law.)

PRESIDENTIAL IMPEACHMENTS AND THE COURT

When McCloskey wrote his book, he no doubt believed that presidential impeachment was a constitutional nullity. It had been attempted once, during the Reconstruction turmoil, but of course even then the egregious Andrew Johnson retained his office (by one vote in the Senate); most observers in 1960 would have predicted that impeachment had disappeared as a genuine possibility within American politics. Those observers, obviously, were dead wrong. Richard Nixon's disastrous decision to participate in covering up the break-in at the Democratic Party headquarters (located in the Watergate apartment complex, which gave its name to the overall scandal) ultimately led, after further missteps by the President, to demands for his impeachment. The Court's role was limited but crucial: In *U.S. v. Nixon* (1974), it delivered the final blow to his efforts to retain his shattered Presidency by ordering him to disclose to the Special Prosecutor tapes of conversations in which Nixon had discussed the break-in. It was these tapes that provided the "smoking gun" of evidence that made it impossible to deny Nixon's involvement. The House Judiciary Committee in July 1974 voted two Articles of Impeachment against Nixon, after which he resigned.

Even *Nixon*, though, sent mixed messages. For the first time, the Court found that the President had a constitutionally based "executive privilege" to withhold material from senatorial or judicial scrutiny, even as it held that the privilege was overridden in the specific circumstances of the *Nixon* case. However dramatic the *Nixon* case is, it surely tells us little about the true power of the Court. At the time of the decision, Nixon was already clearly on the brink of impeachment, deserted even by rapidly increasing numbers of Republicans. The Court's decision immediately drew the support of almost the entire Congress and of the nation at large, thereby enhancing its own popular image as resolute defender of the rule of law. It is difficult otherwise to draw much in the way of a message from the episode.

A quarter century after Nixon's resignation, another President, Bill Clinton, would face many similar problems (though not over similar kinds of misconduct). The Supreme Court's role in the Clinton impeachment again was peripheral but important. In 1988 the Court had, in *Morrison* v. *Olson,* upheld the constitutionality of post-Watergate legislation mandating the appointment by a special panel of federal judges of an "independent prosecutor" in cases where misconduct had been alleged on the part of certain high-level members of the Executive Branch. Justice Scalia wrote a stinging dissent in which he presciently noted that "independence" could become, in effect, synonymous with a lack of accountability and that a zealous independent counsel, unconstrained by normal budgetary or institutional considerations, could wreak havoc on the persons being investigated. Though the Ethics in Government Act of 1978 authorized the appointment of independent counsel and was in fact supported by most Democrats, who relished its use against members of the Reagan Administration during the 1980's, Scalia's fears seemed most amply realized in the multiyear investigation of the Clintons, presided over by former federal judge and Solicitor General (and Republican Party activist) Kenneth Starr. Congress ultimately refused to renew the Act when it expired in 1999. By then, many of its former supporters were suggesting that Scalia's opinion was correct as a constitutional (and not only political) matter, but the Court never explicitly indicated second thoughts about its decision in *Morrison.*

The Court played an even more significant role in the impeachment drama when, in *Clinton* v. *Jones* (1997), it upheld the right of Paula Corbin Jones to move forward with a lawsuit for sexual harassment against President Clinton, thus rejecting the President's claim that he was immune from having to defend himself in such a suit until after leaving office. In what appears, in retrospect, to be an astonishing case of misjudgment about political reality, the Supreme Court, through Justice Stevens, stated that it would not "disrupt" the President's conduct of his duties to defend the lawsuit. It was *Jones* that helped to set up the fateful deposition in January 1998 in which Clinton presented grossly misleading statements about his relationship with White House intern Monica Lewinsky. (Even with *Jones,* the President could have chosen to settle the case prior to the deposition; in retrospect, the financial and political costs of settling, though undoubtedly high, could not possibly have outweighed the costs of proceeding as he did.) Had Clinton not offered his dubious deposition, the independent prosecutor, Kenneth Starr, would have had no reason to summon him before a federal grand jury in August 1998, where Clinton again offered what some (including the Independent Prosecutor and, ultimately, the House of Representatives) deemed perjurious testimony. Still, the principal activities of impeachment were carried out in the House of Representatives and the Senate, though Chief Justice Rehnquist, as required by the constitutional text, presided over the impeachment trial in the Senate, which resulted in Clinton's acquittal for failure to gain the necessary two-thirds vote for conviction.

Interestingly enough, Congress in recent decades has impeached two federal district judges: one of them, Walter Nixon, after his conviction for committing certain federal tax offenses; the other, Alcee Hastings, after his acquittal of charges that he had taken bribes with regard to a case before him. (Hastings later successfully ran for election to the House of Representatives.) One question that arose in both cases was whether the entire Senate had to be convened for a full-scale trial, or whether it would suffice to have the trial, in effect, conducted before a select committee of twelve senators, who would then report their conclusions to the full Senate prior to its debate over removal from office. In a 1993 decision involving Judge Nixon's impeachment, the Court held that the matter was nonjusticiable; in other words, the Senate had "sole discretion" to decide what procedures were acceptable, and the Court would not intervene.

NINE

JUDICIAL MONITORING OF THE NEW AMERICAN WELFARE STATE

B Y THE TURN of the twentieth century, government was accepting increasing responsibility for assuring the welfare of its citizens. It is crucial, however, to recognize that the particular means most often chosen to enhance their welfare was the *regulation* of the private sector. Rarely did the state take on direct responsibilities, including raising monies through taxation and then redistributing these funds to low-income citizens so that they might purchase necessary goods and services in the private market. Many important cases in the next thirty years or so after 1937 continued to address the basic question of regulation and the existence of limits, if any, on Congress' or a state legislature's ability to regulate the private market. The message of almost all of the post-1937 cases is that state governments have extremely wide discretion in this area, subject only to such limits as the inability to order racial segregation and the like.

The message has, however, become considerably more complex with regard to congressional discretion, especially at the turn of the new millennium. In a sharply contested 1995 decision, *United States v. Lopez,* the Court for the first time since 1936 held that a law regulating private individuals went beyond the legitimate domain of Congress' power under the commerce clause. The case involved a ban on guns within 1,000 feet of a school, and the five-justice majority held that Congress had not demonstrated the "substantial" effect on interstate commerce purportedly required by existing cases. Chief Justice William Rehnquist, for the majority, took care to distinguish the case from the classic New Deal cases that had so broadened congressional power. One could not tell at the time whether *Lopez* was a "one-time-only" case, in which the Court expressed

well-justified frustration with Congress' passing almost totally unnecessary "feel-good" legislation designed to assure the voters back home that
legislators care about crime and violence, or, on the contrary, whether the
case presaged a more fundamental shift by the Court, calling into question much of what had been assumed to be settled in the aftermath of the
New Deal.

Those who perceived the potential for a sea change, perhaps even a
"revolution" similar to the changes in doctrine between 1937 and 1942,
were heartened or dismayed by *United States* v. *Morrison* (2000), yet another bitterly contested five-to-four decision. The Court struck down a
key provision of the Violence Against Women Act of 1994 (passed by
Congress after four years of hearings and debate), which allowed victims
alleging such violence to sue their attackers in federal courts. It was held
beyond Congress' power either under the commerce clause or the Fourteenth Amendment. With regard to the commerce clause argument, the
majority held that violence against women, even if it generated consequences for the economy, did not involve a "commercial activity," and
that only such activities could be regulated by Congress. (Farmer Filburn's
production of wheat for his own use in 1942 was described as in effect
competing with wheat that was being sold in the market, whereas there is
no "market," state or local, for the battering of women.) The Fourteenth
Amendment aspect of *Morrison* will be discussed elsewhere in this chapter, but the Court also indicated far more suspicion of wide-ranging congressional power than had been the case in the mid-1960's with such cases
as *Katzenbach* v. *Morgan,* discussed in chapter 8, with reference to what
was there described as "hyperdeference" by the Court to congressional
regulation of "traditional" state interests.

Perhaps analysts in 2010 or 2020 will derive the ultimate lesson that
the willingness of President Franklin Roosevelt's justices to give Congress
enhanced power was later matched by an equal determination of appointees of far more conservative Presidents to rein in the national government.
As if to counter Justice Harlan Stone's memorable 1936 reminder that
Congress must be regarded as capable of effective governance and that the
only cure for judicial overreaching is "self-restraint," Justice Sandra Day
O'Connor wrote in a 1985 case that without aggressive judicial review,
"all that stands between the remaining essentials of state sovereignty and
Congress is the latter's underdeveloped capacity for self-restraint."

The contemporary Court has proved especially receptive to Justice
O'Connor's entreaty regarding congressional commands to states. Even

before her arrival on the Court, it had, in *National League of Cities* v. *Usery* (1976), held that Congress had exceeded its powers under the commerce clause by extending federal wages-and-hours requirements to state employees. This, said the Court, imposed on the "core" interests of the states and thus violated the principle of Federalism, even though it remained perfectly constitutional for Congress to impose similar requirements on private-sector employers. Although the case generated a flurry of scholarship wondering whether the 1937 settlement was being challenged by newly empowered conservatives appointed by President Richard M. Nixon (who, with Potter Stewart, a Republican appointed by President Eisenhower, provided the five-man majority), the Court quickly showed its reluctance to fight. Succeeding cases carefully "distinguished" *Usery* and upheld challenged congressional legislation. Even as a formal matter the case survived only nine years; it was overruled, by only one vote, in 1985. It was not so much that "the Court" had changed its collective mind as that Justice Blackmun, part of the 1976 majority, had changed *his* mind. He no longer believed that the Court could develop a coherent method by which to distinguish legitimate and illegitimate national regulation of the states and announced that the resolution of such questions should basically be left up to the political process. It was in that case, though, that O'Connor delivered her pronouncement and also indicated her hope that it, too, would be overruled when more sympathetic justices joined the Court.

Justices William Brennan and Thurgood Marshall indeed did leave the Court over the next half-dozen years, and were replaced by President George Bush with the considerably more conservative Justices David Souter and Clarence Thomas (though Justice Souter ultimately emerged by the end of the decade as a far more nationalist justice and staunch opponent of the new conservative majority than had first appeared would be the case). In 1992, a reconstituted majority accepted New York's plea to invalidate a congressional requirement that states assume responsibility for the disposal of certain nonstate-created radioactive waste. The majority emphasized that the nuclear waste regulation was not general, as with wage-and-hours legislation that applied to both private and state employers alike, but instead applied only to states. Similarly, in 1997 a five-justice majority struck down a section of the "Brady Bill," passed by Congress to regulate the sale of handguns, which required state police officers to engage in background checks of those who wished to purchase guns. The Court held that this constituted an illegitimate "commandeering" of state officials that was beyond federal power. If Congress wants the information, they should either establish a federal bureaucracy to obtain it or contract with state governments to provide it; what they cannot do is order the states to help implement the federal program.

The esoteric subject of "sovereign immunity" also proved vital in a number of cases, as five-justice majorities, over vigorous—indeed, sometimes vitriolic—dissent, declared that it would impose on the "dignity" of states to force them into federal or state courts to answer claims that they had violated federally established rights. Thus, one decision (*Alden v. Maine* [1999]) held that the state could not be required to respond to charges that the state had willfully failed to pay its employees the level of wages required by federal law. Similar in consequence was *Kimel* v. *Florida Board of Regents* (2000), yet another five-to-four decision in which the majority, in order to hold that states could not be sued under the Federal Age Discrimination Act, determined as well that Congress was without the power to pass such an act under the Fourteenth Amendment. Earlier decisions had held that Congress *could* force states into federal courts as part of enforcing Fourteenth Amendment rights, but *Kimel* strongly reasserted that only the Court could authoritatively interpret the meaning of equal protection. Having held in earlier cases that age discrimination did not violate constitutional norms, the Court was not inclined to accept a contrary conclusion by Congress. Similarly, in a case involving Alabama, the Court, in yet another angry five-to-four division, determined that Alabama could not be sued under the Americans with Disabilities Act for discriminating against the handicapped. The Court was unwilling to treat the handicapped as deserving special judicial solicitude under the Fourteenth Amendment, which, once more, meant that "sovereign immunity" protected the state against litigation by private parties. (Again, the contrast with *Katzenbach* v. *Morgan* is stark.) To be sure, Congress had the power under the commerce clause to regulate age discrimination or discrimination against the handicapped even by states, but *Alden* and other cases decided at the time had held that the clause did not give power to Congress to force states into federal courts or even the states' own courts. Legal scholars debated the practical consequences of these decisions, and it is indeed difficult to ascertain their actual significance. Symbolically, though, they seemed to suggest that "sovereign" states could basically decide which federal laws they wished to comply with. A caustic dissent by Justice John Paul Stevens announced his unwillingness to give precedential weight to the majority's decisions in this area. They represent, he said, "such a radical departure from the proper role of this Court that [they] should be opposed whenever the opportunity arises." Given the level of division on the Court with regard to such issues, it is safe to say that any final resolution will await perhaps two more presidential elections and the appointment of new justices.

At the most theoretical level, the debate concerns the basic structure of the Union. Robert McCloskey correctly described *McCulloch* v. *Maryland* (1819) as "the greatest decision John Marshall ever handed down." Not least among the reasons for this accolade is Marshall's determined rejection of the articulation of Union set out by James Madison and Thomas Jefferson some twenty years before in the Virginia and Kentucky Resolutions of 1798, which put forth the claim that the Constitution was a "compact" entered into by "sovereign states." No, said Marshall: "The government of the Union . . . is emphatically, and truly, a government of the [united] people"; and, he said, it was a mere happenstance that the people happened to meet, in their ratification conventions, in the separate state capitals. At the heart of this enduring struggle over what might be termed "constitutional ontology" is, among other things, the legitimacy of secession, as later Southerners happily embraced the Doctrine of '98 against the far more Marshallian vision of Abraham Lincoln. Not surprisingly, Marshall's nationalist vision was often quoted by the New Deal Supreme Court (and, of course, warmly endorsed by McCloskey).

It was therefore significant when three other justices signed a dissent by Justice Thomas in a 1995 case striking down an attempt by Arkansas to impose term limits on candidates for the House of Representatives and the Senate from that state; Thomas invoked the "compact" language and seemingly rejected the Marshallian theory of Union. (Indeed, Ronald Reagan in his first inaugural address had called on the American people to remember "that the Federal Government did not create the states; the states created the Federal Government"—a direct, albeit unacknowledged, repudiation of Marshall and Lincoln.) At the very least, this should remind us that the great constitutional controversies outlined by McCloskey endure and that it would be a mistake to assume they had been truly resolved, in the sense of being brought to permanent closure, at the end of any given "period" of the Court—an error in thinking to which McCloskey did not succumb.

Many analysts suggest that the practical meaning of these "state sovereignty" cases is vitiated by the ability of Congress to condition the availability of federal funds on the willingness of recipients, including states, to conform with congressional policy. Indeed, Chief Justice Rehnquist, who has joined in almost all of the pro-state decisions since authoring *National League of Cities* in 1976, wrote for the Court in a 1987 case, *South*

Dakota v. *Dole*. The Court upheld Congress' mandate, attached to the receipt of federal highway funds, that states raise their legal drinking age to twenty-one. Putting aside whether Congress could directly raise the drinking age under the commerce clause, the majority emphasized Congress' "spending power" under Article I of the Constitution and the legitimacy of placing strings on the receipt of federal funds. Rehnquist *did* write that "Congress' power under the spending power is not unlimited," but it is hard, as a practical matter, to divine what those limitations are in regard to states. Such declarations, of course, do reserve the Court's power to invalidate some future congressional program, even if it provides no useful guidance beforehand as to when that might occur.

With regard to understanding the Supreme Court's role in monitoring the federal-state relationship, one should also be aware of the "preemption" doctrine, which refers to the extent to which federal law will be viewed as "occupying" the field in some area and thus displace state law. If the state law flatly contradicts federal law, there is no real constitutional difficulty: The Supremacy Clause of Article VI dictates that the national law triumphs. Far more complex is how one analyzes the legitimacy of state laws that "go beyond" the regulatory regime imposed by the national government. An excellent example is regulation of oil-tanker safety requirements. Congress has in fact passed legislation on this topic, but the law did not explicitly prohibit states from passing their own further regulations. However, when Washington State did require a greater degree of (expensive) safety that might prevent, for example, oil spills in Puget Sound, a divided Court struck the state law down, declaring that it had been preempted by the national legislation. This might reflect a continuing nationalist commitment on the part of even a conservative Court; it might also reflect the fact that one consequence of Congress's having become far more conservative as a result of elections in the 1980's and, most dramatically, 1994, is that it is selected states, and not the national government, that are more likely to pass what is perceived as "liberal" regulatory legislation of the kind at issue in the Washington State case. The Court might therefore be more consistently conservative both in limiting the effect of certain legislation on state governments and in preventing states from more vigorous regulation of business.

THE RISE OF THE WELFARE STATE

A *welfare* state, in the sense used in this chapter, involves the active dispensation by the state of funds or services to recipients chosen at least in part on the basis that they have legitimate needs that could not otherwise be supplied through the operation of the standard market—even one subject to the higher level of regulation associated with the New Deal era and afterward. It is the welfare state, far more than the regulatory state, that merits the description (often applied by its opponents) of the "taxing and spending" state. Whatever the importance of such New Deal agencies as the Securities and Exchange Commission or the National Labor Relations Board, they required relatively little additions to the federal budget. That is obviously not true of the kinds of governmental programs (some of them, such as Social Security, very much linked with the New Deal) that typify the welfare state. If the earlier part of the twentieth century features the maturation in the United States of the modern *regulatory* state, then the dominant motif of the last third of the century is the remarkable growth of governmental programs, at both federal and state levels, that involve direct expenditures of tax revenues.

First, some facts. The national budget passed the $100 billion point only in 1962, with the previous high of $95 billion being reached in 1945, the last year of World War II. During the truncated administration of John F. Kennedy, a "war on poverty" was declared, though it was the successor administration of Lyndon Johnson that won major legislative victories in this war. Between 1964 and 1966, for example, Congress passed, at Johnson's behest, a plethora of statutes, including the Food Stamp Act and the legislation establishing Medicare and Medicaid. Although Johnson's successor, Richard Nixon, was scarcely thought of as a liberal, his administration consolidated the changes provoked by Johnson and, indeed, in some cases added to them. By 1975 the federal budget was $326 billion. One should obviously control for inflation. Thus in constant 1972 dollars the federal nondefense budget went from $32.1 billion in 1960 to $60.9 billion in 1969 and fully doubled again, to $115 billion, by 1978. Breaking down these figures functionally, one discovers that federal spending on elementary and secondary education went from $417 million in 1961 to $46.5 billion in 1979, and health care costs climbed from around $150 million in 1961 to $4.9 billion in 1966, immediately after the passage of the 1965 Medicare legislation.

Nor did the coming to power of a significantly more conservative antiwelfare-state Republican like Ronald Reagan fundamentally change things, except to slow down the almost inexorable growth of the welfare state. When Reagan was elected President, in 1980, the nondefense federal budget was approximately $850 billion. A decade later, in the middle of George H. W. Bush's administration, the figure had gone up to $1.25 trillion, and by the middle of his son's presidency, the amount was approaching $1.5 trillion. (All of these figures are in constant 1996 dollars.) Federal expenditures on medical care almost tripled between 1980 and 1990 and then went up approximately 60 percent again in the ensuing decade, to a total of $437 billion. The passage in November 2003 of a prescription drug component of Medicare is predicted to cost at least $525 billion over the next decade, which effectively guarantees at least yet another doubling, to approximately $1 trillion for medical expenses alone, by the turn of the next decade. There has been similar doubling of federal expenditures since 1985 in student assistance expenditures by the Department of Education (over $15 billion in 2002) and an 80 percent increase in Social Security expenditures since 1990 (to almost $400 billion). And none of these figures takes into account state and local welfare expenditures, which have also risen over this time period.

The Court had almost nothing to do with these dramatic developments, other than to get out of the way of the state and national governments. Still, the consequences of these changes in the polity inevitably affected both the business, and ultimately the role, of the Supreme Court during the last third of the twentieth century. Insofar as one of McCloskey's aims was to identify the variation in primary issues confronting the Court—and the different roles the Court would choose to play—it seems legitimate to suggest that the concern about civil liberties and minority rights he identified as the dominant motif of the post-1937 Court began to give way by the 1970's to concern about somewhat newer issues linked to the rise of the welfare state. Indeed, the Court has taken on as one of its principal roles that of *monitor* of this new state. Among the central questions that confront the Court are the following:

(1) To what extent, if at all, was the government *required* to take account of the welfare needs of the populace and to supply at least some of those needs to those having inadequate financial resources? This is the problem of so-called "affirmative rights."

(2) Insofar as most welfare programs are limited to those who establish their specific eligibility for benefits, must the state give some degree of "due process" to persons when making decisions of eligibility?

(3) Even if one concedes that the state must be able to place reasonable conditions on those who receive its funds, are there *limits* on what the state can ask? A linked issue is raised by the vast increase in the number of public employees hired to administer the welfare state. To what extent can the state

impose certain conditions—the inability, for example, to engage in normal political activity—in exchange for the job?

(4) How much freedom does the state have in defining those general classes of persons eligible to receive benefits? For example, can the state distinguish between citizens and noncitizens, long-term residents and newcomers, African-Americans and whites, men and women? To some extent, this issue is treated under the equal protection clause of the Fourteenth Amendment (or, for the federal government, the Fifth Amendment). In addition, though, it raises classic questions about the role that ought to be played by the Court in assuring that legislatures strive to achieve some ascertainable "public interest" rather than become mere agents of politically dominant "private" or "special" interests.

All of these raise obvious problems not only of constitutional doctrine, but also of the effective role that can be played by the Supreme Court as an actor within American politics. In all of these areas, one sees, at least in the four decades between 1963 and 2003, a Court that has been hesitant to declare (or maintain) any sweeping doctrinal visions, whether because of the political fragmentation among the justices that has made consensus unachievable or because of the intrinsic difficulty of the issues themselves.

THE REJECTION OF AFFIRMATIVE ENTITLEMENTS

Generally, constitutional rights within the American system have been viewed as "negative" limitations on state power to deprive its members of certain liberties guaranteed by the Constitution. The Bill of Rights, for example, is basically a series of "thou shalt nots" directed at government. But does the state have "affirmative" duties to give succor to persons rather than merely not directly "mistreat" them? The American legal tradition has generally rejected any "duty to rescue." It is perfectly acceptable, as a legal matter, for an onlooker to refuse to go to the aid of a drowning person even where giving such aid would be without risk to the rescuer. Should it be different if the state is the onlooker? Must it supply lifeguards, or can it leave up to individuals the decision whether to take the risks associated with swimming? One may, of course, regard the decision to swim (or to ski, or, for that matter, to build homes in predictable flood-plain or forest-fire areas) as "voluntary" and therefore feel quite comfortable saying that such decisions need not, indeed *should* not, be subsidized by the state. But is one's vulnerability always the results of one's own decisions?

The "rediscovery" in the early 1960's of poverty in America, coupled with a view that many (most) of the poverty-stricken were the victims of complex social and economic processes well beyond their own control, led to a host of statutes attempting to alleviate the circumstances of those in need (and thus to "rescue" them from their desperate circumstances). Inevitably, the legislative response was limited, whether by budgetary pressures or the simple political unpopularity of certain groups making claims for aid. Just as inevitably, the Supreme Court, increasingly perceived as an ally of liberal reformers, was called upon by political activists to join in solving the plight of those poor unable to win legislative victories.

The first move toward recognizing an affirmative right to economic assistance came in regard to indigent criminal defendants. Although the Sixth Amendment provides that "[i]n all criminal prosecutions, the accused shall enjoy the right . . . to have the Assistance of Counsel for his defense," this had been interpreted only "negatively," as prohibiting the state from interfering with the representation of defendants by lawyers they had hired in the private market (or who were voluntarily contributing their services). It provided nothing to the indigent unable to hire counsel (or to find a volunteer attorney).

Although *Powell* v. *Alabama* (1932) held that indigent defendants in cases in which the death penalty was a possibility had to be provided counsel, the Court had carefully refrained from extending any such right to indigent defendants in general. A 1942 case, *Betts* v. *Brady*, did hold that courts should reverse convictions of defendants having no lawyer where, because of the complexity of the trial, the lack of representation was "fundamentally unfair." Over the next two decades, justices were forced to become intimately familiar with trial records in order to determine whether the lack of representation fatally tainted their procedural fairness.

Finally, in *Gideon* v. *Wainwright* (1963), the Court unanimously overruled *Betts* and adopted a per-se rule to replace the case-by-case general standard of the earlier case. According to Justice Hugo Black, "any person hauled into court, who is too poor to hire a lawyer, cannot be assured a fair trial unless counsel is provided for him. . . . [L]awyers in criminal courts are necessities, not luxuries." Similar cases arising in the mid-1960's extended this right to counsel to any charge that carried with it the threat of jail, as well as to initial appeals from convictions. Later Courts became significantly more restrained in their reading of *Gideon*.

Thus 1974 and 1989 decisions rejected the duty of the state to provide legal assistance in regard to appeals to the Supreme Court itself and—far more important as a practical matter—to petitions for habeas corpus filed in federal courts by convicts challenging the fairness of their convictions in state courts under federal constitutional norms.

Nor did the Court exhibit the slightest enthusiasm for supplying state-paid attorneys to indigents faced with civil litigation, however important the interests involved. Thus the Court in 1981 rejected claims that "fundamental fairness" required legal assistance to an indigent mother threatened with loss of custody of her child because of charges of child neglect. To be sure, Congress and many states began funding limited civil legal services for the poor at the end of the 1960's—a subject of recurrent battle and diminished funding during the Reagan era of the 1980's and thereafter—but this was apparently a matter of legislative grace rather than constitutional necessity.

Gideon and its progeny, if taken seriously, were significantly redistributive in their implications. The Court rarely considered the actual mechanisms by which distribution would take place. It was all too happy to leave to local administrators the details of how the lawyers supplied to the indigent were to be paid. The Court quickly determined, though, that indigent defendants certainly weren't entitled to the level of representation that could be purchased by the well-off; furthermore, it basically refused to hear any of the multitude of "inadequacy of representation" cases challenging the quality of state-provided counsel. Professor Louis Michael Seidman has suggested that the primary impact of *Gideon,* coupled with the Burger Court's upholding of the distinctively American process of "plea bargaining"—by which criminal defendants waive their various constitutional rights, including their right to a jury trial, in return for an "acceptable" level of punishment—is putting in place an essentially bureaucratic structure designed to administer an assembly-line system of criminal justice. Such a system limits, for all practical purposes, the full enjoyment of ostensibly constitutional rights to the well-off and provides state-funded or subsidized attorneys to explain to less-fortunate defendants why resisting the fate wished for them by prosecutors would be a mistake.

An affirmative right of a quite different sort also seemed to be the result of a 1966 case, *Harper* v. *Virginia Board of Elections,* that invalidated Virginia's poll tax as a condition for voting in elections for state offices. (The poll tax for elections for federal officials had been prohibited by the Twenty-fourth Amendment, added to the Constitution in 1964.) Although Justice William O. Douglas spoke of the specific importance of voting, his opinion for the Court also contained language suggesting that classification by ability to pay would now be treated by the Court as an "invidious discrimination" barred by the Fourteenth Amendment. "Voter qualifications," he wrote, "have no relation to wealth." But, of course, the same thing could be said about receiving health care, riding subways, crossing toll bridges, visiting public zoos, or participating in an almost infinite number of other activities that are available only upon payment of fees. One could limit the force of Douglas's statement by putting the emphasis on the importance of voting itself. Visiting a zoo is regarded as a "fundamental interest" by almost no one; the same, obviously, cannot be said about the ability to cast a ballot, perhaps the sine qua non of membership in a democratic polity. Was voting unique as such an interest, or were there others that also had constitutional implications for the operation of state programs?

The argument for more general "welfare rights" appeared to gain momentum in *Shapiro* v. *Thompson,* a 1969 case dealing with the ability of states to require one year of residence before an indigent resident could receive welfare benefits. In striking down the requirement, Justice Brennan suggested that the special vulnerability of the indigent made such welfare a "fundamental interest"; the state therefore had to supply a "compelling state interest" before depriving the indigent of the aid in question. Interestingly enough, one of the three dissenters was Earl Warren himself. As a former (liberal) governor of California, he might well have feared that adoption of the *Shapiro* doctrine would make California's generous welfare policies a "welfare magnet" that would draw indigents from other, far less generous, states. Indeed, these less generous states probably would like nothing more than the emigration of its less-productive, more welfare-dependent citizenry, to the "magnet" states.

In any event, both the general political ambiance of the 1960's and the specific apparent receptivity of a liberal Supreme Court, especially between 1963 and 1969, to egalitarian pleas for redistribution of resources from haves to have-nots, spurred many organizations to seek judicial help. They would be frustrated, however, in part because of changes of membership that left the "Warren Court" (dominated by William Brennan) only a memory. Warren had submitted his resignation early in 1968, to take effect upon the confirmation of his successor. President Johnson, in a rare act of remarkable political maladroitness, nominated Justice Abe Fortas to be Chief Justice and a Texas associate, former congressman Homer Thornberry, to succeed Fortas as an associate justice. Already weakened by Vietnam and his lame-duck status after his March 1968 announcement that he would not seek reelection, Johnson could not organize an effective defense against a Republican filibuster that prevented confirmation of Fortas and, therefore, the creation of a vacancy for Thornberry to fill. In retrospect, one can view this as the first use of the filibuster to defeat a judicial nomination that almost certainly would have been confirmed had the Senate been allowed to vote.

Because of Fortas's defeat, Warren remained in office after the 1968 election. Its winner, Richard Nixon, had explicitly promised to change the direction of what was described as a dangerously liberal, activist Supreme Court. He quickly named, and achieved Senate confirmation for, Warren Burger as the new Chief Justice. (Burger had been a conservative member of the Court of Appeals for the District of Columbia.) Immediately beforehand, Fortas suffered the humiliation of being forced to resign after disclosure of some dubious financial dealings, thereby giving Nixon a second appointment early in his term. After rejecting two Southern conservatives nominated by Nixon, the Senate easily confirmed his third choice, the Minnesotan Harry Blackmun, in 1970. Later that year both Justices Harlan and Black retired because of illnesses, and Nixon successfully replaced them in 1971 with Lewis Powell, a racially moderate but otherwise conservative Southern Democrat, and William Rehnquist, by far the most conservative nominee for the Supreme Court in more than fifty years.

The period between 1970 and 1973 would prove to be a decisive watershed with regard to what some termed "the constitutionalization of the welfare state." By the end of this period, it was clear that the Court had repudiated any suggestions that the state might be under any general duty to rescue indigents from their fate. For example, in *Dandridge* v. *Williams* (1970), the Court upheld a provision of Maryland's law on Aid to Families with Dependent Children that limited the monthly grant to any one family to $150, regardless of its size or computed need. As a result, individual members of a large family received less per capita than the state itself recognized as the minimum required for subsistence. Although Justice Stewart for the majority conceded that the case "involves the most basic economic needs of impoverished human beings," he refused to apply any special scrutiny to Maryland's program. It was, the Court said, just another socioeconomic policy of the state, and the teaching of 1937 is that the state had extensive discretion in establishing or administering such programs. A similar fate met a 1972 claim that the "need for decent shelter" should lead the Court to engage in especially strict supervision of Oregon landlord-tenant law.

A like pattern can be detected in 1977 and 1980 cases dealing with the right of states and the federal government to refuse to include most abortions in medical benefits provided poor women, even though the state would pay for services surrounding childbirth. *Roe* was interpreted as prohibiting only the criminalization of abortion. It did not require active aid by the state for women unable to purchase abortions through the private market.

Perhaps the most dramatic illustration of the Court's resistance to finding affirmative rights within the Constitution came in the 1989 *De-Shaney* case involving a Wisconsin youngster beaten into a permanently brain-damaged state by his father after state welfare authorities had become aware that the child was possibly being abused. They had, in fact, temporarily removed the child from parental custody before returning him to the father. Should Wisconsin, then, have to accept financial responsibility for the fate visited upon "poor Joshua" (as he was called by Justice Blackmun in dissent)? No, said the Court. "The affirmative duty to protect"—in effect, to rescue—"arises not from the State's knowledge of the individual predicament"—the state is scarcely unaware that many people are in precarious or even desperate straits—"or from its expressions of intent to help him, but from the limitation which it has imposed on his freedom to act on his own behalf." Wisconsin "played no part in [the] creation of the child's plight, nor did it do anything to render him any more vulnerable to them."

After 1969, then, the Court basically rejected almost all invitations to declare new rights of the poor that suggested a constitutional duty to rescue them from the dire fate that lack of resources can entail in a market-oriented society—though many of the key decisions saw three or four liberal dissenters challenging the more conservative majority. By a quarter century later, the Court was firmly controlled by conservatives who would certainly continue to resist any such suggestions, and there was relatively little public outcry about the Court's stinginess in this regard. If the public wished to rescue those in need, it had only to elect legislators who promised to raise the necessary taxes. This the public was most definitely unwilling to do, as shown most dramatically by the results of the 1994 election: For the first time in more than forty years, both the House and Senate were returned to Republican control. One of the most important consequences of that election was the 1996 repeal by Congress, in a bill signed by President Bill Clinton, of several basic federal welfare programs with roots in the New Deal and the placement of stringent time limits on those still eligible for welfare funds. A mark of the conservatives' victory was that almost no lawyers suggested that the legislation presented constitutional difficulties or, perhaps more precisely, that it would be worthwhile to litigate any such claims before the present Supreme Court. The extent of the welfare state seems, more than ever, to be a topic for political debate rather than judicial resolution.

USER FEES, EQUALITY, AND THE WELFARE STATE

Just as the Court disappointed liberals who hoped that it would require states to fund new redistributive programs designed to alleviate the plight of the less fortunate, so did it reject most of the challenges, encouraged by decisions like the 1966 *Harper* case, to the extraction of fees for public services. *Boddie* v. *Connecticut* (1971) did hold that Connecticut could not constitutionally impose filing fees from indigents suing for divorce. Justice John Harlan stressed that the state absolutely monopolized the dissolution of legal marriage; it was therefore fundamentally unfair for the state to deprive indigents seeking divorce from access to its courts because of their inability to pay the fees. Two years later, however, in *Kras* v. *U.S.*, a five-justice majority composed of the four Nixon appointees and the relatively conservative Kennedy appointee Byron White refused to find unconstitutionality in the U.S. policy prohibiting access to federal bankruptcy courts by those unable to pay what was then a $50 filing fee. One could, therefore, be too poor to afford bankruptcy—and to gain the "fresh start" that bankruptcy promises to debtors. (The rationale was that there were other ways besides bankruptcy to dissolve one's debt, including negotiating with one's creditors, whereas such "private" alternatives were unavailable with regard to marriage.)

Perhaps the most visible sign of the Court's unwillingness to expand notions of constitutional entitlement—and, just as important, to enter into almost certain political struggle with elected politicians and the publics they represent—was a 1973 case, *San Antonio Independent School District* v. *Rodriguez,* which challenged the Texas system of school finance. Like many states, Texas relied basically on local property taxes, supplemented by some state funds, to finance its public schools. This meant, among other things, that the amount of money available for the education of students within given school districts, even after the state supplement, depended on the wealth of these districts. This, argued the parents in low-wealth districts, violated the equal protection clause insofar as their children would receive diminished education relative to the children of more-fortunate parents living elsewhere. (One could scarcely defend this

difference by arguing that well-off children "need" more educational resources than do poor children.) Four justices—Brennan, Marshall, Douglas, and White, all Democrats—agreed. More importantly, of course,
five justices did not. Education was not, wrote Justice Powell, a "fundamental interest," nor was reliance on district wealth "suspect," the two
judicial mantras signaling heightened judicial intervention. Instead, the
Court asked only if the Texas method of school finance was "rationally"
justified, and the answer was yes, inasmuch as it helped to preserve local
autonomy over public schools.

In the ensuing years, many state supreme courts—including that of
Texas itself—have struck down educational finance systems as violations
of state constitutions. Almost invariably, such decisions have generated
political crises within the states, given the inevitability of significantly increased taxation to pay for the redistribution of funds from the prosper-
ous to the less-fortunate school districts. The class dimension has also, in
many states, intersected with racial and ethnic dimensions: Plaintiffs are
often members of inner-city racial or ethnic minorities who are complaining about the considerably greater resources often available to white sub-
urbanites. State legislatures dominated by suburban members are often
less than eager to comply with judicially imposed mandates to equalize
school finance. In turn, courts have been tested both as to the extent of
their own commitments and, just as significantly, the actual extent of the
political resources available to them to achieve their goals.

Whatever the travails of supervising such court-ordered changes as
reapportionment or even school desegregation, they only rarely involved
spending large sums of money and the concomitant necessity of finding
new funding sources. It is inconceivable that anyone who shares even a
measure of Robert McCloskey's skepticism about the judicial capacity to
move beyond the broad mainstream of public opinion could lament the
failure of the United States Supreme Court to embark on the kind of political tasks that would have been required by a serious commitment to
equalization of financial resources among the literally thousands of American school districts. If courts are going to do this, he might have argued,
far better it be state courts, especially if, as is true in many instances, the
judges are elected and therefore in some measure accountable to the citizenry. Indeed, there is reason to believe that in some instances state legislatures are quite happy to have state judges—especially if they have some
measure of practical political experience prior to their judicial careers—
resolve hot-potato issues like school finance, so long, at least, as they can
be readily tamed if they go "too far" in their demands. Federal courts, how-

ever, are another matter, given the much greater insulation from political control.

One lesson, then, of the first forty years of the "modern" American welfare state is that states and Congress are, with few exceptions, given a relatively free hand in establishing redistributive programs and then deciding upon the level of funding of those programs. One might explain this freedom simply in terms of the majority of justices during this period being politically conservative and thus likely to be unsympathetic to redistributive transfers of wealth. Though there is undoubtedly some truth to this, one should not ignore the fact that even many liberals eventually became more skeptical of the Court's capacity to make the kinds of judgments involved with the construction of a modern welfare state. How, for example, does one really identify the "fundamental interests" of a modern society, and is there any reason to rely on judges to identify them? It should also be clear that any Court that found many interests to be "fundamental" and thus constitutionally entitled to governmental funding (whatever the wishes of tax-passing legislatures) would be simultaneously establishing itself as precisely the kind of "superlegislature" whose legitimacy was denied by the constitutional revolution of 1937. By the time of his death in 1998, even many of those who admired Justice Brennan and shared his deep concern about indignities visited upon the poor wondered if his vision of the Court's role might not have overreached.

DUE PROCESS IN THE ADMINISTRATION OF THE WELFARE STATE

Whatever the minimal constitutional duty to establish any welfare programs in the first place, state legislatures and Congress have obviously chosen to establish many such programs. Many of them, particularly those most likely to be identified by the public as "welfare"—income transfers from the well-off to the less-fortunate—involved the use of so-called "means tests," by which access to the programs was limited only to those who could demonstrate their lack of financial resources. A fear surrounding any means-tested programs is that cheaters will try to take advantage of state largesse by falsely claiming to be eligible or otherwise engaging in what some analysts label "strategic misrepresentation." Almost immediately, questions arose regarding the procedures determining eligibility.

Perhaps the quintessential "Brennan Court" case was *Goldberg* v. *Kelly* (1970). Could New York, in administering its Aid to Families with Dependent Children (AFDC) and Home Relief programs, terminate public assistance payments to those it thought to be cheaters without first giving them a hearing at which they would be informed of the charges and given a chance to respond? In fact, the state offered *posttermination* hearings, but it saw no duty to offer *pretermination* ones. Pretermination hearings would, it argued, not only increase the costs of administering the welfare program but also ultimately result in less overall money being distributed to deserving recipients unless legislatures added the money paid to cheaters in the time before their hearing without taking it from other programs serving the poor. The Court disagreed, emphasizing that welfare payments provide "the means to obtain essential food, clothing, housing, and medical care."

It is worth mentioning that *Goldberg* was decided within weeks of *Dandridge* v. *Williams,* the case mentioned above that upheld Maryland's limitations on welfare stipends to large families. Six of the nine justices clearly believed that the cases were fundamentally similar. That is, three would have upheld the claimants' arguments in both cases, three would have equally rejected them. Only the remaining three justices believed that they were genuinely distinguishable. It is a property of multi-member courts, though, that decision-making power often goes to "median justices," even as most of their colleagues would adopt more "consistent" doctrines. Those seeking to maximize doctrinal clarity should probably support single-member Supreme Courts, though, of course, there are a host of reasons to consider that a terrible idea otherwise.

Once again reflecting the crucial changes in membership, the Court in *Matthews* v. *Eldridge* (1976) considerably cut back on *Goldberg* in a case involving the termination of disability benefits under the Social Security Act. The formality of procedures depended on balancing the importance of the individual need for a government benefit, the state interest in expeditious action, and the likelihood of the state's actually committing error in its (prehearing) process of decision making. Reasoning that "a disabled worker's need is likely to be less than that of a welfare recipient," the Court found posttermination hearings adequate. *Goldberg,* which had been hailed by some as the initial stage of a "due process revolution" in the administration of state and federal welfare programs, thus turned out to be of relatively marginal importance. Even the requirement that persons be given some kind of hearing when they lose their welfare benefits—even if, contrary to the decision in *Goldberg* itself, it need not occur prior to termination—proved vulnerable to formal changes in governmental policy. For example, benefits could be assigned only for a limited time period, with recipients then forced to reapply for funds.

CONDITIONAL FUNDING AND THE MODERN WELFARE STATE

Perhaps the central issue raised by the post–New Deal activist state is whether the Constitution limits the kinds of conditions the state places on its own willingness to deal with the recipients of its largesse. *Dole,* the South Dakota drinking-age case, exemplifies one aspect of the problem, though most of the cases involve private individuals asserting their own claims.

Justice Oliver Wendell Holmes, then on the Supreme Judicial Court of Massachusetts, established one end of the doctrinal spectrum in an 1892 case involving a New Bedford policeman dismissed for violating a departmental regulation against political activism: "Petitioner may have a constitutional right to talk politics, but he has no constitutional right to be a policeman. . . . [H]e takes the employment on the terms which are offered him." The state, then, can in effect require waiver of First Amendment rights as a condition of receiving the "privilege" of a job. This can basically be summarized as adopting the old adage that "the person paying the piper calls the tune." Holmes's analysis was extended in many cases to cover almost all welfare-state benefits, similarly treated as "privileges" to be extended on practically any terms asserted by the granting state.

If Holmes is one end of the spectrum, Justice William O. Douglas is at the other. For him "the central question is whether the government by force of its largesse has the power to 'buy up' rights guaranteed by the Constitution." He delivered this remark in *Wyman* v. *James* (1971), yet another AFDC case testing, in this instance, the state's ability to condition its aid on the recipients' agreeing to accept unannounced "home visits" by welfare caseworkers monitoring the program. Otherwise, such "visits" would require search warrants. The Court, in upholding the state's demand that the warrant requirement in effect be waived, insisted that "the visitation in itself is not forced or compelled. . . . If consent to the visitation is withheld, no visitation takes place. The aid then never begins or merely ceases, as the case may be." Douglas, in dissent, emphasized that the recipient's circumstances made it so difficult to reject the state's offer that it ought not be regarded as a genuinely "voluntary" waiver of rights.

The Court has scarcely explained when it would uphold certain waivers of otherwise-protected constitutional rights or, in contrast, describe them as illegitimate attempts by the state to compel, through the pressure of its offer of welfare benefits, results that it could not legislate directly. Perhaps one explanation for the intellectual intractability of the "unconstitutional conditions conundrum" is its lack of particular political valence, either liberal or conservative, that might tempt a politically sophisticated Court to proffer a single grand theory.

An early critique of Holmesian argumentation was offered, for example, by the very conservative Justice George Sutherland in a 1926 opinion invalidating California's attempt to condition the right of a trucking company to use public roads on its agreeing to charge its customers California-determined prices: "If the state may compel the surrender of one constitutional right as a condition of its favor, it may, in a like manner, compel a surrender of all." The Court found it "inconceivable that guarantees embedded in the Constitution of the United States may thus be manipulated out of existence." Sutherland, of course, was defending the traditional right of private business to set its own prices; Douglas was defending the privacy rights of poor women. Each, though, could readily adopt the rhetoric of the other.

It should therefore occasion little surprise that the Supreme Court has ended up, for all practical purposes, offering case-by-case (or at least issue-by-issue) balancing, studying the importance of the proclaimed state interest versus the actual burden placed on the recipients, as an alternative to sweeping pronouncements designed to cut the Gordian knot. Thus the Court struck down a requirement that noncommercial radio stations that accept any support at all from the United States agree not to engage in any editorializing. The majority, over heated dissent, found this unjustified by a "compelling" state interest, which the Court required because the condition involved a waiver of rights otherwise protected by the First Amendment. The Court also ruled, in a series of cases extending from 1963 to 1989, that the state could not condition unemployment compensation on the willingness of recipients to violate tenets of their religion, such as working on their Sabbath or, if they are religious pacifists, working on military weapons.

On the other hand, in *Rust* v. *Sullivan* (1991) a sharply split Court upheld a so-called gag rule that prohibited doctors in federally funded family planning programs from informing their patients of the availability of abortion as a possible alternative to carrying a pregnancy to term. The majority did not see this as raising serious First Amendment questions at all.

Perhaps the most contentious issue with regard to conditional funding has involved the arts. Can artists who receive federal funds be required to promise that they will not paint sacrilegious pictures or write plays that do not mock basic social values? When one photographer exhibited an "art photograph" of a crucifix in urine, for example, a national outcry ensued, and Congress explicitly attempted to control the granting of funds by the National Endowment for the Arts. When the Supreme Court finally decided a case challenging the new rules, the Court basically straddled the issue, over vigorous dissents, from opposite sides of the spectrum. One side argued that Congress in fact enjoyed relative carte blanche in distributing federal subsidies to artists, given that an artist who wishes to paint objectionable pictures can simply refuse to accept the subsidy and instead seek support from the private market, while the other side insisted just as vigorously that such conditions violated the most basic tenets of the First Amendment's commitment to freedom of expression. There is no reason to believe that the issue will not continue to plague future courts.

If one group is furious about federal funding going to fund "antireligious" art, another is equally upset about funds going to fund "religious" practices or organizations. We will consider this below in the context of religious schools, but the issue also arose with regard to the funding practices of the University of Virginia, which subsidized a variety of student publications but refused to grant a subsidy (raised from compulsory student fees) to an explicitly religious journal. An extremely fragmented Court—with Justice O'Connor taking care, in a concurring opinion, to assert the extremely fact-bound, limited nature of the five-justice majority opinion—struck down the Virginia limitation, arguing that the student authors of the journal were entitled to "equal treatment" and could not be deprived of the subsidy because of their religious commitments. (Earlier cases had struck down attempts by localities and universities to limit the ability of religious organizations to use publicly funded and operated auditoriums or after-hours classroom space.) Four justices dissented, arguing that this constituted precisely the kind of "establishment of religion" that James Madison intended to foreclose with the First Amendment. Of course, Madison wrote well before the emergence of the modern welfare state, and it is not clear why those who reject "original intent" in other contexts—think only of Congress's power to regulate the modern economy—believe that Madison has much to teach with regard to figuring out the parameters of a contemporary state that offers a level of benefits that would have literally been inconceivable to him.

The *Rust* case is significant not only with regard to the issue of conditional funding, but also because it illustrates as well a remarkable deference by the Court to administrative agencies in their interpretations of congressional statutes. The initial congressional statute, passed in

1970, did not impose the "gag rule" on recipients, unlike, say, the radio-editorializing statute mentioned above, which had the "gag" specified in the statute. The abortion "gag" was the result of an administrative inter-pretation offered for the first time late in the second term of the Reagan Administration in 1988. The Court nonetheless upheld this interpreta-tion by invoking a 1984 decision involving the Chevron Oil Company, in which the Court announced that it would, as a general practice, accept the interpretations of congressional statutes offered by administrative agen-cies so long as they were at all reasonable. Some commentators viewed this as a conservative Court's happy acquiescence to the shift of practi-cal decision-making power from a Democratic-dominated Congress to a conservative-dominated Executive Branch. (One of President Clinton's first acts was to change the Reagan Administration interpretation, thus eliminating the "gag rule.") It may be worth noting in this context that the recent Court, in some of the voting-rights decisions discussed in chap-ter 8, has proved notably unwilling to defer to interpretations proffered by the Justice Department, some of them going back thirty years and thus embraced by Democratic and Republican administrations alike. The Court has scarcely offered a comprehensive theory explaining why it de-fers to administrative decision making in some cases but vigorously over-rides such decisions in others.

Similar questions were raised by *Immigration and Naturalization Service* v. *Chadha* (1983), where the Court, through Chief Justice Bur-ger, invalidated the so-called legislative veto by which Congress pre-served, in various statutes, the power to override "offensive" regulations promulgated by administrative agencies. According to the majority, such "vetoes," sometimes requiring resolution only by one house or even a committee of Congress, were in fact new laws and thus required "pre-sentment" to the President. Any glib political analysis is complicated by the fact that one of the two dissenters was Justice Rehnquist (White was the other), and the majority included Justices Brennan and Marshall.

At the time, *Chadha* was thought to be extraordinarily important inasmuch as it called into question literally more than 200 statutes, in-cluding the War Powers Act passed by Congress in 1973 to curb presi-dential power. In its two decades, though, *Chadha* has had little apparent impact: One political scientist has counted more than 200 new bills con-taining legislative vetoes, even though signing statements of Presidents Reagan, Bush, and Clinton often included such declarations as President Bush's promise that "I will treat them as having no legal force or effect in this or any other legislation in which they appear." As a practical matter, this may be irrelevant, inasmuch as administrative agencies have a significant incentive to pay attention to the wishes of the appropriations-controlling Congress. Moreover, an additional possible explanation of congressional "defiance" of *Chadha* is that Congress' own lawyers may read the majority decision far more narrowly than did Justice White in dissent. Dissenters often (though not invariably) adopt a strategy of highlighting the potential mischief of a majority decision, and one should be wary of looking to either majority *or* dissenting opinions for accurate information as to the likely consequences of any given decision.

In any event, both the so-called *Chevron* doctrine and *Chadha* underscore some of the ambiguities involved in the notion of judicial deference to politically accountable decision-makers. Especially in a political system like that of the United States, which often places different political parties in charge of the Legislative and Executive Branches, "we the people" evoked by theories of popular sovereignty speak in decidedly mixed, sometimes flatly contradictory, tones. A court's decision to favor legislature over executive agency, or vice versa, might as often be explained in terms of political preferences or commitment to one particular view of our constitutional tradition as by any notion of abstract judicial deference to "popular" branches of government.

Rust also illustrates the fact that any full analysis of the American Supreme Court should include recognition of the increasingly important role it plays as statutory interpreter. The modern state is quintessentially a state of statutes and of regulations issued by administrative agencies interpreting these statutes. The constitutional-law docket of the Court may in fact draw attention disproportionate to its actual importance in the modern state. Some of the most important civil rights decisions of the Court during the 1980's, for example, offered restrictive interpretations of legislation passed in earlier decades, which in turn led to bitter struggles both within Congress and between it and President Bush before Congress successfully overturned several of the decisions. Similarly, most of the major cases in the 1990s involving "sexual harassment" involved the construction of federal antidiscrimination statutes and regulations issued by federal agencies.

The practical importance of the Court's power to construe statutes was also exemplified in a series of cases during 1999 that involved the meaning of the Americans with Disabilities Act (ADA) passed by Congress during the Bush Administration. Congress was notably unclear on what constituted a disability. The Court chose to give a relatively limited reach to the concept; it rejected, for example, the proposition that needing glasses in order to see clearly was a disability that made illegal the airline requirement that pilots have adequate uncorrected vision. The ADA has the potential to reorder significant aspects of the American work environment, not to mention the imposition of significant monetary burdens with regard, for example, to building accessible facilities. If, as seems likely, Congress is unwilling to return to the issue, the Court will in effect set much of national policy regarding the full integration of the disabled into the American economy.

BUREAUCRACY AND THE WELFARE STATE

One result of the welfare state has been a sharp increase in the number of governmental employees who staff its various bureaucracies. Although the theoretical issues may be the same whether the state employs one person or one thousand, the social consequences obviously increase with the number of persons involved. In 1816 the entire federal government had fewer than 5,000 civilian employees; their number reached 100,000 only in 1881. It took almost another sixty years, until 1940, to reach 1 million employees. As of 2002, there were approximately 2.5 million federal civilian employees; state and local governments employed another 15.6 million "full-time equivalent" workers, a 1.6 percent increase over 2001. (This obviously does not include members of the United States armed forces, nor do these census figures include sizable numbers of employees of the Homeland Security Administration.)

It is clear, then, that a major source of jobs—perhaps as many as one in seven—in contemporary America is government. Inevitably, this raises questions about the limitations on government in its hiring and firing practices. General American law had given employers the right to engage in "employment at will"; that is, an employee could be fired without the demonstration of any justifying cause. Conversely, civil service laws, first passed toward the end of the nineteenth century, grant public employees a variety of protections against arbitrary firing. But does the Constitution itself guarantee any particular process beyond what a legislature chooses to grant?

A 1972 decision, *Board of Regents* v. *Roth,* said yes, at least if the employee has a "justifiable expectation" to continued employment. Whether or not the worker had a "right" to be a policeman (or schoolteacher, social worker, etc.), he or she retained the right not to be dismissed from what could justifiably be perceived as a "permanent" position without at least some due process, including hearings. Subsequent litigation dealt with the timing of any hearings, pre- or posttermination.

But due process is certainly not the only issue presented in the governmental-employment context. As noted in an earlier chapter, the cold war era of the 1950's provoked much litigation about the ability of the state to deny jobs to persons who were members of the Communist Party or who refused to take loyalty oaths that included promises never to join the party. Such litigation continued well into the 1960's, when a series of decisions limited the formal power of the state to consider the political views of prospective hires. Perhaps the most remarkable decision was *Robel v. United States* (1967), which struck down a ban on Communists working in defense plants. The Court basically said that only the kind of behavior that would support a criminal conviction—knowing membership in the Party coupled with actual support for any illegal goals it professed—would justify exclusion from routine public employment. Moreover, the Court in effect eliminated loyalty oaths as a significant qualification for public-sector employment, though a 1971 decision written by Chief Justice Burger upheld a requirement that an employee pledge fidelity to the Constitution. Far more significant "negative" oaths—"I am not a member of the Communist Party" and the like—continued to be forbidden, and the issue has disappeared from American politics.

The Supreme Court has been quite tolerant of the continued desire of governments to limit the political activity of their employees, even when the activity could not reasonably be described as "subversive": The federal government especially justified such limitations on the ground that they contribute to the vitally important perception (and reality) of neutrality on the part of the public bureaucracy. The Supreme Court, first in 1947 and then in 1973, upheld these restraints, finding the loss of employee rights a cheap price to pay for maintaining a civil service divorced from politics.

Equally important was another 1947 decision, in which the Court upheld a federal spending program that conditioned the receipt of highway funds by states on their willingness to prohibit the state officials spending these funds from taking "any active part" in political activities. Whatever the response to such decisions by the states—who have complained, much like the individual recipients of welfare payments, of the unfair pressures placed upon them by the national government—the Court itself can scarcely be viewed as foisting constraints on the hapless states. Here, in a pattern going back at least as far as *McCulloch*, the Court is simply legitimizing the increasingly expansive assertions of federal power by Congress.

Where the Court did take the lead, first in *Elrod* v. *Burns* (1976) and then again in *Branti* v. *Finkel* (1980), was in restricting the traditional role played by political patronage in dispensing state and local governmental jobs. To prefer Democrats or Republicans for nonpolicy-level positions, it said, violated the First Amendment rights of the members of the "wrong" political party; such positions must be filled on a nonpartisan basis. (Justice Powell denounced the Court's disregard of the value of patronage for maintaining strong political parties and the presumed contribution to American democracy of such parties.) Such decisions were extended by the Court in the 1990's to cover, for example, the award of contracts by local governments: No longer, apparently, could mayors and other officials award sanitation or snow-plowing contracts on the basis of whether the owners of the companies had supported them in the previous election.

Similarly, the Warren Court led the way in protecting federal employees against retaliation for engaging in speech critical of the agencies for which they work, though a later Court limited protection only to what it was willing to classify as matters of "public concern." One decision rather surprisingly protected the job of a sheriff's department clerical employee who had expressed sympathy with the attempted assassination of President Reagan. As with other anomalous pairings of cases discussed earlier in this chapter, the key to understanding them centers around the fact that both of these latter decisions reflected five-to-four votes. What is being analyzed, therefore, is far less "the Court" than the refined perceptions of one or two justices.

RACE AND THE WELFARE STATE

Brown v. *Board of Education,* the great civil rights case of the century at least in its mythic import, was the culmination of a series of cases going back to 1938 that tested state policies on public education. Chief Justice Warren described education as "perhaps the most important function of state and local government"; he could have added that public education is the quintessential example of the modern welfare state, accounting for the bulk of both spending and employment by most state and local governments. Nevertheless, the Court was scarcely clear, whether in *Brown* or thereafter, in delineating its position regarding the use of racial criteria in dispensing the goods of the welfare state.

Through heroic efforts or sometimes outright obfuscation, the Court maintained a staunch unanimity in almost all of the major racial segregation cases following *Brown* in 1954. One explanation for this unanimity—beyond its obviously serving the institutional interests of the Court itself—is that the Court in fact did relatively little following the thunderbolt of 1954.

The major act of the Supreme Court, in the ten years after *Brown,* was defending its newly self-appointed role as "ultimate interpreter of the Constitution" in *Cooper* v. *Aaron.* The 1958 case was triggered by the refusal the year before of Arkansas Governor Orval Faubus to enforce a judicial decree ordering the admission of nine African-American students to Central High School in Little Rock. President Dwight Eisenhower ultimately used federal troops to enforce compliance. The Court reaffirmed *Brown* and denounced the refusal of Arkansas authorities to comply with the law. That use of troops was, of course, vitally important in demonstrating that the Court would in fact be supported by the Executive Branch, but it also pointed out the potential difficulties presented by a resisting South. One might interpret the relative quiet of the Court in the decade following *Brown* as a "testing of the waters" to see if its views would garner necessary support from the electorally accountable branches of the national government (and, though this was a more utopian hope, even of the affected Southern states themselves).

When *Brown* was decided in 1954, only twenty-three African-American schoolchildren—this is an absolute number, *not* a percentage—attended secondary or elementary schools with white children in those Southern states that attempted to secede from the Union in 1860–61. In the 1960–61 school year, during which John F. Kennedy was elected, the number of African-American children in the Southern states other than Tennessee and Texas attending racially mixed schools was 432, approximately .02 percent of all African-American schoolchildren in these states. (If Texas and Tennessee were included, the number would rise to approximately 4,300 and the percentage to 1.6 percent.) The border states—Missouri, Kentucky, Maryland, Delaware—and the District of Columbia had a better record: By the 1960 school year, almost half of the African-American children in those states were attending school with whites.

What dramatically changed things was not anything the Court did, but rather the active collaboration of the Congress and President Lyndon B. Johnson, with a shared sense of political purpose, at least between 1964 and 1966, that was probably unprecedented in American history with regard to race. (Whatever else may be said of FDR's ample political vision and congressional support, at least before 1938, it did not extend to making any genuine attack on the segregationist version of America's "peculiar institution," in part because he drew much of his support from Southerners like Hugo Black, who had thought it necessary to join the Ku Klux Klan in order to make his way in Alabama politics.) Johnson and members of Congress, including Republicans, were in turn heavily influenced by the civil rights movement, with its calls for realization of basic American values of equal justice under the law, symbolized by the leadership of Martin Luther King and by the oppressive opposition of Birmingham's "Bull" Connor, who set fire hoses and police dogs, unforgettably captured by television cameras, upon demonstrating African-American children.

The Civil Rights Act of 1964 not only mandated the desegregation of public accommodations and made racial and gender discrimination in employment illegal; it also gave the Department of Justice far more extensive authority to press for school desegregation. Moreover, the federal government was, for the first time in its history, beginning to engage in significant distribution of federal revenue to states for use in public education, and what was then the Department of Health, Education, and Welfare threatened to cut off much-needed funds to school systems that refused to move toward desegregation. Thus by the end of the Johnson Administration, almost a third of all African-American students in the South (including Texas and Tennessee) were attending racially mixed schools, a figure that would leap to more than 90 percent by the end of Richard Nixon's first term as President in 1973.

This outpouring of national support for overcoming at least the worst aspects of discrimination against African-Americans undoubtedly encouraged the Court, in Green v. New Kent County (1968), to invalidate a "freedom of choice" plan by a Virginia county that resulted in overwhelmingly "racially identifiable" schools. According to the Court, the "free choice" was likely to be illusory, a manifestation either of traditional (and no longer acceptable) Southern mores about the desirability of racial separation or, even more ominously, of pressures brought by economically and politically powerful whites upon vulnerable African-American parents to make "choices" that maintained this separation. The government's duty, stated Justice Brennan for the Court, was to "fashion steps which promise realistically to convert promptly to a system without a 'white' school and a 'Negro' school, but just schools."

Green concerned a small, rural county, but its principle of "nonidentifiability" of schools as "white" or "Negro" was applied by many judges in urban settings to require the self-conscious assignment of students in ways likely to produce racially mixed schools, which required as well the "busing" of many of these students to schools relatively distant from their quite likely segregated neighborhoods. Three years after *Green,* a unanimous Court, in *Swann* v. *Charlotte-Mecklenburg Board of Education,* upheld a sweeping order by a North Carolina district judge that required extensive busing in order to achieve, in most schools within the system, "racially balanced" schools. Thereafter, busing became a major political issue, with the Nixon Administration leading the opposition to many of the far-reaching decrees issued by liberal district judges appointed by Lyndon Johnson.

Given the political sea change of the 1970's—Richard Nixon's election in 1968, after all, was partly achieved through the aggressive pursuit of a "Southern strategy" that sought white voters otherwise attracted by Alabama Governor George C. Wallace, who ran as a third-party candidate by promising a greater sensitivity to their concerns—it can scarcely surprise that there was an inexorable movement away from busing during that decade. By the mid-1980's, the controversy over busing had in effect been resolved via a judicial retreat that saw far less ambitious and controversial remedies imposed on those districts found to have engaged in segregated schooling. One might wonder whether the Court would have initially endorsed extensive busing had Congress and the President, seemingly backed by the public, not vigorously thrown their own weight behind the striving for integration; and had many of the busing orders not been issued by district judges who themselves were part of the social and political elites of the communities in question. Moreover, these district judges were often perceived by the Court as unusually courageous in their commitment to enforce desegregation, and the Court was willing to support them. Throughout the 1970's, though, busing became increasingly unpopular, even among many African-Americans (let alone among other minorities, whose specific interests and views were often submerged by a rhetoric that assumed that the "race problem" in America was confined entirely to relations between blacks and whites and that the policy preferences and interests of African-Americans necessarily coincided with, for example, those of Mexican-Americans or any other of the literally hundreds of minority groups that comprise the American mosaic). The Court beat a hasty retreat, and many schools thus remain easily identifiable by race in the United States. By the 1990's, Justice Thomas was writing opinions on the Supreme Court suggesting that *Brown* (and busing) was implicitly racist insofar as it rested on the assumption that African-

Americans could gain a good education only if placed in classrooms with whites.

Busing arose as an issue only after a court had decided that a district was in fact guilty of discrimination in the first place. However, the Supreme Court first had to decide what counted as discrimination, triggering the need for any remedy at all. Two sentences in *Brown* exemplified the potential for confusion: "Separate educational facilities," the Court stated, "are inherently unequal." It also declared, perhaps thinking that it was simply making the same point, that "To separate [children] from others of similar age and qualifications solely because of their race generates a feeling of inferiority as to their status in the community that may affect their hearts and minds in a way unlikely ever to be undone." The first sentence suggests that the constitutional harm lies in the very existence of "separate educational facilities," of what the Court in *Green* later called "racially identifiable schools." The second sentence, however, though on the surface a strong denunciation of the harms of racial discrimination, points in a different direction, suggesting that the Constitution prohibits only those racially separate schools that are the result of intentional assignment based "solely" on racial grounds.

The Warren Court did not really have to wrestle with these questions because its race-oriented docket came almost entirely from Southern and border states that had explicitly used race in their public policies as a means of segregating African-Americans or otherwise keeping them "in their place." For the South the question was remedy rather than the existence of the initial constitutional violation.

By the 1970's, however, an increasing number of school cases were arising outside the South, including such cities as Boston, Cleveland, Detroit, and Denver. Plaintiffs usually argued that the "racial identifiability" of the schools was enough to establish unconstitutionality; the defendants, in response, argued that such "identifiability" was irrelevant unless it was the product of a conscious desire to create and maintain segregated schools—as distinguished, for example, from a defensible desire to assign children to "neighborhood schools." In an important 1974 case involving the Denver, Colorado, public schools, the Court, though finding the system in violation of the Constitution, nonetheless emphasized that plaintiffs would have to show (and did successfully show, in regard to Denver) that the Board of Education "intended" to bring about the separation in question. Thereafter, an increasingly conservative majority became harder to convince that various assignment practices were "in fact" simply subterfuges designed to maintain racial separateness. What this meant is that relatively few Northern school districts were subjected to the radical transformations seen in the South, and "racially identifiable schools" remain an omnipresent reality of most Northern school systems even as they have been significantly limited throughout the Southern and border states whose practices were struck down by *Brown.*

Interestingly enough, Justice Powell, from Richmond, Virginia, had in the Denver case seemingly offered a "bargain," in which he would no longer require the demonstration of an intention to segregate—simple presentation of statistics demonstrating "identifiability" would be enough to establish liability—in return for an agreement to cut back significantly on the scope of the remedy; in other words, less busing. The liberal Justice Brennan, who wrote the opinion, in effect rejected the deal, perhaps because he was confident that the judiciary would remain in the hands of judges quite willing to find the presence of the requisite bad intent and then to order sweeping remedies. If he believed this, he was, of course, flatly mistaken. One can only wonder what might have happened had Justice Powell's offer been accepted. It could hardly have had less effect on Northern school segregation than Justice Brennan's approach has turned out to have.

The Court also assured the practical maintenance of racial identifiability throughout the North when, in *Bradley* v. *Millikin* (1974), it overturned a district judge's decision to force the consolidation of many separate school districts in and around Detroit, Michigan, into one "superdistrict" the size of Delaware for the purposes of achieving desegregation. Many Southern districts, including that of Charlotte, were quite vast "consolidated" city-county districts. The pattern in the North, however, was for urban areas to be subdivided into sometimes literally dozens of separate school districts, themselves often predominantly white or African-American in demographic composition. In a sharply divided five-to-four decision that signified the final (and so-far permanent) collapse of the Court's carefully maintained emphasis on unanimity in cases involving racial matters, the majority held that federal judges were without power to order the consolidation of these formally separate districts unless they had been drawn with the purpose of maintaining racial segregation, which was almost never the case.

RACE AND "AFFIRMATIVE ACTION"

Much of the debate throughout this period was couched in terms of the validity of Justice Harlan's vision, in his *Plessy* dissent, of a "colorblind"

Constitution. Although the justices did not reject this as an "ideal" vision of the Constitution (and, more to the point, of American society), they were sharply divided over the pace at which the Constitution required race to become irrelevant to governmental decision-makers. The very sharpest conflicts took place over "affirmative action," the use of racial classifications for the ostensibly benign purpose of enhancing the access of racial minorities to education, jobs, and other important social goods, the distribution of which is, of course, a principal aspect of the contemporary welfare state.

There was obviously nothing "color-blind" about such programs. What saved them, according to their supporters, was precisely that they were "affirmative" rather than negative in the treatment of the affected minorities. The debate over affirmative action was foreshadowed in the Court's opinion in *Strauder* v. *West Virginia* (1880), the very first case construing the meaning of the equal protection clause in regard to race. The majority had had no trouble striking down a state prohibition on African-Americans serving on juries. It did not do so, though, on the simple ground that the state had used a racial classification. Instead, the Court several times emphasized the "unfriendly" nature of the classification and defined the Fourteenth Amendment as providing "protection against unfriendly action" directed at African-Americans because of racial animus. This left open the possibility that "friendly" action, designed to include rather than exclude, could be legitimate even if based on overt racial classification. Yet *Strauder* also described the Fourteenth Amendment as "ordain[ing] that the law in the States shall be the same for the black as for the white." As with *Brown* seventy-four years later, the Court scarcely spoke with any great precision.

The first major "affirmative action" case to be decided by the Court was *Bakke* v. *Regents of the University of California* (1978), which involved a program at the University of California Medical School at Davis. The program reserved sixteen places in its entering class for persons selected from an applicant pool consisting only of African-, Hispanic-, Asian-, and Native-Americans. (*All* groups were entitled to compete for eighty-four "open" places.) Once again the Court was sharply divided; indeed, presaging many of the future "affirmative action" cases, not even five justices could coalesce around a single "majority" opinion. Four justices argued that one need not even reach the constitutional issue because of the Civil Rights Act of 1964, which stated that "[n]o person in the United States shall, on the ground of race, color, or national origin, be excluded from participation in, be denied the benefits of, or be subjected to discrimination under any program or activity receiving Federal financial assistance" (as Davis did). The majority of justices, however, agreed, in Justice Powell's words, that the Act "must be held to proscribe only those racial classifications that would violate the Equal Protection Clause or the Fifth Amendment," the latter of which had been held, in *Bolling* v. *Sharpe* (the companion case to *Brown* in 1954) to apply equal protection–like limitations to the federal government.

Four justices would have upheld the Davis program in its entirety because of its benign purpose. The ninth, Justice Powell, though taking a wholly idiosyncratic position, wrote what in fact became the most influential opinion in the case. Like the first four, though on constitutional rather than statutory grounds, he invalidated the program. The reason, however, was not that the Constitution required "color blindness"; rather, it prohibited rigid "quotas" of the kind concededly adopted by Davis. Thus Powell agreed with the competing foursome that the Constitution did not prohibit *any* consideration of race in the admissions process, at least so long as there was no rigid quota *and* the university could show that a "compelling state interest," such as achieving diversity of backgrounds in a student body, required the use of the racial classification. Alan Bakke was thus admitted to medical school, but the debate continued (and almost all state universities operated "diversity"-oriented affirmative action programs).

A similarly fragmented Court in 1986 struck down a preference adopted by the Jackson, Michigan, school board that protected recently hired minority teachers against being laid off, even though the traditional practice was "last hired, first fired." Though apparently willing to accept racial preferences in the initial hiring decision, the Court was unwilling to extend its tolerance to a layoff policy that meant that some whites with seniority would be laid off before more recently hired African-Americans.

The Court's fumbling around on the issue probably reflected quite well the public confusion (and ambivalence) regarding racial preferences. For example, although the Nixon Administration was almost flamboyantly conservative on such issues as busing, it promoted the establishment of many of the initial affirmative action programs by private businesses. And even though the public elected Republican Presidents in the 1980's who drew significantly on white antagonism to affirmative action, the same public often elected Democratic representatives and senators—as well as some Republicans—who wished, in the later words of President Clinton, to "mend" rather than "end" the use of racial preferences. The George H. W. Bush Administration, for example, was forced by public opinion to beat a hasty retreat when one of its officials suggested that universities offering race-sensitive scholarships were violating the law. Like Goldilocks, the mainstream of the public seemed to be willing to accept some amount of affirmative action that is "just right," even as it finds many actual programs either "too hot" or "too cold." Discerning the "just right" bowl of porridge, however, continued to be a major item on the Court's agenda.

A majority of the Court did come together in a majority opinion in *City of Richmond, Virginia* v. *Croson* (1989), which struck down a requirement that at least 30 percent of publicly financed building projects go to minority contractors. Yet Justice O'Connor in her majority opinion emphasized some of the specific facts about the city, including its having a majority African-American city council. The program could therefore be viewed less as a "friendly" gesture by the white majority than as a decidedly "unfriendly" effort by a newly empowered African-American majority to direct public funds to its own constituents. Only a year later, Justice Brennan, in his final opinion for the Court, upheld a minority-preference program of the Federal Communications Commission in the allocation of television licenses (which, if not a direct distribution of funds, has been described as a "license to print money" on the part of the lucky license holders); however, the crucial fifth vote for the opinion, from Justice White, was gained by Brennan's emphasizing that Congress had much more latitude in adopting racial preferences than did state legislatures or city councils. The replacement of Justice Marshall by Justice Thomas in 1991 meant, among other things, that the Court reversed itself, holding in the *Adarand* case (1995) that the national government was bound by the same strict standards applying to state governments. Gerald Gunther coined the phrase that the Court's "strict scrutiny" was almost always "fatal in fact"; Justice O'Connor, however, insisted that that would not necessarily be the case, though observers wondered if a majority would ever actually uphold any affirmative action programs.

The answer was provided in 2003, when the Court heard two cases involving admissions programs at the University of Michigan undergraduate and law schools. In one of them, *Gratz* v. *Bollinger,* six justices struck down the undergraduate program inasmuch as it offered a twenty-point bonus (out of 100 needed for admission) to members of selected racial or ethnic groups. But Justices O'Connor and Breyer joined the three dissenters in *Gratz* in upholding the law school's program in *Grutter* v. *Bollinger* because, according to Justice O'Connor's majority opinion, it was more "holistic" and did not make race or ethnicity a "determinative"

factor. Moreover, she embraced in full Justice Powell's "diversity" rationale first articulated in the 1978 *Bakke* case. Whatever might have been
true of other decisions, *Grutter* appeared to typify genuine "judicial restraint" and deference to other decision-making bodies.

As usual, it is difficult to ascertain the true dimensions of the Court's
present position (not to mention what might happen if a member of the
Grutter majority is replaced by a justice selected by President George W.
Bush, whose administration opposed both of the programs in arguments
before the Supreme Court). Justice O'Connor emphasized that "universities occupy a special niche in our constitutional tradition," which might
suggest that *Grutter* (and affirmative action) is limited to those relatively
few "selective" universities. But she also cited in her opinion two briefs—
one by sixty-five major national and multinational corporations and the
other by a stellar list of former military officers and ex-secretaries of defense—both of which emphasized the importance to business and to the
military of "diverse" workforces and military personnel. Thus, according to the latter brief, "[t]he officer corps must continue to be diverse or
the cohesiveness essential to the military mission will be crucially undermined." This is an indirect reference to the fact that almost 40 percent of
the current nonofficer military personnel are members of various minorities. Indeed, there are some observers who believe that the Michigan law
school won its case when Solicitor General Theodore Olson, presenting
the arguments of the George W. Bush Administration against the University, conceded that he just had not thought much about the consequences
of a negative decision upon the admissions programs of the three major national military academies at West Point, Annapolis, and Colorado
Springs.

Sharp divisions on the Court concerning the overt use of race as a
classification were reflected as well in controversies involving the differential *impact* of programs on various racial groups. An important 1971
decision written by Chief Justice Burger, *Griggs* v. *Duke Power Co.*, interpreted the Civil Rights Act of 1964 as prohibiting the use of certain employment criteria by the Duke Power Company on the grounds that their
use served to exclude a disproportionate number of African-Americans
from the employment pool and that the Company could not show that using these criteria was necessary to achieve legitimate business goals. This
suggested to many that the Constitution itself would be similarly interpreted as barring state practices that disproportionately affected African-
American and other vulnerable minorities, at least in the absence of the
state's being able to present a "compelling interest" justifying the practices.

Such hopes were dashed a year later, however, by another case. In *Jefferson v. Hackney,* the Court rejected a suit brought by recipients of Aid for Dependent Children who claimed that Texas was considerably more generous in offering aid to the aged and infirm, who were presumably predominantly white, than to the predominantly African- and Mexican-American beneficiaries of AFDC. Justice Rehnquist rejected the plaintiffs' "naked statistical argument" and also turned down a potential judicial role of "second guess[ing] state officials charged with the difficult responsibility of allocating limited public welfare funds among the myriads of potential recipients." An even more crucial case along these lines was *Washington v. Davis* (1976), which emphasized the absence of intent to discriminate in upholding a test, administered by the District of Columbia police department, that appeared to weed out a disproportionate number of African-American applicants.

Later cases underscored the Court's determination to require proof of the state's *intent* to discriminate; it would not, with rare exceptions, be sufficient to point simply to differential *effects.* Indeed, the 1971 *Duke Power* decision was itself significantly modified by the Court in 1989. Congress responded with legislation overriding the Court's decision (which was an interpretation of the statute's meaning and not based on the Constitution), leading to the first veto by a President of a civil rights bill since the Presidency of Andrew Johnson. Negotiations between President Bush and Congress finally led to the passage of new legislation, but that scarcely has ended the debate, which includes, among other things, the passage by popular referenda, in California and other states, of complete bans on affirmative action.

Gender and the Welfare State

Many welfare programs have been quite explicitly gender linked—sometimes explicitly, sometimes only as a matter of social fact. Neither kind of linkage perturbed the Court prior to the 1970's, when it began restricting the wide latitude it had traditionally given states in using gender as a classification in making public policy. (One reason for the Court's interest, of course, was the placement by Congress of a ban on sex discrimination in the Civil Rights Act of 1964, so that many of the most important cases involving sex and gender discrimination are statutory interpretations rather than interpretations of the Constitution.) The change of legal reality sparked by the Civil Rights Act and the growth of the "second-wave" feminist movement in the 1960's had obvious implications for the American welfare state.

A number of provisions of the Social Security Act, for example, specifically gave "widows" more benefits than "widowers," on the assumption that women were less likely to have alternative sources of income because they had probably not worked outside the home. The Court throughout the 1970's struck down a number of such provisions, emphasizing that they rested on outmoded social stereotypes about either a woman's "proper" role or even her likely behavior, given the dramatically greater number of women participating in the compensated workforce.

Inevitably, gender-segregated education would be challenged in much the same way that racially segregated schools had. Ironically, the main such case to be decided by the Supreme Court, *Mississippi University for Women* v. *Hogan* (1982), involved a complaint by a male, Joe Hogan, who wanted to enter the nursing program at M.U.W. In a five-to-four decision written by Justice Sandra Day O'Connor, appointed in 1981 by President Reagan as the first woman on the Supreme Court, the Court granted Hogan his wish, saying that Mississippi, in order to defend gender-segregated education, had to present a more "substantial" justification than in fact it had done. The dissenters, led by Justice Powell, emphasized the potential benefits to women of being able to choose gender-specific schooling, quoting, among others, the president of Wellesley College. A 1996 case involving the Virginia Military Institute, this time with the majority opinion written by Ruth Bader Ginsburg, reinforced *Hogan* by invalidating the all-male admissions policy of that institution. It remains unclear, though, whether this prohibits as well the operation of "boys'" and "girls'" schools by public school systems.

Interestingly enough, none of the proponents of a "color-blind" Constitution seriously suggested that "gender-blindness" was required. Whether the issue involved the propriety of maintaining separate-sex secondary schools or the ability of the armed forces to exclude women from certain combat roles, the public and the Court, rightly or wrongly, were far more accepting of gender classifications than of racial ones. No one, for example, seriously mounted constitutional challenges to sexually segregated public bathrooms, although, even by the 1960's, any such racially segregated facilities would have instantly been prohibited. Nor were opponents of sex discrimination eager to concede that their position logically required revising American marriage law, which patently discriminates on grounds of sex insofar as it allows dual-sex, but not same-sex, couples to procure marriage licenses. Indeed, state laws prohibiting mixed-race marriages had been struck down as racially discriminatory by the Court in 1967, in the aptly named *Loving* v. *Virginia*. Yet, as Justice Holmes memorably opined, the life of the law is not "logic" but rather "experience," and most of the country, including judges, were unwilling to concede the similarity between racial and sex discrimination regarding the right to choose whom to marry.

As with race, the Court must confront *impact* as well as *intent;* the Court fairly quickly determined that it would require the latter and, relatively speaking, ignore the former in regard to gender. Perhaps the most bizarre illustration of the Court's use of an "intent-impact" distinction in the context of gender and the welfare state was provided in a 1974 challenge to California's exclusion of pregnancy from the health insurance provided its public employees. According to the majority, California "does not exclude anyone from benefit eligibility because of gender but merely removes one physical condition—pregnancy—from the list of compensable disabilities." Although the majority recognized the obvious fact that only women can be pregnant, "[i]t does not follow," said the Court, "that every legislative classification concerning pregnancy is a sex-based [rather than physical condition] classification." The Court's decision was overturned by Congress, which made it illegal for insurance programs to discriminate against pregnant women.

The Court emphasized the importance of intent in the 1979 *Feeney* case upholding a Massachusetts policy that gave all veterans of the armed forces an absolute lifetime preference for positions in the state bureaucracy. Given the officially mandated exclusion of women from the draft and the relatively small number of women who had, up to that time, volunteered for military service, this operated in effect to exclude almost all women from access to jobs in the Massachusetts bureaucracy so long as a male veteran applied for the job as well. The Court, with only Justices Brennan and Marshall dissenting, upheld the program, which, it said, had been passed in order to help veterans, a traditional object of state beneficence, rather than to hurt women. The fact that it did the latter was simply an incidental effect of its doing the former. And, of course, some women, however few, did benefit from the veterans' preference.

This case only underscores the fact that perhaps the most sustained beneficiaries of the American welfare state have been male veterans (and, in many cases, their widows). One scholar has noted that the national commitment, emphasized by the Republican Party after the Civil War, to take care of veterans of the Union Army and their dependents, meant that "for over thirty years prior to World War I the United States national government ran the world's largest and most expensive disability and pension system in the world."

RELIGION AND THE WELFARE STATE

Few issues presented the Court with more problems than determining the intersections of the establishment and free exercise clauses of the First Amendment with the realities of the modern welfare state. In many of the cases discussed above, one can describe the Court as refusing to read the Constitution to require more in the way of welfare expenditures than state legislatures or Congress was willing to appropriate. But sometimes the legislatures proved to be far more generous than the Court was willing to tolerate, as when they included, as part of general programs involving aid to private schools, state aid to religious schools or students as well. The Court frequently struck down such aid as a violation of the establishment clause.

The 1947 case that "incorporated" the establishment clause into the Fourteenth Amendment as a limit on states, *Everson v. New Jersey,* involved a classic welfare-state issue, the payment by the state of transportation fees for students attending parochial schools. The Court upheld such payments, in part because no money went directly to the schools themselves. Four justices dissented. It is hard to read some of the dissenting opinions in that case (and opinions in other cases as well during that era) without seeing in them traces of quite traditional Protestant suspicion of—some have described it as bigotry against—Roman Catholics, who were by far the largest group of beneficiaries of the challenged state policies.

One might also see in many of these opinions illustrations of an ever-increasing secularization on the part of the political elites from whom Supreme Court justices tend to be drawn. This might help to explain, for example, the Court's willingness in the early 1960's to strike down state-compelled prayers in the public schools, extremely controversial decisions triggering much public opposition and more than a little defiance regarding the actualities of classroom behavior. These decisions, however, have survived the transition to a far more conservative Court than that of the 1960's. Thus the Court, albeit divided five to four, in *Lee v. Weisman* (1991) cited them in invalidating prayers offered at the beginning of state-sponsored baccalaureate ceremonies. The most recent iteration, in 2000, of the continuing dispute involved whether students themselves can choose to offer what might be termed institutional prayers at the beginning of athletic events. The issue of prayer and the public schools is especially interesting for anyone interested in the actual role of the Court in structuring low-visibility behavior by literally thousands of public officials. Anyone holding the shallow belief that the Court issues "definitive rulings" that bring closure to public debate and conformity of behavior should study the wide variation in meaning given to the school-prayer cases by "inferior" courts and lawyers.

School prayer is primarily of symbolic importance; aid to parochial schools raises far more basic questions about the nature of a pluralistic state and the ability of government to use public funds to nurture pluralism. An exemplary case was *Committee for Public Education & Liberty* v. *Nyquist* (1973), which involved a New York program giving both direct monetary grants to religious schools and tax credits to parents whose children attend such schools. To qualify for such grants, schools would have to show that they "serv[ed] a high concentration of pupils from low-income families." The New York legislature had found that a "fiscal crisis in nonpublic education" was leading to severe problems; moreover, it noted that the parents of the children attending these schools had often paid substantial taxes for public education which they were not using; and, further, that the public school budgets in effect depended on their *not* having to educate the children attending nonpublic schools. None of these considerations was relevant to the majority of justices, who saw only an interweaving of church and state forbidden by the establishment clause.

Subsequent cases were successful only in issuing what one distinguished scholar called "a series of inconsistent and almost inexplicable decisions: Shifting majorities, almost always of the bare minimum of five justices, declared that certain kinds of aid were, or were not, forbidden establishments." Thus a 1977 decision forbade public subsidy of transportation for student field trips, distinguishing *Everson* on the basis that there were no teachers on the New Jersey buses who might discuss religion with the students. Other decisions upheld the ability of the state to supply textbooks, but rejected the right of state legislatures to loan maps or other instructional materials. While academic commentators poured ridicule upon the Court, politicians (and practicing lawyers) expressed frustration not only about specific results but also about the lack of any coherent guidelines.

The coming to the Court of new justices appointed by Ronald Reagan and George H. W. Bush, who had made explicit appeals to religious groups critical of secular public schools, did not—contrary to some expectations—lead to a dramatic rejection of the prior legal regime, though the Court allowed states to offer parents tax write-offs for at least some of the tuition paid to parochial schools. In addition, some other programs of state aid were upheld in the 1980's that might have been rejected earlier, but the decisions upholding them were almost always narrowly written, adhering, at least as a formal matter, to the more restrictive tenets set out years before in *Nyquist*. In one case, for example, the Court, while upholding state funding of a sign language interpreter for a deaf student attending a religious school, emphasized the minimal nature of the program. Whether this was a heartfelt point or simply a strategic decision by a conservative majority was unclear. A later case explicitly built on this one to overrule, in yet another five-to-four decision, an earlier case restricting aid; but there, too, it was possible to read the Court's opinion as being relatively cautious rather than giving full-scale permission to state and national legislators to aid religious schools however they saw fit—so long as the aid was part of a more general program that would go to other private schools as well.

The dam finally burst, with regard to previous doctrinal structures, with the coming of the new millennium. First, in *Mitchell* v. *Helms* (2000), the Court upheld Louisiana's giving parochial schools, as well as other private schools, computers that its students could use.. Three justices joined Justice Thomas's plurality opinion giving quite free rein to such programs; typically, Justice O'Connor wrote a separate concurring opinion (joined by Justice Breyer) concentrating on the specifics of the program. Two years later, however, in *Zelman* v. *Simmons-Harris,* Chief Justice Rehnquist was able to get five votes (the *Mitchell* plurality plus Justice O'Connor) for a broad opinion upholding a school-voucher program operated by the State of Ohio, where 96 percent of the voucher-using beneficiaries took them to religiously operated schools. The key, according to the majority, was that "the Ohio program is entirely neutral with respect to religion. It provides benefits directly to a wide spectrum of individuals, defined only by financial need and residence in a particular school district." If these individuals choose to spend their vouchers in religious schools, that is *their* choice, not the state's choice. Justice Souter wrote a strong dissent that was joined by the three remaining justices. It is obviously too early to tell if this understanding of the establishment clause in the age of the welfare state will "stick." Like many other topics treated in this chapter, it may depend on the winner of the 2004 election, which judges retire, and who their replacements are.

Taking the *Zelman* doctrine as a given, though, then the next doctrinal battlefield will almost certainly concern whether states *must* allow vouchers to be used in religious schools if they fund vouchers for use in secular schools. *Zelman* held that a state could, if it wished, adopt such a voucher system. However, it is undoubtedly the case that some states, even if they adopt voucher systems, will, for one reason or another—including provisions of some state constitutions that forbid any public funds being used at religious schools—limit their use to secular schools. Does this constitute unacceptable "discrimination" against parents who wish to enroll their children in religious schools?

Guidance as to the likely response by the Supreme Court may have been provided by a 2004 case, *Locke* v. *Davey*. Washington State funded a "Promise Scholarship Program" for low-income students that could be used at any accredited college, including religious schools, to study almost any subject. (After *Zelman*, this is certainly constitutional.) However, the "almost" derives from the fact that a recipient of a Promise Scholarship could not major in "devotional theology." Joshua Davey enrolled in a denominational college, which was perfectly permissible, but he wished to double major in business and devotional theology in order to prepare for a career in the ministry. He was told that was impossible, at least if he wished to retain his state grant. The Ninth Circuit Court of Appeals upheld Mr. Davey's claim that this violated his constitutional rights. Many observers expected the Court to uphold the decision, in part because of the logic of its earlier decision holding unconstitutional the refusal by the University of Virginia to fund an overtly religious evangelical Christian student journal when it was, according to the Court, funding a wide variety of other student journals.

Not only did the Supreme Court reverse the Ninth Circuit, which was (slightly) surprising in itself; more surprisingly, it did so by a seven-to-two vote, with Chief Justice Rehnquist writing for the majority. Rehnquist returned to a theme he has made in other opinions, that the modern welfare state, with its plethora of programs inconceivable to the framers generation, makes it especially difficult to interpret the establishment and free exercise clauses. His own solution (and perhaps the Court's more generally) seems to be the grant to states of a wide degree of discretion in deciding whether they want to help fund (or not fund) religious schools or accommodate (or refuse to accommodate) religious persons who feel burdened by the operation of governmental programs. Thus, as to the Washington State program, Rehnquist wrote that the Constitution allows a certain "play in the joints," so that Washington *could,* if it wished to, subsidize Mr. Davey's study of theology, but that it was not required to. Justice Scalia wrote the principal dissent, joined by Justice Thomas, denouncing this as patently "unequal" and discriminatory treatment by the state against persons who take religion more seriously than does the average person.

It seems doubtful, then, that a majority of the current Court would strike down a state's voucher program that excluded religious schools as possible recipients. One possible explanation of the Court's reluctance to invalidate Washington's restriction (and, therefore, in effect to grant the state a significant degree of discretion in the design of its programs) is a heightened concern, after September 11, 2001, that fundamentalist Islamic groups within the United States might try to use vouchers to help fund their own schools. Since it would, according to almost all lawyers, be patently unconstitutional to single out any given religion for exclusion—that is, allow vouchers to be used at Christian and Jewish schools but not Islamic ones, or only at Islamic schools that teach what the state regards as "safe" theological doctrines—the most prudent course, from this perspective, is to refuse to allow vouchers to be used at *any* religious schools. If such considerations played even a partial role in the thinking of the Justices (though there is no mention of them in the opinion), it only highlights the interplay between constitutional developments and key political events that, as a formal matter, are not part of the case actually in front of the Court.

As suggested above, discretion also increasingly seems to be the key reality with regard to "accommodating" religious persons. In an extremely controversial 1990 decision, *Employment Division, Department of Human Resources of Oregon* v. *Smith,* the Court upheld the right of the state to criminalize the use of peyote even in Native-American religious rituals and, consequently, to deny unemployment compensation to a state employee fired for such use. The free exercise clause, wrote Justice Antonin Scalia for the Court, did not protect religious minorities whose observances would violate "general" legislation that did not overtly target the religious for special (negative) treatment. After a three-year struggle, in 1993 Congress in effect overturned this decision by passing a statute requiring that incursions on important religious interests be accepted only if the state presents a "compelling interest" in their behalf. The Religious Freedom Restoration Act was based on Congress's powers under Section Five of the Fourteenth Amendment, which the Court had suggested in *Katzenbach* v. *Morgan* could serve as a broad source of congressional power to which the Court would defer unless Congress was trying to cut back on individual rights. RFRA was invalidated by the Court in *City of Boerne* v. *Flores* (1997), where the Court thunderously proclaimed its own privileged status as the interpreter of constitutional norms. Although several justices in fact suggested that the Court should revisit (and reverse) *Smith*, there was no dissent from the proposition that the Court was a distinctly senior partner when interpreting the Constitution. This rejection of what some scholars have termed a "dialogical" model of constitutional interpretation typified several important decisions in ensuing years. The decision seems best understood as part of the Court's desire to cut down the discretion enjoyed by Congress with regard to regulating issues that the Court seems to feel are best left to the states themselves. It does not entail that a state could not choose, on its own, to be more accommodating than the free exercise clause directly requires.

Most of the education cases looked at earlier involve persons or groups wishing to get aid from the state in order to supply their children with particular kinds of education. One case, *Wisconsin* v. *Yoder* (1972), on the other hand, involved a claim by the Amish community that Wisconsin, by imposing compulsory education until the age of sixteen, in effect was forcing too much education upon its children. According to leaders of the Amish community, this violated the tenets of their "withdrawn" agrarian religious community, which required less formal education. (The Amish do not vote, for example, and in significant ways they can be described as living within the American political community, territorially, but not as really being part of it in terms of psychological identification.) The Court upheld the claim, though it was careful to limit its decision to groups like the Amish, with their centuries-long history and general record of good behavior. Justice Douglas dissented, claiming that the majority ignored the interests of the children in becoming aware of possible alternatives to the lifestyle desired by their parents.

Attempts to build on *Yoder*, such as claiming that it was unconstitutional to force the Amish to participate in Social Security, proved unsuccessful; it may prove to be what is sometimes called "a sport in the law," having no real general consequences. The case most certainly remains on the books, however, and the issues it raises, which go to the heart of the nature of America's pluralism and, indeed, multiculturalism, are scarcely marginal ones.

DEFINING THE COMMUNITY OF WELFARE RECIPIENTS

The struggle between the Amish and the state of Wisconsin illustrates only one difficulty in defining the nature of the American political community. The Amish were exceptional in attempting to rebuff aid from the state. More typical are attempts by the state to limit its beneficence to those deemed part of the community, while withholding it from those deemed "outsiders." The easiest example of such "outsiders" would be those who are not even formal members of the American political community; that is, noncitizens. No one has seriously argued that the Constitution entitles the children even of Mexico—let alone Azerbaijan—to welfare provided by California or by the national government of the United States. But what about, for example, resident aliens or even illegal ones who live in the United States? Then things get considerably more complicated. Once more, the Supreme Court has monitored the desire of local communities to dispense their various welfare goods—whether defined as direct cash payments, eligibility for access to state institutions like universities, or certain licenses given by the state, for example, to practice law or operate a television station—only to favored insiders.

The Court first addressed the issue of national citizenship and the welfare state in *Graham v. Richardson* (1971), when resident aliens legally entitled to live within the United States challenged state policies that either limited welfare benefits to citizens or required that resident aliens live in the country for a long period of time, such as fifteen years. The Court struck these policies down, arguing that states violated the equal protection clause in distinguishing between citizens and resident aliens. Once the United States as a nation agrees to let persons into the country, states cannot discriminate against them. There are, however, some exceptions. The Court, for example, reached mixed results in deciding a number of cases involving eligibility for public employment or positions requiring state licensure, such as membership in the bar that allows one to practice law. Thus the Court struck down Connecticut's attempt to limit membership in the bar to U.S. citizens, just as it invalidated a similar limitation by New York in regard to eligibility for civil service jobs. On the other hand, later decisions concluded that the state could limit eligibility for "policy-making positions" to citizens, including within the definition of such positions membership in the state highway patrol and teaching in the public schools.

Undoubtedly the most controversial of all such decisions was *Plyler v. Doe* (1982), in which Justice Brennan wrote for a five-justice majority in overturning a Texas law that refused to allocate any state funds to pay for the education of children brought illegally into the United States. The Court provided no particularly cogent analysis as to why conduct that could be criminalized—illegal entry into the United States—could not also serve as a bar to receiving educational benefits. Justice Brennan primarily pointed to the undoubtedly high social costs attached to tolerating the development within the country of an underclass deprived by lack of education of even the chance of bettering its position. Justice Powell, who had written for the Court a decade earlier in the San Antonio case rejecting a constitutional requirement of equal educational spending, provided the crucial fifth vote; he viewed Texas as in effect depriving the children of *any* education at all. Chief Justice Burger, writing for himself and three fellow conservatives, castigated the majority for its activism.

It is difficult to believe that the case would have come out the same way even in 1987, when Justice Anthony Kennedy replaced Justice Powell; and it is certainly impossible to imagine that Justice Thomas shares the view of his predecessor Justice Marshall, even if the other "replacement judges"—Souter, Ginsburg, and Breyer—do in fact maintain the views of the men they replaced. One might have thought that the issue would surely have returned to the Court, whether as the result of California's 1994 adoption, via popular referendum, of Proposition 187, which explicitly bars anyone not legally within the state from receiving most public benefits, or in the aftermath of the 1996 national welfare legislation that, among other things, made ineligible "for any State or local public benefit," save for very limited exceptions, anyone who is an illegal immigrant to the United States. A district judge enjoined enforcement of Proposition 187, claiming that *Plyler* controlled; then-Governor Gray Davis stated that California would accept this decision and not appeal.

Predicting the Supreme Court's response to such cases, if and when they finally arrive in Washington, is made additionally difficult by having to factor the basic issue—the constitutional rights of aliens, including illegal immigrants—into the post-September 11 reality of a country "at war" with foreign terrorism and therefore increasingly suspicious of those deemed strangers. Ironically, five-justice majorities in spring 2001 had ruled that the United States had violated the rights of illegal aliens who had committed relatively minor criminal offense in keeping them permanently confined until some country could be found to which they could be deported. Whether this sympathetic attitude survived September 11 is yet to be known. As noted in the previous chapter, the Court in 2003 granted review with regard to the similarly potentially permanent incarceration of aliens at Guantanamo Bay, Cuba, even though they have in fact not been charged or convicted of specific criminal acts. Although the issues are analytically different, it may be that that decision will cast some light on the likely response to more mundane (and poor) noncitizens who wish access to the benefits of the modern welfare state.

National citizenship raises the most basic questions of political community, but the United States, as a federal system, continues to be faced with residual questions about the meaning of membership in state communities. Recall the quintessential "Brennan Court" decision, *Shapiro* v. *Thompson* (1969), in which Connecticut (among other states) required its new residents to live there at least a year before being eligible for welfare payments. Justice Brennan wrote that such durational-residence requirements violated a constitutionally protected "right to travel" that disallows states from in effect discouraging (or "punishing") immigration from one state to another by depriving newcomers of welfare benefits.

The Court retreated from the more far-reaching implications of *Shapiro* when it affirmed a lower court upholding a Minnesota state law requiring persons to live in the state a full year before being eligible for reduced state-university tuition available only to residents. The district court below had noted the lack of "any dire effects" on the students in question, in presumed contrast to the welfare recipients who were the subject of *Shapiro*. Still, the Court adhered to *Shapiro* in striking down an Arizona law that required a year's residence to be eligible for state-provided medical treatment.

Moreover, even after the shift in membership to a considerably more conservative group of justices, the Court continued to look askance at state efforts to differentiate between short- and long-term residences when distributing benefits. Thus only Justice Rehnquist dissented in *Zobel* v. *Williams* (1982), which struck down Alaska's attempt to distribute to its residents the income from its vast oil reserves on the basis of length of residence. Chief Justice Burger, for the majority, found this "irrational." And in 1999 a solid seven-judge majority overturned a California law—seemingly authorized by the 1996 changes in national welfare policy—by which the state, for the first year of a newcomer's residence, would offer only the dollar amount of benefits that the person would have received from the state of origin. If, for example, Louisiana would pay only $300 per month while California would offer $500, then California insisted on its right to limit the newcomer to the $300. Although many observers expected the Court to reverse *Shapiro,* declaring it a relic of the now-outmoded Warren- (or Brennan-) Court era, it did not do so—although the majority opinion did not explicitly reaffirm *Shapiro* either. Instead the Court suggested that the privileges or immunities clause of the Fourteenth Amendment, basically eviscerated in the aptly named *Slaughter-house Cases* in 1873, might have some bite after all, or at least operated in this case to prevent California from being so stingy to newcomers. What this portends for the future is anyone's guess. Does it announce the beginnings of a bold new doctrinal journey by the Court or, rather, the indirect internment of the equal protection doctrine identified with Justice Brennan and cases like *Shapiro?* The answer, as has been so often suggested in these last two chapters, lies in future electoral developments and the exigencies of judicial retirements and appointments.

CONCLUSION

As these words are written, near the beginning of 2004, it is hard to see any prospects for closure in regard to the Court's role as monitor of the welfare state. Whatever the ideological transformation announced by the 1994 election and President Clinton's acquiescence to the repudiation of classic New Deal legislation (and aspirations) in the 1996 welfare "reforms," it remains altogether obvious that the welfare state is not going to go away. (Indeed, as noted earlier, November 2003 saw the passage of a broad new program bringing prescription drugs into the Medicare program.) There is no clamor by the middle class to get rid of its rich array of entitlements, of which deeply below-market tuition costs at most state universities and professional schools are only the most obvious example likely to interest readers of this book.

No doubt a future reviser of this book will be able to speak of some new modal role of the Court that will have supplanted its role as monitor of the welfare state. One possible candidate, especially given some of the most prominent cases of the 1990's and early 2000's, is the role of an aggressive "umpire" of Federalism, with the judicial thumb being strongly placed on the side of ostensibly beleaguered states facing an overreaching national government. It is, of course, a condition of our being embedded in our own historical situations that developments are often only dimly perceived, if at all, as we concentrate not on the acorns that might be taking root but rather on the existing mighty oaks.

In any event, one suspects that Robert McCloskey would approve of the Court's basic caution in monitoring the welfare state, especially insofar as more assertive decisions might have important impact on public finance and thus, perhaps uniquely, spark public resentment and attack on the Court. But here, as elsewhere, one price of caution may well be acquiescence in unjust treatment of those who are most vulnerable and thus in special need of the services provided by a welfare state. McCloskey, who was relatively liberal in his politics, might respond, though, that alleviation of the plight of the poor will come only if the public itself is sufficiently aroused to support strong legislation (as was, arguably, the case in the 1960's) and not through more-or-less quixotic campaigns by a Court bereft of public support.

He might be more critical of the Court's appointment of itself as the guardian of states' rights, especially if it starts striking down legislation that is genuinely important and/or popular (these are, obviously, not always the same things). Consider first the Americans with Disabilities Act, which has a supportive constituency of millions of people. The Court, in 1999, delivered a series of opinions offering quite restrictive constructions of the statute—thus limiting the number of persons actually protected by the Act; this underscores once more the importance of the Court as statutory interpreter even if it does not challenge the constitutional status of the legislation. But the Court *did* invoke the Constitution in limiting the rights of the disabled to sue states in *University of Alabama* v. *Garrett* (2001). These decisions sparked almost no public outcry, even among groups whose core constituency are the disabled themselves. The same lack of public or interest-group response can be found with regard to the Court's striking down a provision of the Violence Against Women Act in May 2000. Although one can easily believe that McCloskey would have agreed with Justice Souter's warning, in dissent, that the Court was coming ever closer to repeating the "tragedy" of the Old Court in the 1930's, it is also the case that the polity in general is nowhere nearly as upset at the current Court, at least with regard to the "state's rights" decisions, as was the case during the mid- and late-1930's. One may draw two quite different morals from this: Either the public in general is more supportive of a strong Supreme Court than was the case during the New Deal period or, in fact, the current Court has involved itself, with rare exceptions (such as *Bush* v. *Gore*), in relatively peripheral matters whose decisions have relatively little impact on most members of the public.

Epilogue: The Court of Today and the Lessons of History

THOSE WHO STUDY HISTORY and write about it have always been attracted by the idea that the present is illuminated by the past. No doubt they tend to magnify the virtues of their muse and to expect without warrant that others will heed her. Patterns of error in the very historical record they read should serve to remind them that their mistress is not everyone's fancy and that the present is likely, in large measure, to make up its own mind.

Yet they cannot be entirely dissuaded from hoping that today will learn a little from yesterday, that—to come back without further ado to the subject of this book—the Supreme Court of the 1960's will be understood and evaluated in the light of what has gone before. True, the case for such optimism is not overwhelming. As recently as the New Deal period, we saw that some judges of the Supreme Court itself did not know the history of the bench they occupied, or had failed to understand it. From first to last the Court has been attacked and defended in terms of a historical performance that was often completely fictitious.

The Desegregation decision and the 1956–57 subversion decisions seem to have set going one of those irruptions of antijudicial spirit that have from time to time enlivened the chronicles of the Court. And as always the attackers have been met and to a degree countered by a muster of ardent champions. In part, as always, this has been a contest between those who happen for the moment to like the Court because it serves their purpose and those who traduce it because it does not. Such clashes by night are not very edifying, but neither are they very novel or alarming. The Court has survived times more perilous than this. An institution that came through the Jeffersonian revolution, the slavery controversy, and the

New Deal is not likely to expire in the face of this latter-day threat, noisy though it may be.

However, the clamor has been accompanied by a strain of much more responsible and thoughtful evaluation. The strident voices of the ill-informed or ill-intentioned have awakened others to realize that the case for (or against) judicial review merits serious reconsideration in the light of modern circumstances.

This realization was long overdue. The critical assault on judicial review that culminated in the Battle of 1937 did not destroy the Court, but it did impair many of the ancient myths which had long served as justifications for the Court's activities. Thereafter it was no longer possible for the judges and their supporters to take refuge from reasoned criticism behind the old incantations—the idea that the Court was merely the passive mouthpiece of an unambiguous constitution; the idea that the nature and range of the Court's power to intervene was settled once and for all by the Constitution itself or by unmistakable inferences from the Constitution. There had grown up a generation of jurists and scholars convinced that the Court's judges were conscious molders of policy and that the Constitution had left open many questions about its own meaning, including the question of the Court's proper role.

Presumably judicial review could be defended even in the light of these insights; presumably a viable definition of its role could still be worked out. But evidently this could not be accomplished merely by invoking the discredited mystique of the past. It required a new defense and a new set of definitions that took account of the "new realism" about the Court's nature.

For a good many years after 1937, this need for rethinking was pretty thoroughly ignored both by the judges and by informed students of the Court. The judiciary doled out the "yeas" and "nays" and onlookers viewed with approval or alarm, but there seemed little disposition for either the Court or its critics to go beyond the *ad hoc* issues of the individual cases and find a reasoned apologia for judicial review in the modern era. Finally, when the 1950's were nearly over, the cries of the anguished South and its allies helped inaugurate a current of sober and scholarly discussion. In particular the participants in this discussion have been addressing themselves to a problem framed by the most venerable of modern judges in the words: "when a court should intervene." That is, under what circumstances can the judiciary feel warranted in disallowing the acts of the other branches of government? What are the proper limits of judicial review?

This development is healthy and hopeful. It may end by greatly illuminating the problem of judicial review in modern America. But it does seem fair to say that much of the discussion so far, though thoughtful and serious, is marred by inadequate attention to the lessons of history. Of course the Supreme Court of the 1960's must be evaluated as a modern institution, not as an antique. But knowledge of the real (not the fictitious) past of the Court is indispensable to any sound estimate of its capacities in the present and future. The child is father to the man in institutional, as well as individual, life.

In concludi... history of the Court, it mi... sheds on this contemp... vers to the question of ... estions that trouble tod... ser to those answers b...

To begin wi... ques-tion of the Cou... al answer. One of the ... terests and values, and ... ntally and often in the ... ept of the judicial func... inions after 1815 woul... aney's early years. The ... e task required the judi... ction of the Taney Co... Mar-shall claimed, an... lified.

[handwritten marginal note: This could be because public opinion is what shapes the behavior of election-oriented politicians. The Court realizes that these politicians can counteract the Courts actions and so is more inclined not to cross public interest and risk undermining its power.]

Indeed the facts of the Court's history impellingly suggest a flexible and non-dogmatic institution fully alive to such realities as the drift of public opinion and the distribution of power in the American republic. The comparative meekness of the judiciary during the Civil War years, the retreat in 1937 in the face of the election returns—these are only two dramatic examples of a propensity that has been surprisingly constant. As was suggested in the first chapter of this volume, it is hard to find a single historical instance when the Court has stood firm for very long against a really clear wave of public demand. Even the Income Tax law, popular though it was in some circles, was surely not backed by an imperious popular mandate in the 1890's: a constitutional amendment was not even proposed by Congress until fourteen years after the *Pollock* decision.

This is not to suggest that the historical Court has slavishly counted the public pulse, assessed the power relationships that confronted it, and shaped its decisions accordingly. The process in question is a good deal more subtle than that. We might come closer to the truth if we said that the judges have often agreed with the main current of public sentiment because they were themselves part of that current, and not because they feared to disagree with it.

But the salient fact, whatever the explanation, is that the Court has seldom lagged far behind or forged far ahead of America. And the logic of this, as was also suggested at the outset of this volume, was inherent in the conditions of the Court's inception. Judicial review in its peculiar American form exists because America set up popular sovereignty and fundamental law as twin ideals and left the logical conflict between them unresolved. This dualism gave the Court the opportunity for greatness. But it meant that the opportunity was hedged about by reservations and penalties. A tribunal so conceived was not likely to shape its policies without regard for popular sentiment.

It may be deplorable that this is so. There might be something to be said for a Court that imposed loftier ideals and tried to goad the nation faster toward Utopia. But it is at least very doubtful that such a tribunal could have succeeded in holding the scepter it tried to grasp. The American Supreme Court—it should not be forgotten—is the most powerful court known to history. Foreign observers have never ceased to be amazed at the part played by these nine judges in national affairs, and a multitude of students have sought to account for the judiciary's exalted status in this country. The answer I suggest—illustrated over and over in the historical record we have reviewed—is to be found in what has just been said: that the Court seldom strayed very far from the mainstreams of American life and seldom overestimated its own power resources. To put the thing in a different way, the Court learned to be a political institution and to behave accordingly; and this fact above all accounts for its unique position among the judicial tribunals of the world.

All these observations bear directly on the problem of what role the Court should play, or is likely to play, in the modern American order.

For example, the Court's modern shift away from economic rights and toward civil rights can be properly evaluated only when it is seen in historical perspective. There has been a considerable amount of argument over the question of whether the judges ought to have abandoned their old preoccupation with economic matters, should have turned the property-holder as such over to the legislative power to do with as it wished. Perhaps there are still some marginal issues in this area that are open to fruitful discussion, but surely the broad rejoinder is that history, not the Court, made this decision, as it has made similar decisions in the past. Before 1860, America itself was undecided on the question of nation versus states; before 1932, America was undecided about the question of government economic control versus laissez faire. Until those dates the Court could still play a vital part in helping the nation to make up its mind. It happens that the Court's line in the one case was in accord with the final historical decision, and in the other was not. But this makes little difference to the point. If in either case the Court had tried to follow its own course after the Civil War and the New Deal had respectively signalized firm national judgments, the judges would have been talking to themselves. Ethical justifications for these farewells to the past are no doubt still worth seeking, but we should be clear that they are ex post facto.

As for the modern Court's espousal of civil rights as a substitute for the economic rights it once so cherished, this too was less a matter of deliberate choice than of predictable response to the wave of history. As we have seen, the Court has always tended to focus on the great open questions that plagued America as a whole—the nation-state problem from 1789 to 1860, the business-government problem from 1865 to 1937. To be sure, there are some such "great issues" which are probably not meet for judicial treatment. The slavery question in the 1850's seems in retrospect one of these; the question of foreign policy in modern circumstances is, for rather different reasons, another. But within the limits of what it regards as its capacities, the Court can be expected to preoccupy itself with the issues that most preoccupy America. And civil rights is just such an issue—more important perhaps than any modern American problem except foreign affairs, still undecided in spite of what partisans on either side would like to think, and not by its nature inappropriate for some form of judicial intervention. In turning its attention to this subject, the Court was acting in perfect historical character.

It was to be expected, then, and was, historically speaking, "right" that the Court should focus in the modern period on the relationship between government and the individual's rights. But history also has a precept or two to offer in connection with the question of *how* this comparatively new jurisdiction should be administered. What judicial attitudes, what policies, are most likely to serve the cause the judges have so evidently embraced?

In the first place, the record suggests that the principles of this new jurisprudence cannot be reached by a series of leaps and bounds. The Court's great successes in establishing jurisdiction have never been attained that way. We need only recall by way of example the slow and gingerly steps Marshall took from *Marbury* to *Cohens* v. *Virginia* to confirm the Court's supremacy over the states, or the almost painfully gradual accumulation of precedents that led finally to substantive due process in the late nineteenth century. It is in the nature of courts to feel their way along, and it must not be forgotten that this is a court we are speaking of, albeit a most unusual one.

Moreover—it can hardly be said too often—the Supreme Court, being an American institution, is obliged always to reckon with America and her propensities; and America is a nation that moves hesitantly and changes gradually. In spite of our occasional frenzies, the great alterations in the Republic's development have been the result of long experience and slowly growing conviction. There are those on the modern Court—Justices Black and Douglas are the leading exemplars—who would resolve constitutional uncertainties with large, bold, pioneering strokes of the pen. If this is the proper model for judicial governance, then history is indeed an untrustworthy guide.

Rather similar thoughts are aroused when we apply the historical lens to the question that has plagued the modern Court during the past two decades: granting that civil rights are properly within the judicial purview, and granting (at least for argument's sake) that the structure of the new jurisprudence must be built up gradually, how self-assertive should the Court be in imposing the rules it does devise upon the other branches of government? What are the boundaries of modesty on the one hand and "activism" on the other, even in the civil rights field?

Only a rhetorical purpose is served by answering this query in terms that simply ignore the patterns of history. From time to time it is urged that the Court should carry the virtue of modesty to an extreme, adopting a policy of self-restraint that would leave other branches of government almost entirely immune from constitutional restrictions. Whatever the theoretical merits of such a suggestion, the short answer is that it asks the Court to take leave of its heritage. The Court of history has never assessed itself so modestly, and there is not much reason to expect that the Court of the future will deliberately choose such a policy of renunciation. In fact we might almost think that the argument in its pure form had been foreclosed by the passage of time. As I have earlier suggested, the process of policy formation in America has been handled by a rough division of labor: representation of immediate and sometimes imperative interests has been assigned to the legislative branch; the judiciary has been bequeathed a significant share of the responsibility for taking the longer view. If the Court, after nearly two centuries, should cease to perform its wonted share of this work, there is grave doubt that the shirked task would get done at all.

And surely American democracy would be poorer. An impulsive nation like ours, much given to short-run fads, enthusiasms and rages, can little afford to dispense with the one governmental element that is disposed by its nature to take the long-run into account. To be sure, the record suggests that these popular passions are usually followed in the fullness of time by a cooling-off phase. The basic tendency of American politics is surely not extremist. But unfortunately these impulses, if not countered, are likely to leave behind them a brood of foolish laws and unfair practices that are harder to disown than they were to adopt. In 1960 the "McCarthyist" spirit seemed to have subsided quite thoroughly as an active political factor. But legislative and administrative remnants of that spirit lived on. America needs the Court's advice and control to help mitigate its own extravagances.

Neither, however, should history be ignored in determining how judicial control should be exercised and when it should be brought to bear. Surely the record teaches that no useful purpose is served when the judges seek all the hottest political caldrons of the moment and dive into the middle of them. Nor is there much to be said for the idea that a judicial policy of flat and uncompromising negation will halt a truly dominant political impulse. Grave though the McCarthyist threat was, a discreet judiciary would not assail every manifestation of it that appeared, or hope to reverse the tide unaided. The Court's greatest successes have been achieved when it has operated near the margins rather than in the center of political controversy, when it has nudged and gently tugged the nation, instead of trying to rule it. Consider the success of the Taney Court in its early years, compromising or skirting the areas of greatest controversy, yet developing on the peripheries of those areas a moderate but real national jurisprudence. Or consider the long campaign on behalf of laissez faire from 1905 to 1934, with its pattern of concessions to the principle of regulation, dotted here and there with a warning that the principle could be carried too far. And compare the Court of these times with that of 1858 or 1938 after the urge to dominate had enjoyed two moments of triumphant ascendancy. The Court ruled more in each case when it tried to rule less, and that paradox is one of the clearest morals to be drawn from this history.

It is true that such a judicial policy calls for rather extraordinary talents of character and intelligence. The Court must alter its own perspectives as history's perspectives are altered, yet must not move so fast that the idea of continuity is lost. It must allow government some leeway to act either wisely or foolishly, yet must not become so acquiescent that the concept of constitutional limit is revealed as an illusion. This requires judges who possess what a great poet called "negative capability"—who can resist the natural human tendency to push an idea to what seems its logical extreme, to have done with half-measures and uncertainties. It requires judges who can practice the arts of discrimination without losing the light of reason and getting lost in a welter of *ad hoc,* pragmatic judgments. For it is part of the glory and strength of the American constitutional tradition that it assumes the possibility of being rational about the state and its powers and limits.

This is a challenging bill of particulars, and the Supreme Court in the modern era has not met it in all respects. The Court has adjusted impressively to a new environment, has embraced a new set of interests and values, has shouldered great new responsibilities in the field of civil rights. But here and there—as in the free speech field—it has oscillated between a doctrine of limit too strict for enforcement and a doctrine of permissiveness that bordered on judicial abdication. Here and there—as in the segregation case—it has pressed forward at a rate that seems perilous and perhaps self-defeating. Here and there—as in the cases involving state criminal procedures—it has failed to chart a course that is rationally persuasive or even comprehensible. Here and there—as in the Steel Seizure Case—it has presumed to arbitrate an issue charged with the most explosive and immediate political consequences.

Nevertheless the Court of the modern era, like those of the past, has rendered a service of no small significance. From 1789 to the Civil War, the Court labored to establish a reasoned argument for the cause of union. From the war to 1937 it performed a similar function on behalf of laissez faire. Toward the end of each of those periods, the judges overstepped the practical boundaries of judicial power and endangered the place they had earned in the American governmental system. Since 1937, the Court has striven to evolve a civil rights doctrine that will realize the promise of the American libertarian tradition, yet accord with the imperatives of political reality. Even when criticisms are duly acknowledged, the fact remains that the Court has contributed more to an understanding of this issue than any other agency in American life. It would be a pity if the judges, having done so much, should now once more forget the limits that their own history so compellingly prescribes.

CODA

WHATEVER ELSE can be said about the past forty years of the Supreme Court's behavior, it certainly does not appear to accord with Robert McCloskey's advice that it proceed by careful incremental steps and avoid "a series of leaps and bounds." Whether the example be *Reynolds* v. *Sims* and the imposition of the one-person, one-vote rule upon the states; *Roe* v. *Wade* and its sweeping aside of the criminal law of almost all of the states in regard to abortion; or, more recently, the Court's renewed embrace of state sovereignty and concomitant potential destabilization of what had been thought to have been settled by the New Deal, the Court seemed (and seems) more than willing to move boldly. The most spectacular example, needless to say, was the Court's willingness to intervene in the dispute about the 2000 presidential election and, in effect, to declare George W. Bush the winner. The Court appeared to learn as its lesson from the past not the merit of cautious, crablike movement but rather that the American public, for all of its grumbling, was quite willing to accept a great deal of political tutelage from it.

Dozens of constitutional amendments were introduced during this period to overturn one or another of the Court's controversial decisions concerning legislative districting, school prayer, the rights of criminal defendants, abortion, flag burning, and busing to achieve desegregation. None of them even got through Congress. One amendment, the Twenty-sixth, did reverse *Oregon* v. *Mitchell,* a 1970 decision of the Court, though this recourse to the amendment process is probably explained less by a popular outcry in behalf of voting rights for eighteen-year-olds, the subject matter of the amendment, than by the sheer institutional confusion generated by the Court's decision in *Mitchell.* Because of Justice Hugo

Black's entirely idiosyncratic view, one majority of five (with Black providing the fifth vote) held that Congress did not have the power to require states to give eighteen-year-olds the vote in elections for state officials, even as another majority of five (again with Black providing the fifth vote) held that Congress possesses the power to require that eighteen-year-olds be allowed to vote in elections for *federal* offices. As should be obvious, eight of the nine justices agreed that whatever power Congress did or did not possess covered both kinds of elections. Among other things, *Mitchell* illustrates the problems of reaching coherent decisions in a multimember decision-making body like the Supreme Court. In any event, once the Court accepted the proposition that states could be forced to make eighteen-year-olds part of the electorate for at least some elections, then there was no real opposition to the amendment proposed by Congress to override that aspect of the case limiting Congress' power.

Though not trivial, the Twenty-sixth Amendment can hardly be described as a major repudiation of the Court. Otherwise, the formal law of the Constitution remained what the Court said it was.

Perhaps the most interesting attempt of Congress to override the Court is the Religious Freedom Restoration Act (1993), passed to overrule its decision in the *Smith* case that minimized the reach of the free exercise clause. The Court responded in 1997 by invalidating the Act as beyond congressional power, in an opinion repeatedly emphasizing judicial supremacy and diminution of any legitimate congressional role in interpreting disputed tutelage aspects of the Constitution. Even though RFRA passed by overwhelming votes in the House and Senate, there was no serious suggestion that the 1997 *Boerne* decision should be reversed via constitutional amendment—though perhaps one explanation for the lack of any such movement was the recognition that Article V biases the amendment process almost overwhelmingly in favor of those who would resist change.

It would be a mistake, though, to describe the Court as exhibiting any great eagerness to be far in front of those it professed to lead. Perhaps the Leninist dictum of two steps forward, one step backward better characterizes its behavior in that a number of very bold decisions were followed by more cautious retreats. In few areas—abortion may be one of them—can the contemporary Court be described as truly determined to prevail against legislative opposition, though even here it is clear that public opinion generally continues to be relatively supportive of reproductive rights, at least for adult women (as distinguished from young teenagers) who wish to terminate their pregnancies relatively early (as distinguished from late-term abortions). Even the renewed embrace of states'-rights ideology by the contemporary Court, and its resulting invalidation of a number of federal statutes, may be understood as the de facto adoption of the national sentiment possibly revealed by the 1994 elections and the concomitant overthrow of the long-entrenched Democratic majorities in the Senate and, especially, the House of Representatives. Invalidation of pre-1994 legislation cannot self-evidently be described as "countermajoritarian," given the new mood in Congress and the articulation by then-Democratic President Bill Clinton, himself a former governor, that "the era of big government is over." Whatever the circumstances surrounding George W. Bush's gaining the White House, roughly half the country supported him, and the Republican gains in the 2002 congressional elections scarcely bespeak a repudiation of the Republican critique of traditional governmental activism. Relatively speaking, it may still be the case that Congress can do pretty much whatever it wants to, but that it wants to do less than was the case in the period of more overtly activist government.

Ironically, when the Court does insist on its own agenda, the objects of its wrath are as likely to be lower-court judges as legislators or executives. Thus the rampage by the contemporary Court in behalf of capital punishment is directed primarily at liberal judges viewed by its conservative majority as far too lenient with especially vicious murderers—an aftereffect of the Court's jurisprudence of the 1970's is that almost all inmates now on death row have in fact been convicted of brutal killings—and, concomitantly, too indifferent to the victims of the crimes and the public's fears about rampant crime. (Though, even in this area, the Court has also begun expressing concern that some lower courts are perhaps *too* eager to allow executions in the face of irregularities in the procedures by which the inmates were convicted.)

Whether the object of the Court's concern is the judge below or the local administrator of a state welfare system, the student must take up a question that McCloskey addressed only indirectly: To what extent do the pronouncements of the Court actually affect behavior throughout society? Anthony G. Amsterdam once compared the Court to the Delphic Oracle: However impressive her emergence from the Temple might be, especially given the smoke and incense surrounding the Oracle, onlookers were ultimately left scratching their head, wondering what the message actually was. It was then up to the priests to give actual meaning to the truly "delphic" pronouncements. Whether one views the Court as the Delphic Oracle or as the Wizard of Oz, one can still wonder how many ordinary public officials are even aware of its pronouncements, let alone structure their behavior in accordance with the goals presumably sought by the Court.

The essence of lawyering is the making of distinctions. It is usually no great feat, then, for a city attorney faced with a local "affirmative action" ordinance—or, for that matter, one of the judges of the federal courts reviewing the ordinance—to show how the particular case at issue differs from the case proffered by the Court to control the issue. This is all the more true insofar as the Court, as is often its wont, offers fact-intensive analyses that make it difficult to figure out whether its conclusions would be the same in different contexts.

Though Gerald Rosenberg may have been exaggerating in describing the Court as a completely "hollow hope" regarding activists' desire to use it to promote wide-scale changes not otherwise supported by the ordinary political branches, his McCloskeyan note of caution rings true. For the Court to be effective as an agent of change, it must evoke the loyalties of thousands of relatively low-visibility officials who count as "the government" for most ordinary citizens. It could, of course, ruthlessly monitor the behavior of these officials, but that is almost impossible; the Court just does not have the resources to do so, even if it were to accept far more than the roughly eighty to ninety cases per year it has recently been taking—a significant decline from the 125 to 135 cases of the decade before. It remains substantially true, as Hamilton suggested in *Federalist* 78, that the Court possesses neither "purse nor sword" and must depend, therefore, on the willingness of legislative and executive officials to conform their behavior to its judgments.

One might suggest that the likelihood of such conformity is related to what political scientists sometimes describe as the "diffuse support" accorded the Court: the general propensity of the public to pronounce the Court admirable and thus to expect their public servants to comply with its commands. Interpretation of public opinion is an art akin to decoding delphic pronouncements, but it is hard to believe that the Court enjoys enough diffuse support to be able to rely on relatively unproblematic acquiescence to its more controversial policy goals. Both the American public in general, and the legal culture in particular, seem increasingly fragmented in regard to the great issues of the day, and few can plausibly believe that the Court possesses the moral or political authority to resolve bitter disputes about race, freedom of sexual expression, the scope and administration of the welfare state, or crime, to mention only four of the dominant domestic issues at the beginning of the twenty-first century.

A signal moment in American legal culture occurred in 1991, when

Dean Guido Calabresi of the Yale Law School (who would subsequently be appointed to the Second Circuit Court of Appeals by his former student President Clinton) wrote in the pages of the *New York Times* that "I despise the current Supreme Court and find its aggressive, willful, statist behavior disgusting." To be sure, the Court has never been the object of undivided solicitude. It was the famous New York antislavery newspaper editor Horace Greeley who wrote that he would as soon trust the judgment of his dog as that of Roger Taney, and many other such examples can be found over the past two hundred years. "Impeach Earl Warren" billboards were a standard feature of the roadside throughout the 1950's and 60's—and not only in the South.

But the dean of the Yale Law School is not a populist demagogue, or even a fiery newspaper editor. Yale is a special law school, together with Harvard the acknowledged citadel of the American legal elite, with alumni regularly serving on the Supreme Court itself. Indeed, Calabresi made his statement in a column ostensibly supporting the nomination to the Court of Yale alumnus Clarence Thomas. For the dean of that school, in the pages of America's leading newspaper, to express such contempt clearly reveals the contemporary Court's inability to call on even its traditional allies to give testimonials about how the justices are undoubtedly fine persons doing their best to resolve difficult issues and, therefore, that responsible citizens need to rally round the Court regardless of disagreements.

Calabresi's expression of contempt was linked to his generally liberal views. But political conservatives were just as willing to denounce the Court. Thus a November 1996 symposium in the conservative journal *First Things* was titled "The End of Democracy?"; several prominent conservative participants suggested that the Court's unwillingness to validate antiabortion legislation did indeed exemplify the end of democracy. Thus, wrote one of the contributors, "America is not and, please God, will never become Nazi Germany, but it is only blind hubris that denies it can happen here and, in peculiarly American ways, may be happening here" because of the Court's insistence on protecting women's right to abortion. For those who believe, like the symposiasts, that abortion rivals the Holocaust in terms of murdering innocents, the logical next question is the legitimacy of active resistance to the presumptively illegitimate Court. The abortion issue will receive its next test if and when the Court reviews a law passed by Congress in October 2003 that bars what its proponents call "partial-birth" abortions. As a matter of fact, the Court in 2000 struck down a very similar law passed by the Nebraska legislature. Given that the Court's membership has not changed since then—indeed this is threatening to become the longest unchanged Court in American history —there is no particular reason to expect it to be more hospitable to the congressional enactment.

With regard to issues other than abortion, political conservatives were scarcely happy when the Court in June 2003 both upheld affirmative action in the Michigan law school case and, even more importantly, invalidated the Texas anti-sodomy law, just as political liberals were unhappy with a number of other decisions of the recent Court, including, most certainly, *Bush* v. *Gore*. The conservative magazine *Commentary* titled an October 2003 symposium "Has the Supreme Court Gone Too Far?", and its introduction noted that the Court was increasingly being criticized by scholars and activists from both the left and right (though, obviously, they were undoubtedly upset by different decisions). Although the participants reached no consensus on what should be done with regard to the Court, none of them expressed any great regard for its full range of handiwork.

Indirect support for the uncertain status of the contemporary Court may be found in its felt need to repeatedly deem itself the "ultimate interpreter" of the Constitution, lest the citizenry believe that the Court's opinions are only one among a set of legitimate commentaries. Indeed, the Court has gone so far as to assert that *Marbury* declared the "basic principle that the federal judiciary is supreme in the exposition of the law of the Constitution, and that principle has ever since been respected by this Court and the Country as a permanent and indispensable feature of our constitutional system." This statement appeared initially in *Cooper* v. *Aaron* (1958), in which the Court dismissed, in no uncertain terms, arguments by the Little Rock, Arkansas, school board that it was not covered by the Court's rulings in the earlier school segregation cases that had, after all, arisen elsewhere. In that context, one could easily sympathize with the Court's description of its role and, indeed, condemn those who challenged the authority (and domain) of its decision in *Brown*. Yet the Court's statement is really quite preposterous in its depiction of American history. If a student wrote such a statement in a final exam, it would receive a D at best, inasmuch as its validity requires that one ignore, for starters, the thought of Madison, Jefferson, Andrew Jackson, John Calhoun, Lincoln, and Franklin Roosevelt—to name only the best-known critics of overinflated claims of judicial supremacy. Such claims by the Court, both to theoretical ultimacy and, just as significantly, to the popular acceptance of its supremacy, have the overtone of the scared whistler going past the graveyard: ultimately more pathetic than inspiring.

The extent of division within the Court—and the character of its members—was most sharply revealed in the extraordinarily bitter battle over President Ronald Reagan's 1987 nomination of Judge Robert Bork to succeed Lewis Powell on the tribunal. Bork, a former Yale professor and Solicitor General of the United States before being named to the Court of Appeals for the District of Columbia, was one of the most prominent critics of the Warren Court and of the activism that it stood for. Indeed, he denounced it as basically lawless insofar as judges drifted from what he posited as the one true method of constitutional interpretation, the ascertaining and enforcement of the "original meaning" of the Constitution. Bork was particularly savage in his criticism of the Court's return to substantive due process and the enforcement of "unenumerated rights" in cases like *Griswold* v. *Connecticut* and *Roe* v. *Wade.* In the absence of explicit constitutional prohibitions, Bork maintained, political majorities had basically unfettered authority to do what they wished. This is, of course, very close to what Oliver Wendell Holmes argued in the *Lochner* dissent. That dissent, the anthem of liberals during the period preceding the New Deal and for some two decades after, took on a different hue in the era of the Warren Court, which was far less accepting than was Holmes of the duty to uphold what it deemed "tyrannical" legislation.

If Bork was demonized by his opponents, who sometimes described him as blithely indifferent to oppression, then he was just as surely deified by his supporters, who saw him as a Herculean figure ready and willing to clean out the Augean stables desecrated by the jurisprudence of the last several decades. At the end he was rejected, but the scars of the battle remain. And the debacle concerning Clarence Thomas's nomination in 1991 was even greater, as national attention ultimately focused on whether he had in fact sexually harassed an employee.

Never again will the nomination and confirmation of a judge take eight days, as was the case with Byron White in 1961, or even three weeks, as with John Paul Stevens in 1976. Even more will it be impossible for someone like Sherman Minton, who when nominated in 1949 was a member of the Seventh Circuit Court of Appeals, to refuse to testify before the Senate Judiciary Committee on the grounds that it was improper to direct questions at a sitting judge. Yet, ironically, the new public attention paid to Court appointments is evidence that the citizenry expects the Court to play a significant role in defining public policy. It is that expectation that makes it worthwhile for various interest groups to marshal their resources in supporting or rejecting particular nominees. And, in more recent years, one sees the concern over judicial appointments extend to appellate and even district court nominees. Republican Senates refused even to vote out of the Senate Judiciary Committee several of President Clinton's nominees to the federal bench and, in one notable case, defeated the nomination of an African-American justice of the Missouri Supreme Court to join the Eighth Circuit Court of Appeals because of spurious arguments that he was "soft on the death penalty." In turn, the Democratic minority in the post-2002 Senate, unable to block nominations in the Judiciary Committee (as they had when they exercised control prior to that election), engaged in filibusters to defeat the confirmation of six Bush nominees. Almost no one, it appears, can get a "free ride" any longer to lifetime tenure on the federal bench—at least not in the age of divided government or even, in a Senate that confirms presidential nominees, the presence of forty-one senators with enough zeal to threaten a filibuster should a particular nominee's name be brought to the floor for discussion.

To the extent that the rejection of Robert Bork was based, among other things, on his unwillingness to endorse the legitimacy of the Court's protecting the citizenry against certain legislative invasions of "privacy," then the Senate, strongly backed by the public, can be viewed as giving its imprimatur to the rebirth of substantive due process following its apparent demise in 1937. Even Clarence Thomas, apparently more conservative than William Rehnquist or Antonin Scalia, could gain confirmation only by denying to the Senate, truthfully or not, that he had ever thought seriously about *Roe* or had any opinions about the constitutional status of privacy and abortion. To have admitted what quickly became obvious, that he would in fact overrule *Roe,* would have doomed his nomination. Indeed, the Republican Party's failure to mount a serious attack on President Clinton's 1993 nomination to the Court of Ruth Bader Ginsburg, a strong proponent of judicial protection of reproductive choice, signaled its acquiescence to the constitutionalization of basic abortion rights, even if the debate would continue about their scope.

It is chimerical to believe that the Court will ever retire from the political arena and simply adopt the role of some kind of "neutral" referee, making sure that the active players conform to the rules of the constitutional game (which themselves are often in flux because of the desire by one player or another to "push the envelope" and, in effect, establish new rules or, at the least, new understandings of old rules). The Court will continue to assess the rules and, on occasion, to rewrite them, quite independently of the wishes of the other players. The members of the Court therefore have to decide what role they wish to play. At the same time, those responsible for choosing the justices—Presidents, senators, and ultimately the citizenry—must decide as well what sort of person should be placed on the Court. What attributes should one look for? In particular, how does one try to guarantee the presence of the sound political judgment that, as much as legal "expertise," defines the role of the Supreme Court justice?

One of the most striking differences between the Warren and post-Warren Courts concerns the preappointment experiences of the justices. The 1954 Court that decided *Brown,* for example, was headed by the immensely popular former governor of California, which was rapidly becoming the second-largest state. Earl Warren had been a candidate on the Republican ticket in 1948, and he continued to be spoken of as a presidential possibility in 1952. His colleagues included three former senators (Hugo Black, Sherman Minton, and Harold Burton); two of the leading legal academics of their time (Felix Frankfurter and William O. Douglas), both of whom had been involved at the highest level of the Roosevelt Administration during the New Deal; two former Solicitors General (Robert Jackson and Stanley Reed); and two former Attorneys General (Jackson and Tom Clark). Only one of them, Minton, had any prior judicial experience. To be sure, the pattern shifted somewhat thereafter. The other four appointees by President Dwight Eisenhower—William Brennan, John Harlan, Potter Stewart, and Charles Whittaker—all had judicial experience and, perhaps even more to the point, had little or no nonjudicial experience in public life. Only one of John F. Kennedy's and Lyndon Johnson's four appointees—Thurgood Marshall—had judicial experience, and no one seriously would focus on that aspect of Marshall's pre-Court career when assessing his fitness for the Court. Far more important was his status as perhaps the leading public lawyer of the age, the central architect of the NAACP attack on segregation. Marshall would have merited a full-scale biography had he been run over by a truck the day before joining the Court, as would have been true of at least half of the justices that heard his argument in *Brown.* No one appointed since Marshall could conceivably pass this test.

The only subsequent justices whose pre-Court experiences could warrant even a chapter are Lewis Powell, Clarence Thomas, and Ruth Bader Ginsburg. Powell had actively participated in the desegregation of Richmond, Virginia, and was a relatively reformist president of the American Bar Association. Thomas had headed an important federal agency, the

Equal Employment Opportunities Commission, while Ginsburg, as a practicing lawyer and professor of law in the 1970's, devised, and advocated before the Court, important arguments relating to discrimination against women. None, though, could truly be compared to Warren, Black, Frankfurter, Douglas, or Marshall—or past figures like John Marshall, Roger Taney, Salmon P. Chase, Louis Brandeis, William Howard Taft, or Charles Evans Hughes. Whatever their important differences, each of these figures brought real stature to the Court rather than having it thrust upon them by the fact of appointment. That is what I would call the "biography test."

Since Lewis Powell's appointment in 1971, every single subsequent nominee to the Court had already been serving as a member of the judiciary; indeed, with the exception of Sandra Day O'Connor, who was serving on an Arizona state court, they have been chosen from the federal courts of appeals. Published press reports at the time indicated that President Clinton was eager in 1993 and 1994 to appoint someone with significant political experience upon the retirements of Justices White and Blackmun. Most prominently mentioned were former New York Governor Mario Cuomo or former Senate Majority Leader George Mitchell. Yet Clinton's second nominee, Stephen G. Breyer, like his first, Ruth Bader Ginsburg, was a long-time federal appeals judge (and, prior to appointment, law professor) devoid of such background.

Why prior judicial experience is considered an important prerequisite for appointment to the Supreme Court is a mystery. It surely has not been the case that the greatest judges of the past—whether measured by statesmanship, moral sensitivity, or eloquence in behalf of the values we would like to believe undergird the constitutional order—have necessarily had such experience. The best one can say is that a nominee's having served as a judge is not a disqualification, and the nine-justice Court probably needs one or two members who can bring the lessons of that experience to Washington; though, if prior judicial experience is thought relevant, one might wish for occasional nominees who experienced "ground-level" American justice at the trial-court level. Courts of appeals basically work at the same level of abstraction as does the Supreme Court. It is trial court judges who must in fact wrestle with the actualities of the American legal system. No Justice in many years has had such experience.

It is certainly not clear, though, that the habits of thought necessary to performing as a judicial underling are those most truly needed on the Supreme Court. Holmes is the great counterexample, though perhaps all that can be said is that he possessed such transcendent abilities that he survived two decades of service on the Massachusetts Supreme Judicial Court without destroying his capacity for greatness. And even Holmes's opinions are often distinguished by an almost sublime indifference to ground-level realities.

It would be extremely naive to argue that the contempt of court revealed by Dean Calabresi (joined, no doubt, by millions of other Americans of various political stripes) would be assuaged simply by the appointment of at least some political figures who have had their character and judgment tested while running for office or otherwise participating in the brutal battles of public conflict over basic issues. The country may be just too polarized to view any set of appointees as possessing sufficient wisdom to make authoritative decisions in regard to the kind of issues presented the judiciary for resolution. In one of the most stunning passages of the Lincoln-Douglas debates, Stephen Douglas noted that "Mr. Lincoln cannot conscientiously submit, he thinks, to the decision of a court composed of a majority of Democrats. If he cannot, how can he expect us to have confidence in a court composed of a majority of Republicans, selected for the purpose of deciding against the Democracy, and in favor of the Republicans?" According to Douglas, "The very proposition carries with it the demoralization and degradation destructive of the judicial department of the federal government." This may express the great, perhaps almost literally unbearable, tension that exists between the (mythic) view of the Court as truly "above politics," faithful only to the apolitical commands of the Constitution, and the (more accurate) portrait of the Court as invariably part of the political process, with its membership reflecting the particular play of political interests dominant at given moments of appointment and confirmation.

It may be, then, that no Court can really expect to gain the degree of public support and deference that it seeks, especially when the general public is so sharply divided and engaged in what many term a "culture war." Indeed, Justice Scalia, in a bitter dissent from the Court's opinion in the Lawrence case that struck down Texas's anti-sodomy law, accused his colleagues of taking sides in that war by promoting what he termed the "homosexual agenda." It may be that no group of Justices, however distinguished, could bring peace to such deep conflicts in contemporary American society. Yet it is difficult to believe that support will flow to a Supreme Court composed of relative nonentities (chosen for political reasons) who are devoid of practical political experience—and devoid as well of public displays of "grace under pressure" even to the extent of Lewis

Powell's activities in Richmond, let alone Thurgood Marshall's almost infinitely greater courage manifested throughout the Deep South in the 1940's and 1950's.

The Supreme Court of the United States undoubtedly remains the most powerful court of any in the world, and there is no real reason to think that will change in the foreseeable future. However, what we have learned, particularly since the glory days of World War II, is that the possession even of apparently awesome power may not in fact be enough to prevail in an ever-more-complex and fragmented world. After all, the United States—the most powerful country in the world—could not prevail in Vietnam, and nuclear weapons proved irrelevant in keeping the Communist Party in power or, indeed, in preventing the dissolution of the Soviet Union. Deference to established authority seems less and less descriptive of political reality anywhere in the world today, including the United States. The specter of Oz must inhabit the nightmares of anyone who proclaims his or her power.

In an age when incumbent Presidents are now regularly defeated— and, indeed, the state governor of California was successfully "recalled" from office—a lifetime tenured Court may increasingly appear to be an anomaly. One might well ask if a single-term appointment of, say, eighteen years, which would generate a new justice every two years, would really be a blow to the Court's stature or its independence. Interestingly enough, two participants in a 1998 symposium chose lifetime tenure as the "stupidest" feature of the U.S. Constitution. It might be worth noting that very few contemporary constitution writers, such as those in Eastern Europe following the end of the cold war, have chosen to emulate the United States in this regard. As a practical matter, however, it might be impossible to get rid of life tenure because of the enormous difficulties facing anyone who would amend the Constitution.

Certainly nothing has negated McCloskey's 1960 observation that it gets ever harder to take seriously the image of the judge as the impersonal vessel through whom the Constitution speaks. And even if one could continue to believe such things of the judge, it would still remain open to ask whether that Constitution serves us all that well today. State constitutions enjoy none of the veneration accorded the United States Constitution; they are not only often amended, but even, with some frequency, replaced with brand-new versions. It would require the talents of a clairvoyant to predict whether the Supreme Court, powerful though it may be, will continue to escape the storms that seem to be besetting other institutions of government. Yet, as Holmes once wrote, "repose is not the destiny" of humankind. The Supreme Court will remain fascinating, for good or for ill, so long as there is a United States that tries to resolve the tension between popular sovereignty and adherence to fundamental norms even when the majority would prefer to ignore them.

Important Dates

1788   New Hampshire ratifies Constitution
1789   The Republic begins operations
       The Judiciary Act is passed
1791   The Bill of Rights ratified
1793   *Chisholm v. Georgia* (states can be sued in the Federal Courts by
       private citizens of other states)
1798   Eleventh Amendment ratified
       Alien and Sedition Acts
1800   Jefferson elected President
1801   John Marshall appointed Chief Justice
       Judiciary Act of 1801 passed
1802   Judiciary Act of 1801 repealed
1803   *Marbury v. Madison*
1805   Impeachment charges against Justice Chase fail
1810   *Fletcher v. Peck* (the Yazoo land-grant case)
1811   Justice Story appointed
1816   *Martin v. Hunter's Lessee* (state court decisions are reviewable
       by the Supreme Court)
1819   *McCulloch v. Maryland* (the Bank of the United States tax case)
       Dartmouth College v. Woodward
1824   *Gibbons v. Ogden* (the Steamboat Monopoly case)
1833   *Barron v. Baltimore* (the Bill of Rights does not restrict the states)
1835   Death of Marshall
1836   Roger B. Taney appointed Chief Justice
1837   Taney's first term: *Mayor of New York v. Miln; Charles River
       Bridge v. Warren Bridge Co.; Briscoe v. Bank of Kentucky*
1851   *Cooley v. Board of Wardens* (the state can regulate commercial

subjects that do not require a uniform national rule—the doctrine of "selective exclusiveness")

1857   *Dred Scott* case (holding the Missouri Compromise invalid)

1862   Justice Samuel F. Miller appointed

1863   Justice Stephen J. Field appointed

1864   Death of Taney

      Chief Justice Salmon P. Chase appointed

1865   Thirteenth Amendment ratified

1866   *Ex Parte Milligan* (invalidating wartime military trial of civilians)

1868   Fourteenth Amendment ratified

      Thomas M. Cooley's *Constitutional Limitations* published

1870   Fifteenth Amendment ratified

      Hepburn v. *Griswold* (invalidating the Legal Tender Act in certain respects)

1871   *Legal Tender Cases* (upholding the Legal Tender Act in all respects)

1873   *Slaughterhouse Cases* (the Fourteenth Amendment does not forbid a state-granted monopoly)

1874   Chief Justice Morrison R. Waite appointed

1877   *Munn* v. *Illinois* (rate regulation of grain elevator rates by state is not forbidden by the Fourteenth Amendment)

1888   Chief Justice Melville W. Fuller appointed

1890   Minnesota Commission case (state rate regulation without judicial review denies due process)

1895   *United States* v. *E. C. Knight Co.* (the Sherman Antitrust Act cannot constitutionally apply to monopolies in manufacturing)

      Pollock v. *Farmers' Loan and Trust Co.* (the Income Tax case)

1896   *Plessy* v. *Ferguson* (the state may require separate facilities for different races providing that the facilities are equal—the "separate but equal doctrine")

1902   Justice Oliver Wendell Holmes appointed

1904   *McCray* v. *United States* (the Oleomargarine Tax case)

1905   *Lochner* v. *New York* (the Fourteenth Amendment forbids general hours regulation)

      Swift and Co. v. *United States* (the Antitrust Act can validly apply to sales monopolies)

1910   Chief Justice Edward D. White appointed

1913   Sixteenth Amendment ratified

1916   Justice Louis D. Brandeis appointed

1918 *Hammer* v. *Dagenhart* (the Child Labor case)

1919 *Schenck* v. *United States* (the "clear and present danger" rule)

1921 Chief Justice William H. Taft appointed

1923 *Adkins* v. *Children's Hospital* (the Washington, D.C., Minimum Wage case)

1934 *Nebbia* v. *New York* (upholding the validity of a state milk control law)

1935 *Schechter Poultry Corp.* v. *United States* (holding the National Industrial Recovery Act unconstitutional)

1936 *United States* v. *Butler* (holding the Agricultural Adjustment Act unconstitutional)

   Carter v. *Carter Coal Co.* (holding the Bituminous Coal Act unconstitutional)

   Morehead v. *Tipaldo* (holding the New York Minimum Wage Law unconstitutional)

   Franklin D. Roosevelt re-elected

1937 The "court-packing" plan submitted to Congress, February 5.

   West Coast Hotel v. *Parrish* (upholding the Minimum Wage Law of the State of Washington), March 29

   The National Labor Relations Act decisions (upholding the N.L.R.A.), April 12

   Steward Machine Co. v. *Davis* (upholding the Social Security Act), May 24

   Justice Willis Van Devanter retires, June 2

   Justice Hugo L. Black appointed, August 17

1941 Justice Harlan F. Stone appointed Chief Justice

   United States v. *Darby Lumber Co.* (upholding the Fair Labor Standards Act)

1944 *Smith* v. *Allwright* (the White Primary case)

1946 Chief Justice Fred M. Vinson appointed

1947 *Adamson* v. *California* (affirming that the procedural protections of the Bill of Rights are not embodied in the Fourteenth Amendment)

1951 *Dennis* v. *United States* (upholding convictions of Communist party leaders under the Smith Act of 1940)

1952 *Youngstown Co.* v. *Sawyer* (the Steel Seizure case)

1953 Chief Justice Earl Warren appointed

1954 *Brown* v. *Board of Education* (the Public School Desegregation case)

1955 *Brown* v. *Board of Education* (the enforcement decision)

1956   *Pennsylvania* v. *Nelson* (invalidating state sedition laws)

1956   Associate Justice William J. Brennan appointed

1958   *Cooper* v. *Aaron* (Court proclaims itself as "ultimate interpreter" of Constitution while enforcing *Brown* against Little Rock, Arkansas, school board)

1961   *Mapp* v. *Ohio* (applying to state criminal proceedings "exclusionary" rule regarding evidence seized in violation of Fourth Amendment)

1962   *Engel* v. *Vitale* (first school prayer decision)

       Baker v. *Carr* (holding justiciable issue of legislative apportionment)

       Justice Felix Frankfurter retires

1963   *Schempp* v. *Abington Township* (second school prayer decision)

       Gideon v. *Wainwright* (indigents entitled to lawyers in criminal trials)

1964   *New York Times* v. *Sullivan* (constitutionalizing law of libel)

       Reynolds v. *Sims* (one person-one vote)

       Katzenbach v. *McClung* (upholding Civil Rights Act of 1964)

       Malloy v. *Hogan* (incorporation against states of Fifth Amendment right against self-incrimination)

1965   *Griswold* v. *Connecticut* (use of contraceptives constitutionally protected)

1966   *Harper* v. *Virginia Board of Elections* (unconstitutionality of poll taxes in state elections)

       Miranda v. *Arizona* (police must inform criminal defendants of their rights, including right to silence and to aid of lawyer)

1968   *Green* v. *New Kent County* (duty to eliminate racially identifiable schools)

1969   *Brandenburg* v. *Ohio* (speech protected unless an incitement to immediate unlawful conduct)

       Shapiro v. *Thompson* (unconstitutional to require year of residence in order to receive welfare)

       Warren Burger appointed Chief Justice

1970   *Goldberg* v. *Kelly* (due process requires pre-termination hearings for welfare recipients)

       Dandridge v. *Williams* (no constitutional right to subsistence level of welfare)

       Justice Harry Blackmun appointed

1971   *Swann* v. *Charlotte-Mecklenburg Board of Education* (upholding busing as a remedy for school segregation)

Reed v. *Reed* (laws discriminating against women subject to special scrutiny)

New York Times v. *United States* (the Pentagon Papers case)

Justices Hugo L. Black and John Marshall Harlan retire

Justices William Rehnquist and Lewis Powell appointed

1972 *Furman* v. *Georgia* (striking down capital punishment)

Wisconsin v. *Yoder* (exemption of Amish from Wisconsin compulsory education law)

1973 *San Antonio Independent School District* v. *Rodriguez* (14th Amendment does not require equal funding of public school districts)

Roe v. *Wade* (the Abortion case)

Committee for Public Education & Liberty v. *Nyquist* (the Parochial School Funding case)

1974 *Nixon* v. *United States* (the Watergate Tapes case)

Bradley v. *Milliken* (lower courts not permitted to consolidate separate school districts in order to achieve desegregation)

1975 Justice Douglas retires

Justice John Paul Stevens appointed

1976 *Buckley* v. Valeo (the Election Funding case)

National League of Cities v. *Usery* (striking down minimum wage laws applied to state and local governments)

Gregg v. *Georgia* (death penalty not unconstitutional per se)

Mathews v. *Eldridge* (limiting *Goldberg*)

1977 *Coker* v. *Georgia* (death penalty for rape unconstitutional)

Maher v. *Roe* (no constitutional duty to fund abortions)

1978 *Bakke* v. *Regents of University of California* (the Affirmative Action case)

1980 *Branti* v. *Finkel* (the Political Patronage case)

1981 Justice Potter Stewart retires

Justice Sandra Day O'Connor appointed

1982 *Plyler* v. *Doe* (right of children of illegel aliens to education)

Mississippi University for Women v. *Hogan* (states must offer "substantial" reasons to justify gender distinctions)

1983 *Immigration and Naturalization Service* v. *Chadha* (the Legislative Veto case)

1985 *Garcia* v. *San Antonio Metropolitan Transit Authority* (overruling *National League of Cities*)

1986 *Bowers* v. *Hardwick* (constitutional to criminalize homosexual conduct)

Batson v. *Kentucky* (race-based peremptory dismissals of potential jurors unconstitutional)

Chief Justice William Rehnquist succeeds Warren Burger

Justice Antonin Scalia appointed

1987 Justice Lewis Powell retires

Nomination of Judge Robert Bork rejected by Senate, 58–42, October 23

Justice Anthony Kennedy appointed

1989 *DeShaney* v. *Winnebago County Department of Social Services* (no constitutional right to state protection against harm)

1990 Justice William J. Brennan retires

Justice David Souter appointed

1991 *Rust* v. *Sullivan* (the Abortion Gag Rule case)

Justice Thurgood Marshall retires

Justice Clarence Thomas appointed

1992 *Planned Parenthood of Southeastern Pennsylvania* v. *Casey* (reaffirmation of constitutionally protected status of abortion)

New York v. *United States* (invalidating portion of federal regulation of a state as beyond national power)

1993 Justice Byron White retires

Justice Ruth Bader Ginsburg appointed

Shaw v. *Reno* (invalidation of North Carolina redistricting as "racial gerrymander")

1994 Justice Harry Blackmun retires

Justice Stephen Breyer appointed

1995 *U.S.* v. *Lopez* (striking down, for first time in sixty years, congressional regulation of private behavior based on Commerce clause)

Adarand Constructors v. *Pena* (establishing "strict scrutiny" as test for federal as well as state laws involving racial classifications)

1996 *Romer* v. *Evans* (striking down a Colorado constitutional amendment that would prohibit protecting homosexuals against discrimination)

United States v. *Virginia* (invalidating single-sex admissions policy to Virginia Military Institute)

1997 *City of Boerne* v. *Flores* (invalidation of Religious Freedom Restoration Act)

Printz v. *United States* (invalidation of provision of gun-control legislation insofar as it "commandeered" state officials to help enforce national law)

Clinton v. *Jones* (holding that President is subject to civil suit while in office)

Washington v. *Glucksberg* (upholding Washington State's ban on "assisted suicide")

1999 *Saenz* v. *Roe* (striking down a California welfare law that limited new residents to the amount of assistance they received from the state in which they resided before coming to California)

Alden v. *Maine* (one of several five-to-four decisions upholding state "sovereign immunity" against suit in either federal or state courts)

2000 *Nixon* v. *Shrink Missouri Government PAC* (upholding Missouri regulation of campaign contributions)

Kimel v. *Florida Board of Regents* (five-to-four holding that Congress could not declare age discimination by a state to be denial of Fourteenth Amendment "equal protection" and, consequently, that the state could not be sued in federal court for engaging in age discrimination)

United States v. *Morrison* (a five-to-four decision striking down a key provision of the Violence Against Women Act, which allowed victims alleging such violence to sue their attackers in federal courts)

Bush v. *Gore* (five-to-four decision that effectively ended the election procedures in Florida and effectively determined that George W. Bush would become the next President of the United States)

2001 *University of Alabama* v. *Garrett* (five-to-four decision that Congress did not possess power under the Fourteenth Amendment to outlaw discrimination against the handicapped)

2002 *Zelman* v. *Harris* (five-to-four decision upholding a state school-voucher program that largely benefited students attending religious schools)

2003 *Grutter* v. *Bollinger* (five-to-four decision that upheld the use of racial preferences by the University of Michigan Law School, at least so long as they were part of a "holistic" admissions process)

Lawrence v. *Texas* (six-to-three decision striking down Texas's anti-sodomy law)

Nevada Department of Human Resources v. *Hibbs* (five-to-four decision upholding Congress's power under the Fourteenth Amendment to pass the Family and Medical Leave Act of 1993)

McConnell v. *FEC* (five-to-four decision upholding congressional regulation of campaign finance)

2004   *Locke* v. *Davey* (seven-to-two decision upholding Washington's refusal to fund, as part of a scholarship program, a student's major in devotional theology)

Vieth v. *Jubelirer* (five-to-four decision refusing to strike down highly partisan gerrymandering in Pennsylvania)

BIBLIOGRAPHICAL ESSAY

"THE BODY OF LITERATURE pertaining to the Supreme Court of the United States and to American constitutional law is enormous." Thus began Robert McCloskey's original bibliographical essay over four decades ago; the statement is, obviously, even more true today, when a scholarly explosion has made the notion of "keeping up" with the relevant literature almost fanciful. What follows, therefore, does no more than sketch the tip of an ever-growing iceberg; many fine books—and almost all relevant articles—are simply omitted.

A. PRIMARY SOURCES

One should certainly make the direct acquaintance of the Supreme Court by reading some of its actual opinions, which appear in three equally authoritative sources: the *United States Reports,* which is the official publication of the government; and the privately published *Supreme Court Reporter* and *Lawyer's Edition.* Differing somewhat in the amount and kind of accompanying material they provide to aid their users, all three print the Court's opinions in full. They are cited in any legal publication by volume, abbreviated name (U.S., S.Ct., or L.Ed.), and page. Thus 325 U.S. 1 means volume 325, page one, of the *United States Reports.* Until 1875, the official reports were identified by the name of the official reporter (e.g., 7 Wallace 299), though this practice was abandoned with the ninety-first volume; thereafter, the official citation practice is the one just illustrated. This is, incidentally, the standard citation form used by legal academics for scholarly journals as well. Thus 70 *Harvard Law Review* 253 is page 253 of volume 70. And, of course, it has become very easy to gain access to one or another of the on-line services that include, among other things, all judicial decisions and most contemporary law review articles. The most copious such services may require visiting a library that subscribes to them, but one can find an immense amount of useful material simply by logging onto http://www.findlaw.com/. Moreover, http://www

.oyez.org/oyez/portlet/directory/ offers students a way to listen to many oral arguments of past and present cases, as well as much other useful information about the Supreme Court. Del Dickson, in *The Supreme Court in Conference (1940–1985)* (2001), presents edited versions of conference notes taken by various justices during that time period that illuminate the decision-making processes of the justices.

Were this book more about general American constitutional development rather than the specific institution of the United States Supreme Court, there would be significant discussion of constitutional decision-making outside the judiciary. No one should believe that a history of the American Supreme Court is the same thing as a history of American constitutional development more generally; the latter simply cannot be understood without paying ample attention to non-judicial institutions (including mass movements) concerned to generate new understandings of constitutional possibility. James Richardson from 1889–97 published ten volumes of the public papers and messages of the presidents from 1789 to that time, which contain many statements, particularly veto messages, that exemplify presidential constitutional interpretation. Such statements continue to be found in the papers of twentieth-century presidents that have been published since then. Similarly, H. Jefferson Powell, ed., *The Constitution and the Attorneys General* (1999), is a valuable collection of opinions of the Attorneys General of the United States and the Office of Legal Counsel within the Department of Justice on many vital issues.

Anyone interested—whether because of historical curiosity or a commitment to "original intent" as a mode of constitutional interpretation—in the specific background of the 1787 Constitution must consult Max Farrand, *The Records of the Federal Convention of 1787* (4 vols., 1911; 1937). John Kaminski et al., eds., *Documentary History of the Ratification of the Constitution and the Bill of Rights, 1787–1791* (18 vols., 1976–95), is rapidly supplanting the much older (and far less reliable) Jonathan Elliott, *The Debates in the Several State Conventions on the Adoption of the Federal Constitution* (5 vols., 1836). Farrand is available in a Yale University Press paperback edition, which replaces the original volume 4 with a 1987 supplemental volume edited by James Hutson and Leonard Rapport. Bernard Bailyn has edited a marvelous two-volume collection, *The Debate on the Constitution* (1993), that organizes the ratification debate chronologically and includes some illuminating materials from the state debates. Many basic documents can be found on-line at the Avalon Project of the Yale Law School, which has brought together "The American Constitution: A Documentary Record" at http://www.yale.edu/lawweb/avalon/constpap.htm, though the most complete online source is probably that of the Library of Congress, which has Elliot's Debates, Farrand's Records, Letters of Delegates to Continental Congress, and Journals of the Continental Congress available at http://memory.loc.gov/ammem/hlawquery.html.

At least as important as these materials are commentaries on the Constitution produced during the ratification struggle. Certainly the primary example is

The Federalist (or *Federalist Papers*), which were written under the pen name "Publius" by James Madison, Alexander Hamilton, and John Jay primarily in order to encourage ratification by the sharply divided New York convention. The eighty-five essays that comprise them have been too often treated as a disinterested privileged guide to the likely meanings assigned the Constitution at the time of ratification. This is a dubious proposition, even if we ignore the political motivations of their authors, because many of the most important essays were published well after most of the other states had in fact voted to ratify the Constitution. (New York was the eleventh state to ratify.) The standard scholarly edition is that edited by Jacob Cooke (1961). Probably the most widely used edition, indeed the one most often cited by the Supreme Court, is the paperback edited by Clinton Rossiter (1961). They can be found online at http://www.law.emory.edu/FEDERAL/. The papers have spawned an extensive commentary literature of their own. See, for example, Garry Wills, *Explaining America: The Federalist* (1981); David F. Epstein, *The Political Theory of the Federalist* (1984); and Morton White, *Philosophy, The Federalist, and the Constitution* (1987). The Library of America has published valuable collections of the writings of two of the three contributors to *The Federalist, Madison: Writings* (Jack Rakove ed., 1999), and *Hamilton: Writings* (Joanne Freeman ed., 2001).

For the alternative vision of the opponents of the Constitution, the best source is Herbert J. Storing's seven-volume edition of *The Complete Anti-Federalist* (1981). More modest in its coverage, but also excellent, is a reader by Cecilia Kenyon, ed., *The Anti-Federalists* (1966), which includes, among other things, good excerpts from the Virginia, New York, and North Carolina ratifying conventions. Also vital for serious students (and their teachers) is a five-volume *The Founders' Constitution,* edited by Philip B. Kurland and Ralph Lerner (1987). Going through the 1787 Constitution and the first twelve Amendments clause by clause, Kurland and Lerner reprint some of the key historical materials that help to explain why given issues were bones of contention and why given solutions were seized upon by the framers. A special boon is that all five volumes can be found on the Internet at http://press-pubs.uchicago.edu/founders. A short compilation of materials representing the two sides can be found in John P. Kaminski and Richard Leffler, eds., *Federalists and Antifederalists: The Debate over the Ratification of the Constitution* (1998).

Similar in aspiration (and help to anyone interested in constitutional history) are two collections edited by Neil H. Cogan: *The Complete Bill of Rights: The Drafts, Debates, Sources, and Origins* (1997) and *Context of the Constitution* (1999). Somewhat different in orientation is H. Jefferson Powell, *Languages of Power: A Source Book of Early American Constitutional History* (1991), which imaginatively presents a plethora of materials concerning the controversies that wracked the young Republic.

Inevitably, the richest body of easily available primary materials concerns the founding period of 1787–91 (the latter date being the ratification of the Bill of Rights). But, obviously, what happened in the 1860's was of major import. Harold

Hyman, ed., *The Radical Republicans and Reconstruction, 1861–1870* (1967), includes many materials that certainly touch on basic constitutional questions — including, of course, the addition of the so-called "Reconstruction Amendments" that are by far the most important textual additions to the Constitution since the founding period. Daniel A. Farber and Suzanna Sherry, eds., *A History of the American Constitution* (1990), contains a helpful hundred-page section of primary sources on these Amendments. It is a sign, though, of our amnesia about the "second" founding that accompanied the Civil War that there are no scholarly compendia at all comparable to the rich plethora of materials available about the first founding in 1787.

A final primary source of interest to anyone concentrating on the history of the Supreme Court is *Landmark Briefs and Arguments of the Supreme Court of the United States,* initially compiled by Philip Kurland and Gerhard Casper in 1975 and now consisting of approximately two hundred volumes of briefs in most of the important cases heard and decided by the Supreme Court. Briefs of contemporary cases can be found at the Web site of the United States Supreme Court itself, http://www.supremecourtus.gov/.

Several "commentaries" on the Constitution, in addition to *The Federalist,* have become primary sources for the historian of American constitutionalism insofar as they reflect the concerns and thought of a particular time, at least within a segment of the elite bar. James Kent's *Commentaries on American Law* (4 vols., 1830) and Joseph Story's *Commentaries on the Constitution of the United States* (3 vols., 1833; reprinted in a one-volume edition with an introduction by Ronald D. Rotunda and John E. Nowak, 1987) affected constitutional development for many years. (Story, of course, was a leading member of the Court for three decades.) Thomas M. Cooley's *Treatise on the Constitutional Limitations Which Rest upon the Legislative Power of the States of the American Union* (1868) was enormously influential in shaping basic doctrine prior to the great changes associated with the New Deal and its aftermath. There is no modern analogue. Most important among contemporary treatise writers is Harvard law professor Laurence Tribe, whose *American Constitutional Law* (3d ed., vol. 1, 2000) rivals Story in its scope and ambition, even if not in its influence. Less influential, but certainly helpful for students, are John E. Nowak and Ronald D. Rotunda, *Constitutional Law* (6th ed., 2000) and Erwin Chemerinsky, *Constitutional Law: Principles and Policies* (1997). Students should be aware that all of these modern treatises are basically analyses of the decided case law of the Supreme Court, which therefore scants the enormous importance of constitutional developments outside the judiciary.

B. GENERAL REFERENCE WORKS

One of the most welcome developments since 1960 is the publication of many first-rate reference works on the Court. Extremely helpful to any student is Leonard Levy, Kenneth L. Karst, and Dennis J. Mahoney, eds., *Encyclopedia of the*

American Constitution (4 vols., 1986), supplemented by two additional volumes published in 1992 and 2000. The collected volumes include essays by a host of distinguished scholars on almost every relevant topic. A selection of the entries, focusing on historical developments, has been published as *American Constitutional History* (1989). Only slightly less ambitious and helpful is Kermit Hall, ed., *The Oxford Companion to the Supreme Court of the United States* (1992, 2d ed. 2002), consisting of both short entries and sometimes quite extensive essays on practically all aspects of the Court and its work. Paul Finkelman, ed., *Religion and American Law: An Encyclopedia* (2000), is a good source of information on its topic.

Anyone especially interested members of the Supreme Court will certainly want to consult Leon Friedman, ed., *The Justices of the United States Supreme Court: Their Lives and Major Opinions* (5 vols., 1980). More recently, the Supreme Court Historical Society has published *The Supreme Court Justices: Illustrated Biographies, 1789–1993* (Clare Cushman ed., 1993), which offers extremely readable and succinct eight- to twelve-page biographies of every justice save Ruth Ginsburg and Stephen Breyer. Finally, one should mention Kermit L. Hall's five-volume compilation, *A Comprehensive Bibliography of American Constitutional Law and Legal History, 1890–1979* (1984), described by a leading historian as "an incredibly complete collection of virtually everything written on the subject in the last century." An excellent one volume source of information is Lee Epstein et al., *The Supreme Court Compendium: Data, Decisions, and Developments* (3d ed. 2002).

C. GENERAL HISTORICAL OVERVIEWS

Two standard textbooks tell the story of American constitutional development through time: Alfred H. Kelly, Winfred A. Harbison, and Herman Belz, *The American Constitution* (7th ed., 1991) and Melvin I. Urofksy and Paul Finkelman, *A March of Liberty: A Constitutional History of the United States* (2 vols. 2002). A good brief overview is William M. Wiecek, *Liberty under Law: The Supreme Court in American Life* (1988). Bernard Schwartz has also published *A History of the Supreme Court* (1993), more thorough, but less readable, than Wiecek.

One older scholar, Edward S. Corwin, should be singled out for special mention. McCloskey described him in 1960 as "without any serious competitor the foremost living scholar in the field." Corwin wrote about *everything* relevant to the Constitution, from basic history to analyses of leading cases. Corwin is long-since dead, but many of his works remain worth reading, sometimes as de facto primary sources for the ethos of his scholarly generation. Many of his articles can be found in a three-volume collection edited by Richard Loss: *Corwin on the Constitution: Vol. 1: The Foundations of American Constitutional and Political Thought, the Powers of the Congress, and the President's Power of Removal* (1981); *Vol. 2: The Judiciary* (1987); and *Vol. 3: On Liberty against Government* (1988). Mention should also be made of *The President: Office and Powers, 1787–1984*, originally published in 1948, but updated by Randall Bland et al. in 1984.

When Oliver Wendell Holmes died in 1935, he left his money to the United States, and a decision was made to use these funds to commission a "definitive history" of the Supreme Court by various scholars. The standard history at Holmes's death was Charles Warren, *The Supreme Court in United States History* (2 vols., 1925), described by McCloskey as "not a full history of American constitutional law but rather of the Court as an institution; it carries the reader only to 1918; and some may feel that it is marred by excessive pro-judicialism." The Holmes Devise Committee made the questionable decision to divide the project by reference to the tenure of Chief Justices and to assign volumes accordingly. Seven volumes in the Holmes Devise History of the Supreme Court have been published as of 2004: Julius Goebel Jr., *Antecedents and Beginnings to 1801* (1971); George L. Haskins and Herbert A. Johnson, *Foundations of Power: John Marshall, 1801–15* (1981); G. Edward White, *The Marshall Court and Cultural Change, 1815–35* (1988); Carl Brent Swisher, *The Taney Period, 1836–64* (1974); Charles Fairman, *Reconstruction and Reunion, 1864–88, Part One* (1971), *Reconstruction and Reunion, 1864–88, Part Two* (1988), and *Supplement, Five Justices and the Electoral Commission of 1877* (1988); Owen Fiss, *Troubled Beginnings of the Modern State, 1888–1910* (1993); and Alexander M. Bickel and Benno C. Schmidt Jr., *The Judiciary and Responsible Government, 1910–21* (1984). Though the quest for "definitiveness" was undoubtedly futile, they all provide rich detail concerning many of the great (and not-so-great) cases that came before the Court. New volumes are being written by Robert Post on the Taft Court; Richard Friedman, the Hughes Court; William Wiecek, the Stone and Vinson Courts; and Morton J. Horwitz, the Warren Court.

Herbert A. Johnson is the general editor of a useful series on "Chief Justiceships of the United States Supreme Court," less ambitious, but in some ways possibly more useful to the student than the Holmes Devise volumes, which may be written more for the scholar. (The Holmes Devise volumes are also extremely, even unconscionably, expensive and are unaccountably not available in affordable paperback versions.) Published so far are William R. Casto, *The Supreme Court in the Early Republic* (1995); Herbert A. Johnson, *The Chief Justiceship of John Marshall, 1801–1835* (1997); James W. Ely, *The Chief Justiceship of Melville W. Fuller, 1888–1910* (1995); Walter Pratt Jr., *The Supreme Court Under Edward Douglass White, 1910–1921* (1999); Melvin I. Urofsky, *Division and Discord: The Supreme Court under Stone and Vinson, 1941–1953* (1997); and Earl M. Maltz, *The Chief Justiceship of Warren E. Burger, 1969–1986* (2000).

Very much worth a look are two books by David Currie: *The Constitution in the Supreme Court: The First Hundred Years* (1985) and *The Constitution in the Supreme Court: 1886–1986* (1990), though some readers may find this distinguished law professor somewhat ahistorical when he turns to assessing the Court's particular opinions. A classic older general history is Andrew C. McLaughlin, *A Constitutional History of the United States* (1935), which has the added strength of looking beyond the Court for constitutional development.

A sui generis work is Michael Kammen, *A Machine That Would Go of Itself: The Constitution in American Culture* (1986). As one reviewer put it, Kammen "illuminates the amazingly diverse ways in which Americans have interpreted, celebrated, condemned, and ignored their Constitution." Kammen obviously wrote before the bicentennial in 1987. An interesting retrospective look at the bicentennial (and more) is Daniel L. Levin, *Representing Popular Sovereignty: The Constitution in American Political Culture* (1999). John Semonche has offered *Keeping the Faith: A Cultural History of the U.S. Supreme Court* (1998).

An interesting collection of scholarly articles and excerpts from scholarly monographs that goes far beyond case law can be found in Lawrence M. Friedman and Harry N. Scheiber, eds., *American Law and the Constitutional Order: Historical Perspectives* (2d ed., 1988). Similarly, Morton Horwitz's important works, *The Transformation of American Law, 1780–1860* (1977) and *The Transformation of American Law, 1870–1960: The Crisis of Legal Orthodoxy* (1992), though primarily about nonconstitutional law, include illuminating discussions of constitutional development as well. Mention should also be made of the extraordinary book by Bruce Ackerman, *We the People: Transformations* (1998), which offers extremely challenging narratives—as part of his larger theory of constitutional change announced earlier in *We the People: Foundations* (1991)—of the Founding, Reconstruction, and New Deal periods of constitutional innovation. Ackerman's project is subjected to searching review and criticism in a symposium in the May 1999 *Yale Law Journal.*

Robert Burt's *Constitution in Conflict* (1992) also presents a comprehensive overview of American constitutional history that attacks traditional notions of judicial supremacy and instead emphasizes the vital roles played by other branches of government in giving meaning to the Constitution. A more theoretically rich elaboration of the same theme is Stephen M. Griffin, *American Constitutionalism: From Theory to Politics* (1996). The path-breaking book, still very much worth reading, is Donald G. Morgan, *Congress and the Constitution: a Study of Responsibility* (1966). A similarly important recent work, covering important congressional and executive constitutional decisions over the entire period of American history, is Keith Whittington, *Constitutional Construction: Divided Powers and Constitutional Meaning* (1999). There is no fully comprehensive presentation of the constitutional law that is made by Presidents, Congress, administrative agencies, and ordinary citizens in addition to that which is made by the Court, perhaps because a truly "comprehensive presentation" would take many volumes and be the work of a lifetime. Very much worth consulting, though, are two books by Louis Fisher, *Constitutional Dialogues: Interpretation as Political Process* (1988) and *Constitutional Conflicts between Congress and the President* (4th ed., 1997). See also H. Jefferson Powell, *A Community Built on Words: The Constitution in History and Politics* (2002).

There has been special interest in the early process of norm creation outside the judiciary. David P. Currie has published two volumes, *The Constitution in*

Congress: The Federalist Period, 1789–1801 (1997) and *The Constitution in Congress: The Jeffersonians, 1801–1829* (2001). Two more volumes, taking the story up to the Civil War, are promised for 2004. No one interested in the "Constitution outside the courts" should ignore Currie's extraordinary work. Also worth consulting in this regard are Joseph M. Lynch, *Negotiating the Constitution: The Earliest Debates over Original Intent* (1999), and Gerhard Casper, *Separating Power: Essays on the Founding Period* (1997).

There are, of course, many noteworthy studies of particular periods. On the period leading up to the framing and ratification of the Constitution, see Gordon Wood, *The Creation of the American Republic* (1969), a truly magisterial book that places the debates about the Constitution within a dense ideological context. Inevitably, it has provoked its own controversies, but it remains the essential starting point for any serious inquiry. Also superb is Forrest McDonald, *Novus Ordo Seclorum: The Intellectual Origins of the Constitution* (1986). Leonard W. Levy and Dennis J. Mahoney, *The Framing and Ratification of the Constitution* (1987), will quickly bring the student up to date on many of the major current controversies on this topic, as will two collections put together by Peter Onuf, *New American Nation, 1775–1820: Vol. 5, The Federal Constitution* (1991) and *Vol. 6, Ratifying, Amending, and Interpreting the Constitution* (1991). By far the best of more recent books, as essential as Wood's, is Jack N. Rakove, *Original Meanings: Politics and Ideas in the Making of the Constitution* (1996). Also useful are Herman Belz et al., *To Form a More Perfect Union: The Critical Ideas of the Constitution* (1992) and Richard Beeman et al., *Beyond Confederation: Origins of the Constitution and American National Identity* (1987). David C. Hendrickson, *Peace Pact: The Lost World of the American Founding* (2003) manages to say something fresh and interesting about the fear of the framers that the alternative to bringing the thirteen colonies into a general "peace pact" would be their dissolution into (probably three) separate countries that would, inevitably, wage war with one another. Finally, a Swedish scholar, Max M. Edling, argues in *A Revolution in Favor of Government: Origins of the U.S. Constitution and the Making of the American State* (2003) that the framers were, far more than has generally been recognized, attempting to create a strong national government invested with all of the power held by what Edling terms the "fiscal-military states" of eighteenth-century Europe. Not the least important aspect of Edling's book is its comparative emphasis. The same can be said of Philip Bobbitt, *The Shield of Achilles* (2002), a remarkable book that looks at European and American constitutional development over a five-century period and emphasizes the interplay between international and domestic developments.

For the politics of the Constitutional Convention see Calvin C. Jillson, *Constitutional Making: Conflict and Consensus in the Federal Convention of 1787* (1988). Michael Allen Gillespie and Michael Lienesch have edited *Ratifying the Constitution* (1989), a very helpful set of essays examining the state-by-state ratification process. Many of these books and essays refer, in greater or lesser depth, to the classic controversy provoked by Charles A. Beard, *An Economic Interpretation of the Constitution* (1913), which argued that the Constitution's framers were actively seeking to serve their own economic interests in designing the Constitution as they did. Beard's unadorned thesis had been successfully challenged by Robert E. Brown, *Charles Beard and the Constitution* (1954), and by Forrest McDonald, *We the People: The Economic Origins of the Constitution* (1958); but, restated in far more nuanced form, it continues to play a role in scholarly debate.

Obviously the most important textual additions to the original Constitution occurred immediately after ratification, with the passage of what have come to be known as the Bill of Rights. A classic book on this topic is Robert A. Rutland, *The Birth of the Bill of Rights, 1776–1791* (1955). A spectacular recent treatment is Akhil Reed Amar, *The Bill of Rights: Creation and Reconstruction* (1998). As the title suggests, he writes not only of the 1789–91 conceptions of rights but also, and just as significantly, of their reconceptualizations during the second great period of constitutional creativity in the aftermath of the Civil War.

The very earliest work of the Supreme Court is the subject of Maeva Marcus and James. R. Perry, eds., *The Documentary History of the Supreme Court of the United States, 1789–1800* (6 vols., 1985). On the initial fifty years of the Supreme Court, see Charles G. Haines, *The Role of the Supreme Court in American Government and Politics, 1789–1835* (1944). A recent entrant to this list is the brilliant book by Larry Kramer, *The People Themselves: Popular Constitutionalism and Judicial Review* (2004), which argues that the original conception of judicial review was extremely limited and that the most important duties with regard to defending constitutional values were thought to be the responsibilities of the general public.

Charles G. Haines, with Foster H. Sherwood, also wrote *The Role of the Supreme Court in American Government and Politics, 1835–1864* (1957). Another study of the same period is Kent Newmeyer, *The Supreme Court under Marshall and Taney* (1968). Harold Hyman and William Wiecek, *Equal Justice under Law: Constitutional Development 1835–1875* (1982), offers a more cogent periodization than those studies that conclude in the middle of the Civil War, when Taney happened to die. Hyman also wrote the excellent *A More Perfect Union: The Impact of the Civil War and Reconstruction on the Constitution* (1973). Other perspectives are provided by Herman Belz, *Emancipation and Equal Rights: Politics and Constitutionalism in the Civil War Era* (1978) and Philip S. Paludan, *A Covenant with Death: The Constitution, Law, and Equality in the Civil War Era* (1975).

An enduring controversy concerns Abraham Lincoln's devotion to the Constitution during the Civil War. James G. Randall, *Constitutional Problems Under Lincoln* (1951), is the standard account, though one will also want to read Mark E. Neely's prizewinning work, *The Fate of Liberty: Abraham Lincoln and Civil Liberties* (1991). Dan Farber's *Lincoln's Constitution* (2003) presents an excellent recent overview of the topic. Harry Jaffa, whose *Crisis of the House Divided* (1959) is a brilliant examination of the Lincoln-Douglas debates, extended his inquiry in *A New Birth of Freedom: Abraham Lincoln and the Coming of the Civil War* (2000), which is indispensable for anyone interested in wrestling with the full ramifications of Lincoln's thought. One should also be aware of Garry Wills, *Lincoln at Gettysburg: The Words That Remade America* (1992).

One of the most contentious controversies among American historians concerns the "original meaning" of the Fourteenth Amendment, which is certainly the most important textual addition to the Constitution since the Bill of Rights. One polar view is well argued in Raoul Berger, *Government by Judiciary* (1977), which presents an extremely restricted view of the Amendment that limits it basically to guaranteeing only "civil rights" (as distinguished from "political" or "social" rights) to the newly freed African-Americans. The other polar view is well presented in Michael Kent Curtis, *No State Shall Abridge: The Fourteenth Amendment and the Bill of Rights* (1986), which argues, in contrast (and, I believe, with more plausibility), in behalf of a very expansive reading, including the view that the "privileges or immunities" clause of the Amendment was intended to apply the Bill of Rights to the states. Closer to Berger is Earl M. Maltz, *Civil Rights, the Constitution, and Congress, 1863–1869* (1990). Also valuable are William E. Nelson, *The Fourteenth Amendment: From Political Principles to Judicial Doctrine* (1988), which focuses on the libertarian intellectual background of the Amendment; and David A. J. Richards, *Conscience and the Constitution: History, Theory, and Law of the Reconstruction Amendments* (1993), which is more self-consciously philosophical than the other books mentioned. One should also mention Andrew Kull, *The Colorblind Constitution* (1992), an excellent book tracing the idea of that concept in the drafting of the Fourteenth Amendment and thereafter in its interpretation. He demonstrates conclusively that whatever else might be said about the framers, they did not intend to require colorblindness of the American political order, a conclusion that he personally regrets. Finally, Pamela Brandwein, in *Reconstructing Reconstruction: The Supreme Court and the Production of Historical Truth* (1999), offers a fascinating account of the different perspectives on the meaning of slavery, the Civil War, and Reconstruction and how the Supreme Court basically adopted the perspective of Northern Democrats and moderate Republicans as against that held by more "radical" Republicans.

Not the least important aspect of the Fourteenth Amendment is the quite extraordinary process by which it was added to the Constitution. Ackerman, in *We the People: Transformations,* makes this history the linchpin of his argument that many of our most significant constitutional transformations cannot fit within the procrustean limitations of Article V, which, as a formal matter, makes amendment extremely difficult. There has been no genuinely important textual amendment of the Constitution since at least 1951, when the Twenty-second Amendment was added limiting Presidents to two terms. One cannot infer from this lack of amendment that the Constitution does not contain significant "stupidities" that might in fact be changed were amendment not, as a practical matter, next to impossible. See William Eskridge and Sanford Levinson, eds., *Constitutional Stupidities, Con-*

stitutional Tragedies (1998) for a collection of essays on this point. With regard to "non-Article V amendment," see the debate in Sanford Levinson, ed., *Responding to Imperfection: The Theory and Practice of Constitutional Amendment* (1995). Far more traditional (and, I believe, misleading) views of the actualities of amendatory change can be found in David Kyvig, *Explicit and Authentic Acts: Amending the U.S. Constitution, 1776–1995* (1996), and Richard Bernstein, with Jerome Agel, *Amending America: If We Love the Constitution So Much, Why do We Keep Trying to Change It?* (1993). Students will very much profit from John R. Vile's numerous works on constitutional amendment, including his *Encyclopedia of Constitutional Amendments, Proposed Amendments, and Amending Issues, 1789-2002* (2d ed. 2003). Indeed, an interesting perspective is provided by Steven M. Boyd, *Alternative Constitutions for the United States: A Documentary History* (1992), a collection of various proposals, throughout American history, for new constitutions.

The Constitution is brought into the early twentieth century by Loren P. Beth, *Constitutional History, 1877–1917* (1971) and John E. Semonche, *Charting the Future: The Supreme Court Responds to a Changing Society, 1890–1920* (1978). Also illuminating is Arnold M. Paul, *Conservative Crisis and the Rule of Law; Attitudes of Bar and Bench, 1887–1895* (1969). Anyone with an interest in the legal ramifications of the development of the labor movement should read William E. Forbath, *Law and the Shaping of the American Labor Movement* (1989). An interesting set of essays, from a more libertarian perspective, can be found in Ellen Frankel Paul and Howard Dickman, eds., *Liberty, Property, and Government: Constitutional Interpretation Before the New Deal* (1989). The late William F. Swindler wrote an ambitious three-volume study on *Court and Constitution in the Twentieth Century* consisting of *The Old Legality, 1889–1932* (1969); *The New Legality, 1932–1968* (1970); and *The Modern Interpretation* (1974). Much of this same period is covered in Paul L. Murphy, *The Constitution in Crisis Times, 1918–1969* (1972).

McCloskey clearly accepted (and this book reflects) the predominant view during his lifetime (and for years afterward) that 1937 represented a genuine "revolution" within the Court, symbolized by the famous jibe "the switch in time that saved nine." That view has come under significant attack, especially in the work of Barry Cushman, *Rethinking the New Deal Court: The Structure of a Constitutional Revolution* (1998). He finds far more continuity in the opinions of Owen Roberts and Chief Justice Hughes, the two justices said to have "switched," and therefore dates the "revolution" that he agrees did occur several years later with the appointment of new justices by President Roosevelt, who did indeed sweep aside the doctrinal views of the older generation of justices. The older view is ably defended in William Leuchtenburg, *The Supreme Court Reborn: The Constitutional Revolution in the Age of Roosevelt* (1995). Once more, Bruce Ackerman's work is highly relevant (including the *Yale* symposium on his work and articles by Laura Kalman and Leuchtenburg on New Deal constitutionalism). G. Edward

White offers an important overview in *The Constitution and the New Deal* (2000); it is especially good in its discussion of the Court's view of national foreign-affairs powers, where Justice Sutherland played a surprisingly nationalist role.

The *Modern Supreme Court* (1972) is a posthumous book of Robert Mc-Closkey's essays on the Vinson and Warren Courts. Morton Horwitz's short *The Warren Court and the Pursuit of Justice* (1998) presents a very admiring overview of that Court. Bernard Schwartz, *Superchief* (1983), is a not very well-written study of the Warren Court that nonetheless has a lot of valuable material drawn from interviews with, and the private papers of, some of the justices. Lucas A. Powe's magisterial book *The Warren Court and American Politics* (2000) is far more encompassing than anything previously published and, significantly, more skeptical of the enduring significance of much of the Court's handiwork.

Earl M. Maltz, *The Chief Justiceship of Warren E. Burger, 1969–1986* (2000), is now the standard history of that Court, though one should also consult Vincent Blasi, ed., *The Burger Court: The Revolution That Wasn't* (1983) and Bernard Schwartz, *Ascent of Pragmatism: The Burger Court in Action* (1989). All agree that the shift from the liberal Warren Court to the more conservative Burger tribunal brought far less rejection of the earlier precedents than had been anticipated (and, of course, with *Roe* as the major example, in some areas went far beyond its predecessor). The Rehnquist Court has been analyzed by the journalist David G. Savage, *Turning Right: The Making of the Rehnquist Supreme Court* (1992). It is particularly useful in detailing some of the changes in the law of criminal procedure during the 1980's. Ronald Kahn, in *The Supreme Court and Constitutional Theory, 1953–1993* (1994), necessarily includes extensive discussion of the Burger and (early) Rehnquist eras, as well as the earlier period. He takes special issue with those who reduce the changes over his period to simple "judicial politics" or the ideology of the judges involved. Both of these books were written, of course, before the highly controversial decisions of the Rehnquist Court beginning with *Lopez* in 1995 and continuing through the present. A critique from the left is Martin Garbus, *Courting Disaster: The Supreme Court and the Unmaking of American Law* (2002).

One of the most interesting analyses of the current Court is Mark V. Tushnet, *The New Constitutional Order* (2003). Although no admirer of the Rehnquist Court, he criticizes those scholars who have described it as pursuing a "revolutionary" agenda, see, e.g., Jack M. Balkin and Sanford Levinson, "Understanding the Constitutional Revolution," 87 *Virginia Law Review* 1045 (2001). Instead, Tushnet argues that its decisions, however controversial among academic lawyers, were relatively marginal shifts to the right, reflecting to some extent the relative freedom of action enjoyed by the Court during the period of the 1990s when political power was sharply divided between a Republican Congress and a Democratic President. Tushnet's book was written before the Republicans gained control of both the Presidency and Congress in 2002, and it will be interesting to see if this serves to invigorate the majority of the Supreme Court in pursuing an ever-more-conservative agenda (though, by the same token, it would be quite surprising if a Republican Congress passed many, if any, laws that the current Court would deem illegitimate exercises of congressional power).

Finally, mention should be made of William Lasser, *The Limits of Judicial Power: The Supreme Court in American Politics* (1988), which explicitly attempts to counter the thesis enunciated by McCloskey in the original edition of this book. Focusing on *Dred Scott* and its aftermath, the 1937 constitutional revolution, and the Warren and Burger Courts, Lasser argues that the Supreme Court has considerably more latitude for action than was acknowledged by McCloskey, who, Lasser believes, overestimated the likelihood of effective attacks on the Court's exertions of power.

D. JUDICIAL BIOGRAPHIES

One excellent way to learn the history of the Court of a given period is by reading a good biography of a justice. A number of the justices were quite obscure even in their lifetime and have received no scholarly treatment since then; indeed, even some relatively well-known justices have been ignored by biographers, save in such general reference works as those mentioned earlier. One reason, perhaps, is that most justices have probably not led very dramatic lives, and, once they arrive at the Court, their lives become almost entirely cerebral. Still, as one would expect, many important justices have been the subject of major biographies, some of them, indeed, of several biographies, so students will find more than enough to keep themselves busy.

Though it is sometimes difficult to remember, there *was* a Court before John Marshall's arrival in 1801. The first Chief Justice, John Jay, is the subject of *John Jay, the Nation, and the Court* (1967) by the distinguished colonial historian Richard B. Morris. Similarly, James Wilson went from being an especially influential figure at the Philadelphia convention and then the Pennsylvania ratifying convention to the Supreme Court. His life and thought are the subject of an extended introduction to Robert McCloskey, ed., *The Works of James Wilson* (2 vols., 1967). Another of Washington's eight (confirmed) appointees to the Court was Samuel Chase, famous in part because he was unsuccessfully threatened with impeachment by angry Jeffersonians. James Haw and others have written *Stormy Patriot: The Life of Samuel Chase* (1981). Most recent is Scott Douglas Gerber, ed., *Seriatim: The Supreme Court before John Marshall* (1998), a helpful collection of biographical essays.

Still, it is John Marshall who dominates the early history of the Court and the shelves of judicial biographies. United States Senator Albert J. Beveridge, a gifted amateur historian, published a four-volume biography of Marshall in 1916. Although almost idolatrous in its stance toward Marshall, it offers copious insight into the history and political culture of the time. The leading contemporary biographies are Charles F. Hobson, *The Great Chief Justice: John Marshall and the*

Rule of Law (1996) and Jean Edward Smith, *John Marshall, Definer of a Nation* (1996). The most recent comprehensive overview is R. Kent Newmyer, *John Marshall and the Heroic Age of the Supreme Court* (2001). In a more popular vein, James F. Simon analyzes the conflict between Marshall and Thomas Jefferson in *What Kind of Nation: Thomas Jefferson, John Marshall, and the Epic Struggle to Create a United States* (2002). A more self-consciously theoretical analysis of Marshall's jurisprudence can be found in Robert K. Faulkner, *The Jurisprudence of John Marshall* (1968).

An interesting member of the Marshall Court was William Johnson, ably profiled in Donald G. Morgan, *Justice William Johnson: The First Dissenter* (1959). Certainly, though, the most important member of the Court, save for Marshall, was the brilliant legal polymath Joseph Story. The best of several biographies is R. Kent Newmyer, *Supreme Court Justice Joseph Story: Statesman of the Old Republic* (1985).

Marshall's successor, Roger Brooke Taney, was the subject of a 1935 biography by Carl Swisher, supplemented by the somewhat more recent Lewis Walker, *Without Fear or Favor: A Biography of Chief Justice Roger Brooke Taney* (1965). One of Taney's great adversaries is profiled in Francis P. Weisenburer, *The Life of John McLean: A Politician on the Supreme Court* (1937). Peter Daniel, more states-rightist and proslavery than Taney himself, is the subject of John P. Frank, *Justice Daniel Dissenting: Peter V. Daniel* (1964). Sectional tensions on the Court are captured in Alexander A. Lawrence, *James Moore Wayne: Southern Unionist* (1970).

Salmon P. Chase, an extremely important abolitionist leader, Republican activist, and, finally, Lincoln's appointee as Taney's successor (in part to forestall Chase's own ambitions for the Presidency), is the subject of Frederick J. Blue, *Salmon P. Chase, A Life in Politics* (1987) and John Niven, *Salmon P. Chase: A Biography* (1995). An important colleague of Chase, Samuel F. Miller is the subject of a recent book by Michael A. Ross, *Justice of Shattered Dreams: Samuel Freeman Miller and the Supreme Court during the Civil War* (2003); the most recent prior study is Charles Fairman, *Mr. Justice Miller and the Supreme Court, 1862–1890* (1938). Stephen J. Field is another important Justice who has not yet received the modern full-scale biography that he deserves. There are, though, Carl B. Swisher, *Stephen J. Field: Craftsman of the Law* (1930) and, more recently, Paul Kens, *Justice Stephen Field: Shaping Liberty from the Gold Rush to the Gilded Age* (1997), especially illuminating with regard to Field's background in California. New Deal–influenced historians tended to see Field as a simple lackey of capitalist businessmen, a view reflected in McCloskey's first book, *American Conservatism in the Age of Enterprise: A Study of William Graham Sumner, Stephen J. Field, and Andrew Carnegie* (1951). An important corrective to this view, emphasizing his origins in Jacksonian egalitarianism, is Michael Les Benedict, "Laissez-Faire and Liberty: A Re-Evaluation of the Meaning and Origins of Laissez-Faire Constitutionalism," 3 *Law and History Review* 293 (1985).

Mention should be made in this context of Allison Dunham and Philip B. Kurland, eds., *Mr Justice* (1964), primarily because it contains a very useful essay by Charles Fairman on Joseph Bradley, an important colleague (and occasional adversary) of Field's who surely deserves a more substantial treatment.

The first ex-Confederate to be appointed to the Court is the subject of James B. Murphy, *L. Q. C. Lamar: Pragmatic Patriot* (1973). Another former slaveholder who, unlike Lamar, became a great justice, was John Marshall Harlan, who stands out as literally unique among late nineteenth-century justices for his commitment to racial justice. His life is the subject of Loren Beth, *John Marshall Harlan: The Last Whig Justice* (1992); Tinsley E. Yarbrough, *Judicial Enigma: The First Justice Harlan* (1995); and, most recently, Linda Przybyszewski, *The Republic According to John Marshall Harlan* (1999). Harlan and Lamar both served under notably obscure Chief Justices. One can learn all one wants to know about these worthies from C. Peter McGrath, *Morrison R. Waite: The Triumph of Character* (1963); Willard L. King, *Melville Weston Fuller: Chief Justice of the United States* (1950); and Robert B. Highsaw, *Edward Douglass White: Defender of the Conservative Faith* (1981).

Oliver Wendell Holmes is almost certainly the best known of all associate justices, partly as the result of Catherine Drinker Bowen's breathless hagiography, *Yankee from Olympus* (1944), which was turned into a play and then a movie. His remarkable personality, plus his status as, in fact, one of the most important justices in American history, has made him the subject of no fewer than four recent biographies. The best of them is surely G. Edward White's *Justice Oliver Wendell Holmes: Law and the Inner Self* (1993). A superb short treatment of Holmes's life is Gary J. Aichele, *Oliver Wendell Holmes, Jr.: Soldier, Scholar, Judge* (1989). Anyone particularly interested in Holmes's early life will want to consult Mark DeWolfe Howe's first two volumes of a multivolume work that he did not live to complete: *Justice Oliver Wendell Holmes: The Shaping Years* (1957) and *The Proving Years* (1963). Finally, Richard Posner edited a sterling collection of Holmes's writing in *The Essential Holmes: Selections from the Letters, Speeches, Judicial Opinions and Other Writings of Oliver Wendell Holmes, Jr.* (1992). Many readers will wish to graduate to Sheldon M. Novick's three-volume *The Collected Works of Justice Holmes: Complete Public Writings and Selected Judicial Opinions of Oliver Wendell Holmes* (1995). Novick also wrote his own biography of Holmes, *Honorable Justice: The Life of Oliver Wendell Holmes* (1989), which presents the most vivid portrayal of Holmes's extraordinarily significant experiences during the Civil War, when he was thrice wounded, though it is surprisingly weak in analyzing Holmes's thought (on which White is definitely the best work to read). Excellent essays on Holmes's thought can be found in Robert W. Gordon, ed., *The Legacy of Oliver Wendell Holmes, Jr.* (1992).

Holmes's great companion on the Court, Louis D. Brandeis, has also received multiple treatments. Alpheus T. Mason's *Brandeis: A Free Man's Life* (1946) has inevitably been supplanted by works of later scholars having access to more copious sources. The best one-volume study is Philippa Strum, *Louis D. Brandeis: Justice for the People* (1984). More recently, she has written *Brandeis: Beyond Progressivism* (1993) and edited *Brandeis on Democracy* (1995), a collection of Brandeis's writings. A later effort is Stephen W. Baskerville, *Of Laws and Limitations: An Intellectual Portrait of Louis Dembitz Brandeis* (1994). One might also wish to consult Leonard Baker, *Brandeis and Frankfurter: A Dual Biography* (1984) and Allon Gal, *Brandeis of Boston* (1980). Someone often associated with Holmes and Brandeis, Benjamin Nathan Cardozo, in fact made his most important contributions to law as a member of the New York Court of Appeals; and the definitive biography by Andrew Kaufman, *Cardozo* (1998), inevitably (and properly) focuses on that aspect of his career, though he, of course, treats Cardozo's eight years on the Supreme Court. Far less complete, but for most readers much more accessible, is Richard Polenberg, *The World of Benjamin Cardozo: Personal Values and the Judicial Process* (1997).

Holmes and Brandeis spent the bulk of their years together serving under William Howard Taft, whose Chief Justiceship is the subject of Alpheus P. Mason, *William Howard Taft, Chief Justice* (1965). Another of Mason's contributions, and almost certainly his most enduring one, concerns Harlan Fiske Stone, who served with Holmes, Brandeis, Cardozo, and Taft and ultimately became Chief Justice himself. *Harlan Fiske Stone, Pillar of the Law* (1956) drew extensively on Stone's private papers, which were often extremely (and brutally) candid regarding his colleagues. It created a storm when published and continues to repay careful study, especially for persons interested in the internal operations of the Court. Merlo J. Pusey, *Charles Evans Hughes* (1951), is also valuable, in part because it conflicts with some of Mason's judgments about the Court of the 1930's. See also David Danelski and Joseph S. Tulchin, eds., *The Autobiographical Notes of Charles Evans Hughes* (1973). Joel E. Paschal, *Mr. Justice Sutherland* (1951), is a good starting point for understanding the conservative jurisprudence against which Holmes, Brandeis, and Stone (and, at times, Hughes) so forcefully argued. Hadley Arkes, in *The Return of George Sutherland: Restoring a Jurisprudence of Natural Rights* (1994), offers a more theoretically oriented treatment of a very interesting figure. None of the other "four horsemen," Pierce Butler, Willis Van Devanter, and the egregious James McReynolds (an anti-Semite with sufficient principle to refuse to sign the traditional letter conveying regrets upon the retirement of Justice Brandeis), has proved enticing to a biographer. Insight into how truly awful McReynolds was is provided in a remarkable memoir, written by his law clerk during the vital 1936-37 term of court and published posthumously, *The Forgotten Memoir of John Knox: A Year in the Life of a Supreme Court Clerk in FDR's Washington* (2002).

The "Roosevelt Court," many of whose members lasted into the 1960's (and one, William O. Douglas, into the 70's), contained some of the most interesting and vivid personalities in our history. J. Woodford Howard's *Mr. Justice Murphy* (1968) is an invaluable study of this Court. Not only a first-rate study of an interesting life (though a truncated career on the Court), it is also an unusually fine analysis of the inner workings of the Court during an especially contentious period in which it was seeking its way after the tumult of the New Deal and the great retreat of 1937 coupled with the extraordinary issues generated by participation in World War II. Murphy is the subject of a comprehensive three-volume biography by Sidney Fine, the third volume of which, *Frank Murphy: The Washington Years* (1984), includes his service on the Court. Murphy, though, was certainly not one of the "stars" of the Court; he was left behind in the struggle for leadership waged by such titans as Douglas, Felix Frankfurter, Hugo Black, and Robert Jackson (not to mention the nominal Chief Justice, Harlan Fiske Stone). This struggle is depicted in a political science classic, C. Herman Pritchett, *The Roosevelt Court: A Study in Judicial Politics and Values, 1937–1947* (1948).

All of the men mentioned above amply pass the test suggested in the last chapter of this book: Would they merit biographies had they never served on the Court? Thus Michael E. Parrish, *Felix Frankfurter and His Times* (1982), in fact concludes with Frankfurter's appointment to the Court. For this phase of Frankfurter's remarkable career, the student can consult Melvin I. Urofsky, *Felix Frankfurter: Judicial Restraint and Individual Liberties* (1991), or Harry N. Hirsch, *The Enigma of Felix Frankfurter* (1981). Also important is the long biographical essay that Joseph P. Lash wrote to introduce *From the Diaries of Felix Frankfurter* (1975). The diary entries, incidentally, vividly convey Frankfurter's intensity — such as what can only be described as his hatred of some of his colleagues on the Court, including Black (with whom he later became quite friendly) and Douglas (whom he despised to his dying day, fully reciprocated by Douglas). They are the subject of Howard Ball and Phillip J. Cooper, *Of Power and Right: Hugo Black, William O. Douglas, and America's Constitutional Revolution* (1992). Douglas wrote two volumes of autobiography, *Go East Young Man: The Early Years* (1974) and the posthumously published *The Court Years: 1939–1975* (1980), though Ball and Cooper laconically note that "[l]ike most autobiographies, Douglas's must be read with considerable care, particularly *The Court Years,* which he plainly wrote for posterity and not always from fact. His protestations about his generally good relationship with Felix Frankfurter provides an example." James F. Simon has published a helpful biography, *Independent Journey: The Life of William O. Douglas* (1980), though Bruce Allen Murphy, *Wild Bill: The Legend and Life of William O. Douglas* (2003) is now clearly the standard biography (and proves, beyond doubt, how misleading Douglas could be as a source of information about himself). Black has recently been the subject of two good biographies, Roger Newman, *Hugo Black: A Biography* (1994) and Howard Ball, *Hugo L. Black: Cold Steel Warrior* (1996). Tony Freyer has written *On Hugo L. Black and the Dilemma of American Liberalism* (1990).

There is, alas, no equivalent biography for the last of the Roosevelt Court titans, Robert H. Jackson. Eugene C. Gerhart's *America's Advocate: Robert H. Jackson* (1958) is, at best, serviceable. Jackson, one of the most interesting minds (and eloquent writers) ever to serve on the Court, deserves far better. John Q. Barrett is writing an eagerly awaited biography, and fruits of his research can be found in *That Man: An Insider's Portrait of Franklin D. Roosevelt* (2003), a memoir discovered by Barnett in which Jackson wrote about his perceptions of the Roosevelt administration. The "Truman Court" was headed by the hapless Fred Vinson, who remains unchronicled save in general books about the Court of that era. A fellow Truman appointee is the subject of Linda C. Gugin, *Sherman Minton: New Deal Senator, Cold War Justice* (1997). Moreover, because another Truman justice, Harold Burton, left unusually complete notes of the Friday decision-making conferences of the Court, he is the subject of Mary Frances Berry, *Stability, Security, and Continuity: Mr. Justice Burton and Decision-making in the Supreme Court, 1945–1958* (1978). The last of the Truman appointees, Tom C. Clark of Texas, left a wonderful collection of papers to the University of Texas Law School that has provided the grist for several Ph.D. dissertations; there are, however, no published biographies.

Although one refers to the "Roosevelt" and "Truman" Courts, almost no one refers to the Supreme Court of the Eisenhower Administration as the "Eisenhower Court." Instead, of course, it is known by the name of its Chief Justice appointed by Ike, Earl Warren. Warren's life is examined by G. Edward White, *Earl Warren: A Public Life* (1982), and more copiously by Ed Cray, *Chief Justice: A Biography of Earl Warren* (1997). One might also be interested in examining Warren's own view of his life, *The Memoirs of Earl Warren* (1977). The Warren Court was full of strong intellects and personalities. The great conservative counterweight to Black, Douglas, and Warren, following Frankfurter's retirement in 1962, was John Marshall Harlan, the subject of Tinsley E. Yarbrough, *John Marshall Harlan: Great Dissenter of the Warren Court* (1992). Two potentially important members of the Court had unusually truncated careers. Arthur J. Goldberg is the subject of David Stebenne's aptly named *Arthur J. Goldberg: New Deal Liberal* (1996). Laura Kalman, *Abe Fortas* (1990), is an unusually fine biography—though one is curious to know how she might have rewritten it after clear evidence emerged in the late 1990's that Fortas had committed perjury in his Senate testimony, during hearings on his nomination by Lyndon Johnson to succeed Warren as Chief Justice, in denying the extent of his participation in the Johnson Administration after his appointment to the Court. Bruce Allen Murphy had already written a more critical account of Fortas, whose career was cut short by scandal, in *Fortas: The Rise and Ruin of a Supreme Court Justice* (1988).

Three colleagues of Warren's served into the 1990's. One, William J. Brennan, is arguably the most important single justice in this half century. He awaits even his first scholarly biography, though journalist Kim Isaac Eisler published *A Justice for All: William J. Brennan Jr. and the Decisions That Transformed America* (1993). An unusually fine study of his jurisprudence can be found in Frank Michelman, *Brennan and Democracy* (1999); Michelman is not only an especially distinguished law professor at Harvard but also a former clerk and close friend of Brennan's. It is certainly not the first thing one should read, since it requires a sophisticated background in the subject, but it is certainly one of the deepest and most illuminating.

Brennan's close colleague and friend Thurgood Marshall, probably the most important constitutional lawyer of the twentieth century because of his pre-Court career with the NAACP Legal Defense Fund, has already been the subject of a fine two-volume biography by Mark V. Tushnet, *Making Civil Rights Law: Thurgood Marshall and the Supreme Court, 1936–1961* (1994) and *Making Constitutional Law: Thurgood Marshall and the Supreme Court, 1961–1991* (1997). (The latter contains a lot of fascinating material on the inner workings of the Burger Court.) Juan Williams, *Thurgood Marshall: American Revolutionary* (1998), is marred by overstatement, beginning with the preposterous title—if there is anything Marshall was not, it was a "revolutionary"—but it probably is the best available book in terms of offering insight into the persona of the very complex and interesting person who was Thurgood Marshall. Tushnet has also edited *Thurgood Marshall: His Speeches, Writings, Arguments, Opinions, and Reminiscences* (2001). Finally, Byron White, whose tenure on the Court was more notable for its longevity than for its impact on the law, has received full-scale coverage in Dennis Hutchinson, *The Man Who Once Was Whizzer White: A Portrait of Justice Byron R. White* (1998).

Not surprisingly, most members of the post-Warren era have yet to have books written about them, though there are exceptions. Lewis H. Powell is the subject of an excellent biography written by a former clerk, John Jeffries: *Justice Lewis F. Powell, Jr.* (1994). One still-active justice who is already the subject of two books, perhaps because of her status as the first woman on the Court, is Sandra Day O'Connor, treated in Robert W. Van Sickel, *Not a Particularly Different Voice: The Jurisprudence of Sandra Day O'Connor* (1998) and Nancy Maveety, *Justice Sandra Day O'Connor: Strategist on the Supreme Court* (1996). Maveety emphasizes her status as the "swing" vote in a Court divided between two quite strong blocs, a position that has made her an unusually influential Justice during almost the entirety of her career on the Court. Another active justice is the subject of Richard A. Brisbin, *Justice Antonin Scalia and the Conservative Revival* (1997). Sue Davis has published *Justice Rehnquist and the Constitution* (1989). Finally, one might consult Scott Douglas Gerber, *First Principles: The Jurisprudence of Clarence Thomas* (1999). Of these books, only Jeffries's can truly be described as a biography, however.

E. JUDICIAL WRITING AND THE JUDICIAL ROLE

One might well be interested in how judges, when stepping back from the specific task of writing opinions, describe their role as constitutional interpreters. A fine collection is Mark W. Cannon and David M. O'Brien, eds., *Views from the Bench: The Judiciary and Constitutional Politics* (1985). Also still helpful is Alan P. Westin, ed., *The Supreme Court: Views from Inside* (1961).

Probably the classic book authored by a judge remains Benjamin N. Cardozo, *The Nature of the Judicial Process* (1921), written when he was on the New York Court of Appeals. In it he presents a straightforward defense of pragmatic decision-making. Cardozo's argument has been picked up and elaborated most recently by the extraordinarily interesting and provocative Richard Posner, a distinguished University of Chicago law professor and now the chief Judge of the Seventh Circuit Court of Appeals, in *The Problems of Jurisprudence* (1990) and the remarkably titled *Overcoming Law* (1995).

Justice Brennan delivered an important talk, "The Constitution of the United States: Contemporary Ratification," reprinted in Sanford Levinson and Steven Mailloux, eds., *Interpreting Law and Literature: A Hermeneutic Reader* (1988), pp. 13–24. A full-scale attack on such arguments (and any others that ostensibly give too much power to judges) was delivered by Robert Bork, President Reagan's ill-fated nominee for the Supreme Court, in *The Tempting of America: The Political Seduction of the Law* (1990). Chief Justice Rehnquist's primary explication of his view is "The Notion of a Living Constitution," 54 *Texas L. Rev.* 693 (1976). He has also written several books, though none explicitly devoted to setting out a judicial philosophy. See, for example, *The Supreme Court* (2001). Given contemporary realities, one might also be interested in his book *All the Laws But One: Civil Liberties in Wartime* (1998). Antonin Scalia's 1996 Tanner Lectures at Princeton University were published as *A Matter of Interpretation: Federal Courts and the Law* (1997), which includes critical commentaries by Ronald Dworkin and Laurence Tribe.

Older judge-authored books still worth reading are Robert Jackson, *The Supreme Court in the American System of Government* (1951); Hugo Black, *A Constitutional Faith* (1968); and Learned Hand, *The Bill of Rights* (1958). Hand, the most eminent federal appellate judge of his time, is the subject of an unusually subtle biography by Gerald Gunther, *Learned Hand* (1994). Also very interesting is Philip Kurland, *Felix Frankfurter on the Supreme Court: Extrajudicial Essays on the Court and the Constitution* (1970), a collection of Frankfurter's copious writings over a fifty-year period on the general subject. All of these volumes are particularly relevant for students interested in the endless (and not always illuminating) debate about the Supreme Court's "activism" or "self-restraint."

Finally, there is a very interesting reader coedited by federal circuit judge John T. Noonan and Kenneth I. Winston, *The Responsible Judge: Readings in Judicial Ethics* (1993).

F. GREAT CASES

Another good way to learn about the Court is by reading about some of the "great cases" it decided. See, for example, John Garraty, *Quarrels That Shaped the Constitution* (rev. ed., 1987). Peter Irons focuses on civil liberties cases in *The Courage of Their Convictions: Sixteen Americans Who Fought Their Way to the Supreme Court* (1988). Linda Kerber, in *No Constitutional Right to be Ladies: Women and the Obligations of Citizenship* (1998), marvelously details several important cases involving women's rights over the course of American history. Students should also be aware of Peter Irons and Stephanie Guitton, *May It Please the Court* (1993), edited transcripts and cassette tapes of the arguments in twenty-three cases argued before the Supreme Court between 1858 and 1989. One can, for example, hear Thurgood Marshall's stunning argument in *Cooper* v. *Aaron,* the Little Rock school case. No student should miss the opportunity to hear these cases and the interactions between lawyers and justices captured on the tapes.

Marbury v. *Madison* remains a focus of scholarly interest. A superb recent compendium is Mark Graber and Michael Perhac, eds., *Marbury versus Madison: Documents and Commentary* (2002). Robert Clinton, *Marbury* v. *Madison and Judicial Review* (1989), offers a fresh look at that old chestnut, as does Sylvia Snowiss, *Judicial Review and the Law of the Constitution* (1990). William Nelson, *Marbury* v. *Madison and the Rise of Judicial Review* (2000), offers an overview specifically written for an undergraduate audience and is thus especially accessible to students. Mention should also be made of several unusually fine articles, William Van Alstyne, "A Critical Guide to Marbury." 1969 *Duke Law Journal* 1; James O'Fallon, "*Marbury,*" 44 *Stanford Law Review* 219 (1992); David Engdahl, "John Marshall's 'Jeffersonian' Concept of Judicial Review," 42 *Duke Law Journal* (1992); and Jack Rakove, "The Origins of Judicial Review: A Plea for New Contexts," 49 *Stanford Law Review* 1031 (1997). Finally, Louise Weinberg offers what is almost certainly the most thorough defense ever written of *Marbury*'s legal arguments in "Our *Marbury,*" 89 *Virginia Law Review* 1235 (2003). I should note that both Engdahl and O'Fallon criticize what Engdahl describes as "McCloskey's absurd, romanticized account of Marshall's opinion as a 'masterwork of indirection.'" *Marbury,* of course, invariably raises the question of the framers' intent regarding judicial review—on which students should certainly consult Raoul Berger, *Congress* v. *the Supreme Court* (1969). Berger demonstrates quite conclusively that at least some degree of judicial review—the bitter struggles, both then and now, concerned the scope, not the existence—was indeed expected and intended by most of the framers.

The notorious Yazoo Land scandal is the subject of C. Peter McGrath, *Yazoo: Land and Politics in the New Republic, The Case of Fletcher* v. *Peck* (1966). Two other classic Marshall Court cases are treated in Maurice G. Baxter, *The Steamboat Monopoly: Gibbons* v. *Ogden, 1824* (1972) and Francis N. Stiles, *Private Interest and Public Gain: The Dartmouth College Case, 1819* (1972). The most truly significant of all of Marshall's cases, *McCulloch* v. *Maryland,* still awaits the full-scale treatment it deserves, but a good place to start is Gerald Gunther, ed., *John Marshall's Defense of McCulloch* v. *Maryland* (1969). It details the fascinating newspaper debates, in which Marshall participated anonymously, that followed the decision in that case. Though not in a strict sense a constitutional case, *The Antelope,* an 1825 slavery case, is immensely illuminating about the Marshall Court's view of its role, and John Noonan Jr. grippingly tells its story in *The An-*

telope: The Ordeal of the Recaptured Africans in the Administrations of James Monroe and John Quincy Adams (1977). Finally, Mark Graber, in "The Passive-Aggressive Virtues: *Cohens v. Virginia* and the Problematic Establishment of Judicial Review," 12 *Constitutional Commentary* 67 (1995), offers a brief but extremely insightful analysis of *Cohens v. Virginia* (1821), a key case in the struggle between states and Court.

Stanley Kutler's *Privilege and Creative Destruction: The Charles River Bridge Case* (rev. ed., 1977) is a fascinating study of a key Taney Court case about monopolies and the states' role in fostering economic development. Slavery, of course, was the major issue before the Taney Court. Paul Finkelman, *An Imperfect Union: Slavery, Federalism, and Comity* (1981), is an excellent study of a state's duty (if any) to recognize and, in effect, enforce, the laws of other states regarding the status of persons deemed to be slaves. The most important slavery case is the subject of Don Fehrenbacher's truly magisterial *The Dred Scott Case* (1978), which also offers a thorough constitutional history of the entire slavery issue. One is also well advised to consult Fehrenbacher's posthumously published *The Slaveholding Republic: An Account of the United States Government's Relations to Slavery* (2001).

Harold Hyman examines two important post–Civil War cases in *The Reconstruction Justice of Salmon P. Chase: In re Turner and Texas v. White* (1997). As part of the same invaluable series, published by the University of Kansas Press, Ronald M. Labbe and Jonathan Lurie have written *the Slaughterhouse Cases: Regulation, Reconstruction, and the Fourteenth Amendment* (2003). Two other classic cases are well treated in Charles Lofgren, *The Plessy Case: A Legal-Historical Interpretation* (1987) and Paul Kens, *Judicial Power and Reform Politics: The Anatomy of Lochner v. New York* (1990). The important subject of the constitutional status of American Indians has received far too little attention. A good entry into the issue is Sidney L. Harring, *Crow Dog's Case: American Indian Sovereignty, Tribal Law, and United States Law in the Nineteenth Century* (1994). Probably the most systematic religious persecution in American history was that visited upon Mormons in the nineteenth century, the subject of a fine book by Sarah Barringer Gordon, *The Mormon Question: Polygamy and Constitutional Conflict in Nineteenth-Century America* (2002), that necessarily includes discussions of such cases as *Reynolds v. United States,* the 1879 case unanimously upholding the conviction of George Reynolds for bigamy; that episode is the subject of Bruce A. Van Orden, *Prisoner for Conscience Sake: The Life of George Reynolds* (1999), an extremely sympathetic account of his travails.

In *Fighting Faiths: The Abrams Case, the Supreme Court, and Free Speech* (1987), Richard Polenberg examines in depth one of the crucial free-speech cases of the post–World War I era. *Near v. Minnesota* (1931), in which the Court for the first time announced its antagonism to prior restraints, is described in Fred W. Friendly, *Minnesota Rag: The Dramatic Story of the Landmark Court Case That Gave New Meaning to Freedom of the Press* (1981).

Though not about any specific "great case" as such, Peter Irons, in *The New Deal Lawyers* (1981), closely examines the litigation strategies of the Roosevelt Administration in bringing many such cases before the Court. It is a useful complement to Benjamin R. Twiss, *Lawyers and the Constitution: How Laissez Faire Came to the Constitution* (1942), a study of the important role played by lawyers in providing the Court with ideas and supporting argument during the pre-1937 constitutional regime. One of the prototypical New Deal cases is detailed by Richard Cortner, *The Jones & Laughlin Case* (1970). Cortner, who has written many books on specific cases, had earlier written *The Wagner Act Cases* (1964). Students interested in the Supreme Court's willingness to monitor state criminal justice should read Cortner's *A "Scottsboro Case" in Mississippi: The Supreme Court and Brown v. Mississippi* (1986), which focuses on an important 1936 case.

The apparent unity of the Roosevelt justices would founder regarding the protection to be accorded highly unpopular minorities such as the Jehovah's Witnesses. David R. Mainwaring, *Render unto Caesar: The Flag Salute Controversy* (1952), sets out the context of the crucial 1940's cases that first revealed the split. In *Judging Jehovah's Witnesses: Religious Persecution and the Dawn of the Rights Revolution* (2000), Shawn Francis Peters offers a comprehensive overview of the recurrent interaction between Witnesses and the American legal system and of the general consequences of their invoking constitutional protections. Peters has also written a book on a later case involving the right of the Amish to refuse to comply with Wisconsin's compulsory education law, *The Yoder Case: Religious Freedom, Education, and Parental Rights* (2003). It is especially good on its description of the Amish communities that, with some reluctance, brought the litigation.

Among the most scandalous instances of judicial nonprotection of what legal jargon terms a "discrete and insular minority" was the World War II incarceration of Japanese-Americans merely for suspicions that they, uniquely among American ethnic groups, would prove to be more loyal to their country of origin than to their new home. Peter Irons, *Justice at War: The Story of the Japanese American Internment Cases* (1983), details that episode and the particularly shameful behavior of the Executive Branch in regard to the evidence it placed before the Supreme Court. Irons has also edited *Justice Delayed: The Record of the Japanese American Internment Cases* (1989), which includes material relating to the reopening of the cases in the 1980's and the ultimate formal legal vindication of Fred Korematsu and other Japanese-Americans. The general episode of Japanese relocation is the subject of Page Smith, *Democracy on Trial: The Japanese American Evacuation and Relocation in World War II* (1995).

Shelley v. Kraemer, in which the Supreme Court declared unenforceable racially restricting housing covenants, is the subject of Clement Vose, *Caucasians Only: The Supreme Court, the NAACP, and the Restrictive Covenant Cases* (1959)—valuable not only for its insights about the Court but also for explaining the increasingly important role played by agenda-driven groups who had adopted specific litigation strategies regarding their issues of special concern. This is the central subject of Mark V. Tushnet, *The NAACP's Legal Strategy against Segregated Education, 1925–1950* (1987). Maeva Marcus, *Truman and the Steel Seizure Case: The Limits of Presidential Power* (1977), examines another significant Vinson Court case.

The Warren Court is indelibly identified with the most important civil rights case of modern times, *Brown* v. *Board of Education,* the history of which is marvelously set out in Richard Kluger, *Simple Justice* (1975). A more recent, though less detailed, retelling is Robert J. Cottrol, Raymond T. Diamond, and Leland B. Ware, *Brown v. Board of Education: Caste, Culture, and the Constitution* (2003). Mary L. Dudziak, *Cold War Civil Rights: Race and the Image of American Democracy* (2000) makes an important argument that one must understand the strong attack by the Truman and Eisenhower Administrations on the segregationist regime of *Plessy* by reference to foreign policy imperatives generated by the Cold War and the criticisms of American racism by Communists around the world. Also recommended is James T. Patterson, *Brown v. Board of Education: A Civil Rights Milestone and Its Troubled Legacy* (2001). As its title suggests, it is as much a look backward at the uncertain consequences of *Brown* as an analysis of the case itself. Finally, mention should be made of Jack M. Balkin, ed., *What Brown v. Board of Education Should Have Said: The Nation's Top Legal Experts Rewrite America's Landmark Civil Rights Decision* (2001), in which a number of leading law professors offer their versions of what Chief Justice Warren *should* have written in *Brown* (and its companion case of *Bolling* v. *Sharpe*), given the widespread criticism of the opinions that Warren did write. Balkin also offers a very helpful introduction placing the decision in context.

New York Times columnist Anthony Lewis writes of two other classic Warren Court cases in *Gideon's Trumpet* (1964), which tells the background of *Gideon* v. *Wainwright,* the indigent-criminal-defendant case, and *Make No Law: The Sullivan Case and the First Amendment* (1991). Liva Baker writes of *Miranda, Crime, Law and Order* (1983), though it has, of course, been considerably overtaken by subsequent developments.

One of the very early Burger Court cases involved publication of the "Pentagon Papers," the secret history of the Vietnam War. David Rudenstine tells its story very well in *The Day the Presses Stopped : A History of the Pentagon Papers Case* (1996). Surely the most controversial of all Burger Court opinions, though, is *Roe* v. *Wade,* the subject of David Garrow's *Liberty and Sexuality: The Right to Privacy in the Making of Roe v. Wade* (1994). N. E. H. Hull and Peter Charles Hoffer offer a more condensed treatment in *Roe v. Wade: The Abortion Rights Controversy in American History* (2001). Barbara Hinkson Craig and David M. O'Brien, in *Abortion and American Politics* (1993), include a lot of helpful information and political analysis of various cases brought to the Court, as well as the partial texts of some of the key opinions. See also Neal Devins, *Shaping Constitutional Values: Elected Government, the Supreme Court, and the Abortion Debate* (1996) and Mark A. Graber, *Rethinking Abortion: Equal Choice, the Constitution, and Reproductive Politics* (1996).

Lee Epstein and Joseph F. Kobylka offer, in *The Supreme Court and Legal Change* (1992), in-depth case studies of abortion and death penalty litigation. It supplants the earlier book by Michael Meltsner, *Cruel and Unusual: The Supreme Court and Capital Punishment* (1973), written when it appeared that the Court was indeed going to use its power to abolish capital punishment in the United States.

The litigation of another extraordinarily controversial case is analyzed in Timothy J. O'Neill, *Bakke and the Politics of Equality: Friends and Foes in the Classroom of Litigation* (1985). Barbara Hinkson Craig, *Chadha: The Story of an Epic Constitutional Struggle* (1988), details the struggle of an alien plaintiff in challenging the decision of Congress to override, via "legislative veto," an administrative determination that he be allowed to remain in the United States. Jessica Korn's *American Constitutionalism and the Myth of the Legislative Veto* (1996) offers a convincing challenge to Craig's description of *Chadha* as truly epic for anyone else other than Chadha himself. Both books are extremely useful in grasping the tangled constitutional dimensions of congressional-administrative agency relations in the modern state.

The 1990 case of *Oregon* v. *Smith,* concerning the rights of American Indians to use peyote as part of their traditional religious ceremonies, generated two interesting books: Garrett Epps, *To An Unknown God: Religious Freedom On Trial* (2001); Carolyn N. Long, *Religious Freedom and Indian Rights: The Case of Oregon v. Smith* (2000). Long writes almost entirely from the perspective of the American Indian litigants; Epps, though not unsympathetic, offers superb insight into the reasons for which Oregon, through then-Attorney General David Frohnmayer, insisted on defending its ability to criminalize the use of peyote. Another important case of the 1990's is examined in Philippa Strum, *Women in the Barracks: The VMI Case and Equal Rights* (2002). Certainly the most written-about case of the past decade is the Supreme Court's decision in *Bush v. Gore.* Probably the best single book on the case is Howard Gillman, *The Votes That Counted: How the Court Decided the 2000 Presidential Election* (2001). An excellent collection of essays, including both supporters and opponents of the decision, is Cass R. Sunstein and Richard A. Epstein, eds., *The Vote: Bush, Gore, and the Supreme Court* (2001). Students can also get a good basic introduction to the legal issues from Abner Green, *Understanding the 2000 Election: A Guide to the Legal Battles That Decided the Presidency* (2001). Most scholars who have written of the case are distinctly critical of *Bush v. Gore.* The best defense of the decision is Richard A. Posner, *Breaking the Deadlock: The 2000 Election, the Constitution, and the Courts* (2001), though, as a matter of fact, Posner's defense is far more "pragmatic," based on his debatable view that the Court saved the country from political instability, than it is a ringing endorsement of its cogency as legal argument, of which he is rather dismissive. The most unequivocal defense of the legal arguments in *Bush* v. *Gore* is Nelson Lund, "The Unbearable Rightness of *Bush v. Gore,*" 23 *Cardozo Law Review* 219 (2002).

G. GENERAL APPROACHES TO THE CONSTITUTIONAL INTERPRETATION AND THE ROLE OF THE SUPREME COURT

The past quarter century has seen the publication of many important books analyzing (and justifying) various roles of the Supreme Court. The two most influential by far were Alexander Bickel, *The Least Dangerous Branch* (1962) and John Hart Ely, *Democracy and Distrust* (1980). Both attempted to defend, against the apostles of "restraint," a fairly strong role for the Court. Ely put forth a theory of "representation reinforcement," in which the Court would pay special attention to especially vulnerable minority groups but otherwise would refrain from intervening in American politics with regard to decisions about ostensible "fundamental values." (Why would one believe that courts were better than legislators at discerning such values, he asked.) A collection of Ely's essays was published as *On Constitutional Ground* (1996). Bickel focused on the Court's ability to discern certain fundamental values within the American constitutional tradition and to enforce them. (He seemed to pull back, though, in *Politics and the Warren Court* [1965], which seemed far closer to Frankfurter than to Warren in terms of assessing the Court's actions.) Bickel is especially noteworthy for making the notion of "countermajoritarianism" central in discussions of the role of the Court. A fascinating history and analysis of that notion can be found in a series of articles by Barry Friedman, the most relevant of which are "The Birth of an Academic Obsession: The History of the Countermajoritarian Difficulty, Part Five," 112 *Yale Law Journal* 153 (2002) and "The Counter-Majoritarian Problem and the Pathology of Constitutional Scholarship," 95 *Northwestern University Law* Review 933 (2001).

Matthew D. Adler, in "Judicial Restraint in the Administrative State: Beyond the Countermajoritarian Difficulty," 143 *University of Pennsylvania Law Review* 759 (1997), notes that the "difficulty" is present, if at all, only when the Court is assessing legislation passed by a broadly based legislature; he therefore criticizes those who invoke it to call for greater judicial restraint with regard to acts of ubiquitous administrative agencies and other low-visibility decision-makers who cannot plausibly claim the imprimatur of majority approval. Mark Graber offers even more fundamental criticism of the notion in "The Nonmajoritarian Difficulty: Legislative Deference to the Judiciary," 7 *Studies in American Political Development* 35 (1993), which argues that legislators often prefer to send political hot potatoes (like abortion or affirmative action) to the courts rather than pay the political costs of making inevitably politically costly decisions themselves.

Also extremely influential—and defending a far stronger judicial presence than Ely or Bickel—has been the philosopher Ronald Dworkin, *Taking Rights Seriously* (1978); *Law's Empire* (1986); *Life's Dominion: An Argument about Abortion, Euthanasia, and Individual Freedom* (1993); and *Freedom's Law: The Moral Reading of the American Constitution* (1996). Very much influenced by Dworkin, especially his earlier writings, is Richard Markovits, *Matters of Principle: Legitimate Legal Argument and Constitutional Interpretation* (1998).

Other much discussed books defending a strong judicial role are Charles Black, *The People and the Court* (1960); Jesse Choper, *Judicial Review and the National Political Process: A Functional Reconsideration of the Role of the Supreme Court* (1980); and Michael Perry, *The Constitution, the Courts and Human Rights* (1982). More recently, Perry has written *The Constitution in the Courts: Law or Politics?* (1994). Christopher L. Eisgruber also defends a strong judiciary in *Constitutional Self-Government* (2001).

Cass Sunstein, in *One Case at a Time: Judicial Minimalism on the Supreme Court* (1999), offers what has been described as the rediscovery of the merits of the Frankfurterian (or at least Bickelian) position that had been rejected by the Warren Court (and by most legal academics). The ultimate in judicial restraint would be the abnegation of judicial review entirely, a position ably defended by Mark Tushnet, *Taking the Constitution Away from the Courts* (1999). Earlier, Tushnet had cast a skeptical eye on all comprehensive theories in *Red, White, and Blue* (1988). A book taking a similarly skeptical stance is Robert Nagel, *Constitutional Cultures: The Mentality and Consequences of Judicial Review* (1989). Students may also wish to consult Mitchell S. Muncy, ed., *The End of Democracy? The Judicial Usurpation of Politics* (1997) and *The End of Democracy? II. A Crisis of Legitimacy* (1999), both of which are the aftermaths of a November 1996 symposium in the conservative religious journal *First Things* that suggested that the Court had basically become illegitimate and that thoughtful citizens might even contemplate civil disobedience against some of its mandates.

A different light on comprehensive constitutional theory is cast in two books by Philip Bobbitt, *Constitutional Fate* (1982) and *Constitutional Interpretation* (1991). Bobbitt outlines what he calls the "modalities" of constitutional interpretation and then goes on to criticize the notion that there is one privileged method of interpretation. Bobbitt also criticizes books like this one for offering basically "externalist" political, rather than "internal" legal, accounts of most of the Court's significant decisions. Similar in spirit is the defense of self-consciously "pragmatic" decision-making in Daniel A. Farber and Suzanna Sherry, *Desperately Seeking Certainty: The Misguided Quest for Constitutional Foundations* (2002). Terri Jennings Peretti, *In Defense of a Political Court* (1999) offers a rousing defense of a politically self-conscious Court. Probably the most written-about comprehensive theory over the past decade or so has been "originalism," in part because it appeared to be the official theory of the Reagan Administration and its judicial nominees—including, certainly, Robert Bork, who described it as the "only" legitimate approach to constitutional interpretation. There is now a vast literature, pro and con, on the desirability, or even possibility, of actually discerning the framers' intentions and then applying them in our own time. One obvious question linked with originalism is the ability of the lawyers on the Supreme Court, who are usually completely untrained in the skills of the historian, to engage in the kind of historical analyses required by the method. Though written three decades ago, Charles A. Miller, *The Supreme Court and the Uses of History* (1969), remains essential. Strong defenses of originalism are offered by Christopher Wolfe, *The Rise of Modern Judicial Review: From Constitutional Interpretation to Judge-Made Law* (1986); Keith Whittington, *Constitutional Interpretation: Textual Meaning, Original Intent, and Judicial Review* (1999); and Randy Barnett, *Restoring the Lost Constitution* (2004).

Linked in some ways to originalism, though coming, usually, from the opposite end of the political spectrum insofar as originalism became identified with conservative politics in the 1980's, was the rediscovery by political progressives of the ostensibly "republican" (as distinguished from "liberal") roots of the Constitution. This, and much more, is skillfully analyzed in Laura Kalman's invaluable study of the intellectual vicissitudes of the American legal academy, *The Strange Career of Legal Liberalism* (1996).

Also much discussed is "textualism," a close cousin but analytically distinguishable from the more historically saturated "originalism." See Leslie Friedman Goldstein, *In Defense of the Text: Democracy and Constitutional Theory* (1991). A good collection of articles can be found in "Symposium, Textualism and the Constitution," *66 George Washington Law Review* (June/August 1998).

Sotirios A. Barber, *On What the Constitution Means* (1984) and *The Constitution of Judicial Power* (1993) are notable for being among the few books unabashedly to argue that the Court must draw on the teachings of natural law in its own jurisprudence. Also drawing on natural law, but harshly critical of the Court, is Hadley Arkes, *Beyond the Constitution* (1990) and Graham Walker, *Moral Foundations of Constitutional Thought: Current Problems* (1990). Mention should also be made in this context of Duke law professor H. Jefferson Powell's interesting and imaginative study, *The Moral Tradition of American Constitutionalism* (1993).

Rogers Smith, in *Liberalism and American Constitutional Law* (1985), also basically defends moderate judicial activism. Strong critiques of any such role are offered by John Agresto, *The Supreme Court and Constitutional Democracy* (1964) and Eugene W. Hickok and Gary L. McDowell, *Justice vs. Law: Courts and Politics in American Society* (1993). Daniel N. Hoffman offers an interesting perspective in *Our Elusive Constitution: Silences, Paradoxes, Priorities* (1997). Richard H. Fallon, Jr., in *Implementing the Constitution* (2001), valuably reminds readers that the key to understanding the Supreme Court is its approach to enforcing its decisions, a topic that tends to be ignored by professors more interested in the abstract arguments by which the Court determines legal liability in the first place.

Other, more idiosyncratic, books should also be mentioned. William P. Harris's brilliant *The Interpretable Constitution* (1992) is a study of the theoretical foundations of the very idea of constitutionalism as a means of structuring political decision-making by a sovereign people, while Sanford Levinson's *Constitutional Faith* (1988) looks at American constitutionalism as a "civil religion" and analyzes enduring constitutional controversies by reference to classical religious conflicts. The debate about the authority of the Court, for example, is analogized to the debate about the institutional authority of the Roman Catholic Church within Christianity. Gary Jacobsohn, *Apples of Gold: Constitutionalism in Israel and the United States* (1993), is a very suggestive comparison of the roles of the respective Supreme Courts in using constitutional norms to help shape their societies. Lief Carter, in *Contemporary Constitutional Lawmaking* (1985), offers a self-consciously "post-modernist" reading of constitutional interpretation and the role of the Court. Steven D. Smith, though no post-modernist, offers a thoroughgoing critique of much constitutional theory in *The Constitution and the Pride of Reason* (1998). Finally, a number of essays in the latter half of William Eskridge and Sanford Levinson, eds., *Constitutional Stupidities/Constitutional Tragedies* (1998), explicitly address the tension between constitutional theory and the moral acceptability of the results generated by application of one's favorite theory.

Students might want to turn to two good collections of materials on contemporary constitutional theory, John Garvey, T. Alexander Aleinikoff, and Dan Farber, *Modern Constitutional Theory: A Reader* (5th ed., 2003), and Michael J. Gerhardt and Thomas D. Rowe Jr., *Constitutional Theory: Arguments and Perspectives* (1993).

Most of the books named above are normative in their approach. There is also a rich empirical literature focusing on the ability of the Supreme Court, practically speaking, to affect public policy. William K. Muir, *Prayer in the Public Schools* (1968), for example, looks not at the "background" but rather at the subsequent *impact* of the Court's school prayer decisions on the practice of a local school system. One must always remember that Supreme Court decisions are not self-enforcing; many are the public officials, at all levels of government, who must agree to change their behavior before the Court's decisions can be accurately described as in fact affecting the American political landscape. This point is further elaborated in Theodore Becker and Malcolm Feeley, eds., *The Impact of Supreme Court Decisions* (1973).

Gerald Rosenberg's *The Hollow Hope: Can Courts Bring About Social Change?* (1991) caused quite a sensation when published, for it argues very strongly that the answer to his question is basically no, at least if the Court does not have the strong support of other national branches of government; he uses *Brown* and *Roe* as the central examples of his thesis. Michael W. McCann challenges the Rosenberg thesis in *Rights at Work: Pay Equity Reform and the Politics of Legal Mobilization* (1994). "Post-Rosenberg" essays are collected in David A. Schultz, ed., *Leveraging the Law: Using the Courts to Achieve Social Change* (1998). Also highly relevant is Malcolm M. Feeley and Edward L. Rubin, *Judicial Policy Making and the Modern State: How the Courts Reformed America's Prisons* (1998), though it is worth noting that the Supreme Court played a minimal role in these efforts, the major role by far being played by federal district and appellate judges. An older book examining the attempts to use courts to create new constitutional rights is Stuart A. Scheingold, *The Politics of Rights* (1974). All of these books should be read along with Martin Shapiro's *Law and Politics in the Supreme Court: New Approaches to Political Jurisprudence* (1964), which, though obviously written many years ago, remains full of relevant insights. Students should also be familiar with Donald L. Horwitz, *The Courts and Social Policy* (1977), a classic critique of the Court's efforts to make general social policy in regard to empirically complex issues. R. Shep Melnick, *Between the Lines: Interpreting Welfare Rights* (1994), is an excellent study of the Court's increasingly important role as interpreter of statutes, as is William Eskridge's more theoretically oriented *Dynamic Statutory Interpretation* (1994).

The empirical studies necessarily focus on the Court's interaction with other political institutions and, ultimately, on its ability to shape public opinion (and the extent to which the Court's handiwork is itself shaped by public opinion). As to the former, see Maxwell L. Stearns, *Constitutional Process: A Social Choice Analysis of Supreme Court Decision Making* (2000). Walter Murphy, in *Congress and the Supreme Court* (1962), examines the response of Congress to a series of highly controversial decisions viewed by many representatives and senators as too favorable to Communists and criminal defendants. And, of course, Murphy assesses the response of the Court itself to Congress' reaction. (It basically capitulated.) Finally, students should be aware of Howard Gillman and Cornell Clayton, eds., *The Supreme Court in American Politics: New Institutionalist Interpretations* (1999), which attempts to link the Court's behavior to the broad contours of party systems, capitalist development, and the like. Any serious inquiry into the history and behavior of the United States Supreme Court with regard to such issues as protecting vulnerable minorities (as distinguished from the interests of political elites) should take into account Ran Hirschl, *Towards Juristocracy: The Origins and Consequences of the New Constitutionalism* (2004), a comparative analysis of "the judicialization of politics" in Canada, Israel, New Zealand, and South Africa, though written against a background reference to the history of the United States Supreme Court. He argues that strong judiciaries are far more likely to protect powerful economic and social interests by removing otherwise controversial issues from the political process than to advance "progressive" notions of social justice. Walter Murphy is, with Joseph Tannenhaus and Daniel Kastner, an author of *Public Evaluations of Constitutional Courts: Alternative Explanations* (1973), probably the best study of the Court's (in)ability to change public opinion. Thomas R. Marshall, in *Public Opinion and the Supreme Court* (1989), compares public opinion on a broad set of issues with Court opinions dealing with those issues and finds significant congruence.

H. INSTITUTIONAL STUDIES OF THE MODERN COURT

There is, of course, a copious literature on the internal behavior of the Court as an institution. Three good texts include Henry Abraham's classic *The Judiciary: The Supreme Court in the Governmental Process* (10th ed., 1996); David M.

O'Brien, *Storm Center: The Supreme Court in American Politics* (4th ed., 1996); and Lawrence Baum, *The Supreme Court* (6th ed., 1998). One political scientist describes Lee Epstein et al., *The Supreme Court Compendium: Data, Decisions, and Developments* (3d ed., 2002) as "a resource on the Court you can't beat." Susan Low Bloch and Thomas G. Krattenmaker have also edited a very helpful collection, *Supreme Court Politics: The Institution and Its Procedures* (1994).

Mention should be made of two "inside" books on the Supreme Court, Robert Woodward and Scott Armstrong, *The Brethren: Inside the Supreme Court* (1979) and Edward Lazarus, *Closed Chambers: The First Eyewitness Account of the Struggles inside the Supreme Court* (1998). Both books were extremely controversial—Lazarus, a former clerk to Justice Blackmun, was accused by some of behaving unethically—but there is no doubt that they offer important, and disquieting, insights into the dynamics of the contemporary Court. Vastly more scholarly but equally readable is Walter P. Murphy, *Elements of Judicial Strategy* (1964), which focuses on the strategic problems and choices facing justices seeking the approval of a majority of their colleagues for given policy goals. The opinion-writing process is also the subject of Forrest Maltzman, James F. Spriggs II, and Paul J. Wahlbeck, *Crafting Law on the Supreme Court: The Collegial Game* (2000).

How do cases get to the Court? See H. W. Perry, *Deciding to Decide: Agenda Setting in the Supreme Court* (1991), which examines the certiorari process by which the modern Court selects the specific cases it wishes to hear and issue opinions about. Also worth consulting is Doris Marie Provine, *Case Selection in the United States Supreme Court* (1980). How important is oral argument before the Court? More than many scholars had assumed, argues Timothy Johnson in *Oral Arguments and Decision Making on the United States Supreme Court* (2004).

How do persons get to the Supreme Court? (The answer is not, as with the old joke about Carnegie Hall, "practice, practice.") The standard book is Henry J. Abraham, *Justices and Presidents: A Political History of Appointments to the Supreme Court* (3d ed., 1992), though one is also well advised to look at the relevant pages of Michael J. Gerhardt, *The Federal Appointments Process* (2000); Robert A. Katzmann, *Courts and Congress* (1997); and Deborah J. Barrow, Gary Zuk, and Gerard S. Gryski, *The Federal Judiciary and Institutional Change* (1996). A classic study of a specific appointment is David J. Danelski, *A Supreme Court Justice Is Appointed* (1964), which focuses on the 1922 appointment by President Harding (who had been heavily lobbied by Chief Justice Taft, himself a former President) of Pierce Butler, a railroad lawyer from Minnesota. As David Alistair Yalof notes in *Pursuit of Justices: Presidential Politics and the Selection of Supreme Court Nominees* (1999), the nomination process has, following World War II, become a part of the increasingly institutionalized (and often internally disputatious) Presidency, and he provides an important account of the processes from the Truman through the Reagan Administrations that led to the not-always-successful nominations they sent to the Senate for confirmation. The subsequent process of confirmation hearings is treated in John Anthony Maltese, *The Selling of Supreme Court Nominees* (1995) and Mark Silverstein, *Judicious Choices: The New Politics of Supreme Court Confirmations* (1994). Both Maltese and Silverstein are political scientists; for a lawyer's perspective, see Stephen L. Carter, *The Confirmation Mess: Cleaning Up the Federal Appointments Mess* (1994). All were written after the epic battle following Ronald Reagan's unsuccessful nomination of Robert Bork in 1987, the subject of Ethan Bronner, *Battle for Justice* (1989). The Supreme Court is, of course, only the apex of a complex federal judicial system, and the often Delphic pronouncements of the Court are actually given concrete form in the decisions of what the Constitution calls "inferior" courts. Sheldon Goldman is acknowledged to be the leading student of the appointment of judges to the lower federal courts, and his years of study are summarized in *Picking Federal Judges: Lower Court Selections from Roosevelt through Reagan* (1997).

David Atkinson has recently asked an important question: How do judges leave the Court? See *Leaving the Bench: Supreme Court Justices at the End* (1999). He suggests that the answer, for too many, is ungraciously, in part because they stay on the Court long after they have begun losing their powers. (This may be one of the major costs of the constitutional grant of lifetime tenure to members of the Court.)

There is an important body of work on the relationship between the "attitudes" of Supreme Court justices and the way they vote. A full review of the literature by two of the major scholars adopting this approach is Jeffrey A. Segal and Harold J. Spaeth, *The Supreme Court and the Attitudinal Model* (1993) and *The Supreme Court and the Attitudinal Model Revisited* (2002). They also apply their approach in *Majority Rule or Minority Will: Adherence to Precedent on the U.S. Supreme Court* (1999). See also Lee Epstein and Jack Knight, *The Choices Justices Make* (1998). Also highly recommended is Cornell W. Clayton and Howard Gillman, eds., *Supreme Court Decision-Making: New Institutionalist Approaches* (1999), which offers an excellent way of understanding contemporary debates between more politically oriented "strategic" and more traditionally legalistic "interpretivist" approaches to explaining Supreme Court decision-making. Indeed, Nancy Maveety, ed., *The Pioneers of Judicial Behavior* (2003) is an excellent collection of essays on the "pioneers" written by leading contemporary political scientists (such as Howard Gillman's essay on McCloskey). This book should be especially useful to any graduate student preparing for general exams, but it is a treasure trove for anyone looking for a quick way to immerse oneself in the field.

Lawyering before the Court is studied in Charles Epp, *The Rights Revolution: Lawyers, Activists, and Supreme Court in Comparative Perspective* (1998) and Kevin McGuire, *The Supreme Court Bar: Legal Elites in the Washington Community* (1993). Susan E. Lawrence studies a particular portion of the bar in *The Poor in Court: The Legal Services Program and Supreme Court Decision-making* (1990). The most important single lawyer is the Solicitor General, who not only argues many cases before the Supreme Court, but who also presides over an extraordinarily sophisticated group of lawyers vis-à-vis litigation before the Supreme Court. See Rebecca Mae Salokar, *The Solicitor General: The Politics of Law* (1992). A popular (and quite partisan) book criticizing the Reagan Administration's Solicitor Generals is Lincoln Caplan, *The Tenth Justice: The Solicitor General and the Rule of Law* (1987). One of those Generals, Charles Fried, has written *Order and Law: Arguing the Reagan Revolution: A Firsthand Account* (1991). An outstanding biography of an especially active lawyer (and Solicitor General during the administration of Woodrow Wilson) is William H. Harbaugh, *Lawyer's Lawyer: The Life of John W. Davis* (1990).

I. Specific Doctrinal Studies

It would be truly ludicrous to attempt to list all of the literally thousands of articles and books relevant to specific topics of constitutional law (let alone the other important bodies of law, such as administrative law, that the Court contends with). All of the general reference works cited above, as well as other works cited throughout this note, include copious leads to further research in their footnotes and bibliographies.

Two publications that all students should be familiar with are the November issues of the *Harvard Law Review*, which is traditionally devoted to an intensive review of the work of the previous term's decisions by the Supreme Court, and *The Supreme Court Review*, an annual review that includes predictably first-rate articles on several of the most important cases of the previous year. The analyses, however, tend to be highly doctrinal and rarely offer more "political" explanations of the Court's decisions.

Few topics are more important than war and peace, and few topics have been less illuminated by the Supreme Court. Christopher N. May offers a historical overview in *In the Name of War: Judicial Review and the War Powers since 1918* (1989). Among other recent books are Harold Hongju Koh, *The National Security Constitution: Sharing Power after the Iran-Contra Affair* (1990); Michael J. Glennon, *Constitutional Diplomacy* (1990); John Hart Ely, *War and Responsibility: Constitutional Lessons of Vietnam and Its Aftermath* (1993); Louis Fisher, *Presidential War Power* (1995); and Gordon Silverstein, *Imbalance of Powers: Constitutional Interpretation and the Making of American Foreign Policy* (1997). An interesting collection of essays is Richard H. Kohn, *The United States Military under the Constitution of the United States, 1789–1989* (1991).

The problems of war and peace invariably involve the notion of separation of powers, as suggested by the title of Clinton Rossiter, *The Supreme Court and the Commander in Chief* (2d ed., 1976). But the issues generated by the reality of separate branches of government go well beyond war and peace, as demonstrated in an excellent casebook by Harold H. Bruff and Peter M. Shane, *The Law of Presidential Power* (1988). Joseph M. Bessette and Jeffrey Tulis, eds., *The Presi-*

dency in the Constitutional Order (1981), offers a set of essays on the history and contemporary practice of the Presidency. See also the collection of essays in Robert A. Goldwin and Art Kaurman, eds., *Separation of Powers—Does It Still Work?* (1986).

One important manifestation of separation of powers is impeachment, a subject that became unexpectedly salient in 1998. Three classic books on presidential impeachment are those of Raoul Berger, *Impeachment: The Constitutional Problems* (1973); Charles Black, *Impeachment: A Handbook* (1974); and Michael Gerhardt, *The Federal Impeachment Process: A Constitutional and Historical Analysis* (2d ed., 2000). Although Gerhardt has added a discussion of the Clinton impeachment to his new edition, his book is especially useful in regard to the less dramatic, but practically more important, power to impeach federal judges. All three treat the question whether the Supreme Court has any useful role to play in the proceedings, except to furnish its Chief Justice to preside over the Senate trial of the President. Chief Justice Rehnquist published his own book, *Grand Inquests: The Historic Impeachments of Justice Samuel Chase and President Andrew Johnson* (1992). Federal judge Richard Posner offers a fascinating account of the episode in *An Affair of State: The Investigation, Impeachment, and Trial of President Clinton* (1999).

A final aspect of separation of powers, especially in the modern era of the administrative state, is the propriety of Congress' "delegating" to administrative agencies the ability, as a practical matter, to make law by filling in the specifics of otherwise extraordinarily broad legislation. David Schoenbrod, in *Power without Responsibility: How Congress Abuses the People through Delegation* (1993), levels a thoroughgoing attack on the post-1937 acceptance of very broad delegation. Sotirios Barber considers the same subject in *The Constitution and the Delegation of Congressional Power* (1975). Well worth reading is the classic critique of "interest-group" liberalism in Theodore J. Lowi, *The End of Liberalism: The Second Republic of the United States* (2d ed., 1979).

Robert McCloskey once suggested that academics have a "class interest," as it were, in freedom of speech, which may explain why there is so much good writing examining the meaning of that aspect of the First Amendment. The classic account of the development of free-speech doctrine is Zechariah Chafee, *Free Speech in the United States* (1941), though much of its history has been challenged by later scholars: The leading history of freedom of speech is now David Rabban, *Free Speech in Its Forgotten Years* (1997). Also an important corrective to Chafee's account is Mark A. Graber, *Transforming Free Speech: The Ambiguous Legacy of Civil Libertarianism* (1991). Harry Kalven was a leading commentator in the decades following Chafee. *A Worthy Tradition: Freedom of Speech in America* (1988) is a collection of his essays. Among the most gifted contemporary analysts of the increasingly complicated doctrines surrounding freedom of speech is Robert Post, whose *Constitutional Domains: Democracy, Community, Management* (1995) is an unusually subtle treatment of many current issues. See also Steven

Shiffrin, *The First Amendment, Democracy, and Romance* (1990) and *Dissent, Injustice, and the Meanings of America* (1999). One is also well advised to read any of the First Amendment scholarship of Frederick Schauer, who unfortunately has not collected it in book form (though his book, *Free Speech: A Philosophical Enquiry* [1982], is the best single starting point for anyone interested in the theoretical arguments regarding freedom of speech). In addition, he has edited with John Garvey *The First Amendment: A Reader* (2d ed., 1996). A recent collection of excellent essays by leading scholars is Lee C. Bollinger and Geoffrey R. Stone, *Eternally Vigilant: Free Speech in the Modern Era* (2002).

The First Amendment also includes the press clause, of course. Leonard Levy's *Legacy of Suppression: Freedom of Speech and Press in Early American History* (1960), revised and reprinted as *Emergence of a Free Press* (1985), triggered a major debate about its meaning. Levy argued that the framers of the First Amendment had a quite restricted view of freedom of speech, confined primarily to blocking prior restraints (but not, for example, prohibiting subsequent punishment for seditious speech or, certainly, libel suits for defamation). Levy's history was criticized in David Anderson, "The Origins of the Press Clause," 30 *U.C.L.A. Law Review* 453 (1983) and "Levy v. Levy," 84 *Michigan Law Review* (1986). A superb, highly readable general history of the constitutional treatment of the press throughout American history is Lucas Powe, *The Fourth Estate and the Constitution* (1991)—a complement, in a way, to his *American Broadcasting and the First Amendment* (1987), which focuses on the special (and, he argues, indefensible) regulation imposed on the broadcasting industry, in contrast to the unregulated press. Powe accepts the unregulated press as the normative ideal for electronic and new cable media. Cass Sunstein, on the other hand, accepts the regulated broadcasting industry as the normative model for the press in general in *Democracy and the Problem of Free Speech* (1993). Lee Bollinger, on the third hand, argues that the present mixture of regulation and nonregulation is just right in *Images of a Free Press* (1991). All of these topics are also ably examined in Rodney A. Smolla, *Free Speech in an Open Society* (1992).

Donald Downs, *The New Politics of Pornography* (1989), is a good examination of that extremely volatile subject. The most prominent academic advocate of extensive regulation of pornography is Catherine A. MacKinnon. A good short summary of her views is *Only Words* (1993). Anyone interested in this subject should also consult Nadine Strossen, *Defending Pornography: Free Speech, Sex, and the Fight for Women's Rights* (1995). Strossen, the president of the American Civil Liberties Union, defends the traditionally libertarian views associated with that organization against critics like MacKinnon and others.

In thinking about freedom of speech, one usually (and properly) thinks of the state's duties to tolerate private speech. But state speech itself raises some important constitutional issues. Mark G. Yudof, *When Government Speaks: Politics, Law, and Government Expression in America* (1983), is a seminal examination of the constitutional problems linked to government communication with the citizenry, whether through choosing a curriculum for public schools or engaging in direct propaganda in behalf of governmental policies ("Just Say No").

Certainly one of the most important areas of contemporary First Amendment litigation involves regulation of campaign finance and the relationship between money and speech. An excellent introduction is Richard Hasen, *The Supreme Court and Election Law: Judging Equality from* Baker v. Carr *to* Bush v. Gore (2003). As the title suggests, it also includes discussions of constitutional issues surrounding reapportionment and vote-counting in elections, usually litigated under the Equal Protection Clause. One should also be aware of Alexander Keyssar, *The Right to Vote: The Contested History of Democracy in the United States* (2000).

The Bill of Rights in the Modern State (Cass Sunstein, ed., 1992) is an excellent collection, not least because of two articles by Michael McConnell and Kathleen Sullivan that concentrate on the application of traditional theories to the contemporary welfare state. They particularly differ in regard to the constitutional consequences of aid to religious schools, another basic First Amendment controversy. On the early history of this aspect of the First Amendment, see Thomas J. Curry, *The First Freedom: Church and State in America to the Passage of the First Amendment* (1986). The most recent treatment of the religious establishment debate throughout our history (or at least until 1950) is Philip Hamburger, *Separation of Church and State*(2002). A far briefer overview of that topic can be found in Leonard Levy, *The Establishment Clause: Religion and the First Amendment* (1986), though it is marred by its too easy acceptance of the standard liberal view of that clause. Jesse Choper, *Securing Religious Liberty: Principles for Judicial Interpretation of the Religion Clauses* (1995), summarizes the thought of one of the leading analysts of religion and the Constitution (which is not to say that the book is not quite controversial in many of its arguments). John H. Garvey, *What Are Freedoms For?* (1996) is an excellent theoretically oriented examination of the general topic that includes a good discussion of what ought to be protected under the rubric "religious freedom." Somewhat older, but still worth looking at, is a collection of essays from *The Supreme Court Review* in Philip B. Kurland, ed., *Church and State: The Supreme Court and the First Amendment* (1975).

Only in the twentieth century has the First Amendment served as a source of major litigation; the most litigated single clause of the Constitution prior to the Civil War was nothing from the Bill of Rights—basically moribund in its entirety for at least the first century of the United States—but rather the contract clause. Benjamin R. Wright, *The Contract Clause of the Constitution* (1938), remains the essential source. It was in important ways a victim of the post-1937 revolution, though it has never completely died. One function of the contract clause was to protect the property owners, specifically creditors. The more general issue is surveyed in James W. Ely Jr., *The Guardian of Every Other Right: A Constitutional History of Property Rights* (1992). Two helpful works, from opposite ends of the political spectrum, are Jennifer Nedelsky, *Private Property and the Limits of Amer-*

ican Constitutionalism: The Madisonian Framework and Its Legacy (1990) and Richard A. Epstein, *Takings: Private Property and the Power of Eminent Domain* (1985). Nedelsky argues that the very notion of private property rights has become incoherent following the demise of the *Lochner* regime and the legitimation of the modern regulatory state. Epstein, on the other hand, argues that the pre-1937 Court was right and the New Deal revolution therefore illegitimate and ripe for overruling by judges committed to the original vision of constitutional limits. Also very interesting is Bruce A. Ackerman, *Private Property and the Constitution* (1977), which focuses, among other things, on the differences between the economist's and the ordinary lawyer's understanding of "property." John Brigham examines *Property and the Politics of Entitlement* (1990). The more general issue of the ability of traditional constitutional concepts to survive the development of the contemporary expansive state is the topic of Mark Tushnet and Michael Seidman, *Remnants of Belief: Contemporary Constitutional Issues* (1996).

The most extraordinary example of property, of course, was human beings trapped within the institution of chattel slavery. In addition to the Fehrenbacher and Finkelman books mentioned earlier, one is well advised to read William M. Wiecek, *The Sources of Antislavery Constitutionalism in America: 1760–1848* (1972), which, as the title suggests, focuses on the attempts by Lysander Spooner and others to use the Constitution as the basis of the attack on, rather than protection of, slavery. Wiecek is also author of *The Guarantee Clause of the U.S. Constitution* (1972), a study of the "republican form of government" clause that was, as a practical matter, eliminated as a topic of standard constitutional discourse by the Court's decision in *Luther v. Borden* (1847) that it involved a "political question" not appropriate for judicial review.

The most important formal constitutional development after 1791 was surely the addition of the Fourteenth Amendment to the text, which led, among other things, to enhanced judicial monitoring of state legislation. A basic problem in constitutional theory (and basic doctrine) is whether legislative power extends only to passing laws that are in "the public interest" and, more particularly, whether the Supreme Court has the ability to distinguish between such laws and those serve only "private," "partial" interests. An unusually instructive book on this point is Howard Gillman, *The Constitution Beseiged: The Rise and Demise of Lochner Era Police Powers Jurisprudence* (1993). Cass Sunstein examines the issue in *The Partial Constitution* (1994), an excellent general discussion of post–New Deal constitutionalism. Sunstein is also the author of *After the Rights Revolution: Reconceiving the Regulatory State* (1990), which underscores the point that much of the most important contemporary work of the Court involves non-constitutional statutory interpretation and monitoring of the administrative agencies that are the hallmark of the modern state. Peter L. Strauss, *Administrative Justice in the United States* (1989), written initially for a non-American audience, is especially accessible and useful with regard to delineation of the constitutional issues attached to the modern administrative state. Mention should also be made of Martin Shapiro, *Who Guards the Guardians? Judicial Control of Administration* (1988).

The general issue of the welfare state is the subject of Sotirios A. Barber, *Welfare and the Constitution* (2003). Perhaps the most intractable doctrinal problem attached to the modern welfare state concerns the conditions that governments can place on those who receive state funds. Richard Epstein, *Bargaining with the State* (1993), examines such problems at length. Two seminal discussions of the problem are Seth Kreimer, "Allocational Sanctions: The Problem of Negative Rights in a Positive State," 132 *University of Pennsylvania Law Review* 1293 (1984), and Kathleen Sullivan, "Unconstitutional Conditions," 102 *Harvard Law Review* 1413 (1989).

The Fourteenth Amendment is especially noteworthy, of course, for the equal protection clause and its application to problems involving race and gender. Michael Klarman, *From Jim Crow to Civil Rights: The Supreme Court and the Struggle for Racial Equality* (2004), is clearly the major work on the subject. A serviceable overview is Donald G. Nieman, *Promises to Keep: African Americans and the Constitutional Order, 1776 to the Present* (1991). See also Paul Peterson, ed., *Classifying by Race* (1995). Skeptical of recent developments is Herman Belz, *Equality Transformed: A Quarter-Century of Affirmative Action* (1991), as is the case also of Lina A. Graglia, *Disaster by Decree: The Supreme Court Decisions on Race and the Schools* (1976), which focuses on the Court's "busing" decisions. Equally critical, though from the other end of the political spectrum, is Morgan Kousser, *Colorblind Injustice: Minority Voting Rights and the Undoing of the Second Reconstruction* (1999). On gender, see Judith Baer, *Equality under the Constitution: Reclaiming the Fourteenth Amendment* (1983) and *Women in American Law: The Struggle toward Equality from the New Deal to the Present* (2d ed., 1996), as well as David L. Kirp, Mark G. Yudof, and Marlene Strong Franks, *Gender Justice* (1986).

As noted earlier, the treatment of American Indians is an extremely interesting and important issue that has also failed to generate a comprehensive book. See, though, Charles Wilkinson, *American Indians, Time, and the Law: Native Societies in a Modern Constitutional Democracy* (1987). American Indians are a major subject of Alexander Alienikoff, *Semblances of Sovereignty: The Constitution, the State, and American Citizenship* (2002). The book goes on to consider the constitutional ramifications attached to American expansion in the nineteenth and early twentieth centuries, which meant, among other things, the acquisition of territories (or what some might call "colonies") that are not treated as full parts of "the United States of America." A fascinating and important topic in this context is the constitutional status of Puerto Rico, added to the domain of the United States. See Juan R. Torruella, *The Supreme Court and Puerto Rico: The Doctrine of Separate and Unequal* (1988), as well as Christina Duffy Burnett and Burke Marshall, eds., *Foreign in a Domestic Sense: Puerto Rico, American Expansion, and the Constitution* (2001). The general issue of whom the United States decides to welcome into its community and how they are treated is ably discussed in Gerald L. Neuman, *Strangers to the Constitution: Immigrants, Borders, and Fundamental Law* (1996). The most insightful (and troubling) book on the history of American citizenship law (among many other topics) is Rogers Smith, *Civic Ideals* (1997), though James H. Kettner, *The Development of American Citizenship, 1608–1870* (1978), well deserves its status as a classic.

Given its importance throughout American history, and especially after 1937, it is astonishing that there is no great historical treatment of the commerce clause. Two older books worth looking at are Edward S. Corwin, *The Commerce Power versus States Rights* (1959) and Felix Frankfurter, *The Commerce Clause under Marshall, Taney, and Waite* (1937). There is also a very intensive study by Paul R. Benson Jr., *The Supreme Court and the Commerce Clause, 1937–1970* (1970). Probably the best short overview can be found in Lino A. Graglia, "*United States v. Lopez*: Judicial Review Under the Commerce Clause," 74 *Texas Law Review* 719 (1996).

There is also no great book on Federalism, an especially urgent need given the Court's recent rediscovery of its ostensible centrality in the American constitutional order. Useful starting points are S. Rufus Davis, *The Federal Principle: A Journey through Time in Question of Meaning* (1978); David L. Shapiro, *Federalism: A Dialogue* (1995); and Paul Peterson, *The Price of Federalism* (1995). An excellent, highly accessible history of one important strand of Federalism is Forrest McDonald, *States' Rights and the Union: Imperium in Imperio, 1776–1876* (2000), particularly interesting given the contemporary Supreme Court's reassertion of the importance of state "sovereignty." Some especially interesting insights are provided in Leslie Friedman Goldstein, *Constituting Federal Sovereignty: The European Union in Comparative Context* (2001), which includes an important chapter comparing resistance by the American states to national authority between 1790 and 1860 and resistance by the members of the European Community to transnational commands from community institutions. Goldstein's book only underscores the general importance, to anyone interested in understanding the development of American legal institutions, of taking a more comparative perspective. See, e.g., Joseph H. H. Weiler, *The Constitution of Europe: "Do the New Clothes Have an Emperor?"* (1999), which contains several fascinating comparisons between European and American constitutional development. Another obvious point of comparison is American state constitutions, which also has the advantage of deepening one's appreciation for living in a federal political system. The leading scholar of state constitutions is surely G. Alan Tarr, among whose books are *State Supreme Courts in State and Nation* (1988); *Constitutional Politics in the States: Contemporary Controversies and Historical Patterns* (1996); and *Understanding State Constitutions* (1998).

Especially since *Griswold* v. *Connecticut*, the once-forgotten Ninth Amendment has been the subject of interest (and, in some cases, dismay). Randy E. Barnett has edited two excellent collections of materials on the Amendment, *The*

Rights Retained by the People: The History and Meaning of the Ninth Amendment (Vol. 1, 1989; Vol. 2, 1993). The Tenth Amendment is the focus of Wayne Moore, *Constitutional Rights and Powers of the People* (1996). *Griswold*, of course, is the origin of much contemporary protection of sexual autonomy, the most controversial area of which probably remains the constitutional protection to be accorded to non-heterosexuals. A good place to start one's study is William N. Eskridge, *Gaylaw: Challenging the Apartheid of the Closet* (1999), which is obviously critical of the failure to adequately protect gay and lesbian (and bisexual) sexual choices. Also worth reading, from a strikingly different law-and-economics perspective, is Richard A. Posner, *Sex and Reason* (1992).

The criminal procedure provisions of the Bill of Rights are the topic of Akhil Reed Amar's interesting and extremely controversial *Constitution and Criminal Procedure: First Principles* (1997), full of "revisionist" arguments about the historical assumptions underlying the Amendments. Also very much worth reading is Jeffrey Abramson, *We, the Jury: The Jury System and the Ideal of Democracy* (1994). Most criminal charges do not lead to jury trials, however; plea bargaining resolves the overwhelming number of cases, a subject considered in George Fisher, *Plea Bargaining's Triumph: A History of Plea Bargaining in America* (2003). Many persons convicted of crime, of course, file appeals for writs of habeas corpus, a subject well treated in a short book by Eric M. Freedman, *Habeas Corpus: Rethinking the Great Writ of Liberty* (2001). Finally, inasmuch as many of the most important issues of American criminal justice have revolved around the treatment of racial minorities, students are well advised to read Randall Kennedy, *Race, Crime, and the Law* (1997).

Especially interesting as an example of a constitutional clause that is the subject of great popular interest and almost willful judicial ignorance is the Second Amendment, dealing with the ostensible right to bear arms. A good collection of recent articles can be found in Robert J. Cottrol, ed., *Gun Control and the Constitution: Sources and Explorations on the Second Amendment* (1994). A later collection is Carl T. Bogus, ed., *The Second Amendment in Law and History: Historians and Constitutional Scholars on the Right to Bear Arms* (2000); it is, however, marred by the failure to invite participation from any scholar who does not share an "anti-gun-rights" position. Two important recent books are H. Richard Uviller and William G. Merkel, *The Militia and the Right to Arms, or, How the Second Amendment Fell Silent* (2002) and David C. Williams, *The Mythic Meanings of the Second Amendment: Taming Political Violence in a Constitutional Republic*. Both, interestingly enough, accept the view that the most cogent explanation of that Amendment's existence in the Constitution is the felt importance at the time of in effect recognizing the potential legitimacy of armed uprising against a corrupt central government, as had occurred, of course, in 1776. Both of the books argue that the assumptions behind the Amendment no longer obtain and that it should be treated as a more-or-less nullity.

The possibility of armed uprising leads to what may be the most important single constitutional issue in American history, the legitimacy of secession. (That the issue was settled on the field of battle and, blessedly, does not now seem pressing does not lessen its theoretical importance.) See Mark Brandon, *American Slavery and Constitutional Failure* (1998), for an especially interesting treatment of the topic. Harry Jaffa, *A New Birth of Freedom: Abraham Lincoln and the Coming of the Civil War* (2000), treats the thought not only of Lincoln, but also of the Southern secessionists (and his predecessor James Buchanan) to whom he was responding.

INDEX